THE WORLD'S CLASSICS
VICTORY

JOSEPH CONRAD was born Józef Teodor Konrad Korzeniowski in the Russian part of Poland in 1857. His parents were punished by the Russians for their Polish nationalist activities and both died while Conrad was still a child. In 1874 he left Poland for France and in 1878 began a career with the British merchant navy. He spent nearly twenty years as a sailor and did not begin writing novels until he was approaching forty. He became a British citizen in 1886 and settled permanently in England after his marriage to Jessie George in 1896.

Conrad is a writer of extreme subtlety and sophistication; works such as *Heart of Darkness, Lord Jim*, and *Nostromo* display technical complexities which have established Conrad as one of the first English 'Modernists'. He is also noted for the unprecedented vividness with which he communicates a pessimist's view of man's personal and social destiny in such works as *The Secret Agent, Under Western Eyes* and *Victory*. Despite the immediate critical recognition that they received in his lifetime Conrad's major novels did not sell, and he lived in relative poverty until the commercial success of *Chance* (1914) secured for him a wider public and an assured income. In 1923 he visited America, with great acclaim, and he was offered a knighthood (which he declined) shortly before his death in 1924. Since then his reputation has steadily grown and he is now seen as a writer who revolutionized the English novel and was arguably the most important single innovator of the twentieth century.

JOHN BATCHELOR is a Fellow of New College, Oxford. His publications include a critical biography of Mervyn Peake (1974) and *The Edwardian Novelists*, a study of Conrad, Ford Madox Ford, Wells, Bennett, Galsworthy, and Forster (1982) and *H. G. Wells* (1985). He is General Editor of The World's Classics' Conrad and has edited *Lord Jim* for the series.

THE WORLD'S CLASSICS

JOSEPH CONRAD

Victory

An Island Tale

Edited by

JOHN BATCHELOR

with an Introduction by

TONY TANNER

Of calling shapes, and beckoning shadows dire,
And airy tongues that syllable men's names
On sands and shores and desert wildernesses.

COMUS*

OXFORD UNIVERSITY PRESS
1986

Oxford University Press, Walton Street, Oxford OX2 6DP

Oxford New York Toronto
Delhi Bombay Calcutta Madras Karachi
Kuala Lumpur Singapore Hong Kong Tokyo
Nairobi Dar es Salaam Cape Town
Melbourne Auckland

and associated companies in
Beirut Berlin Ibadan Nicosia

Oxford is a trade mark of Oxford University Press

Introduction © Tony Tanner 1986
Bibliography, Chronology © John Batchelor 1983
(revised by Cedric Watts 1986)
Preface, Notes © John Batchelor 1986

This edition first published as a World's Classics paperback 1986

British Library Cataloguing in Publication Data

Conrad, Joseph
Victory: an island tale.—(The World's classics)
I. Title   II. Batchelor, John, 1942–
823'.912[F] PR6005.04

ISBN 0–19–281708–6

Printed in Great Britain by
Hazell Watson & Viney Ltd.
Aylesbury, Bucks

CONTENTS

Editor's Preface	vii
Introduction	ix
Note on the Text	xxi
Select Bibliography	xxii
A Chronology of Joseph Conrad	xxiv
Note to the First Edition	xxxi
Author's Note	xxxiii
VICTORY	1
Explanatory Notes	413

EDITOR'S PREFACE

CHANCE (1913–14) had opened up a huge readership for Conrad in England and America, and *Victory* (1915) was a great popular success. Early critics like Leavis and Miss Bradbrook regarded it as one of Conrad's greatest achievements, but in the 1950s academic resistance to *Victory* set in. It was said that the artistry was very uneven and that the subject was unsuited to Conrad; that it was impossible for a man of Conrad's temperament and experience to dramatize love as a moral positive.[1] But to read *Victory* in this way is to distort it. It may well be the case that Conrad did not, in his own experience, find much consolation in his wife and family for the torments of authorship and poverty (though Jessie was an excellent wife, typing manuscripts, cooking gourmet meals, and putting up with her husband's tantrums and depressions), but whatever disappointments Conrad's own experience of love may have held for him, he is no more to be identified with Heyst than Lena is to be identified with Jessie.

From *Nostromo* onwards Conrad's novels had asserted the power of love but failed to demonstrate that power in action. For Gould and Decoud in *Nostromo*, and for Razumov in *Under Western Eyes*, there is no doubt that the love of a good woman—Emily, Antonia, or Nathalie—holds the promise of salvation (salvation which in these instances is cruelly withheld). In

[1] In the words of a representative and influential academic critic of the 1950s, Conrad's attitude to love was consistently 'negative': 'How could it be otherwise? Conrad sees man as lonely and morally isolated, harried by egoistic longings for power and peace, stumbling along a perilous path, his only hope benumbing labour, or, in rare cases, a little self-knowledge. Conrad could not possibly reconcile so dark a view with a belief in the panacea of love, wife, home and family' (Thomas Moser, *Joseph Conrad: Achievement and Decline*, first published 1957 (Hamden, Conn.; Archon Books, 1966), p. 127).

Chance Roderick and Flora do find wholly satisfying mutual love, once their mutual misunderstandings have been cleared away and Flora's wicked father has been disposed of, but their full married relationship is tragically brief, cut short by Roderick's death. In *Victory* the pattern is changed again; Heyst comes to recognize the saving and fulfilling love that Lena offers him, but this recognition is, of course, too late. His last reported speech marks the distance he has travelled from his earlier stance of isolated nihilistic voyeur: 'Ah, Davidson, woe to the man whose heart has not learned while young to hope, to love—and to put its trust in life!' The 'victory' of the title is Lena's; she succeeds, at the cost of her own life, in freeing Heyst from his father's paralysing influence and forcing from him a final acknowledgement that he loves her. The conclusion to *Victory* is rather simple: life, love, and commitment are absolute human imperatives, while philosophical detachment of the kind commended by Heyst's father is a deforming and arid heresy which has wrecked the son's life. Now that it is too late he can see the full extent of his loss, and since nothing can bring Lena back it seems psychologically fitting, and aesthetically appropriate, that he should set fire to his bungalow and join her. The story which begins with the glowing tip of his cigar and the companionable red glow of the neighbouring volcano ends with this purifying blaze.

INTRODUCTION

BY TONY TANNER*

THERE are two key words in *Victory*, 'gentleman' and 'gossip'. 'Gentleman' usually occurs in reference to Heyst or Mr Jones, but it is deployed in a wide variety of conversations and issues from many different mouths. To gain some deeper sense of what Conrad might have been about in making this word both 'hollow' and central to his novel, it is worth reminding ourselves of the importance of that word in the latter part of the nineteenth century, particularly in England. There is no point in offering a full etymological history of the word—as to how it relates to family or 'blood' or clan; to property or wealth; to the right to bear arms; to the freedom from obligation to engage in manual labour or retail trade, and so on—though we may note that in Samburan, or North Borneo, to the East generally, any such 'anchorings' for the word are removed, so that the appellation 'gentleman', like the people to whom it is applied, has undergone a very considerable emigration from the land and families and society which gave it birth. It is, we may say, up for re-definition, or de-definition, as the case may be. But in England itself, the word was becoming ever harder to define: a few background quotations may be helpful here.

Defoe asserted that 'Our modern Acceptation of a Gentleman is this. A person BORN (for there lies the essence of Quality) of some known, or Ancient Family; whose Ancestors have at least for some time been rais'd above the class of Mechanicks. If we will examine for how long it must be, that is

* This essay is part of an article, 'Gentlemen and Gossip: Aspects of Evolution and Language in Conrad's *Victory*', which is published in full in the *Critical Quarterly*, Summer 1986.

a dangerous Inquiry, we dive too deep, and may indeed strike at the Root of both the Gentry and Nobility; for all must begin somewhere and would be traced to some less Degree in their original than will suit with the Vanity of the Day' (*The Compleat English Gentleman*, 1729). To enquire into genealogy—the *origins* of a crucial social class—could indeed be dangerous because, particularly after Darwin, if you tried to trace a 'family' back to its 'origin', well, there was no saying what you might find—as Darwin found with the 'family' of man. But there had always been an emphasis on the inner qualities of the individual as constituting the real essence of a 'gentleman', thus to a certain extent making it less class-bound and class-defined, if not actually class-free. A Mr F. Lieber, writing in 1847, put it this way:

The term Gentleman in its highest acceptation signifies that character which is distinguished by strict honour, self-possession, forbearance, generous as well as *refined* feelings, and polished deportment—a character to which all manners, explosive irritableness and peevish fretfulness are alien; to which, consequently, a generous candour, scrupulous veracity, courage both moral and physical, dignity, self-respect, a studious avoidance of giving offence to others or oppressing them, and liberality in thought, argument, and conduct, are habitual and have *become natural*. Perhaps we are justified in saying that the character of the gentleman implies an addition of *refinement* of feeling, and loftiness of conduct to the rigid dictates of morality and *purifying* precepts of religion. It seems to me that we always connect the ideas of honour, polish, collectedness of mind and liberal disposition with the word gentleman, and feel that its antagonistic characters are the clown, the *gossip*, the backbiter, the dullard, coward, braggart, fretter, swaggerer and bully. (*Character of the Gentleman*, 1847)

The italics are mine, and are intended to draw attention to words which Conrad uses in his novel—refinement, purification—with a kind of polysemic irony. There is a paradoxical problem which is central to the novel—namely, how do the so-called 'highest', most civilized human attributes 'become natural', for isn't 'nature', in some sense, precisely what is 'refined away' in producing the social creation, the gentleman? 'Gossip'—the other key word—effectively destroys Heyst, his 'courtesy' being powerless against, and annihilated by, the gratuitous 'calumny' of others, mainly emanating from our old friend, or rather Conrad's old *bête noire*, Schomberg. The gentleman, and speech—these were considered two of the 'highest' products of evolution. And in their degraded, perverted, or 'scandalously' travestied forms—Mr Jones and Schomberg's gossip—they can destroy the higher, 'authentic' forms. 'Scandal' is another key word in the book—as it derives from *scandere*, to climb, and *skandalon*, a stumbling block—it appropriately conflates the ideas of ascent and fall, and in one of its many ironic narrative developments, *Victory* does indeed re-enact the 'scandalous' fall of the most 'highly ascended' man; Heyst, Number One, the 'saviour', the namer of things and people (from the German *heissen*—to name), a second Adam, who is himself called many names—'Enchanted Heyst', 'Hard Facts', the 'Spider', the 'Enemy', the 'Hermit'—but succumbs to the slanderous and malicious mal-naming of him by Schomberg's gossip, a kind of verbal 'mud' which sticks to him and drags him back to the old earth of our common origin, from which he can only finally and fully escape by the purifying, terminating fire.

Victory was finished just before the First World War; and after that 'gentlemen' emerged with another name, if indeed there were any left at all. There *is* an elegiac, as well as an 'enchanted' strain to *Victory* (it is Conrad's *Tempest*) and one of the deeds it performs is to rehearse the exequies of the 'puffect g'n'lman'—Heyst. Alongside the image of the 'perfect gentleman' there grew up within his shadow—or perhaps *as* his shadow—another figure, in many ways the opposite of the gentleman, and yet disturbingly akin to him. This is the figure of the 'egoist' who seems to put the instincts of self-survival and self-gratification in the place of that altruism which the gentleman should feel. To take one of Meredith's metaphors, which is appropriate enough for Conrad, 'this one is for the ship, that one is for his life'. In *The Egoist*, Meredith wrote: 'A very little, my love, and everything gained for us by civilization crumbles; we fall back to the first mortarbowl we were bruised and stirred in.' The words are spoken by Sir Willoughby Patterne who hardly knows if he is a gentleman or an egoist, not surprisingly since, in a way, he is both. But what we have in Meredith is the realization that the idea of the 'primitive' and the 'civilized' being separated by great stretches of time and place, and infinite modifications up the evolutionary scale, barely stood up to experience. Not that Darwin and such followers as Huxley denied the possibility of 'regressions', indeed they stressed it; and Darwin often makes observations such as the following: 'The evidence that all civilised nations are the descendants of barbarians, consists, on the one side, of clear traces of their low condition in still-existing customs, beliefs, language, etc.' (*The Descent of Man*). But a clear sense of some ineluctable, if non-teleological progression, from the 'lowest' forms up to Western European contemporary man, effectively permeates Darwin's writings, two or three points from which seem particularly relevant to *Victory*. Thus 'most animals and plants keep to their proper homes, and do not needlessly wander about; we see this even with migratory birds, which almost always return to the same spot' (*Origin of Species*). Heyst lives, precisely, 'by a system of restless wandering, by the detachment of an impermanent dweller amongst changing scenes', believing, most wrongly it transpires, that he will thus remain 'invulnerable because elusive'. He does realize that 'I am a transplanted being. Transplanted. I ought to call myself uprooted—an unnatural state of existence.' We might note that Darwin is also tolerably specific about 'restlessness', when discussing how undesirable moral qualities are in the continual process of being eliminated ('some elimination of the worst dispositions is always in progress even in the most civilised nations'—an example of how Darwin so often manages to sound optimistic about a morally purposive progress in nature without being teleological). 'Violent and quarrelsome men often come to a bloody end': not an observation of dazzling perspicacity; but he continues, 'The restless who will not follow any steady occupation—and this relic of barbarism is a great check to civilization—emigrate to newly settled countries, where they prove useful pioneers' (*Descent of Man*). But Samburan is hardly a newly settled country, and Heyst is far from being a hard-working emigrant or 'useful pioneer'. After fifteen years of 'restless' wandering, after a brief flutter with the mining company, his most steady occupation is not to be occupied in any physical way: is this a 'relic of barbarism' or perhaps an excess of useless refinement? In fact, Darwin makes a point which is oddly relevant to Heyst's situation. In dealing with the phenomenon that, in his own terms, many manifestly 'lowly organized forms' still exist in the world, he discusses this 'retrogression of organization', adding: 'But the main cause lies in the fact that under very simple conditions of life a high organisation would be of no service, possibly would be an actual disservice, as being of a more delicate nature, and more liable to be put out of control and injured.' One could hardly say which is more of a disservice to Heyst in the relatively 'simple conditions' of his island—his impeccable fastidiousness or his complex, physically paralysing, cerebration. (We might also note that Darwin observed that 'a high standard of morality gives but a slight or no advantage to an individual man and his children over the other men of the same tribe'—to be highly moral, as to be highly civilized, on Samburan, has decidedly no 'advantages' when it comes to a struggle for survival with members of the same race, if not exactly the same tribe.) Related to this is another assertion of Darwin's in *The Descent of Man*, namely that 'everyone will admit that man is a social being. We see this in his dislike of solitude, and in his wish for society beyond that of his own family.' No one will pretend that Darwin is the first writer to study the phenomenon of deracination, or the deliberate cultivation of an antisocial solitude, a non-communal alienation, but in Heyst we find a figure who simply seems to prefer 'solitude' and to shun company (Lena apart, but she is in every sense a special case). His attitude is more like that described in *The Egoist*: 'His enemy was the mass, which confounds us in a lump, which has breathed on her whom we have selected, whom we cannot, can never, rub quite clear of her contact with the abominated crowd.' But of course, Heyst's reasons for his disengagement and detachment from the world, or 'the mass', are very different from any of Willoughby's egotistical and society-bound repugnances. And his nausea at the 'breath' of the mass is based on the destructive calumny that 'breath' can produce when formed into that semantic rubbish we call gossip. Heyst goes to an island, in order to be out of the contaminating contact of the crass struggle for existence. Here is Darwin on what I suppose we would call the 'ecology' of an island.

But in the case of an island, or of a country partly surrounded by barriers, into which new and better adapted forms could not freely enter, we should then have places in the economy of nature which would assuredly be better filled up, if some of the original inhabitants were in some manner modified; for, had the area been open to immigration, these same places would have been seized on by intruders. In such cases, slight modifications, which in any way favoured the individuals of any species, by better adapting them to their altered conditions, would tend to be preserved; and natural selection would have free scope for the work of improvement.

In *Victory*, all the main characters are 'intruders' of one sort or another; the 'original inhabitants' retire behind a 'barrier' and whatever is temporarily 'seized' by the intruders is in varying ways relinquished by them: there are no 'modifications': nothing is 'preserved': instead of 'natural selection' we have what we may call natural deletion.

That all the evolutionary options were, as it were, still open, is clear from such comments as the following, when Heyst's attempts to break out of the magic circle of the islands take him in the direction either of New Guinea or Saigon—'to cannibals or to cafés'. As if to say that both modes of existence are present in the world, and, more to the point, there is not a great deal of difference between them. I have referred elsewhere to the importance of 'eating' in Conrad,* and here, as in many other ways, he picks up a theme from *Falk*, in making Schomberg obsessed with the need for mankind to eat at his hotel: 'his ambition was to feed it at a profitable price, and his delight was to talk of it behind its back'. The bad talk is a reflex of, and connected with, the bad food: the ears and the mouth are alike malnourished there. No wonder Heyst avoids that establishment; in the event one might well opt for nature's cannibals over Schomberg's café. And Schomberg's destructive resentment starts from the fact that Heyst does not eat at his 'establishment'. Mr Jones, a 'starved spectre', intense and insatiable, rapacious and insubstantial, is a clear relative of Kurtz in *Heart of Darkness*. But for all his talk of being a 'gentleman' he knows that he is undomesticated. 'We aren't tame,' he casually warns Schomberg (who is terrified of 'ferocity'), adding 'in a voice indifferent, as if issuing from a tomb, that he depended on himself, as if the world were still one great, wild jungle without law'. Mr Jones seems deathly, his vitality exhausted, yet he still has 'the will and the power to sting—something vicious, unconquerable, and deadly'. In all of this he seems the very opposite of the other gentleman, Heyst, who, by contrast, looks 'martial' and capable of active struggle, yet is powerless to 'sting'; who has tried to renounce the lawless jungle of the world without realizing that it is quite out of his power to force it to renounce him.

There are also some odd, and potentially disturbing,

---

* See Tony Tanner, 'Eating and Narration in Conrad' in *Joseph Conrad: A Commemoration*, ed. Norman Sherry (Macmillan, 1976).

similarities. We read much of Heyst's 'inertia', just as we hear a lot about Mr Jones's 'laziness'. Mr Jones assumes that he is—or was—from a similar 'social sphere' as Heyst, just as Ricardo assumes that he and Lena have similar 'origins' 'in the dregs of mankind'. Such offensive, contaminating, and usually dangerous assumptions of identity, or similarity, are common in Conrad—it is the theme of the 'unforeseen partnership', the unsolicited but unseverable alliance, or, as we may say with particular reference to *Victory*, it is related to the overall theme of the uninvited guest. Jones and his team are referred to as 'the guests whom the renounced world had sent [Heyst] at the end of the day', and later Heyst refers ironically to 'the sacred virtue of hospitality! But it leads one into trouble as well as any other.' Anthropologists have shown us how absolutely fundamental the guest/host roles in the rites of hospitality are in all tribes, and 'hospitality' is of course the crucial way of mediating between the known and the unknown, the familiar and the strange, the inside and the outside, the home and the 'guest', which, let us remember, originally meant 'enemy' as well as 'stranger'. Hospitality turns the potentially disruptive enemy, interloper, intruder, into the defined, and therefore safe, figure of the 'guest'—a ritualistic de-fusing of a possible danger. Abrogations or transgressions of the 'sacred' rules of hospitality are felt to be particularly horrendous as they threaten the very stability of civilization—or the house, the city, the tribe, whatever unit of consolidated territory we are dealing with. To be a 'guest' implies that one has accepted being 'domesticated' or 'tamed'—if only temporarily—according to the rules and codes of the house. Heyst's improbably fantastic, phantasmagoric, ferocious, and distinctly uninvited 'guests' are precisely *not* tame or tameable, and Heyst's attempts to continue to act the proper 'host' with these freaks, 'sports', anti-types, or monsters (we can describe them in many ways) show how impossible it is to maintain the conventions of 'civilization' when only one party feels obliged to abide by them. It becomes a black parody of hospitality—with parasitic scavengers trying to act as 'gentlemen' guests.

Another disturbing similarity/difference concerning Heyst and Mr Jones lies in their habitual mode of motion. Though Mr Jones is prone to 'laziness', he has volition and intention, a plotting intelligence which—with the aid and support of Ricardo's 'instinctive savagery' and Pedro's 'brute force'—gives him goals, directions, aims, and ends, albeit these are of the most ruthlessly exploitative and self-profiting kind. Heyst, we remember, before he arrives at what is almost his terminal 'stagnation', chooses to 'drift'. 'He meant to drift altogether and literally, body and soul, like a detached leaf drifting in the wind-currents ... to drift without ever catching on to anything.' How he *does* catch on to something—or someone—and how things catch on to him, with or without his assent, constitute a large part of the action of the book. But to drift without a goal, while making for some kind of detachment and invulnerability, involves a passive capitulation to the wind-currents of the world, or more generally, the driving powers of nature which, working through winds, or men or women, may push the motiveless drifter in any direction they choose. As Heyst explains: 'I had no schemes, no plans ... I was simply moving on, while the others, perhaps, were going somewhere. An indifference as to roads and purposes makes one meeker, as it were.' Hence the irony of Heyst's getting temporarily involved in the coal-mining venture with its illusions of progress—the '"stride forward", as he expressed it, in the general organization of the universe'. The theoretical 'stride forward' rapidly becomes a series of moves backwards, aptly illustrated in the spectacle of the 'abandoned settlement invaded by the jungle' on Samburan, just as the large sign-board advertising the progressive, enterprising presence of the 'Tropical Belt Coal Company' is slowly being reclaimed by the non-signifying, though not, therefore, insignificant, indigenous vegetation. First the enterprise goes, then the men, the buildings, finally the very 'signs' of the human, intruding presence. The equivocal aspects of 'drifting'—that it works at least two ways, bringing things in your way you wanted to avoid, even while you think you are avoiding the traps and travails of more conventional 'roads and purposes'—are clearly indicated by the fact that it is the wind-currents, and not the planning and steering of Mr Jones and his 'crew', which finally bring them to Samburan. 'The explanation lay in the two simple facts that the light winds and strong current of the Java Sea had drifted the boat about until they partly lost their bearings.' (Compare, in chapter 1 of *Nostromo*: 'On crossing the imaginary line drawn from Punta Mala to Azuera the ships from Europe bound to Sulaco lose at once the strong breezes of the ocean. They become the prey of capricious airs that play with them for thirty hours at a stretch sometimes.') In seeking to avoid the purposive planning of men, it is impossible to avoid the unpredictable caprices of nature. Heyst drifts—only to be drifted *into*. He thinks to renounce the world—mentally: but as long as he is, has, a body, he cannot renounce participation in the world's physicality, and it will not renounce him: it plays with him, capriciously, cruelly, catastrophically. The gentleman at rest is visited by the 'gentleman at large' who travels randomly but deliberately, driven by currents of greed and aggressive spite, and purposefully but 'driftingly', driven by the winds and currents of nature.

Heyst's 'detachment' from the world is 'not complete'. He has a flaw: he can still be 'touched'. So, despite his deep distrust of 'action', despite his sense that this is 'a world not worth touching, and perhaps not substantial enough to grasp', despite his having 'nothing worth holding on to', he is vulnerable, penetrable, 'touchable'. He has, he admits, asked himself 'in what way would life try to get hold of me?' but later says to Lena that 'when one's heart has been broken into in the way you have broken into mine, all sorts of weaknesses are free to enter'. His convicition is that 'He who forms a tie is lost.'

'Touch' is of course a key pun or ambiguity in the book. You can be 'touched' in the sense of being emotionally stirred, as when he first sees Alma, Heyst feels 'a secret touch on the heart'; or you can be 'touched', handled, 'grabbed' by any of the alien predators drifting around the world. Heyst is, of course, touched in both senses. As he is 'touched'—i.e. reached, smirched, marked, muddied, by gossip and calumny. 'Mud' provides an interesting leitmotiv in the book. Schomberg is a 'mud turtle', a creature of the slime. The nearby volcano inflicts an unexpected 'mud shower' on Heyst's apparently immaculate island; while Mr Jones, at the peak of his anger with Ricardo, refers to his assistants as 'mud souls, obscene and cunning: mud bodies, too—the mud of the gutter'. Heyst thought to have 'no connection with earthly affairs and passions' and, like other Conradian quixotic idealists, he is habitually dressed in spotless white. But as he realizes, after forming the 'tie' with Alma/Lena, 'there must be a lot of the original Adam in me, after all'. Despite his mental contempt for matter and materiality, the original and originating mud of things, he himself, even Heyst, is ultimately of the earth, earthy.

He reflected, too, with the sense of making a discovery, that this primeval ancestor [i.e. Adam] is not easily repressed. The oldest voice in the world is just the one that never ceases to speak. If anybody could have silenced its imperative echoes, it should have been Heyst's father, with his contemptuous, inflexible negation of all effort; but apparently he could not. There was in the son a lot of that first ancestor who, as soon as he could uplift his muddy frame from the celestial mould, started inspecting and naming the animals of that paradise which he was so soon to lose.

The oldest ancestor, Adam, speaks through Heyst when his carefully maintained aloofness dissolves at the deep touch of desire—of attraction towards another, an instinct or 'drive' to take hold which thus precipitates him—much against his apparent 'will'—into the world of action.

It has long seemed to me that *Victory* offers, among other things, a dramatic testing of a man pervaded, and perhaps perverted, by Schopenhauerian philosophy; and a demonstration of how, amidst the contingencies of actual, acted, life, such a philosphy could be found hopelessly, fatally wanting. Schopenhauer's warning that 'we must not suppose that ... when the denial of the will to live has once appeared, it never wavers or vacillates' is peculiarly apt for Heyst, whose 'apostasy' is, as we are reminded, imperfect, not complete. The only deliverance from an existence such as ours, says Schopenhauer, is through the complete denial of the will to live. We must shake off the world. With the complete denial of the will, all phenomena are abolished—'No will: no ideas: no world'. What then is left? This is the conclusion of *The World as Will and Idea*: 'We freely acknowledge that what remains after the entire abolition of will is for all those who are still full of will certainly nothing; but, conversely, to those in whom the will has turned and denied itself, this our world, which is so real, with all its suns and milky ways—is nothing.' The same word concludes *Victory*. Heyst, the gentleman, the man of 'refinement', admits at one point that '"I have managed to refine everything away. I've said to the Earth that bore me 'I am I and you are a shadow.' And, by Jove, it is so. But it appears that such words cannot be uttered with impunity"'. And so, at the end, we have the final 'refinement' by fire, which 'purifies everything', but leaves—'Nothing'. And so Conrad ends *his* book. The mood is very different from the air of almost mystic ecstasy which pervades Schopenhauer's conclusion.

NOTE ON THE TEXT

Victory was first published in serial form in *Munsey's Magazine* (New York) and in the *Star*, in 1915, and in book form the same year. This text is based on the Dent Library edition, which is based on the first edition of 1915. *Victory* was originally planned as a short story to be called 'The Dollars' and grew into one of Conrad's longest novels. The manuscript version is substantially longer than the published text; Conrad made more cuts between manuscript and publication than in any of his other works.

SELECT BIBLIOGRAPHY

Dent's Collected Edition (1946–55) contains almost all Conrad's works except the fragment called *The Sisters*, the dramatizations, and a tale written in collaboration with Ford Madox Hueffer (who later became Ford Madox Ford), *The Nature of a Crime. Congo Diary and Other Uncollected Pieces* (ed. Zdzislaw Najder, 1978) contains Conrad's Congo notebooks, *The Sisters, The Nature of a Crime* and other minor pieces. Cambridge University Press is preparing a scholarly edition of the canon.

Important editions of Conrad's letters are as follows: G. Jean-Aubry: *Joseph Conrad: Life and Letters* (two volumes, 1927); *Letters from Conrad, 1895 to 1924* (ed. Edward Garnett, 1928); *Letters of Joseph Conrad to Marguerite Poradowska* (tr. and ed. J. A. Gee and P. J. Sturm, 1940); and *Conrad's Polish Background* (ed. Z. Najder, 1964). There are further collections by Richard Curle (1928), G. Jean-Aubry (1930), William Blackburn (1958), D. B. J. Randall (1968) and Cedric Watts (1969). In 1983 volume I (ed. F. R. Karl and Laurence Davies) of *The Collected Letters of Joseph Conrad* appeared; further volumes have been prepared.

Informative memoirs of Conrad include those by Ford Madox Ford (1924), Jessie Conrad (1926 and 1935), Richard Curle (1928), Bertrand Russell (1967), Borys Conrad (1970), and John Conrad (1981). Notable critical biographies have been written by Jocelyn Baines (1960), Bernard Meyer (a 'psychoanalytic' biography, 1967), Frederick Karl (1979) and Ian Watt (*Conrad in the Nineteenth Century*, 1980), and there is a biography by Roger Tennant (1981). An important scholarly account is Zdzislaw Najder's *Joseph Conrad: A Chronicle* (1983).

Probably the most influential of the biographically related studies which make substantial use of documentary material are: J. D. Gordan, *Joseph Conrad: The Making of a Novelist* (1940), and Norman Sherry, *Conrad's Eastern World* (1966) and *Conrad's Western World* (1971). There are further relevant studies by Richard Curle

(1914), Edward Crankshaw (1936), Gustav Morf (1930 and 1976), R. L. Mégroz (1931), J. H. Retinger (1941), Jerry Allen (1965), and Norman Sherry (1972).

Of the numerous critical books on Conrad, the following may be found fruitful: Douglas Hewitt, *Conrad: A Reassessment* (1952), Thomas Moser, *Joseph Conrad: Achievement and Decline* (1957), Albert Guerard, *Conrad the Novelist* (1958), Eloise Knapp Hay, *The Political Novels of Joseph Conrad* (1963), Avrom Fleishman, *Conrad's Politics* (1967), and Jacques Berthoud, *Joseph Conrad: The Major Phase* (1978). Other studies of interest are by Paul Kirschner (1968), Bruce Johnson (1971), and Jan Verleun (1978 and 1979). There are important essays on Conrad in F. R. Leavis, *The Great Tradition* (1948) and *'Anna Karenina' and Other Essays* (1967), J. Hillis Miller, *Poets of Reality* (1966), and Norman Sherry, ed., *Joseph Conrad: A Commemoration* (1976). Fredric Jameson, *The Political Unconscious* (1981), has an important chapter on Conrad.

Of particular interest for readers of *Victory* are Bruce Johnson, *Conrad's Models of Mind* (1971), Daniel Schwarz, *Conrad: The Later Fiction* (1982), Frederick R. Karl, *'Victory*: its origins and development', *Conradiana*, XV, no. 1 (1983), pp. 23–51, and H. M. Daleski, *'Victory* and Patterns of Self-Division', *Conrad Revisited*, ed. Ross C. Murfin (1985), pp. 1078–24.

A CHRONOLOGY OF JOSEPH CONRAD

1857   3 December: Born Józef Teodor Konrad Korzeniowski, in the Ukraine.

1861   His father, poet and translator Apollo Korzeniowski, arrested for patriotic conspiracy.

1862   Conrad's parents exiled to Vologda, Russia; their son accompanies them.

1865   Death of his mother.

1869   Death of Apollo Korzeniowski in Kraków; Conrad becomes the ward of his uncle, Tadeusz Bobrowski.

1874   Leaves Poland for Marseilles to become a trainee seaman with the French merchant navy.

1876   As a 'steward' on the *Sainte-Antoine*, becomes acquainted with Dominic Cervoni (who appears in *The Mirror of the Sea*, *A Personal Record*, and *The Arrow of Gold*, and who is a source for Nostromo and for Peyrol in *The Rover*).

1877   Possibly involved in smuggling arms from Marseilles to the 'Carlists' (Spanish royalists).

1878   March: Shoots himself in the chest but is not seriously injured; as a direct result of this suicide attempt his uncle clears his debts. April: Joins his first British ship, the *Mavis*, and later in the year joins the *Skimmer of the Sea*.

1886   August: Becomes a British citizen. (Formerly, as a Russian citizen and the son of a convict, Conrad was liable for Russian military service.) November: Passes the examination for a Master's certificate.

1887   In hospital in Singapore with an injury sustained on the *Highland Forest*.

1887–8   Gets to know the Malay Archipelago as an officer of the *Vidar*.

1888 Master of the *Otago*, his only command. (The *Otago* voyages provided a basis of 'Falk', 'The Secret Sharer', *The Shadow-Line*, and 'A Smile of Fortune'.)

1889 Resigns from the *Otago*, settles briefly in London, and begins to write *Almayer's Folly*. Begins a lasting friendship with Marguerite Poradowska.

1890 Works in the Belgian Congo for the Société Anonyme pour le Commerce du Haut-Congo.

1891–3 His pleasantest experience at sea, as an officer of the *Torrens*; meets John Galsworthy, who is among the passengers and becomes a loyal friend.

1893 Autumn: Meets Jessie George.

1894 February: Death of Tadeusz Bobrowski. October: *Almayer's Folly* accepted by Unwin. Meets Edward Garnett, Unwin's reader and an influential literary friend.

1895 *Almayer's Folly* published.

1896 *An Outcast of the Islands* published. Becomes acquainted with H. G. Wells. 24 March: Marriage to Jessie George. Begins work on *The Rescue* and initiates correspondence with Henry James.

1897 Corresponds with R. B. Cunninghame Graham (to be a close friend and a source for Gould in *Nostromo*). *The Nigger of the 'Narcissus'* published.

1898 *Tales of Unrest* ('Karain', 'The Idiots', 'An Outpost of Progress', 'The Return', 'The Lagoon') published. Enters into collaboration with Ford Madox Ford (then surnamed Hueffer). Takes over from Ford the lease of a Kentish farmhouse, 'The Pent'. Friendship with Stephen Crane. Borys Conrad born.

1899 'Heart of Darkness' serialized in *Blackwood's Magazine*. J. B. Pinker becomes Conrad's literary agent.

1899–1900 *Lord Jim* serialized in *Blackwood's*.

1900 Stephen Crane dies. *Lord Jim* published as a book.

1901 *The Inheritors* (collaboration with Ford) published.

1902   *Youth: A Narrative; and Two Other Stories* ('Youth', 'Heart of Darkness', 'The End of the Tether') published. *Typhoon* published in New York.

1903   *Typhoon and Other Stories* ('Typhoon', 'Amy Foster', 'Falk', 'Tomorrow') and *Romance* (collaboration with Ford) published.

1904   Jessie Conrad injures her knees and is partially disabled for life. *Nostromo* published.

1906   Meets Arthur Marwood, who becomes a close friend. John Conrad born. *The Mirror of the Sea* published.

1907   The Conrads move to The Someries, Luton Hoo. *The Secret Agent* published.

1908   *A Set of Six* ('Gaspar Ruiz', 'The Informer', 'The Brute', 'An Anarchist', 'The Duel', 'Il Conde') published.

1909   Quarrels with Ford over his contributions to *The English Review*. The Conrads move to a cottage at Aldington, near 'The Pent'.

1910   Completion of *Under Western Eyes* accompanied by a nervous breakdown; Conrad lies in bed holding 'converse with the characters' of the novel. On his recovery the Conrads move to Capel House, Orlestone.

1911   *Under Western Eyes* published.

1912   *A Personal Record* and *'Twixt Land and Sea* ('A Smile of Fortune', 'The Secret Sharer', 'Freya of the Seven Isles') published. *Chance* serialized in *New York Herald*.

1913   *Chance* published as book.

1914   *Chance* has very good sales, especially in America; the earlier works now find a larger public. The Conrads visit Poland and are nearly trapped by the outbreak of war.

1915   *Within the Tides* ('The Planter of Malata', 'The Partner', 'The Inn of the Two Witches') and *Victory* published.

1917   *The Shadow-Line* published. Conrad begins to write 'Author's Notes' for a collected edition of his works.

1919   *The Arrow of Gold* published. The Conrads move to Oswalds, Bishopsbourne, near Canterbury.

1920   *The Rescue* published, 24 years after it was begun.

1921   Visit to Corsica for research on *Suspense*. Conrad in poor health. *Notes on Life and Letters* published.

1923   Conrad visits America and is lionized. *The Rover* published.

1924   May: Declines the offer of a knighthood. 3 August: Dies of a heart attack at Oswalds; buried at Canterbury. *The Nature of a Crime* (collaboration with Ford) published.

1925   *Tales of Hearsay* ('The Warrior's Soul', 'Prince Roman', 'The Tale', 'The Black Mate') and *Suspense* published.

1926   *Last Essays* published.

1928   *The Sisters* (fragment) published.

1917   After three years of non-regulation... The Cuban move to Zürich; Dadaist movement, Tristan...

1920   The Kroon publishes *Je vais m'en aller* operating...

1922   Visit to Greece for research on *El greco*. Ordered to put health. *Prospect* delayed lecture published.

1923   Travel with Angelos, and a brother for... Theodore published.

1924   *Mega Tsichina* ibid Book... Cavafy on Aristotle. Tree of...

1925   *Ode to Women*... The Women... ibid *Prince Roman*... The Cahiers, ibid Matter...

1929   The... (repeated) published.

To
PERCEVAL
and
MAISIE GIBBON

NOTE TO THE FIRST EDITION

THE last word of this novel was written on the 29th of May, 1914. And that last word was the single word of the title.

Those were the times of peace. Now that the moment of publication approaches I have been considering the discretion of altering the title-page. The word Victory, the shining and tragic goal of noble effort, appeared too great, too august, to stand at the head of a mere novel. There was also the possibility of falling under the suspicion of commercial astuteness deceiving the public into the belief that the book had something to do with war.

Of that, however, I was not afraid very much. What influenced my decision most were the obscure promptings of that pagan residuum of awe and wonder which lurks still at the bottom of our old humanity. Victory was the last word I had written in peace time. It was the last literary thought which had occurred to me before the doors of the Temple of Janus flying open with a crash shook the minds, the hearts, the consciences of men all over the world. Such coincidence could not be treated lightly. And I made up my mind to let the word stand, in the same hopeful spirit in which some simple citizen of Old Rome would have "accepted the Omen."

The second point on which I wish to offer a remark is the existence (in the novel) of a person named Schomberg.

That I believe him to be true goes without saying. I

am not likely to offer pinchbeck wares to my public consciously. Schomberg is an old member of my company. A very subordinate personage in Lord Jim as far back as the year 1899, he became notably active in a certain short story of mine published in 1902. Here he appears in a still larger part, true to life (I hope), but also true to himself. Only, in this instance, his deeper passions come into play, and thus his grotesque psy- chology is completed at last.

I don't pretend to say that this is the entire Teutonic psychology; but it is indubitably the psychology of a Teuton. My object in mentioning him here is to bring out the fact that, far from being the incarnation of re- cent animosities, he is the creature of my old, deep- seated and, as it were, impartial conviction.

J. C.

AUTHOR'S NOTE

ON APPROACHING the task of writing this Note for
"Victory" the first thing I am conscious of is the actual
nearness of the book, its nearness to me personally, to
the vanished mood in which it was written and to the
mixed feelings aroused by the critical notices the book
obtained when first published almost exactly a year
after the beginning of the great war. The writing of it
was finished in 1914 long before the murder of an Aus-
trian Archduke sounded the first note of warning for a
world already full of doubts and fears.

The contemporaneous very short Author's Note
which is preserved in this edition bears sufficient witness to the feelings with which I consented to the publication of the book. The fact of the book having
been published in the United States early in the year
made it difficult to delay its appearance in England any
longer. It came out in the thirteenth month of the
war, and my conscience was troubled by the awful
incongruity of throwing this bit of imagined drama into
the welter of reality, tragic enough in all conscience
but even more cruel than tragic and more inspiring
than cruel. It seemed awfully presumptuous to think
there would be eyes to spare for those pages in a community which in the crash of the big guns and in the din of
brave words expressing the truth of an indomitable faith
could not but feel the edge of a sharp knife at its throat.

The unchanging Man of history is wonderfully adap-
table both by his power of endurance and in his capacity for detachment. The fact seems to be that the
play of his destiny is too great for his fears and too

mysterious for his understanding. Were the trump of the Last Judgment to sound suddenly on a working day the musician at his piano would go on with his performance of Beethoven's Sonata and the cobbler at his stall stick to his last in undisturbed confidence in the virtues of the leather. And with perfect propriety. For what are we to let ourselves be disturbed by an angel's vengeful music too mighty for our ears and too awful for our terrors? Thus it happens to us to be struck suddenly by the lightning of wrath. The reader will go on reading if the book pleases him and the critic will go on criticizing with that faculty of detachment born perhaps from a sense of infinite littleness and which is yet the only faculty that seems to assimilate man to the immortal gods.

It is only when the catastrophe matches the natural obscurity of our fate that even the best representative of the race is liable to lose his detachment. It is very obvious that on the arrival of the gentlemanly Mr. Jones, the single-minded Ricardo and the faithful Pedro, Heyst, the man of universal detachment, loses his mental self-possession, that fine attitude before the universally irremediable which wears the name of stoicism. It is all a matter of proportion. There should have been a remedy for that sort of thing. And yet there is no remedy. Behind this minute instance of life's hazards Heyst sees the power of blind destiny. Besides, Heyst in his fine detachment had lost the habit of asserting himself. I don't mean the courage of self-assertion, either moral or physical, but the mere way of it, the trick of the thing, the readiness of mind and the turn of the hand that come without reflection and lead the man to excellence in life, in art, in crime, in virtue, and for the matter of that, even in love. Thinking is the great enemy of perfection. The habit of profound reflection, I am compelled to say, is the most pernicious of all the habits formed by the civilized man.

But I wouldn't be suspected even remotely of making fun of Axel Heyst. I have always liked him. The flesh and blood individual who stands behind the infinitely more familiar figure of the book I remember as a mysterious Swede right enough. Whether he was a baron, too, I am not so certain. He himself never laid a claim to that distinction. His detachment was too great to make any claims, big or small, on one's credulity. I will not say where I met him because I fear to give my readers a wrong impression, since a marked incongruity between a man and his surroundings is often a very misleading circumstance. We became very friendly for a time and I would not like to expose him to unpleasant suspicions though, personally, I am sure he would have been indifferent to suspicions as he was indifferent to all the other disadvantages of life. He was not the whole Heyst of course; he is only the physical and moral foundation of my Heyst laid on the ground of a short acquaintance. That it was short was certainly not my fault for he had charmed me by the mere amenity of his detachment which, in this case, I cannot help thinking he had carried to excess. He went away from his rooms without leaving a trace. I wondered where he had gone to—but now I know. He vanished from my ken only to drift into this adventure that, unavoidable, waited for him in a world which he persisted in looking upon as a malevolent shadow spinning in the sunlight. Often in the course of years an expressed sentiment, the particular sense of a phrase heard casually, would recall him to my mind so that I have fastened on to him many words heard on other men's lips and belonging to other men's less perfect, less pathetic moods.

The same observation will apply *mutatis mutandis*

to Mr. Jones, who is built on a much slenderer connection. Mr. Jones (or whatever his name was) did
not drift away from me. He turned his back on me
and walked out of the room. It was in a little hotel in
the Island of St. Thomas in the West Indies (in the
year '75) where we found him one hot afternoon
extended on three chairs, all alone in the loud buzzing of
flies to which his immobility and his cadaverous aspect
gave a most gruesome significance. Our invasion must
have displeased him because he got off the chairs
brusquely and walked out, leaving with me an indelibly
weird impression of his thin shanks. One of the men
with me said that the fellow was the most desperate
gambler he had ever come across. I said: "A profes-
sional sharper?" and got for answer: "He's a terror;
but I must say that up to a certain point he will play
fair. . . . " I wonder what the point was. I
never saw him again because I believe he went straight
on board a mail-boat which left within the hour for
other ports of call in the direction of Aspinall. Mr.
Jones' characteristic insolence belongs to another man of
a quite different type. I will say nothing as to the origins of his mentality because I don't intend to make any
damaging admissions.

It so happened that the very same year Ricardo—the
physical Ricardo—was a fellow passenger of mine on
board an extremely small and extremely dirty little
schooner, during a four days' passage between two
places in the Gulf of Mexico whose names don't matter.
For the most part he lay on deck aft as it were at my feet,
and raising himself from time to time on his elbow would
talk about himself and go on talking, not exactly to
me or even at me (he would not even look up but kept
his eyes fixed on the deck) but more as if communing
in a low voice with his familiar devil. Now and then

he would give me a glance and make the hairs of his stiff little moustache stir quaintly. His eyes were green and every cat I see to this day reminds me of the exact contour of his face. What he was travelling for or what was his business in life he never confided to me. Truth to say, the only passenger on board that schooner who could have talked openly about his activities and purposes was a very snuffy and conversationally delightful friar, the Superior of a convent, attended by a very young lay brother, of a particularly ferocious countenance. We had with us also, lying prostrate in the dark and unspeakable cuddy of that schooner, an old Spanish gentleman, owner of much luggage and, as Ricardo assured me, very ill indeed. Ricardo seemed to be either a servant or the confidant of that aged and distinguished-looking invalid, who early on the passage held a long murmured conversation with the friar, and after that did nothing but groan feebly, smoke cigarettes and now and then call for Martin in a voice full of pain. Then he who had become Ricardo in the book would go below into that beastly and noisome hole, remain there mysteriously, and coming up on deck again with a face on which nothing could be read, would as likely as not resume for my edification the exposition of his moral attitude toward life illustrated by striking particular instances of the most atrocious complexion. Did he mean to frighten me? Or seduce me? Or astonish me? Or arouse my admiration? All he did was to arouse my amused incredulity. As scoundrels go he was far from being a bore. For the rest my innocence was so great then that I could not take his philosophy seriously. All the time he kept one ear turned to the cuddy in the manner of a devoted servant, but I had the idea that in some way or other he had imposed the connection on the invalid for some end of his own. The reader, therefore, won't be surprised to hear that one morning I was told without any particular emotion by the padrone of the schooner that the "Rich man" down there was dead: He had died in the night. I don't remember ever being so moved by the desolate end of a complete stranger. I looked down the skylight, and there was the devoted Martin busy cording cowhide trunks belonging to the deceased whose white beard and hooked nose were the only parts I could make out in the dark depths of a horrible stuffy bunk.

As it fell calm in the course of the afternoon and continued calm during all that night and the terrible, flaming day, the late "Rich man" had to be thrown overboard at sunset, though as a matter of fact we were in sight of the low pestilential mangrove-lined coast of our destination. The excellent Father Superior mentioned to me with an air of immense commiseration: "The poor man has left a young daughter." Who was to look after her I don't know, but I saw the devoted Martin taking the trunks ashore with great care just before I landed myself. I would perhaps have tracked the ways of that man of immense sincerity for a little while, but I had some of my own very pressing business to attend to, which in the end got mixed up with an earthquake and so I had no time to give to Ricardo. The reader need not be told that I have not forgotten him, though.

My contact with the faithful Pedro was much shorter and my observation of him was less complete but incomparably more anxious. It ended in a sudden inspiration to get out of his way. It was in a hovel of sticks and mats by the side of a path. As I went in there only to ask for a bottle of lemonade I have not to this day the slightest idea what in my appearance or actions could have roused his terrible ire. It became manifest to me less than two minutes after I had set eyes on him for the first time, and though immensely surprised of course I didn't stop to think it out. I took the nearest short cut—through the wall. This bestial apparition and a certain enormous buck nigger encountered in Haiti only a couple of months afterwards, have fixed my conception of blind, furious, unreas ning rage, as manifested in the human animal, to the end of my days. Of the nigger I used to dream for years afterwards. Of Pedro never. The impression was less vivid. I got away from him too quickly.

It seems to me but natural that those three buried in a corner of my memory should suddenly get out into the light of the world—so natural that I offer no excuse for their existence. They were there, they had to come out; and this is a sufficient excuse for a writer of tales who had taken to his trade without preparation, or premeditation, and without any moral intention but that which pervades the whole scheme of this world of senses.

Since this Note is mostly concerned with personal contacts and the origins of the persons in the tale, I am bound also to speak of Lena, because if I were to leave her out it would look like a slight; and nothing would be further from my thoughts than putting a slight on Lena. If of all the personages involved in the "mystery of Samburan" I have lived longest with Heyst (or with him I call Heyst) it was at her, whom I call Lena, that I have looked the longest and with a most sustained attention. This attention originated in idleness for which I have a natural talent. One evening I wandered into a café, in a town not of the tropics but of the South of France. It was filled with tobacco smoke, the hum of voices, the rattling of dominoes and the sounds of strident music. The orchestra was rather

smaller than the one that performed at Schomberg's
hotel, had the air more of a family party than of an
enlisted band, and, I must confess, seemed rather more
respectable than the Zangiacomo musical enterprise. It
was less pretentious also, more homely and familiar,
so to speak, insomuch that in the intervals when all
the performers left the platform one of them went
amongst the marble tables collecting offerings of sous
and francs in a battered tin receptacle recalling the
shape of a sauceboat. It was a girl. Her detachment
from her task seems to me now to have equalled or
even surpassed Heyst's aloofness from all the mental
degradations to which a man's intelligence is exposed in
its way through life. Silent and wide-eyed she went
from table to table with the air of a sleep-walker and
with no other sound but the slight rattle of the coins
to attract attention. It was long after the sea-chapter
of my life had been closed but it is difficult to discard
completely the characteristics of half a life-time, and
it was in something of the Jack-ashore spirit that I
dropped a five-franc piece into the sauceboat; whereupon
the sleep-walker turned her head to gaze at me and said
"Merci, Monsieur," in a tone in which there was no gratitude but only surprise. I must have been idle indeed to
take the trouble to remark on such slight evidence that
the voice was very charming and when the performers
resumed their seats I shifted my position slightly in
order not to have that particular performer hidden
from me by the little man with the beard who conducted, and who might for all I know have been her
father, but whose real mission in life was to be a model
for the Zangiacomo of "Victory." Having got a clear
line of sight I naturally (being idle) continued to look
at the girl through all the second part of the programme.
The shape of her dark head inclined over the violin

was fascinating, and, while resting between the pieces of that interminable programme she was, in her white dress and with her brown hands reposing in her lap, the very image of dreamy innocence. The mature, bad-tempered woman at the piano might have been her mother, though there was not the slightest resemblance between them. All I am certain of in their personal relation to each other is that cruel pinch on the upper part of the arm. That I am sure I have seen! There could be no mistake. I was in a too idle mood to imagine such a gratuitous barbarity. It may have been playfulness, yet the girl jumped up as if she had been stung by a wasp. It may have been playfulness. Yet I saw plainly poor "dreamy innocence" rub gently the affected place as she filed off with the other performers down the middle aisle between the marble tables in the uproar of voices, the rattling of dominoes, through a blue atmosphere of tobacco smoke. I believe that those people left the town next day.

Or perhaps they had only migrated to the other big café, on the other side of the Place de la Comédie. It is very possible. I did not go across to find out. It was my perfect idleness that had invested the girl with a peculiar charm, and I did not want to destroy it by any superfluous exertion. The receptivity of my indolence made the impression so permanent that when the moment came for her meeting with Heyst I felt that she would be heroically equal to every demand of the risky and uncertain future. I was so convinced of it that I let her go with Heyst, I won't say without a pang but certainly without misgivings. And in view of her triumphant end what more could I have done for her rehabilitation and her happiness?

1920.   J. C.

PART I

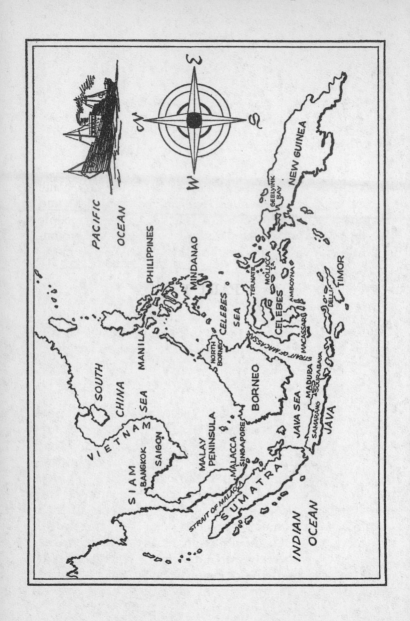

VICTORY

I

THERE is, as every schoolboy knows in this scientific age, a very close chemical relation between coal and diamonds.* It is the reason, I believe, why some people allude to coal as "black diamonds." Both these commodities represent wealth; but coal is a much less portable form of property. There is, from that point of view, a deplorable lack of concentration in coal. Now, if a coal-mine could be put into one's waistcoat pocket—but it can't! At the same time, there is a fascination in coal, the supreme commodity of the age in which we are camped like bewildered travellers in a garish, unrestful hotel. And I suppose those two considerations, the practical and the mystical, prevented Heyst—Axel Heyst*—from going away.

The Tropical Belt Coal Company went into liquidation. The world of finance is a mysterious world in which, incredible as the fact may appear, evaporation precedes liquidation. First the capital evaporates, and then the company goes into liquidation.* These are very unnatural physics, but they account for the persistent inertia of Heyst, at which we "out there" used to laugh among ourselves—but not inimically. An inert body can do no harm to any one, provokes no hostility, is scarcely worth derision. It may, indeed, be in the way sometimes; but this could not be said of Axel Heyst. He was out of everybody's way, as if he were perched on the highest peak of the Himalayas, and in a sense as conspicuous. Every one in that part of the world knew of him, dwelling on his little island. An island is but the top of a mountain. Axel Heyst, perched on it immovably, was surrounded, instead of the imponderable stormy and transparent ocean of air merging into infinity, by a tepid, shallow sea; a passionless offshoot of the great waters which embrace the continents of this globe. His most frequent visitors were shadows, the shadows of clouds, relieving the monotony of the inanimate, brooding sunshine of the tropics. His nearest neighbour—I am speaking now of things showing some sort of animation—was an indolent volcano which smoked faintly all day with its head just above the northern horizon, and at night levelled at him, from amongst the clear stars, a dull red glow, expanding and collapsing spasmodically like the end of a gigantic cigar puffed at intermittently in the dark. Axel Heyst was also a smoker; and when he lounged out on his verandah with his cheroot, the last thing before going to bed, he made in the night the same sort of glow and of the same size as that other one so many miles away.

In a sense, the volcano was company to him in the shades of the night—which were often too thick, one would think, to let a breath of air through. There was seldom enough wind to blow a feather along. On most evenings of the year Heyst could have sat outside with a naked candle to read one of the books left him by his late father. It was not a mean store. But he never did that. Afraid of mosquitoes, very likely. Neither was he ever tempted by the silence to address any casual remarks to the companion glow of the volcano. He was not mad. Queer chap—yes, that may have been said, and in fact was said; but there is a tremendous difference between the two, you will allow.

On the nights of full moon the silence around Samburan*—the "Round Island" of the charts—was dazzling; and in the flood of cold light Heyst could see his immediate surroundings, which had the aspect of an abandoned settlement invaded by the jungle: vague roofs above low vegetation, broken shadows of bamboo fences in the sheen of long grass, something like an overgrown bit of road slanting among ragged thickets towards the shore only a couple of hundred yards away, with a black jetty and a mound of some sort, quite inky on its unlighted side. But the most conspicuous object was a gigantic blackboard raised on two posts and presenting to Heyst, when the moon got over that side, the white letters "T. B. C. Co." in a row at least two feet high. These were the initials of the Tropical Belt Coal Company, his employers—his late employers, to be precise.

According to the unnatural mysteries of the financial world, the T. B. C. Company's capital having evaporated in the course of two years, the company went into liquidation—forced, I believe, not voluntary. There was nothing forcible in the process, however. It was slow; and while the liquidation—in London and Amsterdam—pursued its languid course, Axel Heyst, styled in the prospectus "manager in the tropics," remained at his post on Samburan, the No. 1 coaling-station of the company.

And it was not merely a coaling-station. There was a coal-mine there, with an outcrop in the hillside less than five hundred yards from the rickety wharf and the imposing blackboard. The company's object had been to get hold of all the outcrops on tropical islands and exploit them locally. And, Lord knows, there were any amount of outcrops. It was Heyst who had located most of them in this part of the tropical belt during his rather aimless wanderings, and being a ready letter-writer had written pages and pages about them to his friends in Europe. At least, so it was said.

We doubted whether he had any visions of wealth—for himself, at any rate. What he seemed mostly concerned for was the "stride forward," as he expressed it, in the general organisation of the universe, apparently. He was heard by more than a hundred persons in the islands talking of a "great stride forward for these regions." The convinced wave of the hand which accompanied the phrase suggested tropical distances being impelled onward. In connection with the finished courtesy of his manner, it was persuasive, or at any rate silencing—for a time, at least. Nobody cared to argue with him when he talked in this strain. His earnestness could do no harm to anybody. There was no danger of any one taking seriously his dream of tropical coal, so what was the use of hurting his feelings?

Thus reasoned men in reputable business offices where he had his entrée as a person who came out East with letters of introduction—and modest letters of credit, too —some years before these coal-outcrops began to crop up in his playfully courteous talk. From the first there was some difficulty in making him out. He was not a traveller. A traveller arrives and departs, goes on somewhere. Heyst did not depart. I met a man once—the manager of the branch of the Oriental Banking Corporation in Malacca*—to whom Heyst exclaimed, in no connection with anything in particular (it was in the billiard-room of the club):

"I am enchanted with these islands!"

He shot it out suddenly, à propos des bottes,* as the French say, and while chalking his cue. And perhaps it was some sort of enchantment. There are more spells than your commonplace magicians ever dreamed of.

Roughly speaking, a circle with a radius of eight hundred miles drawn round a point in North Borneo was in Heyst's case a magic circle. It just touched Manila, and he had been seen there. It just touched Saigon, and he was likewise seen there once. Perhaps these were his attempts to break out. If so, they were failures. The enchantment must have been an unbreakable one. The manager—the man who heard the exclamation—had been so impressed by the tone, fervour, rapture, what you will, or perhaps by the incongruity of it that he had related the experience to more than one person.

"Queer chap, that Swede," was his only comment; but this is the origin of the name "Enchanted Heyst" which some fellows fastened on our man.

He also had other names. In his early years, long before he got so becomingly bald on the top, he went to present a letter of introduction to Mr. Tesman of Tesman Brothers, a Sourabaya firm—tip-top house. Well, Mr. Tesman was a kindly, benevolent old gentleman. He did not know what to make of that caller. After telling him that they wished to render his stay among the islands as pleasant as possible, and that they were ready to assist him in his plans, and so on, and after receiving Heyst's thanks—you know the usual kind of conversation—he proceeded to query in a slow, paternal tone:

"And you are interested in——?"

"Facts," broke in Heyst in his courtly voice. "There's nothing worth knowing but facts. Hard facts! Facts alone, Mr. Tesman."

I don't know if old Tesman agreed with him or not, but he must have spoken about it, because, for a time,

our man got the name of "Hard Facts." He had the
singular good fortune that his sayings stuck to him
and became part of his name. Thereafter he mooned
about the Java Sea in some of the Tesman's trading
schooners, and then vanished, on board an Arab ship,
in the direction of New Guinea. He remained so long
in that outlying part of his enchanted circle that he
was nearly forgotten before he swam into view again
in a native proa*full of Goram*vagabonds, burnt black
by the sun, very lean, his hair much thinned, and a port-
folio of sketches under his arm. He showed these
willingly, but was very reserved as to anything else.
He had had an "amusing time," he said. A man who
will go to New Guinea for fun—well!

Later, years afterward, when the last vestiges of
youth had gone off his face and all the hair off the top
of his head, and his red-gold pair of horizontal moustaches had grown to really noble proportions, a certain
disreputable white man fastened upon him an epithet.
Putting down with a shaking hand a long glass emptied
of its contents—paid for by Heyst—he said, with that
deliberate sagacity which no mere water-drinker ever
attained:

"Heyst's a puffect g'n'lman. Puffect! But he's a
ut-uto-utopist."

Heyst had just come out of the place of public
refreshment where this pronouncement was voiced.
Utopist, eh? Upon my word, the only thing I heard
him say which might have had a bearing on the point
was his invitation to old McNab himself. Turning
with that finished courtesy of attitude, movement,
voice, which was his obvious characteristic, he had said
with delicate playfulness:

"Come along and quench your thirst with us, Mr.
McNab!"

Perhaps that was it. A man who could propose, even playfully, to quench old McNab's thirst must have been an utopist, a pursuer of chimæras;* for of downright irony Heyst was not prodigal. And, may be, this was the reason why he was generally liked. At that epoch in his life, in the fulness of his physical development, of a broad, martial presence, with his bald head and long moustaches, he resembled the portraits of Charles XII;* of adventurous memory. However, there was no reason to think that Heyst was in any way a fighting man.

II

IT WAS about this time that Heyst became associated with Morrison on terms about which people were in doubt. Some said he was a partner, others said he was a sort of paying guest, but the real truth of the matter was more complex. One day Heyst turned up in Timor.* Why in Timor, of all places in the world, no one knows. Well, he was mooning about Delli,* that highly pestilential place, possibly in search of some undiscovered facts, when he came in the street upon Morrison, who, in his way, was also an "enchanted" man. When you spoke to Morrison of going home— he was from Dorsetshire—he shuddered. He said it was dark and wet there; that it was like living with your head and shoulders in a moist gunny-bag.* That was only his exaggerated style of talking. Morrison was "one of us."* He was owner and master of the *Capricorn*, trading brig, and was understood to be doing well with her, except for the drawback of too much altruism. He was the dearly beloved friend of a quantity of God-forsaken villages up dark creeks and obscure bays, where he traded for "produce." He would often sail through awfully dangerous channels up to some miserable settlement, only to find a very hungry population clamorous for rice, and without so much "produce" between them as would have filled Morrison's suit-case. Amid general rejoicings, he would land the rice all the same, explain to the people that it was an advance, that they were in debt to him now; would preach to them energy and industry, and make an elaborate note in a pocket-diary which he always carried; and this would be the end of that transaction. I don't know if Morrison thought so, but the villagers had no doubt whatever about it. Whenever a coast village sighted the brig it would begin to beat all its gongs and hoist all its streamers, and all its girls would put flowers in their hair and the crowd would line the river bank, and Morrison would beam and glitter at all this excitement through his single eyeglass with an air of intense gratification. He was tall and lantern-jawed, and clean-shaven, and looked like a barrister who had thrown his wig to the dogs.

We used to remonstrate with him:

"You will never see any of your advances if you go on like this, Morrison."

He would put on a knowing air.

"I shall squeeze them yet some day—never you fear. And that reminds me"—pulling out his inseparable pocketbook—"there's that So-and-So village. They are pretty well off again; I may just as well squeeze them to begin with."

He would make a ferocious entry in the pocketbook:

Memo:—Squeeze the So-and-So village at the first time of calling.

Then he would stick the pencil back and snap the elastic on with inflexible finality; but he never began the squeezing. Some men grumbled at him. He was spoiling the trade. Well, perhaps to a certain extent; not much. Most of the places he traded with were unknown not only to geography but also to the traders' special lore which is transmitted by word of mouth, without ostentation, and forms the stock of mysterious local knowledge. It was hinted also that Morrison had a wife in each and every one of them, but the majority of us repulsed these innuendoes with indignation.

He was a true humanitarian and rather ascetic than otherwise.

When Heyst met him in Delli, Morrison was walking along the street, his eyeglass tossed over his shoulder, his head down, with the hopeless aspect of those hardened tramps one sees on our roads trudging from workhouse to workhouse. Being hailed across the street he looked up with a wild worried expression. He was really in trouble. He had come the week before into Delli, and the Portuguese authorities, on some pretence of irregularity in his papers, had inflicted a fine upon him and had arrested his brig.

Morrison never had any spare cash in hand. With his system of trading it would have been strange if he had; and all these debts entered in the pocketbook weren't good enough to raise a *millrei**on—let alone a shilling. The Portuguese officials begged him not to distress himself. They gave him a week's grace, and then proposed to sell the brig at auction. This meant ruin for Morrison; and when Heyst hailed him across the street in his usual courtly tone, the week was nearly out.

Heyst crossed over, and said with a slight bow, and in the manner of a prince addressing another prince on a private occasion:

"What an unexpected pleasure. Would you have any objection to drink something with me in that infamous wine-shop over there? The sun is really too strong to talk in the street."

The haggard Morrison followed obediently into a sombre, cool hovel which he would have disdained to enter at any other time. He was distracted. He did not know what he was doing. You could have led him over the edge of a precipice just as easily as into that wine-shop. He sat down like an automaton. He was speechless, but he saw a glass full of rough red wine before him, and emptied it. Heyst meantime, politely watchful, had taken a seat opposite.

"You are in for a bout of fever, I fear," he said sympathetically.

Poor Morrison's tongue was loosened at last.

"Fever!" he cried. "Give me fever. Give me plague. They are diseases. One gets over them. But I am being murdered. I am being murdered by the Portuguese. The gang here downed me at last among them. I am to have my throat cut the day after to-morrow."

In the face of this passion Heyst made, with his eyebrows, a slight motion of surprise which would not have been misplaced in a drawing-room. Morrison's despairing reserve had broken down. He had been wandering with a dry throat all over that miserable town of mud hovels, silent, with no soul to turn to in his distress, and positively maddened by his thoughts; and suddenly he had stumbled on a white man, figuratively and actually white—for Morrison refused to accept the racial whiteness of the Portuguese officials. He let himself go for the mere relief of violent speech, his elbows planted on the table, his eyes bloodshot, his voice nearly gone, the brim of his round pith hat shading an unshaven, livid face. His white clothes, which he had not taken off for three days, were dingy. He looked already gone to the bad, past redemption. The sight was shocking to Heyst; but he let nothing of it appear in his bearing, concealing his impression under that consummate good-society manner of his. Polite attention, what's due from one gentleman listening to another, was what he showed; and, as usual, it was catching; so that Morrison pulled himself together and finished his narrative in a conversational tone, with a man-of-the-world air.

"It's a villainous plot. Unluckily, one is helpless. That scoundrel Cousinho—Andreas, you know—has been coveting the brig for years. Naturally, I would never sell. She is not only my livelihood; she's my life. So he has hatched this pretty little plot with the chief of the customs. The sale, of course, will be a farce. There's no one here to bid. He will get the brig for a song—no, not even that—a line of a song. You have been some years now in the islands, Heyst. You know us all; you have seen how we live. Now you shall have the opportunity to see how some of us end; for it is the end, for me. I can't deceive myself any longer. You see it,—don't you?"

Morrison had pulled himself together, but one felt the snapping strain on his recovered self-possession. Heyst was beginning to say that he "could very well see all the bearings of this unfortunate——" when Morrison interrupted him jerkily.

"Upon my word, I don't know why I have been telling you all this. I suppose seeing a thoroughly white man made it impossible to keep my trouble to myself. Words can't do it justice; but since I've told you so much I may as well tell you more. Listen. This morning on board, in my cabin I went down on my knees and prayed for help. I went down on my knees!"

"You are a believer, Morrison?" asked Heyst with a distinct note of respect.

"Surely I am not an infidel."

Morrison was swiftly reproachful in his answer, and there came a pause, Morrison perhaps interrogating his conscience, and Heyst preserving a mien of unperturbed, polite interest.

"I prayed like a child, of course. I believe in children praying—well, women, too, but I rather think God expects men to be more self-reliant. I don't hold with a man everlastingly bothering the Almighty with his silly troubles. It seems such cheek. Anyhow, this morning I—I have never done any harm to any God's creature knowingly—I prayed. A sudden impulse—I went flop on my knees; so you may judge——"

They were gazing earnestly into each other's eyes. Poor Morrison added, as a discouraging afterthought: "Only this is such a God-forsaken spot."

Heyst inquired with a delicate intonation whether he might know the amount for which the brig was seized.

Morrison suppressed an oath, and named curtly a sum which was in itself so insignificant that any other person than Heyst would have exclaimed at it. And even Heyst could hardly keep incredulity out of his politely modulated voice as he asked if it was a fact that Morrison had not that amount in hand.

Morrison hadn't. He had only a little English gold, a few sovereigns, on board. He had left all his spare cash with the Tesmans, in Samarang, to meet certain bills which would fall due while he was away on his cruise. Anyhow, that money would not have been any more good to him than if it had been in the innermost depths of the infernal regions. He said all this brusquely. He looked with sudden disfavour at that noble forehead, at those great martial moustaches, at the tired eyes of the man sitting opposite him. Who the devil was he? What was he, Morrison, doing there, talking like this? Morrison knew no more of Heyst than the rest of us trading in the Archipelago did. Had the Swede suddenly risen and hit him on the nose, he could not have been taken more aback than when this stranger, this nondescript wanderer, said with a little bow across the table:

"Oh! If that's the case I would be very happy if you'd allow me to be of use!"

Morrison didn't understand. This was one of those things that don't happen—unheard of things. He had no real inkling of what it meant, till Heyst said definitely:

"I can lend you the amount."

"You have the money?" whispered Morrison. "Do you mean here, in your pocket?"

"Yes, on me. Glad to be of use."

Morrison, staring open-mouthed, groped over his shoulder for the cord of the eyeglass hanging down his back. When he found it, he stuck it in his eye hastily. It was as if he expected Heyst's usual white suit of the tropics to change into a shining garment flowing down to his toes, and a pair of great dazzling wings to sprout on the Swede's shoulders—and didn't want to miss a single detail of the transformation. But if Heyst was an angel from on high, sent in answer to prayer, he did not betray his heavenly origin by outward signs. So, instead of going on his knees, as he felt inclined to do, Morrison stretched out his hand, which Heyst grasped with formal alacrity and a polite murmur in which "Trifle—delighted—of service," could be just distinguished.

"Miracles do happen," thought the awestruck Morrison. To him, as to all of us in the islands, this wandering Heyst, who didn't toil or spin visibly, seemed the very last person to be the agent of Providence in an affair concerned with money. The fact of his turning up in Timor or anywhere else was no more wonderful than the settling of a sparrow on one's window-sill at any given moment. But that he should carry a sum of money in his pocket seemed somehow inconceivable.

So inconceivable that as they were trudging together through the sand of the roadway to the custom-house— another mud hovel—to pay the fine, Morrison broke into a cold sweat, stopped short, and exclaimed in faltering accents:

"I say! You aren't joking, Heyst?"

"Joking!" Heyst's blue eyes went hard as he turned them on the discomposed Morrison. "In what way, may I ask?" he continued with austere politeness.

Morrison was abashed.

"Forgive me, Heyst. You must have been sent by God in answer to my prayer. But I have been nearly off my chump for three days with worry; and it suddenly struck me: 'What if it's the Devil who has sent him?'"

"I have no connection with the supernatural," said Heyst graciously, moving on. "Nobody has sent me. I just happened along."

"I know better," contradicted Morrison. "I may be unworthy, but I have been heard. I know it. I feel it. For why should you offer——"

Heyst inclined his head, as from respect for a conviction in which he could not share. But he stuck to his point by muttering that in the presence of an odious fact like this, it was natural——

Later in the day, the fine paid, and the two of them on board the brig, from which the guard had been removed, Morrison—who, besides being a gentleman, was also an honest fellow—began to talk about repayment. He knew very well his inability to lay by any sum of money. It was partly the fault of circumstances and partly of his temperament; and it would have been very difficult to apportion the responsibility between the two. Even Morrison himself could not say, while confessing to the fact. With a worried air he ascribed it to fatality.

"I don't know how it is that I've never been able to save. It's some sort of curse. There's always a bill or two to meet."

He plunged his hand into his pocket for the famous notebook so well known in the islands, the fetish of his hopes, and fluttered the pages feverishly.

"And yet—look," he went on. "There it is—more than five thousand dollars owing. Surely that's something."

He ceased suddenly. Heyst, who had been all the time trying to look as unconcerned as he could, made reassuring noises in his throat. But Morrison was not only honest. He was honourable, too; and on this stressful day, before this amazing emissary of Providence and in the revulsion of his feelings, he made his great renunciation. He cast off the abiding illusion of his existence.

"No. No. They are no good. I'll never be able to squeeze them. Never. I've been saying for years I would; but I give it up. I never really believed I could. Don't reckon on that, Heyst. I have robbed you."

Poor Morrison actually laid his head on the cabin table, and remained in that crushed attitude while Heyst talked to him soothingly with the utmost courtesy. The Swede was as much distressed as Morrison; for he understood the other's feelings perfectly. No decent feeling was ever scorned by Heyst. But he was incapable of outward cordiality of manner, and he felt acutely his defect. Consummate politeness is not the right tonic for an emotional collapse. They must have had, both of them, a fairly painful time of it in the cabin of the brig. In the end Morrison, casting desperately for an idea in the blackness of his despondency, hit upon the notion of inviting Heyst to travel with him in his brig and have a share in his trading ventures up to the amount of his loan.

It is characteristic of Heyst's unattached, floating existence that he was in a position to accept this pro-

posal. There is no reason to think that he wanted
particularly just then to go poking aboard the brig
into all the holes and corners of the Archipelago where
Morrison picked up most of his trade. Far from it; but
he would have consented to almost any arrangement in
order to put an end to the harrowing scene in the cabin.
There was at once a great transformation act: Morrison
raising his diminished head and sticking the glass in
his eye to look affectionately at Heyst, a bottle being
uncorked, and so on. It was agreed that nothing
should be said to any one of this transaction. Morrison,
you understand, was not proud of the episode, and he
was afraid of being unmercifully chaffed.

"An old bird like me! To let myself be trapped by
those damned Portuguese rascals! I should never hear
the last of it. We must keep it dark."

From quite other motives, among which his native
delicacy was the principal, Heyst was even more anxious
to bind himself to silence. A gentleman would naturally shrink from the part of heavenly messenger that
Morrison would force upon him. It made Heyst uncomfortable, as it was. And perhaps he did not care
that it should be known that he had some means,
whatever they might have been—sufficient, at any rate,
to enable him to lend money to people. These two
had a duet down there, like conspirators in a comic
opera, of "Sh—ssh, shssh! Secrecy! Secrecy!" It
must have been funny, because they were very serious
about it.

And for a time the conspiracy was successful in so far
that we all concluded that Heyst was boarding with the
good-natured—some said: sponging on the imbecile—
Morrison, in his brig. But you know how it is with
all such mysteries. There is always a leak somewhere.
Morrison himself, not a perfect vessel by any means,

was bursting with gratitude, and under the stress he must have let out something vague—enough to give the island gossip a chance. And you know how kindly the world is in its comments on what it does not understand. A rumour sprang out that Heyst, having obtained some mysterious hold on Morrison, had fastened himself on him and was sucking him dry. Those who had traced these mutters back to their origin were very careful not to believe them. The originator, it seems, was a certain Schomberg,* a big, manly, bearded creature of the Teutonic persuasion, with an ungovernable tongue which surely must have worked on a pivot. Whether he was a Lieutenant of the Reserve,* as he declared, I don't know. Out there he was by profession a hotel-keeper, first in Bangkok,* then somewhere else, and ultimately in Sourabaya.* He dragged after him up and down that section of the tropical belt a silent, frightened little woman with long ringlets, who smiled at one stupidly, showing a blue tooth. I don't know why so many of us patronized his various establishments. He was a noxious ass, and he satisfied his lust for silly gossip at the cost of his customers. It was he who, one evening, as Morrison and Heyst went past the hotel— they were not his regular patrons—whispered mysteriously to the mixed company assembled on the verandah:

"The spider and the fly just gone by, gentlemen." Then, very important and confidential, his thick paw at the side of his mouth: "We are among ourselves; well, gentlemen, all I can say is, don't you ever get mixed up with that Swede. Don't you ever get caught in his web."

III

HUMAN nature being what it is, having a silly side to it as well as a mean side, there were not a few who pretended to be indignant on no better authority than a general propensity to believe every evil report; and a good many others who found it simply funny to call Heyst the Spider—behind his back, of course. He was as serenely unconscious of this as of his several other nicknames. But soon people found other things to say of Heyst; not long afterward he came very much to the fore in larger affairs. He blossomed out into something definite. He filled the public eye as the manager on the spot of the Tropical Belt Coal Company with offices in London and Amsterdam, and other things about it that sounded and looked grandiose. The offices in the two capitals may have consisted—and probably did—of one room in each; but at that distance, out East there, all this had an air. We were more puzzled than dazzled, it is true; but even the most sober-minded among us began to think that there was something in it. The Tesmans appointed agents, a contract for government mail-boats secured, the era of steam beginning for the islands—a great stride forward—Heyst's stride!

And all this sprang from the meeting of the cornered Morrison and of the wandering Heyst, which may or may not have been the direct outcome of a prayer. Morrison was not an imbecile, but he seemed to have got himself into a state of remarkable haziness as to his exact position towards Heyst. For, if Heyst had been sent with money in his pocket by a direct decree of the Almighty in answer to Morrison's prayer then there was no reason for special gratitude, since obviously he could not help himself. But Morrison believed both in the efficacy of prayer and in the infinite goodness of Heyst. He thanked God with awed sincerity for His mercy, and could not thank Heyst enough for the service rendered as between man and man. In this (highly creditable) tangle of strong feelings Morrison's gratitude insisted on Heyst's partnership in the great discovery. Ultimately we heard that Morrison had gone home through the Suez Canal in order to push the magnificent coal idea personally in London. He parted from his brig and disappeared from our ken; but we heard that he had written a letter or letters to Heyst, saying that London was cold and gloomy; that he did not like either the men or things, that he was "as lonely as a crow in a strange country." In truth, he pined after the *Capricorn*—I don't mean only the tropic; I mean the ship too. Finally he went into Dorsetshire to see his people, caught a bad cold, and died with extraordinary precipitation in the bosom of his appalled family. Whether his exertions in the City of London had enfeebled his vitality I don't know; but I believe it was this visit which put life into the coal idea. Be it as it may, the Tropical Belt Coal Company was born very shortly after Morrison, the victim of gratitude and his native climate, had gone to join his forefathers in a Dorsetshire churchyard.

Heyst was immensely shocked. He got the news in the Moluccas* through the Tesmans, and then disappeared for a time. It appears that he stayed with a Dutch government doctor in Amboyna,* a friend of his who looked after him for a bit in his bungalow. He became visible again rather suddenly, his eyes sunk in his head, and with a sort of guarded attitude, as if afraid someone would reproach him with the death of Morrison.

Naïve Heyst! As if anybody would. . . . Nobody amongst us had any interest in men who went home. They were all right; they did not count any more. Going to Europe was nearly as final as going to Heaven. It removed a man from the world of hazard and adventure.

As a matter of fact, many of us did not hear of this death till months afterward—from Schomberg, who disliked Heyst gratuitously and made up a piece of sinister whispered gossip:

"That's what comes of having anything to do with that fellow. He squeezes you dry like a lemon, then chucks you out—sends you home to die. Take warning by Morrison."

Of course, we laughed at the innkeeper's suggestions of black mystery. Several of us heard that Heyst was prepared to go to Europe himself, to push on his coal enterprise personally; but he never went. It wasn't necessary. The company was formed without him, and his nomination of manager in the tropics came out to him by post.

From the first he had selected Samburan, or Round Island, for the central station. Some copies of the prospectus issued in Europe, having found their way out East, were passed from hand to hand. We greatly admired the map which accompanied them for the edification of the shareholders. On it Samburan was represented as the central spot of the Eastern Hemisphere with its name engraved in enormous capitals. Heavy lines radiated from it in all directions through the tropics, figuring a mysterious and effective star—lines of influence or lines of distance, or something of that sort. Company promoters have an imagination of their own. There's no more romantic temperament on earth than the temperament of a company promoter. Engineers came out, coolies were imported, bungalows were put up on Samburan, a gallery driven into the hillside, and actually some coal got out.

These manifestations shook the soberest minds. For a time everybody in the islands was talking of the Tropical Belt Coal, and even those who smiled quietly to themselves were only hiding their uneasiness. Oh, yes; it had come, and anybody could see what would be the consequences—the end of the individual trader, smothered under a great invasion of steamers. We could not afford to buy steamers. Not we. And Heyst was the manager.

"You know, Heyst, enchanted Heyst."

"Oh, come! He has been no better than a loafer around here as far back as any of us can remember."

"Yes, said he was looking for facts. Well, he's got hold of one that will do for all of us," commented a bitter voice.

"That's what they call development—and be hanged to it!" muttered another.

Never was Heyst talked about so much in the tropical belt before.

"Isn't he a Swedish baron or something?"

"He, a baron? Get along with you!"

For my part I haven't the slightest doubt that he was. While he was still drifting amongst the islands, enigmatical and disregarded like an insignificant ghost, he told me so himself on a certain occasion. It was a long time before he materialized in this alarming way into the destroyer of our little industry—Heyst the Enemy.

It became the fashion with a good many to speak of

Heyst as the Enemy. He was very concrete, very
visible now. He was rushing all over the Archipelago,
jumping in and out of local mail-packets as if they had
been tram-cars, here, there, and everywhere—organizing
with all his might. This was no mooning about. This
was business. And this sudden display of purposeful
energy shook the incredulity of the most sceptical
more than any scientific demonstration of the value
of these coal-outcrops could have done. It was impressive. Schomberg was the only one who resisted
the infection. Big, manly in a portly style, and pro-
fusely bearded, with a glass of beer in his thick paw,
he would approach some table where the topic of the
hour was being discussed, would listen for a moment,
and then come out with his invariable declaration:

"All this is very well, gentlemen; but he can't throw
any of his coal-dust in my eyes. There's nothing in it.
Why, there can't be anything in it. A fellow like that
for manager? Phoo!"

Was it the clairvoyance of imbecile hatred, or mere
stupid tenacity of opinion, which ends sometimes by
scoring against the world in a most astonishing manner?
Most of us can remember instances of triumphant folly;
and that ass Schomberg triumphed. The T. B. C. Co.
went into liquidation, as I began by telling you. The
Tesmans washed their hands of it. The Government
cancelled those famous contracts. The talk died out,
and presently it was remarked here and there that
Heyst had faded completely away. He had become
invisible, as in those early days when he used to make
a bolt clear out of sight in his attempts to break away
from the enchantment of "these isles," either in the
direction of New Guinea or in the direction of Saigon—
to cannibals or to cafés. The enchanted Heyst! Had
he at last broken the spell? Had he died? We were

too indifferent to wonder over-much. You see we had on the whole liked him well enough. And liking is not sufficient to keep going the interest one takes in a human being. With hatred, apparently, it is otherwise. Schomberg couldn't forget Heyst. The keen, manly Teutonic creature was a good hater. A fool often is.

"Good evening, gentlemen. Have you got everything you want? So! Good! You see? What was I always telling you? Aha! There was nothing in it. I knew it. But what I would like to know is what became of that—Swede."

He put a stress on the word Swede as if it meant scoundrel. He detested Scandinavians generally. Why? Goodness only knows. A fool like that is unfathomable. He continued:

"It's five months or more since I have spoken to anybody who has seen him."

As I have said, we were not much interested; but Schomberg, of course, could not understand that. He was grotesquely dense. Whenever three people came together in his hotel, he took good care that Heyst should be with them.

"I hope the fellow did not go and drown himself," he would add with a comical earnestness that ought to have made us shudder; only our crowd was superficial, and did not apprehend the psychology of this pious hope.

"Why? Heyst isn't in debt to you for drinks, is he?" somebody asked him once with shallow scorn.

"Drinks! Oh, dear, no!"

The innkeeper was not mercenary. Teutonic temperament seldom is. But he put on a sinister expression to tell us that Heyst had not paid perhaps three visits altogether to his "establishment." This was

Heyst's crime, for which Schomberg wished him nothing less than a long and tormented existence. Observe the Teutonic sense of proportion and nice forgiving temper.

At last, one afternoon, Schomberg was seen approaching a group of his customers. He was obviously in high glee. He squared his manly chest with great importance.

"Gentlemen, I have news of him. Who? Why, that Swede. He is still on Samburan. He's never been away from it. The company is gone, the engineers are gone, the clerks are gone, the coolies are gone, everything's gone; but there he sticks. Captain Davidson, coming by from the westward, saw him with his own eyes. Something white on the wharf; so he steamed in and went ashore in a small boat. Heyst, right enough. Put a book into his pocket, always very polite. Been strolling on the wharf and reading. 'I remain in possession here,' he told Captain Davidson. What I want to know is what he gets to eat there. A piece of dried fish now and then—what? That's coming down pretty low for a man who turned up his nose at my table-d'hôte!"

He winked with immense malice. A bell started ringing, and he led the way to the dining-room as if into a temple, very grave, with the air of a benefactor of mankind. His ambition was to feed it at a profitable price, and his delight was to talk of it behind its back. It was very characteristic of him to gloat over the idea of Heyst having nothing decent to eat.

IV

A FEW of us who were sufficiently interested went to Davidson for details. These were not many. He told us that he passed to the north of Samburan on purpose to see what was going on. At first, it looked as if that side of the island had been altogether abandoned. This was what he expected. Presently, above the dense mass of vegetation that Samburan presents to view, he saw the head of the flagstaff without a flag. Then, while steaming across the slight indentation which for a time was known officially as Black Diamond Bay, he made out with his glass the white figure on the coaling-wharf. It could be no one but Heyst.

"I thought for certain he wanted to be taken off, so I steamed in. He made no signs. However, I lowered a boat. I could not see another living being anywhere. Yes. He had a book in his hand. He looked exactly as we have always seen him—very neat, white shoes, cork helmet. He explained to me that he had always had a taste for solitude. It was the first I ever heard of it, I told him. He only smiled. What could I say? He isn't the sort of man one can speak familiarly to. There's something in him. One doesn't care to.

"'But what's the object? Are you thinking of keeping possession of the mine?' I asked him.

"'Something of the sort,' he says. 'I am keeping hold.'

"'But all this is as dead as Julius Cæsar,' I cried. 'In fact, you have nothing worth holding on to, Heyst.'

"'Oh, I am done with facts,' says he, putting his

hand to his helmet sharply with one of his short bows."

Thus dismissed, Davidson went on board his ship, swung her out, and as he was steaming away he watched from the bridge Heyst walking shoreward along the wharf. He marched into the long grass and vanished— all but the top of his white cork helmet, which seemed to swim in a green sea. Then that too disappeared, as if it had sunk into the living depths of the tropical vegetation, which is more jealous of men's conquests than the ocean, and which was about to close over the last vestiges of the liquidated Tropical Belt Coal Company—A. Heyst, manager in the East.

Davidson, a good, simple fellow in his way, was strangely affected. It is to be noted that he knew very little of Heyst. He was one of those whom Heyst's finished courtesy of attitude and intonation most strongly disconcerted. He himself was a fellow of fine feeling, I think, though of course he had no more polish than the rest of us. We were naturally a hail-fellow-well-met crowd, with standards of our own— no worse, I daresay, than other people's; but polish was not one of them. Davidson's fineness was real enough to alter the course of the steamer he commanded. Instead of passing to the south of Samburan, he made it his practice to take the passage along the north shore, within about a mile of the wharf.

"He can see us if he likes to see us," remarked Davidson. Then he had an after-thought: "I say! I hope he won't think I am intruding, eh?"

We reassured him on the point of correct behaviour. The sea is open to all.

This slight deviation added some ten miles to Davidson's round trip, but as that was sixteen hundred miles it did not matter much.

"I have told my owner of it," said the conscientious commander of the *Sissie*.

His owner had a face like an ancient lemon. He was small and wizened—which was strange, because generally a Chinaman, as he grows in prosperity, puts on inches of girth and stature. To serve a Chinese firm is not so bad. Once they become convinced you deal straight by them, their confidence becomes unlimited. You can do no wrong. So Davidson's old Chinaman squeaked hurriedly:

"All right, all right, all right. You do what you like, captain."

And there was an end of the matter; not altogether, though. From time to time the Chinaman used to ask Davidson about the white man. He was still there, eh?

"I never see him," Davidson had to confess to his owner, who would peer at him silently through round, horn-rimmed spectacles, several sizes too large for his little old face. "I never see him."

To me, on occasions, he would say:

"I haven't a doubt he's there. He hides. It's very unpleasant." Davidson was a little vexed with Heyst. "Funny thing," he went on. "Of all the people I speak to, nobody ever asks after him but that Chinaman of mine—and Schomberg," he added after a while.

Yes, Schomberg, of course. He was asking everybody about everything, and arranging the information into the most scandalous shape his imagination could invent. From time to time he would step up, his blinking, cushioned eyes, his thick lips, his very chestnut beard, looking full of malice.

"'Evening, gentlemen. Have you got all you want? So! Good! Well, I am told the jungle has choked the very sheds in Black Diamond Bay. Fact. He's a hermit in the wilderness now. But what can this manager get to eat there? It beats me."

Sometimes a stranger would inquire with natural curiosity:

"Who? What manager?"

"Oh, a certain Swede,"—with a sinister emphasis, as if he were saying "a certain brigand."—"Well known here. He's turned hermit from shame. That's what the devil does when he's found out."

Hermit. This was the latest of the more or less witty labels applied to Heyst during his aimless pilgrimage in this section of the tropical belt, where the inane clacking of Schomberg's tongue vexed our ears.

But apparently Heyst was not a hermit by temperament. The sight of his kind was not invincibly odious to him. We must believe this, since for some reason or other he did come out from his retreat for a while. Perhaps it was only to see whether there were any letters for him at the Tesmans. I don't know. No one knows. But this reappearance shows that his detachment from the world was not complete. And incompleteness of any sort leads to trouble. Axel Heyst ought not to have cared for his letters—or whatever it was that brought him out after something more than a year and a half in Samburan. But it was of no use. He had not the hermit's vocation! That was the trouble, it seems.

Be this as it may, he suddenly reappeared in the world, broad chest, bald forehead, long moustaches, polite manner, and all—the complete Heyst, even to the kindly, sunken eyes on which there still rested the shadow of Morrison's death. Naturally, it was Davidson who had given him a lift out of his forsaken island. There were no other opportunities, unless some native craft were passing by—a very remote and unsatisfactory chance to wait for. Yes, he came out with Davidson, to whom he volunteered the statement that it was only for a short time—a few days, no more. He meant to go back to Samburan.

Davidson expressing his horror and incredulity of such foolishness, Heyst explained that when the company came into being he had his few belongings sent out from Europe.

To Davidson as to any of us, the idea of Heyst, the wandering, drifting, unattached Heyst, having any belongings of the sort that can furnish a house was startlingly novel. It was grotesquely fantastic. It was like a bird owning real property.

"Belongings? Do you mean chairs and tables?" Davidson asked with unconcealed astonishment.

Heyst did mean that. "My poor father* died in London. It has been all stored there ever since," he explained.

"For all these years?" exclaimed Davidson, thinking how long we all had known Heyst flitting from tree to tree in a wilderness.

"Even longer," said Heyst, who had understood very well.

This seemed to imply that he had been wandering before he came under our observation. In what regions? At what early age? Mystery. Perhaps he was a bird that had never had a nest.

"I left school early," he remarked once to Davidson, on the passage. "It was in England. A very good school. I was not a shining success there."

The confessions of Heyst. Not one of us—with the probable exception of Morrison, who was dead—had ever heard so much of his history. It looks as if the experience of hermit life had the power to loosen one's tongue, doesn't it?

During that memorable passage, in the *Sissie*, which took about two days, he volunteered other hints—for you could not call it information—about his history. And Davidson was interested. He was interested not because the hints were exciting but because of that innate curiosity about our fellows which is a trait of human nature. Davidson's existence too, running the *Sissie* along the Java Sea* and back again, was distinctly monotonous and, in a sense, lonely. He never had any sort of company on board. Native deck-passengers in plenty, of course, but never a white man, so the presence of Heyst for two days must have been a godsend. Davidson was telling us all about it afterward. Heyst said that his father had written a lot of books. He was a philosopher.

"Seems to me he must have been something of a crank, too," was Davidson's comment. "Apparently he had quarrelled with his people in Sweden. Just the sort of father you would expect Heyst to have. Isn't he a bit of a crank himself? He told me that directly his father died he lit out into the wide world on his own, and had been on the move till he fetched up against this famous coal business. Fits the son of his father somehow, don't you think?"

For the rest, Heyst was as polite as ever. He offered to pay for his passage; but when Davidson refused to hear of it he seized him heartily by the hand, gave one of his courtly bows, and declared that he was touched by his friendly proceedings.

"I am not alluding to this trifling amount which you decline to take," he went on, giving a shake to Davidson's hand. "But I am touched by your humanity." Another shake. "Believe me, I am profoundly aware of having been an object of it." Final shake of the hand. All this meant that Heyst understood in a proper sense the little *Sissie's* periodical appearance in sight of his hermitage.

"He's a genuine gentleman," Davidson said to us. "I was really sorry when he went ashore."

We asked him where he had left Heyst.

"Why, in Sourabaya—where else?"

The Tesmans had their principal counting-house in Sourabaya. There had long existed a connection between Heyst and the Tesmans. The incongruity of a hermit having agents did not strike us, nor yet the absurdity of a forgotten cast-off, derelict manager of a wrecked, collapsed, vanished enterprise, having business to attend to. We said Sourabaya, of course, and took it for granted that he would stay with one of the Tesmans. One of us even wondered what sort of reception he would get; for it was known that Julius Tesman was unreasonably bitter about the Tropical Belt Coal fiasco. But Davidson set us right. It was nothing of the kind. Heyst went to stay in Schomberg's hotel, going ashore in the hotel launch. Not that Schomberg would think of sending his launch alongside a mere trader like the *Sissie*. But she had been meeting a coasting mail-packet, and had been signalled to. Schomberg himself was steering her.

"You should have seen Schomberg's eyes bulge out when Heyst jumped in with an ancient brown leather bag!" said Davidson. "He pretended not to know who it was—at first, anyway. I didn't go ashore with them. We didn't stay more than a couple of hours altogether. Landed two thousand cocoanuts and cleared out. I have agreed to pick him up again on my next trip in twenty days' time."

V

DAVIDSON happened to be two days late on his return trip; no great matter, certainly, but he made a point of going ashore at once, during the hottest hour of the afternoon, to look for Heyst. Schomberg's hotel stood back in an extensive enclosure containing a garden, some large trees, and, under their spreading boughs, a detached "hall available for concerts and other performances," as Schomberg worded it in his advertisements. Torn and fluttering bills, intimating in heavy red capitals "Concerts every night," were stuck on the brick pillars on each side of the gateway.

The walk had been long and confoundedly sunny. Davidson stood wiping his wet neck and face on what Schomberg called "the piazza." Several doors opened on to it, but all the screens were down. Not a soul was in sight, not even a China boy—nothing but a lot of painted iron chairs and tables. Solitude, shade, and gloomy silence—and a faint, treacherous breeze which came from under the trees and quite unexpectedly caused the melting Davidson to shiver slightly—the little shiver of the tropics which in Sourabaya, especially, often means fever and the hospital to the incautious white man.

The prudent Davidson sought shelter in the nearest darkened room. In the artificial dusk, beyond the levels of shrouded billiard-tables, a white form heaved up from two chairs on which it had been extended. The middle of the day, table d'hôte tiffin once over, was Schomberg's easy time. He lounged out, portly, deliberate, on the defensive, the great fair beard like a cuirass*over his manly chest. He did not like Davidson, never a very faithful client of his. He hit a bell on one of the tables as he went by, and asked in a distant, Officer-of-the-Reserve*manner:

"You desire?"

The good Davidson still sponging his wet neck, declared with simplicity that he had come to fetch away Heyst, as agreed.

"Not here!"

A Chinaman appeared in response to the bell. Schomberg turned to him very severely:

"Take the gentleman's order."

Davidson had to be going. Couldn't wait—only begged that Heyst should be informed that the *Sissie* would leave at midnight.

"Not—here, I am telling you!"

Davidson slapped his thigh in concern.

"Dear me! Hospital, I suppose." A natural enough surmise in a very feverish locality.

The Lieutenant of the Reserve only pursed up his mouth and raised his eyebrows without looking at him. It might have meant anything, but Davidson dismissed the hospital idea with confidence. However, he had to get hold of Heyst between this and midnight.

"He has been staying here?" he asked.

"Yes, he was staying here."

"Can you tell me where he is now?" Davidson went on placidly. Within himself he was beginning to grow anxious, having developed the affection of a self-appointed protector towards Heyst. The answer he got was:

"Can't tell. It's none of my business," accompanied by majestic oscillations of the hotel-keeper's head, hinting at some awful mystery.

Davidson was placidity itself. It was his nature.
He did not betray his sentiments, which were not
favourable to Schomberg.

"I am sure to find out at the Tesmans' office," he
thought. But it was a very hot hour, and if Heyst was
down at the port he would have learned already that
the *Sissie* was in. It was even possible that Heyst
had already gone on board, where he could enjoy a
coolness denied to the town. Davidson, being stout,
was much preoccupied with coolness and inclined to
immobility. He lingered awhile, as if irresolute.
Schomberg, at the door, looking out, affected perfect
indifference. He could not keep it up, though. Suddenly he turned inward and asked with brusque rage:

"You wanted to see him?"

"Why, yes," said Davidson. "We agreed to meet——"

"Don't you bother. He doesn't care about that
now."

"Doesn't he?"

"Well, you can judge for yourself. He isn't here, is
he? You take my word for it. Don't you bother about
him. I am advising you as a friend."

"Thank you," said Davidson, inwardly startled at
the savage tone. "I think I will sit down for a moment
and have a drink, after all."

This was not what Schomberg had expected to hear.
He called brutally:

"Boy!"

The Chinaman approached, and after referring him
to the white man by a nod the hotel-keeper departed,
muttering to himself. Davidson heard him gnash his
teeth as he went.

Davidson sat alone with the billiard-tables as if
there had been not a soul staying in the hotel. His
placidity was so genuine that he was not unduly fretting

himself over the absence of Heyst or the mysterious manners Schomberg had treated him to. He was considering these things in his own fairly shrewd way. Something had happened; and he was loath to go away to investigate, being restrained by a presentiment that somehow enlightenment would come to him there. A poster of "Concerts Every Evening," like those on the gate, but in a good state of preservation, hung on the wall fronting him. He looked at it idly and was struck by the fact—then not so very common—that it was a ladies' orchestra; "Zangiacomo's eastern tour—eighteen performers." The poster stated that they had had the honour of playing their select repertoire before various colonial excellencies, also before pashas, sheiks, chiefs, H. H. the Sultan of Mascate, etc., etc.

Davidson felt sorry for the eighteen lady-performers. He knew what that sort of life was like, the sordid conditions and brutal incidents of such tours led by such Zangiacomos who often were anything but musicians by profession. While he was staring at the poster, a door somewhere at his back opened, and a woman came in who was looked upon as Schomberg's wife, no doubt with truth. As somebody remarked cynically once, she was too unattractive to be anything else. The opinion that he treated her abominably was based on her frightened expression. Davidson lifted his hat to her. Mrs. Schomberg gave him an inclination of her sallow head and incontinently sat down behind a sort of raised counter, facing the door, with a mirror and rows of bottles at her back. Her hair was very elaborately done with two ringlets on the left side of her scraggy neck; her dress was of silk, and she had come on duty for the afternoon. For some reason or other Schomberg exacted this from her, though she added nothing to the fascinations of the place. She sat there in the smoke and noise, like an enthroned idol, smiling stupidly over the billiards from time to time, speaking to no one, and no one speaking to her. Schomberg himself took no more interest in her than may be implied in a sudden and totally unmotived scowl. Otherwise the very Chinamen ignored her existence.

She had interrupted Davidson in his reflections. Being alone with her, her silence and open-eyed immobility made him uncomfortable. He was easily sorry for people. It seemed rude not to take any notice of her. He said, in allusion to the poster: "Are you having these people in the house?"

She was so unused to being addressed by customers that at the sound of his voice she jumped in her seat. Davidson was telling us afterward that she jumped exactly like a figure made of wood, without losing her rigid immobility. She did not even move her eyes; but she answered him freely, though her very lips seemed made of wood.

"They stayed here over a month. They are gone now. They played every evening."

"Pretty good, were they?"

To this she said nothing; and as she kept on staring fixedly in front of her, her silence disconcerted Davidson. It looked as if she had not heard him—which was impossible. Perhaps she drew the line of speech at the expression of opinions. Schomberg might have trained her, for domestic reasons, to keep them to herself. But Davidson felt in honour obliged to converse; so he said, putting his own interpretation on this surprising silence:

"I see—not much account. Such bands hardly ever are. An Italian lot, Mrs. Schomberg, to judge by the name of the boss?"

She shook her head negatively.

"No. He is a German really; only he dyes his hair

and beard black for business. Zangiacomo is his business name."

"That's a curious fact," said Davidson. His head being full of Heyst, it occurred to him that she might be aware of other facts. This was a very amazing discovery to any one who looked at Mrs. Schomberg. Nobody had ever suspected her of having a mind, I mean even a little of it, I mean any at all. One was inclined to think of her as an It—an automaton, a very plain dummy, with an arrangement for bowing the head at times and smiling stupidly now and then. Davidson viewed her profile with a flattened nose, a hollow cheek, and one staring, unwinking, goggle eye. He asked himself: Did that speak just now? Will it speak again? It was as exciting, for the mere wonder of it, as trying to converse with a mechanism. A smile played about the fat features of Davidson; the smile of a man making an amusing experiment. He spoke again to her:

"But the other members of that orchestra were real Italians, were they not?"

Of course, he didn't care. He wanted to see whether the mechanism would work again. It did. It said they were not. They were of all sorts, apparently. It paused, with the one goggle eye immovably gazing down the whole length of the room and through the door opening on to the "piazza." It paused, then went on in the same low pitch:

"There was even one English girl."

"Poor devil!" said Davidson. "I suppose these women are not much better than slaves really. Was that fellow with the dyed beard decent in his way?"

The mechanism remained silent. The sympathetic soul of Davidson drew its own conclusions.

"Beastly life for these women!" he said. "When you say an English girl, Mrs. Schomberg, do you really mean a young girl? Some of these orchestra girls are no chicks."

"Young enough," came the low voice out of Mrs. Schomberg's unmoved physiognomy.

Davidson, encouraged, remarked that he was sorry for her. He was easily sorry for people.

"Where did they go to from here?" he asked.

"She did not go with them. She ran away."

This was the pronouncement Davidson obtained next. It introduced a new sort of interest.

"Well! Well!" he exclaimed placidly; and then, with the air of a man who knows life: "Who with?" he inquired with assurance.

Mrs. Schomberg's immobility gave her an appearance of listening intently. Perhaps she was really listening; but Schomberg must have been finishing his sleep in some distant part of the house. The silence was profound, and lasted long enough to become startling. Then, enthroned above Davidson, she whispered at last:

"That friend of yours."

"Oh, you know I am here looking for a friend," said Davidson hopefully. "Won't you tell me——"

"I've told you."

"Eh?"

A mist seemed to roll away from before Davidson's eyes, disclosing something he could not believe.

"You can't mean it!" he cried. "He's not the man for it." But the last words came out in a faint voice. Mrs. Schomberg never moved her head the least bit. Davidson, after the shock which made him sit up, went slack all over.

"Heyst! Such a perfect gentleman!" he exclaimed weakly.

Mrs. Schomberg did not seem to have heard him.

This startling fact did not tally somehow with the idea
Davidson had of Heyst. He never talked of women,
he never seemed to think of them, or to remember that
they existed; and then all at once—like this! Running
off with a casual orchestra girl!

"You might have knocked me down with a feather,"
Davidson told us some time afterward.

By then he was taking an indulgent view of both the
parties to that amazing transaction. First of all, on
reflection, he was by no means certain that it prevented
Heyst from being a perfect gentleman, as before. He
confronted our open grins or quiet smiles with a serious
round face. Heyst had taken the girl away to Samburan; and that was no joking matter. The loneliness,
the ruins of the spot, had impressed Davidson's simple
soul. They were incompatible with the frivolous
comments of people who had not seen it. That black
jetty, sticking out of the jungle into the empty sea;
these roof-ridges of deserted houses peeping dismally
above the long grass! Ough! The gigantic and funeral
blackboard sign of the Tropical Belt Coal Company,
still emerging from a wild growth of bushes like an
inscription stuck above a grave figured by the tall
heap of unsold coal at the shore end of the wharf, added
to the general desolation.

Thus the sensitive Davidson. The girl must have
been miserable indeed to follow a strange man to such
a spot. Heyst had, no doubt, told her the truth. He
was a gentleman. But no words could do justice to
the conditions of life on Samburan. A desert island
was nothing to it. Moreover, when you were cast
away on a desert island—why, you could not help
yourself; but to expect a fiddle-playing girl out of an
ambulant ladies' orchestra to remain content there
for a day, for one single day, was inconceivable. She

would be frightened at the first sight of it. She would scream.

The capacity for sympathy in these stout, placid men! Davidson was stirred to the depths; and it was easy to see that it was about Heyst that he was concerned. We asked him if he had passed that way lately.

"Oh, yes. I always do—about half a mile off."

"Seen anybody about?"

"No, not a soul. Not a shadow."

"Did you blow your whistle?"

"Blow the whistle? You think I would do such a thing?"

He rejected the mere possibility of such an unwarrantable intrusion. Wonderfully delicate fellow, Davidson!

"Well, but how do you know that they are there?" he was naturally asked.

Heyst had entrusted Mrs. Schomberg with a message for Davidson—a few lines in pencil on a scrap of crumpled paper. It was to the effect that an unforeseen necessity was driving him away before the appointed time. He begged Davidson's indulgence for the apparent discourtesy. The woman of the house—meaning Mrs. Schomberg—would give him the facts, though unable to explain them, of course.

"What was there to explain?" wondered Davidson dubiously. "He took a fancy to that fiddle-playing girl, and——"

"And she to him, apparently," I suggested.

"Wonderfully quick work," reflected Davidson. "What do you think will come of it?"

"Repentance, I should say. But how is it that Mrs. Schomberg has been selected for a confidante?"

For indeed a waxwork figure would have seemed more useful than that woman whom we all were accustomed to see sitting elevated above the two billiard-tables—without expression, without movement, without voice, without sight.

"Why, she helped the girl to bolt," said Davidson turning at me his innocent eyes, rounded by the state of constant amazement in which this affair had left him, like those shocks of terror or sorrow which sometimes leave their victim afflicted by nervous trembling. It looked as though he would never get over it.

"Mrs. Schomberg jerked Heyst's note, twisted like a pipe-light, into my lap while I sat there unsuspecting," Davidson went on. "Directly I had recovered my senses, I asked her what on earth she had to do with it that Heyst should leave it with her. And then, behaving like a painted image rather than a live woman, she whispered, just loud enough for me to hear:

"'I helped them. I got her things together, tied them up in my own shawl, and threw them into the compound out of a back window. I did it.'

"That woman that you would say hadn't the pluck to lift her little finger!" marvelled Davidson in his quiet, slightly panting voice. "What do you think of that?"

I thought she must have had some interest of her own to serve. She was too lifeless to be suspected of impulsive compassion. It was impossible to think that Heyst had bribed her. Whatever means he had, he had not the means to do that. Or could it be that she was moved by that disinterested passion for delivering a woman to a man which in respectable spheres is called matchmaking?—a highly irregular example of it!

"It must have been a very small bundle," remarked Davidson further.

"I imagine the girl must have been specially attractive," I said.

"I don't know. She was miserable. I don't suppose

it was more than a little linen and a couple of these white frocks they wear on the platform."

Davidson pursued his own train of thought. He supposed that such a thing had never been heard of in the history of the tropics. For where could you find any one to steal a girl out of an orchestra? No doubt fellows here and there took a fancy to some pretty one— but it was not for running away with her. Oh dear no! It needed a lunatic like Heyst.

"Only think what it means," wheezed Davidson, imaginative under his invincible placidity. "Just only try to think! Brooding alone on Samburan has upset his brain. He never stopped to consider, or he couldn't have done it. No sane man. . . . How is a thing like that to go on? What's he going to do with her in the end? It's madness."

"You say that he's mad. Schomberg tells us that he must be starving on his island; so he may end yet by eating her,'"*I suggested.

Mrs. Schomberg had had no time to enter into details, Davidson told us. Indeed, the wonder was that they had been left alone so long. The drowsy afternoon was slipping by. Footsteps and voices resounded on the verandah—I beg pardon, the piazza; the scraping of chairs, the ping of a smitten bell. Customers were turning up. Mrs. Schomberg was begging Davidson hurriedly, but without looking at him, to say nothing to any one, when on a half-uttered word her nervous whisper was cut short. Through a small inner door Schomberg came in, his hair brushed, his beard combed neatly, but his eyelids still heavy from his nap. He looked with suspicion at Davidson, and even glanced at his wife; but he was baffled by the natural placidity of the one and the acquired habit of immobility in the other.

"Have you sent out the drinks?" he asked surlily.

She did not open her lips, because just then the head boy appeared with a loaded tray, on his way out. Schomberg went to the door and greeted the customers outside, but did not join them. He remained blocking half the doorway, with his back to the room, and was still there when Davidson, after sitting still for a while, rose to go. At the noise he made Schomberg turned his head, watched him lift his hat to Mrs. Schomberg and receive her wooden bow accompanied by a stupid grin, and then looked away. He was loftily dignified. Davidson stopped at the door, deep in his simplicity.

"I am sorry you won't tell me anything about my friend's absence," he said. "My friend Heyst, you know. I suppose the only course for me now is to make inquiries down at the port. I shall hear something there, I don't doubt."

"Make inquiries of the devil!" replied Schomberg in a hoarse mutter.

Davidson's purpose in addressing the hotel-keeper had been mainly to make Mrs. Schomberg safe from suspicion; but he would fain have heard something more of Heyst's exploit from another point of view. It was a shrewd try. It was successful in a rather startling way, because the hotel-keeper's point of view was horribly abusive. All of a sudden, in the same hoarse sinister tone, he proceeded to call Heyst many names, of which "pig-dog" was not the worst, with such vehemence that he actually choked himself. Profiting from the pause, Davidson, whose temperament could withstand worse shocks, remonstrated in an undertone:

"It's unreasonable to get so angry as that. Even if he had run off with your cash-box——"

The big hotel-keeper bent down and put his infuriated face close to Davidson's.

"My cash-box! My—he—look here, Captain Davidson! He ran off with a girl. What do I care for the
girl? The girl is nothing to me."

He shot out an infamous word which made Davidson
start. That's what the girl was; and he reiterated the
assertion that she was nothing to him. What he
was concerned for was the good name of his house.
Wherever he had been established, he had always had
"artist parties" staying in his house. One recom-
mended him to the others; but what would happen
now, when it got about that leaders ran the risk in his
house—his house—of losing members of their troupe?
And just now, when he had spent seven hundred and
thirty-four guilders in building a concert-hall in his
compound. Was that a thing to do in a respectable
hotel? The cheek, the indecency, the impudence,
the atrocity! Vagabond, imposter, swindler, ruffian,
Schwein-Hund !*

He had seized Davidson by a button of his coat,
detaining him in the doorway, and exactly in the line
of Mrs. Schomberg's stony gaze. Davidson stole a
glance in that direction and thought of making some
sort of reassuring sign to her, but she looked so bereft
of senses, and almost of life, perched up there, that it
seemed not worth while. He disengaged his button
with firm placidity. Thereupon, with a last stifled
curse, Schomberg vanished somewhere within, to try
and compose his spirits in solitude. Davidson stepped
out on the verandah. The party of customers there
had become aware of the explosive interlude in the
doorway. Davidson knew one of these men, and nodded to him in passing; but his acquaintance called
out:

"Isn't he in a filthy temper? He's been like that ever
since."

The speaker laughed aloud, while all the others sat smiling. Davidson stopped.

"Yes, rather." His feelings were, he told us, those of bewildered resignation; but of course that was no more visible to the others than the emotions of a turtle when it withdraws into its shell.

"It seems unreasonable," he murmured thoughtfully.

"Oh, but they had a scrap!" the other said.

"What do you mean? Was there a fight!—a fight with Heyst?" asked Davidson, much perturbed, if somewhat incredulous.

"Heyst? No, these two—the bandmaster, the fellow who's taking these women about and our Schomberg. Signor Zangiacomo ran amuck in the morning, and went for our worthy friend. I tell you, they were rolling on the floor together on this very verandah, after chasing each other all over the house, doors slamming, women screaming, seventeen of them, in the dining-room; Chinamen up the trees—Hey, John! You climb tree to see the fight, eh?"

The boy, almond-eyed and impassive, emitted a scornful grunt, finished wiping the table, and withdrew.

"That's what it was—a real, go-as-you-please scrap. And Zangiacomo began it. Oh, here's Schomberg. Say, Schomberg, didn't he fly at you, when the girl was missed, because it was you who insisted that the artists should go about the audience during the interval?"

Schomberg had reappeared in the doorway. He advanced. His bearing was stately, but his nostrils were extraordinarily expanded, and he controlled his voice with apparent effort.

"Certainly. That was only business. I quoted him special terms and all for your sake, gentlemen. I was thinking of my regular customers. There's nothing to do in the evenings in this town. I think, gentlemen, you were all pleased at the opportunity of hearing a little good music; and where's the harm of offering a grenadine,* or what not, to a lady artist? But that fellow—that Swede—he got round the girl. He got round all the people out here. I've been watching him for years. You remember how he got round Morrison."

He changed front abruptly, as if on parade, and marched off. The customers at the table exchanged glances silently. Davidson's attitude was that of a spectator. Schomberg's moody pacing of the billiard-room could be heard on the verandah.

"And the funniest part is," resumed the man who had been speaking before—an English clerk in a Dutch house—"the funniest part is that before nine o'clock that same morning those two were driving together in a gharry* down to the port, to look for Heyst and the girl. I saw them rushing around making inquiries. I don't know what they would have done to the girl, but they seemed quite ready to fall upon your Heyst, Davidson, and kill him on the quay."

He had never, he said, seen anything so queer. Those two investigators working feverishly to the same end were glaring at each other with surprising ferocity. In hatred and mistrust they entered a steam-launch, and went flying from ship to ship all over the harbour, causing no end of sensation. The captains of vessels, coming on shore later in the day, brought tales of a strange invasion, and wanted to know who were the two offensive lunatics in a steam-launch, apparently after a man and a girl, and telling a story of which one could make neither head nor tail. Their reception by the roadstead was generally unsympathetic, even to the point of the mate of an American ship bundling them out over the rail with unseemly precipitation.

Meantime Heyst and the girl were a good few miles away, having gone in the night on board one of the Tesman schooners bound to the eastward. This was known afterward from the Javanese boatmen whom Heyst hired for the purpose at three o'clock in the morning. The Tesman schooner had sailed at daylight with the usual land breeze, and was probably still in sight in the offing at the time. However, the two pursuers after their experience with the American mate made for the shore. On landing, they had another violent row in the German language. But there was no second fight; and finally, with looks of fierce animosity, they got together into a gharry—obviously with the frugal view of sharing expenses—and drove away, leaving an astonished little crowd of Europeans and natives on the quay.

After hearing this wondrous tale, Davidson went away from the hotel verandah, which was filling with Schomberg's regular customers. Heyst's escapade was the general topic of conversation. Never before had that unaccountable individual been the cause of so much gossip, he judged. No! Not even in the beginnings of the Tropical Belt Coal Company when becoming for a moment a public character he was the object of silly criticism and unintelligent envy for every vagabond and adventurer in the islands. Davidson concluded that people liked to discuss that sort of scandal better than any other.

I asked him if he believed that this was such a great scandal after all.

"Heavens, no!" said that excellent man who, himself, was incapable of any impropriety of conduct. "But it isn't a thing I would have done myself; I mean even if I had not been married."

There was no implied condemnation in the statement;

rather something like regret. Davidson shared my suspicion that this was in its essence the rescue of a distressed human being. Not that we were two romantics, tingeing the world to the hue of our temperament, but that both of us had been acute enough to discover a long time ago that Heyst was.

"I shouldn't have had the pluck," he continued. "I see a thing all round, as it were; but Heyst doesn't, or else he would have been scared. You don't take a woman into a desert jungle without being made sorry for it sooner or later, in one way or another; and Heyst being a gentleman only makes it worse."

VI

WE SAID no more about Heyst on that occasion, and it so happened that I did not meet Davidson again for some three months. When we did come together, almost the first thing he said to me was:

"I've seen him."

Before I could exclaim, he assured me that he had taken no liberty, that he had not intruded. He was called in. Otherwise he would not have dreamed of breaking in upon Heyst's privacy.

"I am certain you wouldn't," I assured him, concealing my amusement at his wonderful delicacy. He was the most delicate man that ever took a small steamer to and fro amongst the islands. But his humanity, which was not less strong and praiseworthy, had induced him to take his steamer past Samburan wharf (at an average distance of a mile) every twenty-three days—exactly. Davidson was delicate, humane and regular.

"Heyst called you in?" I asked, interested.

Yes, Heyst had called him in as he was going by on his usual date. Davidson was examining the shore through his glasses with his unwearied and punctual humanity as he steamed past Samburan.

"I saw a man in white. It could only have been Heyst. He had fastened some sort of enormous flag to a bamboo pole, and was waving it at the end of the old wharf."

Davidson didn't like to take his steamer alongside—for fear of being indiscreet, I suppose; but he steered

close inshore, stopped his engines, and lowered a boat.
He went himself in that boat, which was manned, of
course, by his Malay seamen.

Heyst, when he saw the boat pulling towards him,
dropped his signalling-pole; and when Davidson arrived, he was kneeling down engaged busily in unfasten-
ing the flag from it.

"Was there anything wrong?" I inquired, Davidson
having paused in his narrative and my curiosity being
naturally aroused. You must remember that Heyst as
the Archipelago knew him was not—what shall I say—
was not a signalling sort of man.

"The very words that came out of my mouth," said
Davidson, "before I laid the boat against the piles. I
could not help it."

Heyst got up from his knees and began carefully
folding up the flag thing, which struck Davidson as
having the dimensions of a blanket.

"No, nothing wrong," he cried. His white teeth
flashed agreeably below the coppery horizontal bar of
his long moustaches.

I don't know whether it was his delicacy or his obes-
ity which prevented Davidson from clambering upon
the wharf. He stood up in the boat, and, above him,
Heyst stooped low with urbane smiles, thanking him
and apologizing for the liberty, exactly in his usual
manner. Davidson had expected some change in the
man, but there was none. Nothing in him betrayed
the momentous fact that within that jungle there was
a girl, a performer in a ladies' orchestra, whom he had
carried straight off the concert platform into the wilderness. He was not ashamed or defiant or abashed about
it. He might have been a shade confidential when addressing Davidson. And his words were enigmatical.

"I took this course of signalling to you," he said to

Davidson, "because to preserve appearances might be of the utmost importance. Not to me, of course. I don't care what people may say, and of course no one can hurt me. I suppose I have done a certain amount of harm, since I allowed myself to be tempted into action. It seemed innocent enough, but all action is bound to be harmful. It is devilish. That is why this world is evil upon the whole. But I have done with it! I shall never lift a little finger again. At one time I thought that intelligent observation of facts was the best way of cheating the time which is allotted to us whether we want it or not; but now I have done with observation, too."

Imagine poor, simple Davidson being addressed in such terms alongside an abandoned, decaying wharf jutting out of tropical bush. He had never heard anybody speak like this before; certainly not Heyst, whose conversation was concise, polite, with a faint ring of playfulness in the cultivated tones of his voice.

"He's gone mad," Davidson thought to himself.

But, looking at the physiognomy above him on the wharf, he was obliged to dismiss the notion of common, crude lunacy. It was truly most unusual talk. Then he remembered—in his surprise he had lost sight of it—that Heyst now had a girl there. This bizarre discourse was probably the effect of the girl. Davidson shook off the absurd feeling, and asked, wishing to make clear his friendliness, and not knowing what else to say:

"You haven't run short of stores or anything like that?"

Heyst smiled and shook his head.

"No, no. Nothing of the kind. We are fairly well off here. Thanks, all the same. If I have taken the liberty to detain you, it is not from any uneasiness for myself and my—companion. The person I was thinking of when I made up my mind to invoke your assistance is Mrs. Schomberg."

"I have talked with her," interjected Davidson.

"Oh! You? Yes, I hoped she would find means to——"

"But she didn't tell me much," interrupted Davidson, who was not averse from hearing something—he hardly knew what.

"H'm—yes. But that note of mine? Yes? She found an opportunity to give it to you? That's good, very good. She's more resourceful than one would give her credit for."

"Women often are," remarked Davidson. The strangeness from which he had suffered, merely because his interlocutor had carried off a girl, wore off as the minutes went by. "There's a lot of unexpectedness about women," he generalized with a didactic aim which seemed to miss its mark; for the next thing Heyst said was:

"This is Mrs. Schomberg's shawl." He touched the stuff hanging over his arm. "An Indian thing, I believe," he added, glancing at his arm sideways.

"It isn't of particular value," said Davidson truthfully.

"Very likely. The point is that it belongs to Schomberg's wife. That Schomberg seems to be an unconscionable ruffian—don't you think so?"

Davidson smiled faintly.

"We out here have got used to him," he said, as if excusing a universal and guilty toleration of a manifest nuisance. "I'd hardly call him that. I only know him as a hotel-keeper."

"I never knew him even as that—not till this time, when you were so obliging as to take me to Sourabaya, I went to stay there from economy. The Netherlands

House is very expensive, and they expect you to bring
your own servant with you. It's a nuisance."

"Of course, of course," protested Davidson hastily.

After a short silence Heyst returned to the matter of
the shawl. He wanted to send it back to Mrs. Schomberg. He said that it might be very awkward for her
if she were unable, if asked, to produce it. This had
given him, Heyst, much uneasiness. She was terrified
of Schomberg. Apparently she had reason to be.

Davidson had remarked that, too. Which did not
prevent her, he pointed out, from making a fool of him,
in a way, for the sake of a stranger.

"Oh! You know!" said Heyst. "Yes, she helped
me—us."

"She told me so. I had quite a talk with her,"
Davidson informed him. "Fancy any one having a
talk with Mrs. Schomberg! If I were to tell the fellows
they wouldn't believe me. How did you get round her,
Heyst? How did you think of it? Why, she looks too
stupid to understand human speech and too scared to
shoo a chicken away. Oh, the women, the women!
You don't know what there may be in the quietest of
them."

"She was engaged in the task of defending her position in life," said Heyst. "It's a very respectable
task."

"Is that it? I had some idea it was that," confessed
Davidson.

He then imparted to Heyst the story of the violent
proceedings following on the discovery of his flight.
Heyst's polite attention to the tale took on a sombre
cast; but he manifested no surprise, and offered no
comment. When Davidson had finished he handed
down the shawl into the boat, and Davidson promised
to do his best to return it to Mrs. Schomberg in some

secret fashion. Heyst expressed his thanks in a few simple words, set off by his manner of finished courtesy. Davidson prepared to depart. They were not looking at each other. Suddenly Heyst spoke:

"You understand that this was a case of odious persecution, don't you? I became aware of it and——"

It was a view which the sympathetic Davidson was capable of appreciating.

"I am not surprised to hear it," he said placidly. "Odious enough, I dare say. And you, of course—not being a married man—were free to step in. Ah, well!"

He sat down in the stern-sheets, and already had the steering lines in his hands when Heyst observed abruptly:

"The world is a bad dog. It will bite you if you give it a chance; but I think that here we can safely defy the fates."

When relating all this to me, Davidson's only comment was:

"Funny notion of defying the fates—to take a woman in tow!"

VII

SOME considerable time afterward—we did not meet very often—I asked Davidson how he had managed about the shawl and heard that he had tackled his mission in a direct way, and had found it easy enough. At the very first call he made in Samarang he rolled the shawl as tightly as he could into the smallest possible brown paper parcel, which he carried ashore with him. His business in the town being transacted, he got into a gharry with the parcel and drove to the hotel. With his previous experience, he timed his arrival accurately for the hour of Schomberg's siesta. Finding the place empty as on the former occasion, he marched into the billiard-room, took a seat at the back, near the sort of dais which Mrs. Schomberg would in due course come to occupy, and broke the slumbering silence of the house by thumping a bell vigorously. Of course a Chinaman appeared promptly. Davidson ordered a drink and sat tight.

"I would have ordered twenty drinks one after another, if necessary," he said—Davidson's a very abstemious man— "rather than take that parcel out of the house again. Couldn't leave it in a corner without letting the woman know it was there. It might have turned out worse for her than not bringing the thing back at all."

And so he waited, ringing the bell again and again, and swallowing two or three iced drinks which he did not want. Presently, as he hoped it would happen, Mrs. Schomberg came in, silk dress, long neck, ringlets,

scared eyes, and silly grin—all complete. Probably
that lazy beast had sent her out to see who was the
thirsty customer waking up the echoes of the house at
this quiet hour. Bow, nod—and she clambered up
to her post behind the raised counter, looking so helpless, so inane, as she sat there, that if it hadn't been
for the parcel, Davidson declared, he would have
thought he had merely dreamed of all that had passed
between them. He ordered another drink, to get
the Chinaman out of the room, and then seized the
parcel, which was reposing on a chair near him, and
with no more than a mutter—"This is something of
yours"—he rammed it swiftly into a recess in the
counter, at her feet. There! The rest was her affair.
And just in time, too. Schomberg turned up, yawning
affectedly, almost before Davidson had regained his
seat. He cast about suspicious and irate glances. An
invincible placidity of expression helped Davidson
wonderfully at the moment, and the other, of course,
could have no grounds for the slightest suspicion of
any sort of understanding between his wife and this
customer.

As to Mrs. Schomberg, she sat there like a joss.
Davidson was lost in admiration. He believed, now,
that the woman had been putting it on for years. She
never even winked. It was immense! The insight
he had obtained almost frightened him; he couldn't
get over his wonder at knowing more of the real Mrs.
Schomberg than anybody in the Islands, including
Schomberg himself. She was a miracle of dissimula-
tion. No wonder Heyst got the girl away from under
two men's noses, if he had her to help with the job!

The greatest wonder, after all, was Heyst getting
mixed up with petticoats. The fellow's life had been
open to us for years and nothing could have been more

detached from feminine associations. Except that
he stood drinks to people on suitable occasions, like
any other man, this observer of facts seemed to have no
connection with earthly affairs and passions. The
very courtesy of his manner, the flavour of playfulness
in the voice set him apart. He was like a feather
floating lightly in the work-a-day atmosphere which
was the breath of our nostrils. For this reason whenever this looker-on took contact with things he
attracted attention. First, it was the Morrison partnership of mystery; then came the great sensation of the
Tropical Belt Coal where indeed varied interests were
involved: a real business matter. And then came this
elopement, this incongruous phenomenon of self-assertion, the greatest wonder of all, astonishing and amusing.

Davidson admitted to me that the hubbub was subsiding; and the affair would have been already forgotten,
perhaps, if that ass Schomberg had not kept on gnashing
his teeth publicly about it. It was really provoking
that Davidson should not be able to give one some
idea of the girl. Was she pretty? He didn't know.
He had stayed the whole afternoon in Schomberg's
hotel, mainly for the purpose of finding out something
about her. But the story was growing stale. The
parties at the tables on the verandah had other, fresher,
events to talk about and Davidson shrank from making
direct inquiries. He sat placidly there, content to be
disregarded and hoping for some chance word to turn
up. I shouldn't wonder if the good fellow hadn't
been dozing. It's difficult to give you an adequate
idea of Davidson's placidity.

Presently Schomberg, wandering about, joined a
party that had taken the table next to Davidson's.

"A man like that Swede, gentlemen, is a public

danger," he began. "I remember him for years. I
won't say anything of his spying—well, he used to say
himself he was looking for out-of-the-way facts, and
what is that if not spying? He was spying into everybody's business. He got hold of Captain Morrison,
squeezed him dry, like you would an orange, and
scared him off to Europe to die there. Everybody
knows that Captain Morrison had a weak chest.
Robbed first and murdered afterward! I don't
mince words—not I. Next he gets up that swindle
of the Belt Coal. You all know about it. And now,
after lining his pockets with other people's money,
he kidnaps a white girl belonging to an orchestra which
is performing in my public room for the benefit of my
patrons, and goes off to live like a prince on that island,
where nobody can get at him. A dam' silly girl . . .
It's disgusting—tfui!"

He spat. He choked with rage—for he saw visions,
no doubt. He jumped up from his chair, and went
away to flee from them—perhaps. He went into
the room where Mrs. Schomberg sat. Her aspect
could not have been very soothing to the sort of torment from which he was suffering.

Davidson did not feel called upon to defend Heyst.
His proceeding was to enter into conversation, with
one and another, casually, and showing no particular
knowledge of the affair, in order to discover something
about the girl. Was she anything out of the way? Was
she pretty? She couldn't have been markedly so. She
had not attracted special notice. She was young—on
that everybody agreed. The English clerk of Tesmans
remembered that she had a sallow face. He was respectable and highly proper. He was not the sort to
associate with such people. Most of these women
were fairly battered specimens. Schomberg had them

housed in what he called the Pavilion, in the grounds, where they were hard at it mending and washing their white dresses, and could be seen hanging them out to dry between the trees, like a lot of washerwomen. They looked very much like middle-aged washerwomen on the platform, too. But the girl had been living in the main building along with the boss, the director, the fellow with the black beard, and a hard-bitten, oldish woman who took the piano and was understood to be the fellow's wife.

This was not a very satisfactory result. Davidson stayed on, and even joined the table d'hôte dinner, without gleaning any more information. He was resigned.

"I suppose," he wheezed placidly, "I am bound to see her some day."

He meant to take the Samburan channel every trip, as before, of course.

"Yes," I said. "No doubt you will. Some day Heyst will be signalling to you again; and I wonder what it will be for."

Davidson made no reply. He had his own ideas about that, and his silence concealed a good deal of thought. We spoke no more of Heyst's girl. Before we separated, he gave me a piece of unrelated observation.

"It's funny," he said, "but I fancy there's some gambling going on in the evening at Schomberg's place, on the quiet. I've noticed men strolling away in twos and threes towards that hall where the orchestra used to play. The windows must be specially well shuttered, because I could not spy the smallest gleam of light from that direction; but I can't believe that those beggars would go in there only to sit and think of their sins in the dark."

"That's strange. It's incredible that Schomberg should risk*that sort of thing," I said.

PART II

I

As WE know, Heyst had gone to stay in Schomberg's hotel in complete ignorance that his person was odious to that worthy. When he arrived, Zangiacomo's Ladies' Orchestra had been established there for some time.

The business which had called him out from his seclusion in his lost corner of the Eastern seas was with the Tesmans, and it had something to do with money. He transacted it quickly, and then found himself with nothing to do while he awaited Davidson, who was to take him back to his solitude; for back to his solitude Heyst meant to go. He whom we used to refer to as the Enchanted Heyst was suffering from thorough disenchantment. Not with the islands, however. The Archipelago has a lasting fascination. It is not easy to shake off the spell of island life. Heyst was disenchanted with life as a whole. His scornful temperament, beguiled into action, suffered from failure in a subtle way unknown to men accustomed to grapple with the realities of common human enterprise. It was like the gnawing pain of useless apostasy, a sort of shame before his own betrayed nature; and, in addition, he also suffered from plain, downright remorse. He deemed himself guilty of Morrison's death. A rather absurd feeling, since no one could possibly have foreseen the horrors of the cold, wet summer lying in wait for poor Morrison at home.

It was not in Heyst's character to turn morose; but his mental state was not compatible with a sociable

mood. He spent his evenings sitting apart on the
verandah of Schomberg's hotel. The lamentations
of string instruments issued from the building in the
hotel compound, the approaches to which were decorated with Japanese paper lanterns strung up between
the trunks of several big trees. Scraps of tunes more or
less plaintive reached his ears. They pursued him even
into his bedroom, which opened into an upstairs verandah.
The fragmentary and rasping character of these sounds
made their intrusion inexpressibly tedious in the long
run. Like most dreamers, to whom it is given sometimes to hear the music of the spheres, Heyst, the wanderer of the Archipelago, had a taste for silence which
he had been able to gratify for years. The islands are
very quiet. One sees them lying about, clothed in
their dark garments of leaves, in a great hush of silver
and azure, where the sea without murmurs meets the
sky in a ring of magic stillness.* A sort of smiling
somnolence broods over them; the very voices of their
people are soft and subdued, as if afraid to break some
protecting spell.

Perhaps this was the very spell which had enchanted
Heyst in the early days. For him, however, that was
broken. He was no longer enchanted, though he was
still a captive of the islands. He had no intention to
leave them ever. Where could he have gone to, after
all these years? Not a single soul belonging to him
lived anywhere on earth. Of this fact—not such a
remote one, after all—he had only lately become aware;
for it is failure that makes a man enter into himself and
reckon up his resources. And though he had made up
his mind to retire from the world in hermit fashion, yet
he was irrationally moved by this sense of loneliness
which had come to him in the hour of renunciation.
It hurt him. Nothing is more painful than the shock

of sharp contradictions that lacerate our intelligence
and our feelings.

Meantime Schomberg watched Heyst out of the
corner of his eye. Towards the unconscious object of
his enmity he preserved a distant Lieutenant-of-the-
Reserve demeanour. Nudging certain of his customers
with his elbow, he begged them to observe what airs
"that Swede" was giving himself.

"I really don't know why he has come to stay in my
house. This place isn't good enough for him. I wish to
goodness he had gone somewhere else to show off his
superiority. Here I have got up this series of concerts
for you gentlemen, just to make things a little brighter
generally; and do you think he'll condescend to step in
and listen to a piece or two of an evening? Not he. I
know him of old. There he sits at the dark end of the
piazza, all the evening long—planning some new swindle,
no doubt. For twopence I would ask him to go and
look for quarters somewhere else; only one doesn't like
to treat a white man like that out in the tropics. I
don't know how long he means to stay, but I'm willing
to bet a trifle that he'll never work himself up to the
point of spending the fifty cents of entrance money
for the sake of a little good music."

Nobody cared to bet, or the hotel-keeper would have
lost. One evening Heyst was driven to desperation
by the rasped, squeaked, scraped snatches of tunes
pursuing him even to his hard couch, with a mattress
as thin as a pancake and a diaphanous mosquito net.
He descended among the trees, where the soft glow of
Japanese lanterns picked out parts of their great rugged
trunks, here and there, in the great mass of darkness
under the lofty foliage. More lanterns, of the shape
of cylindrical concertinas, hanging in a row from a slack
string, decorated the doorway of what Schomberg

called grandiloquently "my concert-hall." In his desperate mood Heyst ascended three steps, lifted a
calico curtain, and went in.

The uproar in that small, barn-like structure, built of
imported pine boards, and raised clear of the ground,
was simply stunning. An instrumental uproar, screaming, grunting, whining, sobbing, scraping, squeaking
some kind of lively air; while a grand piano, operated
upon by a bony, red-faced woman with bad-tempered
nostrils, rained hard notes like hail through the tempest
of fiddles. The small platform was filled with white
muslin dresses and crimson sashes slanting from shoulders provided with bare arms, which sawed away
without respite. Zangiacomo conducted. He wore a
white mess-jacket, a black dress waistcoat, and white
trousers. His longish, tousled hair and his great beard
were purple-black. He was horrible. The heat was
terrific. There were perhaps thirty people having
drinks at several little tables. Heyst, quite overcome by
the volume of noise, dropped into a chair. In the quick
time of that music, in the varied, piercing clamour of the
strings, in the movements of the bare arms, in the
low dresses, the coarse faces, the stony eyes of the
executants, there was a suggestion of brutality—something cruel, sensual and repulsive.

"This is awful!" Heyst murmured to himself.

But there is an unholy fascination in systematic
noise. He did not flee from it incontinently, as one
might have expected him to do. He remained, astonished at himself for remaining, since nothing could
have been more repulsive to his tastes, more painful to
his senses, and, so to speak, more contrary to his genius,
than this rude exhibition of vigour. The Zangiacomo
band was not making music; it was simply murdering
silence with a vulgar, ferocious energy. One felt as

if witnessing a deed of violence; and that impression
was so strong that it seemed marvellous to see the
poeple sitting so quietly on their chairs, drinking so
calmly out of their glasses, and giving no signs of distress, anger or fear. Heyst averted his gaze from the
unnatural spectacle of their indifference.

When the piece of music came to an end, the relief
was so great that he felt slightly dizzy, as if a chasm of
silence had yawned at his feet. When he raised his
eyes, the audience, most perversely, was exhibiting
signs of animation and interest in their faces, and the
women in white muslin dresses were coming down in
pairs from the platform into the body of Schomberg's
"concert-hall." They dispersed themselves all over
the place. The male creature with the hooked nose
and purple-black beard disappeared somewhere. This
was the interval during which, as the astute Schomberg
had stipulated, the members of the orchestra were encouraged to favour the members of the audience with
their company—that is, such members as seemed inclined to fraternize with the arts in a familiar and generous manner; the symbol of familiarity and generosity
consisting in offers of refreshment.

The procedure struck Heyst as highly incorrect.
However, the impropriety of Schomberg's ingenious
scheme was defeated by the circumstance that most
of the women were no longer young, and that none of
them had ever been beautiful. Their more or less
worn cheeks were slightly rouged; but apart from that
fact, which might have been simply a matter of routine,
they did not seem to take the success of the scheme
unduly to heart. The impulse to fraternize with the
arts being obviously weak in the audience, some of the
musicians sat down listlessly at unoccupied tables, while
others went on perambulating the central passage arm

in arm, glad enough, no doubt, to stretch their legs while resting their arms. Their crimson sashes gave a factitious touch of gaiety to the smoky atmosphere of the concert-hall; and Heyst felt a sudden pity for these beings, exploited, hopeless, devoid of charm and grace, whose fate of cheerless dependence invested their coarse and joyless features with a touch of pathos.

Heyst was temperamentally sympathetic. To have them passing and repassing close to his little table was painful to him. He was preparing to rise and go out when he noticed that two white muslin dresses and crimson sashes had not yet left the platform. One of these dresses concealed the raw-boned frame of the woman with the bad-tempered curve to her nostrils. She was no less a personage than Mrs. Zangiacomo. She had left the piano, and, with her back to the hall, was preparing the parts for the second half of the concert, with a brusque, impatient action of her ugly elbows. This task done, she turned, and, perceiving the other white muslin dress motionless on a chair in the second row, she strode towards it between the music-stands with an aggressive and masterful gait. On the lap of that dress there lay, unclasped and idle, a pair of small hands, not very white, attached to well-formed arms. The next detail Heyst was led to observe was the arrangement of the hair—two thick brown tresses rolled round an attractively shaped head.

"A girl, by Jove!" he exclaimed mentally.

It was evident that she was a girl. It was evident in the outline of the shoulders, in the slender white bust springing up, barred slantwise by the crimson sash, from the bell-shaped spread of muslin skirt hiding the chair on which she sat averted a little from the body of the hall. Her feet, in low white shoes, were crossed prettily.

She had captured Heyst's awakened faculty of observation; he had the sensation of a new experience. That was because his faculty of observation had never before been captured by any feminine creature in that marked and exclusive fashion. He looked at her anxiously, as no man ever looks at another man; and he positively forgot where he was. He had lost touch with his surroundings. The big woman, advancing, concealed the girl from his sight for a moment. She bent over the seated youthful figure, in passing it very close, as if to drop a word into its ear. Her lips did certainly move. But what sort of word could it have been to make the girl jump up so swiftly? Heyst, at his table, was surprised into a sympathetic start. He glanced quickly round. Nobody was looking towards the platform; and when his eyes swept back there again, the girl, with the big woman treading at her heels, was coming down the three steps from the platform to the floor of the hall. There she paused, stumbled one pace forward, and stood still again, while the other —the escort, the dragoon, the coarse big woman of the piano—passed her roughly, and, marching truculently down the centre aisle between the chairs and tables, went out to rejoin the hook-nosed Zangiacomo somewhere outside. During her extraordinary transit, as if everything in the hall were dirt under her feet, her scornful eyes met the upward glance of Heyst, who looked away at once towards the girl. She had not moved. Her arms hung down; her eyelids were lowered.

Heyst laid down his half-smoked cigar and compressed his lips. Then he got up. It was the same sort of impulse which years ago had made him cross the sandy street of the abominable town of Delli in the island of Timor and accost Morrison, practically a

stranger to him then, a man in trouble, expressively
harassed, dejected, lonely.

It was the same impulse. But he did not recognize
it. He was not thinking of Morrison then. It may
be said that, for the first time since the final abandon-
ment of the Samburan coal mine, he had completely
forgotten the late Morrison. It is true that to a certain extent he had forgotten also where he was. Thus,
unchecked by any sort of self-consciousness, Heyst
walked up the central passage.

Several of the women, by this time, had found
anchorage here and there among the occupied tables.
They talked to the men, leaning on their elbows, and
suggesting funnily—if it hadn't been for the crimson
sashes—in their white dresses an assembly of middle-
aged brides with free and easy manners and hoarse
voices. The murmuring noise of conversations carried
on with some spirit filled Schomberg's concert-room.
Nobody remarked Heyst's movements; for indeed he
was not the only man on his legs there. He had been
confronting the girl for some time before she became
aware of his presence. She was looking down, very
still, without colour, without glances, without voice,
without movement. It was only when Heyst addressed
her in his courteous tone that she raised her eyes.

"Excuse me," he said in English, "but that horrible
female has done something to you. She has pinched
you, hasn't she? I am sure she pinched you just now,
when she stood by your chair."

The girl received this overture with the wide, motionless stare of profound astonishment. Heyst, vexed
with himself, suspected that she did not understand
what he said. One could not tell what nationality
these women were, except that they were of all sorts.
But she was astonished almost more by the near pres-

ence of the man himself, by this largely bald head, by the white brow, the sunburnt cheeks, the long, horizontal moustaches of crinkly bronze hair, by the kindly expression of the man's blue eyes looking into her own. He saw the stony amazement in hers give way to a momentary alarm, which was succeeded by an expression of resignation.

"I am sure she pinched your arm most cruelly," he murmured, rather disconcerted now at what he had done.

It was a great comfort to hear her say:

"It wouldn't have been the first time. And suppose she did—what are you going to do about it?"

"I don't know," he said with a faint, remote playfulness in his tone which had not been heard in it lately, and which seemed to catch her ear pleasantly. "I am grieved to say that I don't know. But can I do anything? What would you wish me to do? Pray command me."

Again the greatest astonishment became visible in her face; for she now perceived how different he was from the other men in the room. He was as different from them as she was different from the other members of the ladies' orchestra.

"Command you?" she breathed, after a time, in a bewildered tone. "Who are you?" she asked a little louder.

"I am staying in this hotel for a few days. I just dropped in casually here. This outrage——"

"Don't you try to interfere," she said so earnestly that Heyst asked, in his faintly playful tone:

"Is it your wish that I should leave you?"

"I haven't said that," the girl answered. "She pinched me because I didn't get down here quick enough."

"I can't tell you how indignant I am," said Heyst. "But since you are down here now," he went on, with the ease of a man of the world speaking to a young lady in a drawing-room, "hadn't we better sit down?"

She obeyed his inviting gesture, and they sat down on the nearest chairs. They looked at each other across a little round table with a surprised, open gaze, self-consciousness growing on them so slowly that it was a long time before they averted their eyes; and very soon they met again, temporarily, only to rebound, as it were. At last they steadied in contact, but by that time, say some fifteen minutes from the moment when they sat down, the "interval" came to an end.

So much for their eyes. As to the conversation, it had been perfectly insignificant, because naturally they had nothing to say to each other. Heyst had been interested by the girl's physiognomy. Its expression was neither simple nor yet very clear. It was not distinguished—that could not be expected—but the features had more fineness than those of any other feminine countenance he had ever had the opportunity to observe so closely. There was in it something indefinably audacious and infinitely miserable—because the temperament and the existence of that girl were reflected in it. But her voice! It seduced Heyst by its amazing quality. It was a voice fit to utter the most exquisite things, a voice which would have made silly chatter supportable and the roughest talk fascinating. Heyst drank in its charm as one listens to the tone of some instrument without heeding the tune.

"Do you sing as well as play?" he asked her abruptly.

"Never sang a note in my life," she said, obviously surprised by the irrelevant question; for they had not been discoursing of sweet sounds. She was clearly unaware of her voice. "I don't remember that I ever had much reason to sing since I was little," she added.

That inelegant phrase, by the mere vibrating, warm nobility of sound, found its way into Heyst's heart. His mind, cool, alert, watched it sink there with a sort of vague concern at the absurdity of the occupation, till it rested at the bottom, deep down, where our unexpressed longings lie.

"You are English, of course?" he said.

"What do you think?" she answered in the most charming accents. Then, as if thinking that it was her turn to place a question: "Why do you always smile when you speak?"

It was enough to make any one look grave; but her good faith was so evident that Heyst recovered himself at once.

"It's my unfortunate manner," he said with his delicate, polished playfulness. "Is it very objectionable to you?"

She was very serious.

"No. I only noticed it. I haven't come across so many pleasant people as all that, in my life."

"It's certain that this woman who plays the piano is infinitely more disagreeable than any cannibal I have ever had to do with."

"I believe you!" She shuddered. "How did you come to have anything to do with cannibals?"

"It would be too long a tale," said Heyst, with a faint smile. Heyst's smiles were rather melancholy, and accorded badly with his great moustaches, under which his mere playfulness lurked as comfortably as a shy bird in its native thicket. "Much too long. How did you get amongst this lot here?"

"Bad luck," she answered briefly.

"No doubt, no doubt," Heyst assented with slight

nods. Then, still indignant at the pinch which he had divined rather than actually seen inflicted: "I say, couldn't you defend yourself somehow?"

She had risen already. The ladies of the orchestra were slowly regaining their places. Some were already seated, idle, stony-eyed, before the music-stands. Heyst was standing up, too.

"They are too many for me," she said.

These few words came out of the common experience of mankind; yet by virtue of her voice, they thrilled Heyst like a revelation. His feelings were in a state of confusion, but his mind was clear.

"That's bad. But it isn't actual ill-usage that this girl is complaining of," he thought lucidly after she left him.

II

THAT was how it began. How it was that it ended as we know it did end, is not so easy to state precisely. It is very clear that Heyst was not indifferent. I won't say to the girl, but to the girl's fate. He was the same man who had plunged after the submerged Morrison whom he hardly knew otherwise than by sight and through the usual gossip of the islands. But this was another sort of plunge altogether, and likely to lead to a very different kind of partnership.

Did he reflect at all? Probably. He was sufficiently reflective. But if he did, it was with insufficient knowledge. For there is no evidence that he paused at any time between the date of that evening and the morning of the flight. Truth to say, Heyst was not one of those men who pause much. Those dreamy spectators of the world's agitation are terrible once the desire to act gets hold of them. They lower their heads and charge a wall with an amazing serenity which nothing but an indisciplined imagination can give.

He was not a fool. I suppose he knew—or at least he felt—where this was leading him. But his complete inexperience gave him the necessary audacity. The girl's voice was charming when she spoke to him of her miserable past, in simple terms, with a sort of unconscious cynicism inherent in the truth of the ugly conditions of poverty. And whether because he was humane or because her voice included all the modulations of pathos, cheerfulness and courage in its compass, it was not disgust that the tale awakened in him, but the sense of an immense sadness.

On a later evening, during the interval between the two parts of the concert, the girl told Heyst about herself. She was almost a child of the streets. Her father was a musician in the orchestras of small theatres. Her mother ran away from him while she was little, and the landladies of various poor lodging-houses had attended casually to her abandoned childhood. It was never positive starvation and absolute rags, but it was the hopeless grip of poverty all the time. It was her father who taught her to play the violin. It seemed that he used to get drunk sometimes, but without pleasure, and only because he was unable to forget his fugitive wife. After he had a paralytic stroke, falling over with a crash in the well* of a music-hall* orchestra during the performance, she had joined the Zangiacomo company. He was now in a home for incurables.

"And I am here," she finished, "with no one to care if I make a hole in the water the next chance I get or not."

Heyst told her that he thought she could do a little better than that, if it was only a question of getting out of the world. She looked at him with special attention, and with a puzzled expression which gave to her face an air of innocence.

This was during one of the "intervals" between the two parts of the concert. She had come down that time without being incited thereto by a pinch from the awful Zangiacomo woman. It is difficult to suppose that she was seduced by the uncovered intellectual forehead and the long reddish moustaches of her new friend. New is not the right word. She had never had a friend before; and the sensation of this friendliness going out to her was exciting by its novelty alone.   Besides, any man who did not resemble Schomberg appeared for that very reason attractive.   She was afraid of the hotel-keeper, who, in the daytime, taking advantage of the fact that she lived in the hotel itself, and not in the Pavilion with the other "artists," prowled round her, mute, hungry, portentous behind his great beard, or else assailed her in quiet corners and empty passages with deep, mysterious murmurs from behind, which, notwithstanding their clear import, sounded horribly insane somehow.

The contrast of Heyst's quiet, polished manner gave her special delight and filled her with admiration.   She had never seen anything like that before.   If she had, perhaps, known kindness in her life, she had never met the forms of simple courtesy.   She was interested by it as by a very novel experience, not very intelligible, but distinctly pleasurable.

"I tell you they are too many for me," she repeated, sometimes recklessly, but more often shaking her head with ominous dejection.

She had, of course, no money at all.   The quantities of "black men" all about frightened her.   She really had no definite idea where she was on the surface of the globe.   The orchestra was generally taken from the steamer to some hotel, and kept shut up there till it was time to go on board another steamer.   She could not remember the names she heard.

"How do you call this place again?" she used to ask Heyst.

"Sourabaya," he would say distinctly, and would watch the discouragement at the outlandish sound coming into her eyes, which were fastened on his face.

He could not defend himself from compassion.   He suggested that she might go to the consul, but it was his conscience that dictated this advice, not his conviction. She had never heard of the animal or of its uses. A consul! What was it? Who was he? What could he do? And when she learned that perhaps he could be induced to send her home, her head dropped on her breast.

"What am I to do when I get there?" she murmured with an intonation so just, with an accent so penetrating —the charm of her voice did not fail her even in whispering—that Heyst seemed to see the illusion of human fellowship on earth vanish before the naked truth of her existence, and leave them both face to face in a moral desert as arid as the sands of Sahara, without restful shade, without refreshing water.

She leaned slightly over the little table, the same little table at which they had sat when they first met each other; and with no other memories but of the stones in the streets her childhood had known, in the distress of the incoherent, confused, rudimentary impressions of her travels inspiring her with a vague terror of the world, she said rapidly, as one speaks in desperation:

"*You* do something! You are a gentleman. It wasn't I who spoke to you first, was it? I didn't begin, did I? It was you who came along and spoke to me when I was standing over there. What did you want to speak to me for? I don't care what it is, but you must do something."

Her attitude was fierce and entreating at the same time—clamorous, in fact, though her voice had hardly risen above a breath. It was clamorous enough to be noticed. Heyst, on purpose, laughed aloud. She nearly choked with indignation at this brutal heartlessness.

"What did you mean, then, by saying 'command me'?" she almost hissed.

Something hard in his mirthless stare, and a quiet final "All right," steadied her.

"I am not rich enough to buy you out," he went on, speaking with an extraordinary detached grin, "even if it were to be done; but I can always steal you."

She looked at him profoundly, as though these words had a hidden and very complicated meaning.

"Get away now," he said rapidly, "and try to smile as you go."

She obeyed with unexpected readiness; and as she had a set of very good white teeth, the effect of the mechanical, ordered smile was joyous, radiant. It astonished Heyst. No wonder, it flashed though his mind, women can deceive men so completely. The faculty was inherent in them; they seemed to be created with a special aptitude. Here was a smile the origin of which was well known to him; and yet it had conveyed a sensation of warmth, had given him a sort of ardour to live which was very new to his experience.

By this time she was gone from the table, and had joined the other "ladies of the orchestra." They trooped towards the platform, driven in truculently by the haughty mate of Zangiacomo, who looked as though she were restraining herself with difficulty from punching their backs. Zangiacomo followed, with his great, pendulous dyed beard and short mess-jacket, with an aspect of hang-dog concentration imparted by his drooping head and the uneasiness of his eyes, which were set very close together. He climbed the steps last of all, turned about, displaying his purple beard to the hall, and tapped with his bow. Heyst winced in anticipation of the horrible racket. It burst out immediately unabashed and awful. At the end of the platform the woman at the piano, presenting her cruel profile, her head tilted back, banged the keys without looking at the music.

Heyst could not stand the uproar for more than a

minute. He went out, his brain racked by the rhythm of some more or less Hungarian dance music. The forests inhabited by the New Guinea cannibals where he had encountered the most exciting of his earlier futile adventures were silent. And this adventure, not in its execution, perhaps, but in its nature, required even more nerve than anything he had faced before. Walking among the paper lanterns suspended to trees he remembered with regret the gloom and the dead stillness of the forests at the back of Geelvink Bay,* perhaps the wildest, the unsafest, the most deadly spot on earth from which the sea can be seen. Oppressed by his thoughts, he sought the obscurity and peace of his bedroom; but they were not complete. The distant sounds of the concert reached his ear, faint indeed but still disturbing. Neither did he feel very safe in there; for that sentiment depends not on extraneous circumstances but on our inward conviction. He did not attempt to go to sleep; he did not even unbutton the top button of his tunic. He sat in a chair and mused. Formerly, in solitude and in silence, he had been used to think clearly and sometimes even profoundly, seeing life outside the flattering optical delusion of everlasting hope, of conventional self-deceptions, of an ever-expected happiness. But now he was troubled; a light veil seemed to hang before his mental vision; the awakening of a tenderness, indistinct and confused as yet, towards an unknown woman.

Gradually silence, a real silence, had established itself round him. The concert was over; the audience had gone; the concert-hall was dark; and even the Pavilion, where the ladies' orchestra slept after its noisy labours, showed not a gleam of light. Heyst suddenly felt restless in all his limbs. As this reaction from the long immobility would not be denied, he humoured it by passing quietly along the back verandah and out into the grounds at the side of the house, into the black shadows under the trees, where the extinguished paper lanterns were gently swinging their globes like withered fruit.

He paced there to and fro for a long time, a calm, meditative ghost in his white drill suit, revolving in his head thoughts absolutely novel, disquieting, and seductive; accustoming his mind to the contemplation of his purpose, in order that by being faced steadily it should appear praiseworthy and wise. For the use of reason is to justify the obscure desires that move our conduct, impulses, passions, prejudices and follies, and also our fears.

He felt that he had engaged himself by a rash promise to an action big with incalculable consequences. And then he asked himself if the girl had understood what he meant. Who could tell? He was assailed by all sorts of doubts. Raising his head, he perceived something white flitting between the trees. It vanished almost at once; but there could be no mistake. He was vexed at being detected roaming like this in the middle of the night. Who could that be? It never occurred to him that perhaps the girl, too, would not be able to sleep. He advanced prudently. Then he saw the white, phantom-like apparition again; and next moment all his doubts as to the state of her mind were laid at rest, because he felt her clinging to him after the manner of suppliants all the world over. Her whispers were so incoherent that he could not understand anything; but this did not prevent him from being profoundly moved. He had no illusions about her; but his sceptical mind was dominated by the fulness of his heart.

"Calm yourself, calm yourself," he murmured in her ear, returning her clasp at first mechanically, and afterward with a growing appreciation of her distressed humanity. The heaving of her breast and the trembling of all her limbs, in the closeness of his embrace, seemed to enter his body, to infect his very heart. While she was growing quieter in his arms, he was becoming more agitated, as if there were only a fixed quantity of violent emotion on this earth. The very night seemed more dumb, more still, and the immobility of the vague, black shapes surrounding him more perfect.

"It will be all right," he tried to reassure her, with a tone of conviction, speaking into her ear, and of necessity clasping her more closely than before.

Either the words or the action had a very good effect. He heard a light sigh of relief. She spoke with a calmed ardour.

"Oh, I knew it would be all right from the first time you spoke to me! Yes, indeed, I knew directly you came up to me that evening. I knew it would be all right, if you only cared to make it so; but of course I could not tell if you meant it. 'Command me,' you said. Funny thing for a man like you to say. Did you really mean it? You weren't making fun of me?"

He protested that he had been a serious person all his life.

"I believe you," she said ardently. He was touched by this declaration. "It's the way you have of speaking as if you were amused with people," she went on. "But I wasn't deceived. I could see you were angry with that beast of a woman. And you are clever. You spotted something at once. You saw it in my face, eh? It isn't a bad face—say? You'll never be sorry. Listen—I'm not twenty yet. It's the truth, and I can't be so bad looking, or else—I will tell you straight that I have been worried and pestered by fellows like this before. I don't know what comes to them——"

She was speaking hurriedly. She choked, and then exclaimed, with an accent of despair:

"What is it? What's the matter?"

Heyst had removed his arms from her suddenly, and had recoiled a little. "Is it my fault? I didn't even look at them, I tell you straight. Never! Have I looked at you? Tell me. It was you that began it."

In truth, Heyst had shrunk from the idea of competition with fellows unknown, with Schomberg the hotel-keeper. The vaporous white figure before him swayed pitifully in the darkness. He felt ashamed of his fastidiousness.

"I am afraid we have been detected," he murmured. "I think I saw somebody on the path between the house and the bushes behind you."

He had seen no one. It was a compassionate lie, if there ever was one. His compassion was as genuine as his shrinking had been, and in his judgment more honourable.

She didn't turn her head. She was obviously relieved.

"Would it be that brute?" she breathed out, meaning Schomberg, of course. "He's getting too forward with me now. What can you expect? Only this evening, after supper, he—but I slipped away. You don't mind him, do you? Why, I could face him myself now that I know you care for me. A girl can always put up a fight. You believe me? Only it isn't easy to stand up for yourself when you feel there's nothing and nobody at your back. There's nothing so lonely in the world as a girl who has got to look after herself. When I left poor dad in that home—it was in the country, near a village—I came out of the gates with seven shillings and three-pence in my old purse, and my railway ticket. I tramped a mile, and got into a train——"

She broke off, and was silent for a moment.

"Don't you throw me over now," she went on. "If you did, what should I do? I should have to live, to be sure, because I'd be afraid to kill myself; but you would have done a thousand times worse than killing a body. You told me you had been always alone, you had never had a dog, even. Well, then, I won't be in anybody's way if I live with you—not even a dog's. And what else did you mean when you came up and looked at me so close?"

"Close? Did I?" he murmured unstirring before her in the profound darkness. "So close as that?"

She had an outbreak of anger and despair in subdued tones.

"Have you forgotten, then? What did you expect to find? I know what sort of girl I am; but all the same I am not the sort that men turn their backs on—and you ought to know it, unless you aren't made like the others. Oh, forgive me! You aren't like the others; you are like no one in the world I ever spoke to. Don't you care for me? Don't you see——?"

What he saw was that, white and spectral, she was putting out her arms to him out of the black shadows like an appealing ghost. He took her hands, and was affected, almost surprised, to find them so warm, so real, so firm, so living in his grasp. He drew her to him, and she dropped her head on his shoulder with a deep sigh.

"I am dead tired," she whispered plaintively.

He put his arms around her, and only by the convulsive movements of her body became aware that she was sobbing without a sound. Sustaining her, he lost himself in the profound silence of the night. After a while she became still, and cried quietly. Then, suddenly, as if waking up, she asked:

"You haven't seen any more of that somebody you thought was spying about?"

He started at her quick, sharp whisper, and answered that very likely he had been mistaken.

"If it was anybody at all," she reflected aloud, "it wouldn't have been any one but that hotel woman— the landlord's wife."

"Mrs. Schomberg?" Heyst said, surprised.

"Yes. Another one that can't sleep o' nights. Why? Don't you see why? Because, of course, she sees what's going on. That beast doesn't even try to keep it from her. If she had only the least bit of spirit! She knows how I feel, too, only she's too frightened even to look him in the face, let alone open her mouth. He would tell her to go hang herself."

For some time Heyst said nothing. A public, active contest with the hotel-keeper was not to be thought of. The idea was horrible. Whispering gently to the girl, he tried to explain to her that as things stood, an open withdrawal from the company would be probably opposed. She listened to his explanation anxiously, from time to time pressing the hand she had sought and got hold of in the dark.

"As I told you, I am not rich enough to buy you out; so I shall steal you as soon as I can arrange some means of getting away from here. Meantime it would be fatal to be seen together at night. We mustn't give ourselves away. We had better part at once. I think I was mistaken just now; but if, as you say, that poor Mrs. Schomberg can't sleep of nights, we must be more careful. She would tell the fellow."

The girl had disengaged herself from his loose hold while he talked, and now stood free of him, but still clasping his hand firmly.

"Oh, no," she said with perfect assurance. "I tell you she daren't open her mouth to him. And she isn't as silly as she looks. She wouldn't give us away. She

knows a trick worth two of that. She'll help—that's
what she'll do, if she dares do anything at all."

"You seem to have a very clear view of the situation," said Heyst, and received a warm, lingering kiss
for this commendation.

He discovered that to part from her was not such an
easy matter as he had supposed it would be.

"Upon my word," he said before they separated, "I
don't even know your name."

"Don't you? They call me Alma. I don't know
why. Silly name! Magdalen too. It doesn't matter;
you can call me by whatever name you choose. Yes,
you give me a name. Think of one you would like the
sound of—something quite new. How I should like to
forget everything that has gone before, as one forgets
a dream that's done with, fright and all! I would try."

"Would you really?" he asked in a murmur. "But
that's not forbidden. I understand that women easily
forget whatever in their past diminishes them in their
eyes."

"It's your eyes that I was thinking of, for I'm sure
I've never wished to forget anything till you came up
to me that night and looked me through and through. I
know I'm not much account; but I know how to stand by
a man. I stood by father ever since I could understand.
He wasn't a bad chap. Now that I can't be of any use
to him, I would just as soon forget all that and make a
fresh start. But these aren't things that I could talk to
you about. What could I ever talk to you about?"

"Don't let it trouble you," Heyst said. "Your voice
is enough. I am in love with it, whatever it says."

She remained silent for a while, as if rendered breathless by this quiet statement.

"Oh! I wanted to ask you——"

He remembered that she probably did not know his

name, and expected the question to be put to him now;
but after a moment of hesitation she went on:

"Why was it that you told me to smile this evening in
the concert-room there—you remember?"

"I thought we were being observed. A smile is the
best of masks. Schomberg was at a table next but
one to us, drinking with some Dutch clerks from the
town. No doubt he was watching us—watching you,
at least. That's why I asked you to smile."

"Ah, that's why. It never came into my head."

"And you did it very well, too—very readily, as if
you had understood my intention."

"Readily!" she repeated. "Oh, I was ready enough
to smile then. That's the truth. It was the first time
for years I may say that I felt disposed to smile. I've
not had many chances to smile in my life, I can tell you;
especially of late."

"But you do it most charmingly—in a perfectly
fascinating way."

He paused. She stood still, waiting for more with
the stillness of extreme delight, wishing to prolong the
sensation.

"It astonished me," he added. "It went as straight
to my heart as though you had smiled for the purpose of
dazzling me. I felt as if I had never seen a smile before in my life. I thought of it after I left you. It
made me restless."

"It did all that?" came her voice, unsteady, gentle,
and incredulous.

"If you had not smiled as you did, perhaps I should
not have come out here to-night," he said, with his
playful earnestness of tone. "It was your triumph."

He felt her lips touch his lightly, and the next moment she was gone. Her white dress gleamed in the
distance, and then the opaque darkness of the house

seemed to swallow it. Heyst waited a little before he went the same way, round the corner, up the steps of the verandah, and into his room, where he lay down at last—not to sleep, but to go over in his mind all that had been said at their meeting.

"It's exactly true about that smile," he thought. There he had spoken the truth to her; and about her voice, too. For the rest—what must be must be.

A great wave of heat passed over him. He turned on his back, flung his arms crosswise on the broad, hard bed, and lay still, open-eyed under the mosquito net, till daylight entered his room, brightened swiftly, and turned to unfailing sunlight. He got up then, went to a small looking-glass hanging on the wall, and stared at himself steadily. It was not a new-born vanity which induced this long survey. He felt so strange that he could not resist the suspicion of his personal appearance having changed during the night. What he saw in the glass, however, was the man he knew before. It was almost a disappointment—a belittling of his recent experience. And then he smiled at his naïveness; for, being over five and thirty years of age, he ought to have known that in most cases the body is the unalterable mask of the soul, which even death itself changes but little, till it is put out of sight where no changes matter any more, either to our friends or to our enemies.

Heyst was not conscious of either friends or of enemies. It was the very essence of his life to be a solitary achievement, accomplished not by hermit-like withdrawal with its silence and immobility, but by a system of restless wandering, by the detachment of an impermanent dweller amongst changing scenes. In this scheme he had perceived the means of passing through life without suffering and almost without a single care in the world—invulnerable because elusive.

III

For fifteen years Heyst had wandered, invariably courteous and unapproachable, and in return was generally considered a "queer chap." He had started off on these travels of his after the death of his father, an expatriated Swede who died in London, dissatisfied with his country and angry with all the world, which had instinctively rejected his wisdom.

Thinker, stylist, and man of the world in his time, the elder Heyst had begun by coveting all the joys, those of the great and those of the humble, those of the fools and those of the sages. For more than sixty years he had dragged on this painful earth of ours the most weary, the most uneasy soul that civilisation had ever fashioned to its ends of disillusion and regret. One could not refuse him a measure of greatness, for he was unhappy in a way unknown to mediocre souls. His mother Heyst had never known, but he kept his father's pale, distinguished face in affectionate memory. He remembered him mainly in an ample blue dressing-gown in a large house of a quiet London suburb. For three years, after leaving school at the age of eighteen, he had lived with the elder Heyst, who was then writing his last book. In this work, at the end of his life, he claimed for mankind that right to absolute moral and intellectual liberty of which he no longer believed them worthy.

Three years of such companionship at that plastic and impressionable age were bound to leave in the boy a profound mistrust of life. The young man learned to reflect, which is a destructive process, a reckoning

of the cost. It is not the clear-sighted who lead the
world. Great achievements are accomplished in a
blessed, warm mental fog, which the pitiless cold blasts
of the father's analysis had blown away*from the son.

"I'll drift," Heyst had said to himself deliberately.

He did not mean intellectually or sentimentally or
morally. He meant to drift altogether and literally,
body and soul, like a detached leaf drifting in the wind-
currents under the immovable trees of a forest glade;
to drift without ever catching on to anything.

"This shall be my defence against life," he had said to
himself with a sort of inward consciousness that for the
son of his father there was no other worthy alternative.

He became a waif and stray, austerely, from conviction, as others do through drink, from vice, from some
weakness of character—with deliberation, as others
do in despair. This, stripped of its facts, had been
Heyst's life up to that disturbing night. Next day,
when he saw the girl called Alma, she managed
to give him a glance of frank tenderness, quick as
lightning, and leaving a profound impression, a secret
touch on the heart. It was in the grounds of the hotel,
about tiffin time, while the ladies of the orchestra were
strolling back to their pavilion after rehearsal, or practice, or whatever they called their morning musical
exercises in the hall. Heyst, returning from the town,
where he had discovered that there would be difficulties
in the way of getting away at once, was crossing the
compound, disappointed and worried. He had walked
almost unwittingly into the straggling group of Zangiacomo's performers. It was a shock to him, on coming
out of his brown study, to find the girl so near him, as if
one waking suddenly should see the figure of his dream
turned into flesh and blood.* She did not raise her
shapely head, but her glance was no dream thing. It

was real, the most real impression of his detached existence—so far.

Heyst had not acknowledged it in any way, though it seemed to him impossible that its effect on him should not be visible to any one who happened to be looking on. And there were several men on the verandah, steady customers of Schomberg's table d'hôte, gazing in his direction—at the ladies of the orchestra, in fact. Heyst's dread arose, not out of shame or timidity, but from his fastidiousness. On getting amongst them, however, he noticed no signs of interest or astonishment on their faces, any more than if they had been blind men. Even Schomberg himself, who had to make way for him at the top of the stairs, was completely unperturbed, and continued the conversation he was carrying on with a client.

Schomberg, indeed, had observed "that Swede" talking with the girl in the intervals. A crony of his had nudged him; and he had thought that it was so much the better; the silly fellow would keep everybody else off. He was rather pleased than otherwise and watched them out of the corner of his eye with a malicious enjoyment of the situation—a sort of Satanic glee. For he had little doubt of his personal fascination, and still less of his power to get hold of the girl, who seemed too ignorant to know how to help herself, and who was worse than friendless, since she had for some reason incurred the animosity of Mrs. Zangiacomo, a woman with no conscience. The aversion she showed him as far as she dared (for it is not always safe for the helpless to display the delicacy of their sentiments), Schomberg pardoned on the score of feminine conventional silliness. He had told Alma, as an argument, that she was a clever enough girl to see that she could do no better than to put her trust in a man of substance, in the prime of life, who knew his way about. But for the excited trembling of his voice, and the extraordinary way in which his eyes seemed to be starting out of his crimson, hirsute countenance, such speeches had every character of calm, unselfish advice—which, after the manner of lovers, passed easily into sanguine plans for the future.

"We'll soon get rid of the old woman," he whispered to her hurriedly, with panting ferocity. "Hang her! I've never cared for her. The climate don't suit her; I shall tell her to go to her people in Europe. She will have to go, too! I will see to it. *Eins, zwei,* march! And then we shall sell this hotel and start another somewhere else."

He assured her that he didn't care what he did for her sake; and it was true. Forty-five is the age of recklessness for many men, as if in defiance of the decay and death waiting with open arms in the sinister valley at the bottom of the inevitable hill. Her shrinking form, her downcast eyes, when she had to listen to him, cornered at the end of an empty corridor, he regarded as signs of submission to the overpowering force of his will, the recognition of his personal fascinations. For every age is fed on illusions, lest men should renounce life early and the human race come to an end.

It's easy to imagine Schomberg's humiliation, his shocked fury, when he discovered that the girl who had for weeks resisted his attacks, his prayers, and his fiercest protestations, had been snatched from under his nose by "that Swede," apparently without any trouble worth speaking of. He refused to believe the fact. He would have it, at first, that the Zangiacomos, for some unfathomable reason, had played him a scurvy trick; but when no further doubt was possible, he changed his view of Heyst. The despised Swede became for Schomberg the deepest, the most dangerous, the most hateful of scoundrels. He could not believe that the creature he had coveted with so much force and with so little effect, was in reality tender, docile to her impulses, and had almost offered herself to Heyst without a sense of guilt, in a desire of safety, and from a profound need of placing her trust where her woman's instinct guided her ignorance. Nothing would serve Schomberg but that she must have been circumvented by some occult exercise of force or craft, by the laying of some subtle trap. His wounded vanity wondered ceaselessly at the means "that Swede" had employed to seduce her away from a man like him— Schomberg—as though those means were bound to have been extraordinary, unheard of, inconceivable. He slapped his forehead openly before his customers; he would sit brooding in silence or else would burst out unexpectedly declaiming against Heyst without measure, discretion or prudence, with swollen features and an affectation of outraged virtue which could not have deceived the most childlike of moralists for a moment— and greatly amused his audience.

It became a recognised entertainment to go and hear his abuse of Heyst, while sipping iced drinks on the verandah of the hotel. It was, in a manner, a more successful draw than the Zangiacomo concerts had ever been—intervals and all. There was never any difficulty in starting the performer off. Anybody could do it, by almost any distant allusion. As likely as not he would start his endless denunciations in the very billiard-room where Mrs. Schomberg sat enthroned as usual, swallowing her sobs, concealing her tortures of abject humiliation and terror under her stupid, set, everlasting grin, which, having been provided for her by nature, was an excellent mask, inasmuch as noth-

ing—not even death itself, perhaps—could tear it
away.

But nothing lasts in this world, at least without changing its physiognomy. So, after a few weeks, Schomberg regained his outward calm, as if his indignation
had dried up within him. And it was time. He was
becoming a bore with his inability to talk of anything
else but Heyst's unfitness to be at large, Heyst's wickedness, his wiles, his astuteness, and his criminality.
Schomberg no longer pretended to despise him. He
could not have done it. After what had happened
he could not pretend, even to himself. But his bottled-
up indignation was fermenting venomously. At the
time of his immoderate loquacity one of his customers,
an elderly man, had remarked one evening:

"If that ass keeps on like this, he will end by going
crazy."

And this belief was less than half wrong. Schomberg
had Heyst on the brain. Even the unsatisfactory
state of his affairs, which had never been so unprom-
ising since he came out East directly after the Franco-
Prussian War,* he referred to some subtly noxious
influence of Heyst. It seemed to him that he could
never be himself again till he had got even with that artful Swede. He was ready to swear that Heyst had ruined
his life. The girl so unfairly, craftily, basely decoyed
away would have inspired him to success in a new start.
Obviously Mrs. Schomberg, whom he terrified by
savagely silent moods combined with underhand,
poisoned glances, could give him no inspiration.
He had grown generally neglectful, but with a partiality
for reckless expedients, as if he did not care when and
how his career as a hotel-keeper was to be brought to
an end. This demoralized state accounted for what
Davidson had observed on his last visit to the Schom-

berg establishment, some two months after Heyst's secret departure with the girl to the solitude of Samburan.

The Schomberg of a few years ago—the Schomberg of the Bangkok days, for instance, when he started the first of his famed table-d'hôte dinners—would never have risked anything of the sort. His genius ran to catering, "white man for white men," and to the inventing, elaborating, and retailing of scandalous gossip with asinine unction and impudent delight. But now his mind was perverted by the pangs of wounded vanity and of thwarted passion. In this state of moral weakness Schomberg allowed himself to be corrupted.

IV

THE business was done by a guest who arrived one fine morning by mail-boat—immediately from Celebes, having boarded her in Macassar; but generally, Schomberg understood, from up China Sea way; a wanderer clearly, even as Heyst was, but not alone and of quite another kind.

Schomberg, looking up from the stern-sheets of his steam-launch, which he used for boarding passenger ships on arrival, discovered a dark, sunken stare plunging down on him over the rail of the first-class part of the deck. He was no great judge of physiognomy. Human beings, for him, were either the objects of scandalous gossip or else the recipients of narrow strips of paper, with proper bill-heads stating the name of his hotel.—"W. Schomberg, proprietor; accounts settled weekly."

So in the clean-shaven, extremely thin face hanging over the mail-boat's rail Schomberg saw only the face of a possible "account." The steam-launches of other hotels were also alongside, but he obtained the preference.

"You are Mr. Schomberg, aren't you?" the face asked quite unexpectedly.

"I am, at your service," he answered from below; for business is business, and its forms and formulas must be observed, even if one's manly bosom is tortured by that dull rage which succeeds the fury of baffled passion, like the glow of embers after a fierce blaze.

Presently the possessor of the handsome but emaci-

ated face was seated beside Schomberg in the stern-
sheets of the launch. His body was long and loose-
jointed; his slender fingers, intertwined, clasped the
leg resting on his knee, as he lolled back in a careless
yet tense attitude. On the other side of Schomberg
sat another passenger, who was introduced by the
clean-shaven man as—

"My secretary. He must have the room next to
mine."

"We can manage that easily for you."

Schomberg steered with dignity, staring straight
ahead, but very much interested by these two prom-
ising "accounts." Their belongings, a couple of large
leather trunks browned by age and a few smaller pack-
ages, were piled up in the bows. A third individual—
a nondescript, hairy creature—had modestly made his
way forward and had perched himself on the luggage.
The lower part of his physiognomy was over-developed;
his narrow and low forehead, unintelligently furrowed
by horizontal wrinkles, surmounted wildly hirsute
cheeks and a flat nose with wide, baboon-like nostrils.
There was something equivocal in the appearance of his
shaggy, hair-smothered humanity. He, too, seemed to
be a follower of the clean-shaven man, and apparently
had travelled on deck with native passengers, sleeping
under the awnings. His broad, squat frame denoted
great strength. Grasping the gunwales of the launch,
he displayed a pair of remarkably long arms, terminating in thick, brown hairy paws of simian aspect.

"What shall we do with that fellow of mine?" the
chief of the party asked Schomberg. "There must be a
boarding-house somewhere near the port—some grog-
shop where they could let him have a mat to sleep on?"

Schomberg said there was a place kept by a Portuguese half-caste.

"A servant of yours?" he asked.

"Well, he hangs on to me. He is an alligator-hunter. I picked him up in Colombia, you know. Ever been in Colombia?"

"No," said Schomberg, very much surprised. "An alligator-hunter? Funny trade! Are you coming from Colombia, then?"

"Yes, but I have been coming for a long time. I come from a good many places. I am travelling west, you see."

"For sport, perhaps?" suggested Schomberg.

"Yes. Sort of sport. What do you say to chasing the sun?"

"I see—a gentleman at large," said Schomberg, watching a sailing canoe about to cross his bow, and ready to clear it by a touch of the helm.

The other passenger made himself heard suddenly.

"Hang these native craft! They always get in the way."

He was a muscular, short man with eyes that gleamed and blinked, a harsh voice, and a round, toneless, pockmarked face ornamented by a thin, dishevelled moustache sticking out quaintly under the tip of a rigid nose. Schomberg made the reflection that there was nothing secretarial about him. Both he and his long, lank principal wore the usual white suit of the tropics, cork helmets, pipe-clayed white shoes—all correct. The hairy nondescript creature perched on their luggage in the bow had a check shirt and blue dungaree trousers. He gazed in their direction from forward in an expectant, trained-animal manner.

"You spoke to me first," said Schomberg in his manly tones. "You were acquainted with my name. Where did you hear of me, gentlemen, may I ask?"

"In Manila,"* answered the gentleman at large,

readily. "From a man with whom I had a game of cards one evening in the Hotel Castille."

"What man? I've no friends in Manila that I know of," wondered Schomberg with a severe frown.

"I can't tell you his name. I've clean forgotten it; but don't you worry. He was anything but a friend of yours. He called you all the names he could think of. He said you set a lot of scandal going about him once, somewhere—in Bangkok, I think. Yes, that's it. You were running a table d'hôte in Bangkok at one time, weren't you?"

Schomberg, astounded by the turn of the information, could only throw out his chest more and exaggerate his austere Lieutenant-of-the-Reserve manner. A table d'hôte? Yes, certainly. He always—for the sake of white men. And here in this place, too? Yes, in this place, too.

"That's all right, then." The stranger turned his black, cavernous, mesmerising glance away from the bearded Schomberg, who sat gripping the brass tiller in a sweating palm. "Many people in the evening at your place?"

Schomberg had recovered somewhat.

"Twenty covers or so, take one day with another," he answered feelingly, as befitted a subject on which he was sensitive. "Ought to be more, if only people would see that it's for their own good. Precious little profit I get out of it. You are partial to table d'hôtes, gentlemen?"

The new guest made answer that he liked a hotel where one could find some local people in the evening. It was infernally dull otherwise. The secretary, in sign of approval, emitted a grunt of astonishing ferocity, as if proposing to himself to eat the local people. All this sounded like a longish stay, thought Schomberg, satis-

fied under his grave air; till, remembering the girl
snatched away from him by the last guest who had
made a prolonged stay in his hotel, he ground his teeth
so audibly that the other two looked at him in wonder.
The momentary convulsion of his florid physiognomy
seemed to strike them dumb. They exchanged a quick
glance. Presently the clean-shaven man fired out
another question in his curt, unceremonious manner:

"You have no women in your hotel, eh?"

"Women!" Schomberg exclaimed indignantly, but
also as if a little frightened. "What on earth do you
mean by women? What women? There's Mrs. Schomberg, of course," he added, suddenly appeased, with
lofty indifference.

"If she knows how to keep her place, then it will do.
I can't stand women near me. They give me the
horrors," declared the other. "They are a perfect
curse!"

During this outburst the secretary wore a savage grin.
The chief guest closed his sunken eyes, as if exhausted,
and leaned the back of his head against the stanchion of
the awning. In this pose, his long, feminine eyelashes
were very noticeable, and his regular features, sharp
line of the jaw, and well-cut chin were brought into
prominence, giving him a used-up, weary, depraved
distinction. He did not open his eyes till the steam-
launch touched the quay. Then he and the other man
got ashore quickly, entered a carriage, and drove away
to the hotel, leaving Schomberg to look after their luggage and take care of their strange companion. The
latter, looking more like a performing bear abandoned
by his showmen than a human being, followed all
Schomberg's movements step by step, close behind his
back, muttering to himself in a language that sounded
like some sort of uncouth Spanish. The hotel-keeper

felt uncomfortable till at last he got rid of him at an
obscure den where a very clean, portly Portuguese half-
caste, standing serenely in the doorway, seemed to
understand exactly how to deal with clients of every
kind. He took from the creature the strapped bundle
it had been hugging closely through all its peregrinations
in that strange town, and cut short Schomberg's attempts at explanation by a most confident—

"I comprehend very well, sir."

"It's more than I do," thought Schomberg, going
away thankful at being relieved of the alligator-
hunter's company. He wondered what these fellows
were, without being able to form a guess of sufficient
probability. Their names he learned that very day
by direct inquiry—"to enter in my books," he explained
in his formal military manner, chest thrown out, beard
very much in evidence.

The shaven man, sprawling in a long chair, with his
air of withered youth, raised his eyes languidly.

"My name? Oh, plain Mr. Jones*—put that down
—a gentleman at large. And this is Ricardo." The
pock-marked man, lying prostrate in another long
chair, made a grimace, as if something had tickled the
end of his nose, but did not come out of his supineness.
"Martin Ricardo, secretary. You don't want any
more of our history, do you? Eh, what? Occupation?
Put down, well—tourists. We've been called harder
names before now; it won't hurt our feelings. And
that fellow of mine—where did you tuck him away?
Oh, he will be all right. When he wants anything he'll
take it. He's Peter. Citizen of Colombia, Peter,
Pedro—I don't know that he ever had any other
name. Pedro, alligator-hunter. Oh, yes—I'll pay
his board with the half-caste. Can't help myself.
He's so confoundedly devoted to me that if I were to

give him the sack he would fly at my throat. Shall
I tell you how I killed his brother in the wilds of Colombia? Well, perhaps some other time—it's a rather long
story. What I shall always regret is that I didn't kill
him, too. I could have done it without any extra
trouble then; now it's too late. Great nuisance; but
he's useful sometimes. I hope you are not going to
put all this in your book?"

The offhand, hard manner and the contemptuous
tone of "plain Mr. Jones" disconcerted Schomberg
utterly. He had never been spoken to like this in his
life. He shook his head in silence and withdrew, not
exactly scared—though he was in reality of a timid
disposition under his manly exterior—but distinctly
mystified and impressed.

V

Three weeks later, after putting his cash-box away in the safe which filled with its iron bulk a corner of their bedroom, Schomberg turned towards his wife, but without looking at her exactly, and said:

"I must get rid of these two. It won't do!"

Mrs. Schomberg had entertained that very opinion from the first; but she had been broken years ago into keeping her opinions to herself. Sitting in her night attire in the light of a single candle, she was careful not to make a sound, knowing from experience that her very assent would be resented. With her eyes she followed the figure of Schomberg, clad in his sleeping suit, and moving restlessly about the room.

He never glanced her way, for the reason that Mrs. Schomberg, in her night attire, looked the most unattractive object in existence—miserable, insignificant, faded, crushed, old. And the contrast with the feminine form he had ever in his mind's eye made his wife's appearance painful to his esthetic sense.

Schomberg walked about swearing and fuming for the purpose of screwing his courage up to the sticking point.

"Hang me if I ought not to go now, at once, this minute, into his bedroom, and tell him to be off—him and that secretary of his—early in the morning. I don't mind a round game of cards, but to make a decoy of my table d'hôte—my blood boils! He came here because some lying rascal in Manila told him I kept a table d'hôte."

He said these things, not for Mrs. Schomberg's information, but simply thinking aloud, and trying to work his fury up to a point where it would give him courage enough to face "plain Mr. Jones."

"Impudent, overbearing, swindling sharper," he went on. "I have a good mind to——"

He was beside himself in his lurid, heavy, Teutonic manner, so unlike the picturesque, lively rage of the Latin races; and though his eyes strayed about irresolutely, yet his swollen, angry features awakened in the miserable woman over whom he had been tyrannising for years a fear for his precious carcass, since the poor creature had nothing else but that to hold on to in the world. She knew him well; but she did not know him altogether. The last thing a woman will consent to discover in a man whom she loves, or on whom she simply depends, is want of courage. And, timid in her corner, she ventured to say pressingly:

"Be careful, Wilhelm! Remember the knives and revolvers in their trunks."

In guise of thanks for that anxious reminder, he swore horribly in the direction of her shrinking person. In her scanty night-dress, and barefooted, she recalled a mediæval penitent being reproved for her sins in blasphemous terms. Those lethal weapons were always present to Schomberg's mind. Personally, he had never seen them. His part, ten days after his guests' arrival, had been to lounge in manly, careless attitudes on the verandah—keeping watch—while Mrs. Schomberg, provided with a bunch of assorted keys, her discoloured teeth chattering and her globular eyes absolutely idiotic with fright, was "going through" the luggage of these strange clients. Her terrible Wilhelm had insisted on it.

"I'll be on the look-out, I tell you," he said. "I

shall give you a whistle when I see them coming back.
You couldn't whistle. And if he were to catch you
at it, and chuck you out by the scruff of the neck, it
wouldn't hurt you much; but he won't touch a woman.
Not he! He has told me so. Affected beast. I must
find out something about their little game, and so
there's an end of it. Go in! Go now! Quick march!"

It had been an awful job; but she did go in, because
she was much more afraid of Schomberg than of any
possible consequences of the act. Her greatest concern
was lest no key of the bunch he had provided her with
should fit the locks. It would have been such a disappointment for Wilhelm. However, the trunks, she
found, had been left open; but her investigation did not
last long. She was frightened of firearms, and generally of all weapons, not from personal cowardice, but
as some women are, almost superstitiously, from an
abstract horror of violence and murder. She was out
again on the verandah long before Wilhelm had any
occasion for a warning whistle. The instinctive, motiveless fear being the most difficult to overcome, nothing
could induce her to return to her investigations, neither
threatening growls nor ferocious hisses, nor yet a poke
or two in the ribs.

"Stupid female!" muttered the hotel-keeper, perturbed by the notion of that armoury in one of his bed-
rooms. This was from no abstract sentiment; with
him it was constitutional. "Get out of my sight!" he
snarled. "Go and dress yourself for the table d'hôte."

Left to himself, Schomberg had meditated. What
the devil did this mean? His thinking processes were
sluggish and spasmodic; but suddenly the truth came
to him.

"By heavens, they are desperadoes!" he thought.

Just then he beheld "plain Mr. Jones" and his secretary with the ambiguous name of Ricardo entering the grounds of the hotel. They had been down to the port on some business, and now were returning; Mr. Jones lank, spare, opening his long legs with angular regularity like a pair of compasses, the other stepping out briskly by his side. Conviction entered Schomberg's heart. They *were* two desperadoes—no doubt about it. But as the funk which he experienced was merely a general sensation, he managed to put on his most severe Officer-of-the-Reserve*manner, long before they had closed with him.

"Good morning, gentlemen."

Being answered with derisive civility, he became confirmed in his sudden conviction of their desperate character. The way Mr. Jones turned his hollow eyes on one, like an incurious spectre, and the way the other, when addressed, suddenly retracted his lips and exhibited his teeth without looking round—here was evidence enough to settle that point. Desperadoes! They passed through the billiard-room, inscrutably mysterious, to the back of the house, to join their violated trunks.

"Tiffin bell will ring in five minutes, gentlemen," Schomberg called after them, exaggerating the deep manliness of his tone.

He had managed to upset himself very much. He expected to see them come back infuriated and begin to bully him with an odious lack of restraint. Desperadoes! However they didn't; they had not noticed anything unusual about their trunks and Schomberg recovered his composure and said to himself that he must get rid of this deadly incubus as soon as practicable. They couldn't possibly want to stay very long; this was not the town—the colony—for desperate characters. He shrank from action. He dreaded any kind of dis-

turbance—"fracas," he called it—in his hotel. Such
things were not good for business. Of course, sometimes one had to have a "fracas"; but it had been a
comparatively trifling task to seize the frail Zangiacomo
—whose bones were no larger than a chicken's—round
the ribs, lift him up bodily, dash him to the ground,
and fall on him. It had been easy. The wretched,
hook-nosed creature lay without movement, buried
under its purple beard.

Suddenly, remembering the occasion of that "fracas,"
Schomberg groaned with the pain as of a hot coal under
his breastbone, and gave himself up to desolation. Ah,
if he only had that girl with him he would have been
masterful and resolute and fearless—fight twenty desperadoes—care for nobody on earth! Whereas the possession of Mrs. Schomberg was no incitement to a display of manly virtues. Instead of caring for no one,
he felt that he cared for nothing. Life was a hollow
sham; he wasn't going to risk a shot through his lungs
or his liver in order to preserve its integrity. It had
no savour—damn it!

In his state of moral decomposition, Schomberg,
master as he was of the art of hotel-keeping, and careful
of giving no occasion for criticism to the powers regulating that branch of human activities, let things take
their course; though he saw very well where that course
was tending. It began first with a game or two after
dinner—for the drinks, apparently—with some lingering customer, at one of the little tables ranged against
the walls of the billiard-room. Schomberg detected
the meaning of it at once. That's what it was! This
was what they were! And, moving about restlessly
(at that time his morose silent period had set in), he
cast sidelong looks at the game; but he said nothing.
It was not worth while having a row with men who were

so overbearing. Even when money appeared in connection with these postprandial games, into which more and more people were being drawn, he still refrained from raising the question; he was reluctant to draw unduly the attention of "plain Mr. Jones" and of the equivocal Ricardo, to his person. One evening, however, after the public rooms of the hotel had become empty, Schomberg made an attempt to grapple with the problem in an indirect way.

In a distant corner the tired China boy dozed on his heels, his back against the wall. Mrs. Schomberg had disappeared, as usual, between ten and eleven. Schomberg walked about slowly, in and out of the room and the verandah, thoughtful, waiting for his two guests to go to bed. Then suddenly he approached them, militarily, his chest thrown out, his voice curt and soldierly.

"Hot night, gentlemen."

Mr. Jones, lolling back idly in a chair, looked up. Ricardo, as idle, but more upright, made no sign.

"Won't you have a drink with me before retiring?" went on Schomberg, sitting down by the little table.

"By all means," said Mr. Jones lazily.

Ricardo showed his teeth in a strange, quick grin. Schomberg felt painfully how difficult it was to get in touch with these men, both so quiet, so deliberate, so menacingly unceremonious. He ordered the Chinaman to bring in the drinks. His purpose was to discover how long these guests intended to stay. Ricardo displayed no conversational vein, but Mr. Jones appeared communicative enough. His voice somehow matched his sunken eyes. It was hollow without being in the least mournful; it sounded distant, uninterested, as though he were speaking from the bottom of a well. Schomberg learned that he would have the privilege of lodging and boarding these gentlemen for at least a month more. He could not conceal his discomfiture at this piece of news.

"What's the matter? Don't you like to have people in your house?" asked plain Mr. Jones languidly. "I should have thought the owner of a hotel would be pleased."

He lifted his delicate and beautifully pencilled eyebrows. Schomberg muttered something about the locality being dull and uninteresting to travellers—nothing going on—too quiet altogether; but he only provoked the declaration that quiet had its charms sometimes, and even dulness was welcome as a change.

"We haven't had time to be dull for the last three years," added plain Mr. Jones, his eyes fixed darkly on Schomberg, whom he furthermore invited to have another drink, this time with him, and not to worry himself about things he did not understand; and especially not to be inhospitable—which in a hotel-keeper was highly unprofessional.

"I don't understand," grumbled Schomberg. "Oh, yes, I understand perfectly well. I——"

"You are frightened," interrupted Mr. Jones. "What *is* the matter?"

"I don't want any scandal in my place. That's what's the matter."

Schomberg tried to face the situation bravely, but that steady, black stare affected him. And when he glanced aside uncomfortably, he met Ricardo's grin uncovering a lot of teeth, though the man seemed absorbed in his thoughts all the time.

"And, moreover," went on Mr. Jones in that distant tone of his, "you can't help yourself. Here we are and here we stay. Would you try to put us out? I dare say you could do it; but you couldn't do it without get-

ting badly hurt—very badly hurt. We can promise
him that, can't we, Martin?"

The secretary retracted his lips and looked up sharply
at Schomberg, as if only too anxious to leap upon him
with teeth and claws.

Schomberg managed to produce a deep laugh.

"Ha! Ha! Ha!"

Mr. Jones closed his eyes wearily, as if the light hurt
them, and looked remarkably like a corpse for a moment. This was bad enough; but when he opened
them again, it was almost a worse trial for Schomberg's
nerves. The spectral intensity of that glance, fixed
on the hotel-keeper (and this was most frightful), without any definite expression, seemed to dissolve the
last grain of resolution in his character.

"You don't think, by any chance, that you have to do
with ordinary people, do you?" inquired Mr. Jones, in
his lifeless manner, which seemed to imply some sort
of menace from beyond the grave.

"He's a gentleman," testified Martin Ricardo with a
sudden snap of the lips, after which his moustaches
stirred by themselves in an odd, feline manner.

"Oh, I wasn't thinking of that," said plain Mr. Jones,
while Schomberg, dumb and planted heavily in his
chair, looked from one to the other, leaning forward a
little. "Of course I am that; but Ricardo attaches too
much importance to a social advantage. What I mean,
for instance, is that he, quiet and inoffensive as you
see him sitting here, would think nothing of setting
fire to this house of entertainment of yours. It would
blaze like a box of matches. Think of that! It
wouldn't advance your affairs much, would it?—
whatever happened to us."

"Come, come, gentlemen," remonstrated Schomberg
in a murmur. "This is very wild talk!"

"And you have been used to deal with tame people, haven't you? But we aren't tame. We once kept a whole angry town at bay for two days, and then we got away with our plunder. It was in Venezuela.* Ask Martin here—he can tell you."

Instinctively Schomberg looked at Ricardo, who only passed the tip of his tongue over his lips with an uncanny sort of gusto, but did not offer to begin.

"Well, perhaps it would be a rather long story," Mr. Jones conceded after a short silence.

"I have no desire to hear it, I am sure," said Schomberg. "This isn't Venezuela. You wouldn't get away from here like that. But all this is silly talk of the worst sort. Do you mean to say you would make deadly trouble for the sake of a few guilders that you and that other"—eyeing Ricardo suspiciously, as one would look at a strange animal—"gentleman can win of an evening? 'Tisn't as if my customers were a lot of rich men with pockets full of cash. I wonder you take so much trouble and risk for so little money."

Schomberg's argument was met by Mr. Jones's statement that one must do something to kill time. Killing time was not forbidden. For the rest, being in a communicative mood, Mr. Jones said languidly and in a voice indifferent, as if issuing from a tomb, that he depended on himself, as if the world were still one great, wild jungle without law. Martin was something like that, too—for reasons of his own.

All these statements Ricardo confirmed by short, inhuman grins. Schomberg lowered his eyes, for the sight of these two men intimidated him; but he was losing patience.

"Of course, I could see at once that you were two desperate characters—something like what you say.

But what would you think if I told you that I am pretty
near as desperate as you two gentlemen? 'Here's that
Schomberg has an easy time running his hotel,' people
think; and yet it seems to me I would just as soon let
you rip me open and burn the whole show as not.
There!"

A low whistle was heard. It came from Ricardo, and
was derisive. Schomberg, breathing heavily, looked on
the floor. He was really desperate. Mr. Jones remained languidly sceptical.

"Tut, tut! You have a tolerable business. You are
perfectly tame; you——" He paused, then added in
a tone of disgust: "You have a wife."

Schomberg tapped the floor angrily with his foot and
uttered an indistinct, laughing curse.

"What do you mean by flinging that damned trouble
at my head?" he cried. "I wish you would carry her
off with you somewhere to the devil! I wouldn't run
after you."

The unexpected outburst affected Mr. Jones strangely.
He had a horrified recoil, chair and all, as if Schomberg
had thrust a wriggling viper in his face.

"What's this infernal nonsense?" he muttered thickly.
"What do you mean? How dare you?"

Ricardo chuckled audibly.

"I tell you I am desperate," Schomberg repeated. "I
am as desperate as any man ever was. I don't care a
hang what happens to me!"

"Well, then"—Mr. Jones began to speak with a
quietly threatening effect, as if the common words of
daily use had some other deadly meaning to his mind—
"well, then, why should you make yourself ridiculously
disagreeable to us? If you don't care, as you say, you
might just as well let us have the key of that music-
shed of yours for a quiet game; a modest bank—a

dozen candles or so. It would be greatly appreciated by your clients, as far as I can judge from the way they betted on a game of écarté*I had with that fair, baby-faced man—what's his name? They just yearn for a modest bank. And I am afraid Martin here would take it badly if you objected; but of course you won't. Think of the calls for drinks!"

Schomberg, raising his eyes, at last met the gleams in two dark caverns under Mr. Jones's devilish eyebrows, directed upon him impenetrably. He shuddered as if horrors worse than murder had been lurking there, and said, nodding towards Ricardo:

"I dare say he wouldn't think twice about sticking me, if he had you at his back! I wish I had sunk my launch, and gone to the bottom myself in her, before I boarded the steamer you came by. Ah, well, I've been already living in hell for weeks, so you don't make much difference. I'll let you have the concert-room—and hang the consequences. But what about the boy on late duty? If he sees cards and actual money passing, he will be sure to blab, and it will be all over the town in no time."

A ghastly smile stirred the lips of Mr. Jones.

"Ah, I see you want to make a success of it. Very good. That's the way to get on. Don't let it disturb you. You chase all the Chinamen to bed early, and we'll get Pedro here every evening. He isn't the conventional waiter's cut, but he will do to run to and fro with the tray, while you sit here from nine to eleven serving out drinks and gathering the money."

"There will be three of them now," thought the unlucky Schomberg.

But Pedro, at any rate, was just a simple, straightforward brute, if a murderous one. There was no mystery about him, nothing uncanny, no suggestion of a stealthy, deliberate wild-cat turned into a man, or of an insolent spectre on leave from Hades, endowed with skin and bones and a subtle power of terror. Pedro with his fangs, his tangled beard and queer stare of his little bear's eyes was, by comparison, delightfully natural. Besides, Schomberg could no longer help himself.

"That will do very well," he assented mournfully. "But mind, gentlemen, if you had turned up here only three months ago—ay, less than three months ago— you would have found somebody very different from what I am now to talk to you. It's true. What do you think of that?"

"I scarcely know what to think. I should think it was a lie. You were probably as tame three months ago as you are now. You were born tame, like most people in the world."

Mr. Jones got up spectrally, and Ricardo imitated him with a snarl and a stretch. Schomberg, in a brown study, went on, as if to himself:

"There has been an orchestra here—eighteen women."

Mr. Jones let out an exclamation of dismay, and looked about as if the walls around him and the whole house had been infected with plague. Then he became very angry, and swore violently at Schomberg for daring to bring up such subjects. The hotel-keeper was too much surprised to get up. He gazed from his chair at Mr. Jones's anger, which had nothing spectral in it, but was not the more comprehensible for that.

"What's the matter?" he stammered out. "What subject? Didn't you hear me say it was an orchestra? There's nothing wrong in that. Well, there was a girl amongst them——" Schomberg's eyes went stony; he clasped his hands in front of his breast with such force that his knuckles came out white. "Such a girl! Tame, am I? I would have kicked everything to pieces about me for her. And she, of course. . . . I am in the prime of life. . . . Then a fellow bewitched her—a vagabond, a false, lying, swindling, underhand, stick-at-nothing brute. Ah!''

His entwined fingers cracked as he tore his hands apart, flung out his arms, and leaned his forehead on them in a passion of fury. The other two looked at his shaking back—the attenuated Mr. Jones with mingled scorn and a sort of fear, Ricardo with the expression of a cat which sees a piece of fish in the pantry out of reach. Schomberg flung himself backwards. He was dry-eyed, but he gulped as if swallowing sobs.

"No wonder you can do with me what you like. You have no idea—just let me tell you of my trouble——"

"I don't want to know anything of your beastly trouble," said Mr. Jones, in his most lifelessly positive voice.

He stretched forth an arresting hand, and, as Schomberg remained open-mouthed, he walked out of the billiard-room in all the uncanniness of his thin shanks. Ricardo followed at his leader's heels; but he showed his teeth to Schomberg over his shoulder.

VI

From that evening dated those mysterious but significant phenomena in Schomberg's establishment which attracted Captain Davidson's casual notice when he dropped in, placid yet astute, in order to return Mrs. Schomberg's Indian shawl. And, strangely enough, they lasted some considerable time. It argued either honesty and bad luck or extraordinary restraint on the part of "plain Mr. Jones and Co." in their discreet operations with cards.

It was a curious and impressive sight, the inside of Schomberg's concert-hall, encumbered at one end by a great stack of chairs piled up on and about the musicians' platform, and lighted at the other by two dozen candles disposed about a long trestle table covered with green cloth. In the middle, Mr. Jones, a starved spectre turned into a banker, faced Ricardo, a rather nasty, slow-moving cat turned into a croupier. By contrast, the other faces round that table, anything between twenty and thirty, must have looked like collected samples of intensely artless, helpless humanity—pathetic in their innocent watch for the small turns of luck which indeed might have been serious enough for them. They had no notice to spare for the hairy Pedro, carrying a tray with the clumsiness of a creature caught in the woods and taught to walk on its hind legs.

As to Schomberg, he kept out of the way. He remained in the billiard-room, serving out drinks to the unspeakable Pedro with an air of not seeing the growling monster, of not knowing where the drinks went, of

ignoring that there was such a thing as a music-room
over there under the trees within fifty yards of the
hotel. He submitted himself to the situation with a
low-spirited stoicism compounded of fear and resignation. Directly the party had broken up (he could see
dark shapes of the men drifting singly and in knots
through the gate of the compound), he would withdraw
out of sight behind a door not quite closed, in order
to avoid meeting his two extraordinary guests; but he
would watch through the crack their contrasted forms
pass through the billiard-room and disappear on their
way to bed. Then he would hear doors being slammed
upstairs; and a profound silence would fall upon the
whole house, upon his hotel appropriated, haunted by
those insolently outspoken men provided with a whole
armoury of weapons in their trunks. A profound
silence. Schomberg sometimes could not resist the
notion that he must be dreaming. Shuddering, he
would pull himself together, and creep out, with movements strangely inappropriate to the Lieutenant-of-
the-Reserve bearing by which he tried to keep up his
self-respect before the world.

A great loneliness oppressed him. One after another
he would extinguish the lamps, and move softly towards
his bedroom, where Mrs. Schomberg waited for him—
no fit companion for a man of his ability and "in the
prime of life." But that life, alas, was blighted. He
felt it; and never with such force as when on opening
the door he perceived that woman sitting patiently
in a chair, her toes peeping out under the edge of her
night-dress, an amazingly small amount of hair on her
head drooping on the long stalk of scraggy neck, with
that everlasting scared grin showing a blue tooth and
meaning nothing—not even real fear. For she was
used to him.

Sometimes he was tempted to screw the head off the stalk. He imagined himself doing it—with one hand, a twisting movement. Not seriously, of course. Just a simple indulgence for his exasperated feelings. He wasn't capable of murder. He was certain of that. And, remembering suddenly the plain speeches of Mr. Jones, he would think: "I suppose I *am* too tame for that"—quite unaware that he had murdered the poor woman morally years ago. He was too unintelligent to have the notion of such a crime. Her bodily presence was bitterly offensive, because of its contrast with a very different feminine image. And it was no use getting rid of her. She was a habit of years, and there would be nothing to put in her place. At any rate, he could talk to that idiot half the night if he chose.

That night he had been vapouring before her as to his intention to face his two guests and, instead of that inspiration he needed, had merely received the usual warning: "Be careful, Wilhelm." He did not want to be told to be careful by an imbecile female. What he needed was a pair of woman's arms which, flung round his neck, would brace him up for the encounter. Inspire him, he called it to himself.

He lay awake a long time; and his slumbers, when they came, were unsatisfactory and short. The morning light had no joy for his eyes. He listened dismally to the movements in the house. The Chinamen were unlocking and flinging wide the doors of the public rooms which opened on the verandah. Horrors! Another poisoned day to get through somehow! The recollection of his resolve made him feel actually sick for a moment. First of all the lordly, abandoned attitudes of Mr. Jones disconcerted him. Then there was his contemptuous silence. Mr. Jones never addressed him-

self to Schomberg with any general remarks, never
opened his lips to him unless to say "Good morning"—
two simple words which, uttered by that man, seemed
a mockery of a threatening character. And, lastly,
it was not a frank physical fear he inspired—for, as to
that, even a cornered rat will fight—but a superstitious
shrinking awe, something like an invincible repugnance
to seek speech with a wicked ghost. That it was a
daylight ghost, surprisingly angular in his attitudes, and
for the most part spread out on three chairs, did not
make it any easier. Daylight only made him a more
weird, a more disturbing and unlawful apparition.
Strangely enough in the evening, when he came out
of his mute supineness, this unearthly side of him was
less obtrusive. At the gaming-table, when actually
handling the cards, it was probably sunk quite out
of sight; but Schomberg, having made up his mind in
ostrich-like fashion to ignore what was going on, never
entered the desecrated music-room. He had never
seen Mr. Jones in the exercise of his vocation—or perhaps it was only his trade.

"I will speak to him to-night," Schomberg said to
himself, while he drank his morning tea, in pyjamas,
on the verandah, before the rising sun had topped the
trees of the compound, and while the undried dew still
lay silvery on the grass, sparkled on the blossoms of
the central flower-bed, and darkened the yellow gravel
of the drive. "That's what I'll do. I won't keep out
of sight to-night. I shall come out and catch him as
he goes to bed carrying the cash-box."

After all, what was the fellow but a common desperado? Murderous? Oh, yes; murderous enough,
perhaps—and the muscles of Schomberg's stomach
had a quivering contraction under his airy attire. But
even a common desperado would think twice or, more

likely, a hundred times, before openly murdering an inoffensive citizen in a civilised, European-ruled town. He jerked his shoulders. Of course! He shuddered again, and paddled back to his room to dress himself. His mind was made up, and he would think no more about it; but still he had his doubts. They grew and unfolded themselves with the progress of the day, as some plants do. At times they made him perspire more than usual, and they did away with the possibility of his afternoon siesta. After turning over on his couch more than a dozen times, he gave up this mockery of repose, got up, and went downstairs.

It was between three and four o'clock, the hour of profound peace. The very flowers seemed to doze on their stalks set with sleepy leaves. Not even the air stirred, for the sea-breeze was not due till later. The servants were out of sight, catching naps in the shade somewhere behind the house. Mrs. Schomberg, in a dim upstair room with closed jalousies, was elaborating those two long pendant ringlets which were such a feature of her hair-dressing for her afternoon duties. At that time no customers ever troubled the repose of the establishment. Wandering about his premises in profound solitude, Schomberg recoiled at the door of the billiard-room, as if he had seen a snake in his path. All alone with the billiards, the bare little tables, and a lot of untenanted chairs, Mr. Secretary Ricardo sat near the wall, performing with lightning rapidity something that looked like tricks with his own personal pack of cards, which he always carried about in his pocket. Schomberg would have backed out quietly if Ricardo had not turned his head. Having been seen, the hotel-keeper elected to walk in as the lesser risk of the two. The consciousness of his inwardly abject attitude towards these men caused him always to throw his chest out and assume a severe expression. Ricardo watched his approach, clasping the pack of cards in both hands.

"You want something, perhaps?" suggested Schomberg in his Lieutenant-of-the-Reserve voice.

Ricardo shook his head in silence and looked expectant. With him Schomberg exchanged at least twenty words every day. He was infinitely more communicative than his patron. At times he looked very much like an ordinary human being of his class; and he seemed to be in an amiable mood at that moment. Suddenly spreading some ten cards face downward in the form of a fan, he thrust them towards Schomberg.

"Come, man, take one quick!"

Schomberg was so surprised that he took one hurriedly, after a very perceptible start. The eyes of Martin Ricardo gleamed phosphorescent in the halflight of the room screened from the heat and glare of the tropics.

"That's a king of hearts you've got," he chuckled, showing his teeth in a quick flash.

Schomberg, after looking at the card, admitted that it was, and laid it down on the table.

"I can make you take any card I like nine times out of ten," exulted the secretary, with a strange curl of his lips and a green flicker in his raised eyes.

Schomberg looked down at him dumbly. For a few seconds neither of them stirred; then Ricardo lowered his glance, and, opening his fingers, let the whole pack fall on the table. Schomberg sat down. He sat down because of the faintness in his legs, and for no other reason. His mouth was dry. Having sat down, he felt that he must speak. He squared his shoulders in parade style.

"You are pretty good at that sort of thing," he said.

"Practice makes perfect," replied the secretary.

His precarious amiability made it impossible for Schomberg to get away. Thus, from his very timidity, the hotel-keeper found himself engaged in a conversation the thought of which had filled him with apprehension. It must be said, in justice to Schomberg, that he concealed his funk very creditably. The habit of throwing out his chest and speaking in a severe voice stood him in good stead. With him, too, practice made perfect; and he would probably have kept it up to the end, to the very last moment, to the ultimate instant of breaking strain which would leave him grovelling on the floor. To add to his secret trouble, he was at a loss what to say. He found nothing else but the remark:

"I suppose you are fond of cards."

"What would you expect?" asked Ricardo in a simple, philosophical tone. "Is it likely I should not be?" Then, with sudden fire: "Fond of cards? Ay, passionately!"

The effect of this outburst was augmented by the quiet lowering of the eyelids, by a reserved pause as though this had been a confession of another kind of love. Schomberg cudgelled his brains for a new topic, but he could not find one. His usual scandalous gossip would not serve this turn. That desperado did not know any one anywhere within a thousand miles. Schomberg was almost compelled to keep to the subject.

"I suppose you've always been so—from your early youth."

Ricardo's eyes remained cast down. His fingers toyed absently with the pack on the table.

"I don't know that it was so early. I first got in the way of it playing for tobacco—in forecastles of ships, you know—common sailor games. We used to spend whole watches below at it, round a chest, under a slush lamp. We would hardly spare the time to get a bite of salt horse—neither eat nor sleep. We could hardly stand when the watches were mustered on deck. Talk of gambling!" He dropped the reminiscent tone to add the information, "I was bred to the sea from a boy, you know."

Schomberg had fallen into a reverie, but without losing the sense of impending calamity. The next words he heard were:

"I got on all right at sea, too. Worked up to be mate. I was mate of a schooner—a yacht, you might call her—a special good berth too, in the Gulf of Mexico; a soft job that you don't run across more than once in a lifetime. Yes, I was mate of her when I left the sea to follow him."

Ricardo tossed up his chin to indicate the room above; from which Schomberg, his wits painfully aroused by this reminder of Mr. Jones's existence, concluded that the latter had withdrawn into his bedroom. Ricardo, observing him from under lowered eyelids, went on:

"It so happened that we were shipmates."

"Mr. Jones, you mean? Is he a sailor too?"

Ricardo raised his eyelids at that.

"He's no more Mr. Jones than you are," he said with obvious pride. "He a sailor! That just shows your ignorance. But there! A foreigner can't be expected to know any better. I am an Englishman, and I know a gentleman at sight. I should know one drunk, in the gutter, in jail, under the gallows. There's a something —it isn't exactly the appearance, it's a—no use me trying to tell you. You ain't an Englishman; and if you were, you wouldn't need to be told."

An unsuspected stream of loquacity had broken its

dam somewhere deep within the man, had diluted his
fiery blood and softened his pitiless fibre. Schomberg
experienced mingled relief and apprehension, as if
suddenly an enormous savage cat had begun to wind
itself about his legs in inexplicable friendliness. No
prudent man under such circumstances would dare to
stir. Schomberg didn't stir. Ricardo assumed an
easy attitude, with an elbow on the table. Schomberg
squared his shoulders afresh.

"I was employed, in that there yacht—schooner,
whatever you call it—by ten gentlemen at once. That
surprises you, eh? Yes, yes, ten. Leastwise there were
nine of them gents good enough in their way, and one
downright gentleman, and that was . . ."

Ricardo gave another upward jerk of his chin as
much as to say: He! The only one.

"And no mistake," he went on. "I spotted him
from the first day. How? Why? Ay, you may ask.
Hadn't seen that many gentlemen in my life. Well,
somehow I did. If you were an Englishman, you
would——"

"What was your yacht?" Schomberg interrupted as
impatiently as he dared; for this harping on nationality
jarred on his already tried nerves. "What was the
game?"

"You have a headpiece on you! Game! 'Xactly.
That's what it was—the sort of silliness gentlemen will
get up among themselves to play at adventure. A
treasure-hunting expedition. Each of them put down so
much money, you understand, to buy the schooner.
Their agent in the city engaged me and the skipper.
The greatest secrecy and all that. I reckon he had a
twinkle in his eye all the time—and no mistake. But
that wasn't our business. Let them bust their money
as they like. The pity of it was that so little of it

came our way. Just fair pay and no more. And damn any pay, much or little, anyhow—that's what I say!"

He blinked his eyes greenishly in the dim light. The heat seemed to have stilled everything in the world but his voice. He swore at large, abundantly, in snarling undertones, it was impossible to say why; then calmed down as inexplicably and went on, as a sailor yarns.

"At first there were only nine of them adventurous sparks; then, just a day or two before the sailing date, *he* turned up. Heard of it somehow, somewhere—I would say from some woman, if I didn't know him as I do. He would give any woman a ten-mile berth. He can't stand them. Or maybe in a flash bar. Or maybe in one of them grand clubs in Pall Mall.* Anyway the agent netted him in all right—cash down, and only about four and twenty hours for him to get ready; but he didn't miss his ship. Not he! You might have called it a pier-head jump—for a gentleman. I saw him come along. Know the West India Docks,* eh?"

Schomberg did not know the West India Docks. Ricardo looked at him pensively for a while, and then continued, as if such ignorance had to be disregarded.

"Our tug was already alongside. Two loafers were carrying his dunnage behind him. I told the dockmen at our moorings to keep all fast for a minute. The gangway was down already; but he made nothing of it. Up he jumps, one leap, swings his long legs over the rail, and there he is on board. They pass up his swell dunnage,* and he puts his hand in his trousers pocket and throws all his small change on the wharf for them chaps to pick up. They were still promenading that wharf on all fours when we cast off. It was only then that he looked at me—quietly, you know; in a slow way. He wasn't so thin then as he is now; but I noticed he

wasn't so young as he looked—not by a long chalk. He
seemed to touch me inside somewhere. I went away
pretty quick from there; I was wanted forward
anyhow. I wasn't frightened. What should I be fright-
tened for? I only felt touched—on the very spot.
But Jee-miny, if anybody had told me we should be
partners before the year was out—well, I would
have——"

He swore a variety of strange oaths, some common,
other quaintly horrible to Schomberg's ears, and all
mere innocent exclamations of wonder at the shifts and
changes of human fortune. Schomberg moved slightly
in his chair. But the admirer and partner of "plain
Mr. Jones" seemed to have forgotten Schomberg's
existence for the moment. The stream of ingenuous
blasphemy—some of it in bad Spanish—had run dry,
and Martin Ricardo, connoisseur in gentlemen, sat
dumb with a stony gaze as if still marvelling inwardly
at the amazing elections, conjunctions and associations
of events which influence man's pilgrimage on this earth.

At last Schomberg spoke tentatively:

"And so the—the gentleman, up there, talked you
over into leaving a good berth?"

Ricardo started.

"Talked me over! Didn't need to talk me over. He
just beckoned to me, and that was enough. By that
time we were in the Gulf of Mexico. One night we
were lying at anchor, close to a dry sandbank—to this
day I am not sure where it was—off the Colombian
coast or thereabouts. We were to start digging the
next morning, and all hands had turned in early, expecting a hard day with the shovels. Up he comes,
and in his quiet, tired way of speaking—you can tell a
gentleman by that as much as by anything else almost
—up he comes behind me and says, just like that into

my ear, in a manner: 'Well, and what do you think of our treasure hunt now?'

"I didn't even turn my head; 'xactly as I stood, I remained, and I spoke no louder than himself:

"'If you want to know, sir, it's nothing but just damned tomfoolery.'

"We had, of course, been having short talks together at one time or another during the passage. I dare say he had read me like a book. There ain't much to me, except that I have never been tame, even when walking the pavement and cracking jokes and standing drinks to chums—ay, and to strangers, too. I would watch them lifting their elbows at my expense, or splitting their sides at my fun—I *can* be funny when I like, you bet!"

A pause for self-complacent contemplation of his own fun and generosity checked the flow of Ricardo's speech. Schomberg was concerned to keep within bounds the enlargement of his eyes, which he seemed to feel growing bigger in his head.

"Yes, yes," he whispered hastily.

"I would watch them and think: 'You boys don't know who I am. If you did——!' With girls, too. Once I was courting a girl. I used to kiss her behind the ear and say to myself: 'If you only knew who's kissing you, my dear, you would scream and bolt!' Ha! ha! Not that I wanted to do them any harm; but I felt the power in myself. Now, here we sit, friendly like, and that's all right. You aren't in my way. But I am not friendly to you. I just don't care. Some men do say that; but I really don't. You are no more to me one way or another than that fly there. Just so. I'd squash you or leave you alone. I don't care what I do."

If real force of character consists in overcoming our sudden weaknesses, Schomberg displayed plenty of that quality. At the mention of the fly, he re-enforced the severe dignity of his attitude as one inflates a collapsing toy balloon with a great effort of breath. The easygoing, relaxed attitude of Ricardo was really appalling. "That's so," he went on. "I am that sort of fellow. You wouldn't think it, would you? No. You have to be told. So I am telling you, and I dare say you only half believe it. But you can't say to yourself that I am drunk, stare at me as you may. I haven't had anything stronger than a glass of iced water all day. Takes a real gentleman to see through a fellow. Oh, yes—he spotted me. I told you we had a few talks at sea about one thing or another. And I used to watch him down the skylight, playing cards in the cuddy with the others. They had to pass the time away somehow. By the same token he caught me at it once, and it was then that I told him I was fond of cards—and generally lucky in gambling, too. Yes, he had sized me up. Why not? A gentleman's just like any other man— and something more."

It flashed through Schomberg's mind that these two were indeed well matched in their enormous dissimilarity, identical souls in different disguises.

"Says he to me"—Ricardo started again in a gossiping manner—"'I'm packed up. It's about time to go, Martin.'

"It was the first time he called me Martin. Says I: "'Is that it, sir?'

"'You didn't think I was after that sort of treasure, did you? I wanted to clear out from home quietly. It's a pretty expensive way of getting a passage across, but it has served my turn.'

"I let him know very soon that I was game for anything, from pitch and toss to wilful murder, in his company.

"'Wilful murder?' says he in his quiet way. 'What the deuce is that? What are you talking about? People do get killed sometimes when they get in one's way, but that's self-defence—you understand?'

"I told him I did. And then I said I would run below for a minute, to ram a few of my things into a sailor's bag I had. I've never cared for a lot of dunnage; I believed in going about flying light when I was at sea. I came back and found him strolling up and down the deck, as if he were taking a breath of fresh air before turning in, like on any other evening.

"'Ready?'

"'Yes, sir.'

"He didn't even look at me. We had had a boat in the water astern ever since we came to anchor in the afternoon. He throws the stump of his cigar overboard.

"'Can you get the captain out on deck?' he asks.

"That was the last thing in the world I should have thought of doing. I lost my tongue for a moment.

"'I can try,' says I.

"'Well, then, I am going below. You get him up and keep him with you till I come back on deck. Mind! Don't let him go below till I return.'

"I could not help asking why he told me to rouse a sleeping man, when we wanted everybody on board to sleep sweetly till we got clear of the schooner. He laughs a little and says that I didn't see all the bearings of this business.

"'Mind,' he says, 'don't let him leave you till you see me come up again.' He puts his eyes close to mine. 'Keep him with you at all costs.'

"'And that means?' says I.

"'All costs to him—by every possible or impossible

means. I don't want to be interrupted in my business down below. He would give me lots of trouble. I take you with me to save myself trouble in various circumstances; and you've got to enter on your work right away.'

"'Just so, sir,' says I; and he slips down the companion.

"With a gentleman you know at once where you are; but it was a ticklish job. The skipper was nothing to me one way or another, any more than you are at this moment, Mr. Schomberg. You may light your cigar or blow your brains out this minute, and I don't care a hang which you do, both or neither. To bring the skipper up was easy enough. I had only to stamp on the deck a few times over his head. I stamped hard. But how to keep him up when he got there?

"'Anything the matter, Mr. Ricardo?' I heard his voice behind me.

"There he was, and I hadn't thought of anything to say to him; so I didn't turn around. The moonlight was brighter than many a day I could remember in the North Sea.

"'Why did you call me? What are you staring at out there, Mr. Ricardo?'

"He was deceived by my keeping my back to him. I wasn't staring at anything, but his mistake gave me a notion.

"'I am staring at something that looks like a canoe over there,' I said very slowly.

"The skipper got concerned at once. It wasn't any danger from the inhabitants, whoever they were.

"'Oh, hang it!' says he. 'That's very unfortunate.' He had hoped that the schooner being on the coast would not get known so very soon. 'Dashed awkward, with the business we've got in hand, to have a lot of

niggers watching operations. But are you certain this
is a canoe?'

"'It may be a drift-log,' I said; 'but I thought you
had better have a look with your own eyes. You may
make it out better than I can.'

"His eyes weren't anything as good as mine. But he
says:

"'Certainly. Certainly. You did quite right.'

"And it's a fact I had seen some drift-logs at sunset.
I saw what they were then and didn't trouble my head
about them, forgot all about it till that very moment.
Nothing strange in seeing drift-logs off a coast like
that; and I'm hanged if the skipper didn't make one
out in the wake of the moon. Strange what a little
thing a man's life hangs on sometimes—a single word!
Here you are, sitting unsuspicious before me, and you
may let out something unbeknown to you that would
settle your hash. Not that I have any ill-feeling. I
have no feelings. If the skipper had said, 'Oh, bosh!'
and had turned his back on me, he would not have gone
three steps towards his bed; but he stood there and
stared. And now the job was to get him off the deck
when he was no longer wanted there.

"'We are just trying to make out if that object there
is a canoe or a log,' says he to Mr. Jones.

"Mr. Jones had come up, lounging as carelessly as
when he went below. While the skipper was jawing
about boats and drifting logs, I asked by signs, from
behind, if I hadn't better knock him on the head and
drop him quietly overboard. The night was slipping
by, and we had to go. It couldn't be put off till next
night no more. No. No more. And do you know
why?"

Schomberg made a slight negative sign with his
head. This direct appeal annoyed him, jarred on the

induced quietude of a great talker forced into the part of a listener and sunk in it as a man sinks into slumber. Mr. Ricardo struck a note of scorn.

"Don't know why? Can't you guess? No? Because the boss had got hold of the skipper's cash-box by then. See?"

VII

"A COMMON thief!"

Schomberg bit his tongue just too late, and woke up completely as he saw Ricardo retract his lips in a cat-like grin; but the companion of "plain Mr. Jones" didn't alter his comfortable, gossiping attitude.

"Garn! What if he did want to see his money back, like any tame shopkeeper, hash-seller,* gin-slinger,* or ink-spewer does? Fancy a mud-turtle like you trying to pass an opinion on a gentleman! A gentleman isn't to be sized up so easily. Even I ain't up to it sometimes. For instance, that night, all he did was to waggle his finger at me. The skipper stops his silly chatter, surprised.

"'Eh? What's the matter?' asks he.

"The matter! It was his reprieve—that's what was the matter.

"'Oh, nothing, nothing,' says my gentleman. 'You are perfectly right. A log—nothing but a log.'

"Ha, ha! Reprieve, I call it, because if the skipper had gone on with his silly argument much longer he would have had to be knocked out of the way. I could hardly hold myself in on account of the precious minutes. However, his guardian angel put it into his head to shut up and go back to his bed. I was ramping mad about the lost time.

"'Why didn't you let me give him one on his silly coconut, sir?' I asks.

"'No ferocity, no ferocity,' he says, raising his finger at me as calm as you please.

"You can't tell how a gentleman takes that sort of thing. They don't lose their temper. It's bad form. You'll never see him lose his temper—not for anybody to see, anyhow. Ferocity ain't good form, either—that much I've learned by this time, and more, too. I've had that schooling that you couldn't tell by my face if I meant to rip you up the next minute—as of course I could do in less than a jiffy. I have a knife up the leg of my trousers."

"You haven't!" exclaimed Schomberg incredulously.

Mr. Ricardo was as quick as lightning in changing his lounging, idle attitude for a stooping position, and exhibiting the weapon with one jerk at the left leg of his trousers. Schomberg had just a view of it, strapped to a very hairy limb, when Mr. Ricardo, jumping up, stamped his foot to get the trouser-leg down, and resumed his careless pose with one elbow on the table.

"It's a more handy way to carry a tool than you would think," he went on, gazing abstractedly into Schomberg's wide-open eyes. "Suppose some little difference comes up during a game. Well, you stoop to pick up a dropped card, and when you come up— there you are ready to strike, or with the thing up your sleeve ready to throw. Or you just dodge under the table when there's some shooting coming. You wouldn't believe the damage a fellow with a knife under the table can do to ill-conditioned skunks that want to raise trouble, before they begin to understand what the screaming's about, and make a bolt—those that can, that is."

The roses of Schomberg's cheek at the root of his chestnut beard faded perceptibly. Ricardo chuckled faintly.

"But no ferocity—no ferocity! A gentleman knows. What's the good of getting yourself into a state? And no shirking necessity, either. No gentleman ever shirks. What I learn I don't forget. Why! We gambled on the plains, with a damn lot of cattlemen in ranches; played fair, mind—and then had to fight for our winnings afterwards as often as not. We've gambled on the hills and in the valleys and on the sea-shore, and out of sight of land—mostly fair. Generally it's good enough. We began in Nicaragua first, after we left that schooner and her fool errand. There were one hundred and twenty-seven sovereigns and some Mexican dollars in that skipper's cash-box. Hardly enough to knock a man on the head for from behind, I must confess; but that the skipper had a narrow escape, the governor himself could not deny afterwards."

" 'Do you want me to understand, sir, that you mind there being one life more or less on this earth?' I asked him, a few hours after we got away.

" 'Certainly not,' says he.

" 'Well, then, why did you stop me?'

" 'There's a proper way of doing things. You'll have to learn to be correct. There's also unnecessary exertion. That must be avoided, too—if only for the look of the thing.' A gentleman's way of putting things to you,—and no mistake!

"At sunrise we got into a creek, to lie hidden in case the treasure-hunt party had a mind to take a spell hunting for us. And dash me if they didn't! We saw the schooner away out, running to leeward, with ten pairs of binoculars sweeping the sea, no doubt, on all sides. I advised the governor to give her time to beat back again before we made a start. So we stayed up that creek something like ten days, as snug as can be. On the seventh day we had to kill a man, though—the brother of this Pedro here. They were alligator-hunters, right enough. We got our lodgings in their hut. Neither the

boss nor I could *habla Español*—speak Spanish, you
know—much then. Dry bank, nice shade, jolly ham-
mocks, fresh fish, good game, everything lovely. The
governor chucked them a few dollars to begin with;
but it was like boarding with a pair of savage apes,
anyhow. By and by we noticed them talking a lot
together. They had twigged the cash-box, and the
leather portmanteaus, and my bag—a jolly lot of
plunder to look at. They must have been saying to each
other:

"'No one's ever likely to come looking for these two
fellows, who seem to have fallen from the moon. Let's
cut their throats.'

"Why, of course! Clear as daylight. I didn't need
to spy one of them sharpening a devilish long knife behind some bushes, while glancing right and left with his
wild eyes, to know what was in the wind. Pedro was
standing by, trying the edge of another long knife. They
thought we were away on our look-out at the mouth
of the river, as was usual with us during the day. Not
that we expected to see much of the schooner, but it
was just as well to make certain, if possible; and then
it was cooler out of the woods, in the breeze. Well,
the governor was there right enough, lying comfortable
on a rug, where he could watch the offing, but I had
gone back to the hut to get a chew of tobacco out of my
bag. I had not broken myself of the habit then, and I
couldn't be happy unless I had a lump as big as a baby's
fist in my cheek."

At the cannibalistic comparison, Schomberg muttered
a faint sickly "don't." Ricardo hitched himself up in
his seat and glanced down his outstretched legs complacently.

"I am tolerably light on my feet, as a general thing,"
he went on. "Dash me if I don't think I could drop a

pinch of salt on a sparrow's tail, if I tried. Anyhow, they didn't hear me. I watched them two brown, hairy brutes not ten yards off. All they had on was white linen drawers rolled up on their thighs. Not a word they said to each other. Antonio was down on his thick hams, busy rubbing the knife on a flat stone; Pedro was leaning against a small tree and passing his thumb along the edge of his blade. I got away quieter than a mouse, you bet.

"I didn't say anything to the boss then. He was leaning on his elbow on his rug, and didn't seem to want to be spoken to. He's like that—sometimes that familiar you might think he would eat out of your hand, and at others he would snub you sharper than a devil—but always quiet. Perfect gentleman, I tell you. I didn't bother him then; but I wasn't likely to forget them two fellows, so business-like with their knives. At that time we had only one revolver between us two—the governor's six-shooter, but loaded only in five chambers; and we had no more cartridges. He had left the box behind in a drawer in his cabin. Awkward! I had nothing but an old clasp-knife—no good at all for anything serious.

"In the evening we four sat round a bit of fire outside the sleeping-shed, eating broiled fish off plantain leaves, with roast yams for bread—the usual thing. The governor and I were on one side, and these two beauties, cross-legged on the other, grunting a word or two to each other now and then, hardly human speech at all, and their eyes down, fast on the ground. For the last three days we couldn't get them to look us in the face. Presently I began to talk to the boss quietly, just as I am talking to you now, careless like, and I told him all I had observed. He goes on picking up pieces of fish and putting them into his mouth as calm as anything.

It's a pleasure to have anything to do with a gentleman. Never looked across at them once.

"'And now,' says I, yawning on purpose, 'we've got to stand watch at night, turn about, and keep our eyes skinned all day, too, and mind we don't get jumped upon suddenly.'

"'It's perfectly intolerable,' says the governor. 'And you with no weapon of any sort!'

"'I mean to stick pretty close to you, sir, from this on, if you don't mind,' says I.

"He just nods the least bit, wipes his fingers on the plantain leaf, puts his hand behind his back, as if to help himself to rise from the ground, snatches his revolver from under his jacket, and plugs a bullet plumb centre into Mr. Antonio's chest. See what it is to have to do with a gentleman. No confounded fuss, and things done out of hand. But he might have tipped me a wink or something. I nearly jumped out of my skin. Scared ain't in it! I didn't even know who had fired. Everything had been so still just before that the bang of the shot seemed the loudest noise I had ever heard. The honourable Antonio pitches forward—they always do, towards the shot; you must have noticed that yourself—yes, he pitches forward on to the embers, and all that lot of hair on his face and head flashes up like a pinch of gunpowder. Greasy, I expect; always scraping the fat off them alligators' hides——"

"Look here," exclaimed Schomberg violently, as if trying to burst some invisible bonds, "do you mean to say that all this happened?"

"No," said Ricardo coolly. "I am making it all up as I go along, just to help you through the hottest part of the afternoon. So down he pitches, his nose on the red embers, and up jumps our handsome Pedro and I at the same time, like two Jacks-in-the-box. He starts to bolt away, with his head over his shoulder, and I, hardly knowing what I was doing, spring on his back. I had the sense to get my hands round his neck at once, and it's about all I could do to lock my fingers tight under his jaw. You saw the beauty's neck, didn't you? Hard as iron, too. Down we both went. Seeing this the governor puts his revolver in his pocket.

"'Tie his legs together, sir,' I yell. 'I'm trying to strangle him.'

"There was a lot of their fibre-lines lying about. I gave him a last squeeze and then got up.

"'I might have shot you,' says the governor, quite concerned.

"'But you are glad to have saved a cartridge, sir,' I tell him.

"My jump did save it. It wouldn't have done to let him get away in the dark like that, and have the beauty dodging around in the bushes, perhaps, with the rusty flint-lock gun they had. The governor owned up that the jump was the correct thing.

"'But he isn't dead,' says he, bending over him.

"Might as well hope to strangle an ox. We made haste to tie his elbows back, and then, before he came to himself, we dragged him to a small tree, sat him up, and bound him to it, not by the waist but by the neck—some twenty turns of small line round his throat and the trunk, finished off with a reef-knot under his ear. Next thing we did was to attend to the honourable Antonio, who was making a great smell frizzling his face on the red coals. We pushed and rolled him into the creek, and left the rest to the alligators.

"I was tired. That little scrap took it out of me something awful. The governor hadn't turned a hair. That's where a gentleman has the pull of you. He don't get excited. No gentleman does—or hardly ever. I fell asleep all of a sudden and left him smoking by the fire I had made up, his railway rug round his legs, as calm as if he were sitting in a first-class carriage. We hardly spoke ten words to each other after it was over, and from that day to this we have never talked of the business. I wouldn't have known he remembered it if he hadn't alluded to it when talking with you the other day—you know, with regard to Pedro.

"It surprised you, didn't it? That's why I am giving you this yarn of how he came to be with us, like a sort of dog—dashed sight more useful, though. You know how he can trot around with trays? Well, he could bring down an ox with his fist, at a word from the boss, just as cleverly. And fond of the governor! Oh, my word! More than any dog is of any man."

Schomberg squared his chest.

"Oh, and that's one of the things I wanted to mention to Mr. Jones," he said. "It's unpleasant to have that fellow round the house so early. He sits on the stairs at the back for hours before he is needed here, and frightens people so that the service suffers. The Chinamen——"

Ricardo nodded and raised his hand.

"When I first saw him he was fit to frighten a grizzly bear, let alone a Chinaman. He's become civilised now to what he once was. Well, that morning, first thing on opening my eyes, I saw him sitting there, tied up by the neck to the tree. He was blinking. We spent the day watching the sea, and we actually made out the schooner working to windward, which showed that she had given us up. Good! When the sun rose again, I took a squint at our Pedro. He wasn't blinking. He was rolling his eyes, all white one minute and black the next, and his tongue was hanging out a yard. Being tied up short by the neck like this would daunt the arch devil himself—in time—in time, mind! I don't know but that even a real gentleman would find it difficult to keep a stiff lip to the end. Presently we went to work getting our boat ready. I was busying myself setting up the mast, when the governor passes the remark:

"'I think he wants to say something.'

"I had heard a sort of croaking going on for some time, only I wouldn't take any notice; but then I got out of the boat and went up to him, with some water. His eyes were red—red and black and half out of his head. He drank all the water I gave him, but he hadn't much to say for himself. I walked back to the governor.

"'He asks for a bullet in his head before we go,' I said. I wasn't at all pleased.

"'Oh, that's out of the question altogether,' says the governor.

"He was right there. Only four shots left, and ninety miles of wild coast to put behind us before coming to the first place where you could expect to buy revolver cartridges.

"'Anyhow,' I tells him, 'he wants to be killed some way or other, as a favour.'

"And then I go on setting up the boat's mast. I didn't care much for the notion of butchering a man bound hand and foot and fastened by the neck besides. I had a knife then—the honourable Antonio's knife; and that knife is this knife."

Ricardo gave his leg a resounding slap.

"First spoil in my new life," he went on with harsh joviality. "The dodge of carrying it down there I learned later. I carried it stuck in my belt that day. No, I hadn't much stomach for the job; but when you work with a gentleman of the real right sort you may

depend on your feelings being seen through your skin.
Says the governor suddenly:

"'It may even be looked upon as his right'—you
hear a gentleman speaking there?—'but what do you
think of taking him with us in the boat?'

"And the governor starts arguing that the beggar
would be useful in working our way along the coast.
We could get rid of him before coming to the first place
that was a little civilised. I didn't want much talking
over. Out I scrambled from the boat.

"'Ay, but will he be manageable, sir?'

"'Oh, yes. He's daunted. Go on, cut him loose
—I take the responsibility.'

"'Right you are, sir.'

"He sees me come along smartly with his brother's
knife in my hand—I wasn't thinking how it looked from
his side of the fence, you know—and jiminy, it nearly
killed him! He stared like a crazed bullock and began
to sweat and twitch all over, something amazing. I was
so surprised that I stopped to look at him. The drops
were pouring over his eyebrows, down his beard, off his
nose—and he gurgled. Then it struck me that he
couldn't see what was in my mind. By favour or by
right he didn't like to die when it came to it; not in that
way, anyhow. When I stepped round to get at the
lashing, he let out a sort of soft bellow. Thought I
was going to stick him from behind, I guess. I cut
all the turns with one slash, and he went over on his
side, flop, and started kicking with his tied legs. Laugh!
I don't know what there was so funny about it, but I
fairly shouted. What between my laughing and his
wriggling, I had a job in cutting him free. As soon as he
could feel his limbs he makes for the bank, where the
governor was standing, crawls up to him on his hands
and knees, and embraces his legs. Gratitude, eh? You

could see that being allowed to live suited that chap
down to the ground. The governor gets his legs away
from him gently and just mutters to me:

"'Let's be off. Get him into the boat.'

"It was not difficult," continued Ricardo, after
eyeing Schomberg fixedly for a moment. "He was
ready enough to get into the boat, and—here he is.
He would let himself be chopped into small pieces—
with a smile, mind; with a smile!—for the governor.
I don't know about him doing that much for me; but
pretty near, pretty near. I did the tying up and the
untying, but he could see who was the boss. And then
he knows a gentleman. A dog knows a gentleman—
any dog. It's only some foreigners that don't know;
and nothing can teach them, either."

"And you mean to say," asked Schomberg, disregarding what might have been annoying for himself
in the emphasis of the final remark, "you mean to say
that you left steady employment at good wages for a
life like this?"

"There!" began Ricardo quietly. "That's just what
a man like you would say. You are that tame! I
follow a gentleman. That ain't the same thing as to
serve an employer. They give you wages as they'd
fling a bone to a dog, and they expect you to be grateful.
It's worse than slavery. You don't expect a slave that's
bought for money to be grateful. And if you sell your
work—what is it but selling your own self? You've
got so many days to live and you sell them one after
another. Hey? Who can pay me enough for my
life? Ay! But they throw at you your week's money
and expect you to say, 'thank you' before you pick it
up."

He mumbled some curses, directed at employers
generally, as it seemed, then blazed out:

"Work be damned! I ain't a dog walking on its hind legs for a bone; I am a man who's following a gentleman. There's a difference which you will never understand, Mr. Tame Schomberg."

He yawned slightly. Schomberg, preserving a military stiffness reinforced by a slight frown, had allowed his thoughts to stray away. They were busy detailing the image of a young girl—absent—gone—stolen from him. He became enraged. There was that rascal looking at him insolently. If the girl had not been shamefully decoyed away from him, he would not have allowed any one to look at him insolently. He would have made nothing of hitting that rogue between the eyes. Afterwards he would have kicked the other without hesitation. He saw himself doing it; and in sympathy with this glorious vision Schomberg's right foot and right arm moved convulsively.

At this moment he came out of his sudden reverie to note with alarm the wide-awake curiosity of Mr. Ricardo's stare.

"And so you go like this about the world, gambling," he remarked inanely, to cover his confusion. But Ricardo's stare did not change its character, and he continued vaguely:

"Here and there and everywhere." He pulled himself together, squared his shoulders. "Isn't it very precarious?" he said firmly.

The word precarious seemed to be effective, because Ricardo's eyes lost their dangerously interested expression.

"No, not so bad," Ricardo said, with indifference. "It's my opinion that men will gamble as long as they have anything to put on a card. Gamble? That's nature. What's life itself? You never know what may turn up. The worst of it is that you never can tell exactly what sort of cards you are holding yourself. What's trumps?— that is the question. See? Any man will gamble if only he's given a chance, for anything or everything. You too——"

"I haven't touched a card now for twenty years," said Schomberg in an austere tone.

"Well, if you got your living that way you would be no worse than you are now, selling drinks to people— beastly beer and spirits, rotten stuff fit to make an old he-goat yell if you poured it down its throat. Pooh! I can't stand the confounded liquor. Never could. A whiff of neat brandy in a glass makes me feel sick. Always did. If everybody was like me, liquor would be going a-begging. You think it's funny in a man, don't you?"

Schomberg made a vague gesture of toleration. Ricardo hitched up in his chair and settled his elbow afresh on the table.

"French siros I must say I do like. Saigon's the place for them. I see you have siros in the bar. Hang me if I ain't getting dry, conversing like this with you. Come, Mr. Schomberg, be hospitable, as the governor says."

Schomberg rose and walked with dignity to the counter. His footsteps echoed loudly on the floor of polished boards. He took down a bottle labelled *Sirop de Groseille.** The little sounds he made, the clink of glass, the gurgling of the liquid, the pop of the soda-water cork had a preternatural sharpness. He came back carrying a pink and glistening tumbler. Mr. Ricardo had followed his movements with oblique, coyly expectant yellow eyes, like a cat watching the preparation of a saucer of milk; and the satisfied sound after he had drunk might have been a slightly modified form of purring, very soft and deep in his throat. It

affected Schomberg unpleasantly as another example
of something inhuman in those men wherein lay the
difficulty of dealing with them. A spectre, a cat,
an ape—there was a pretty association for a mere man
to remonstrate with, he reflected with an inward shudder; for Schomberg had been overpowered, as it were,
by his imagination, and his reason could not react
against that fanciful view of his guests. And it was not
only their appearance. The morals of Mr. Ricardo
seemed to him to be pretty much the morals of a cat.
Too much. What sort of argument could a mere man
offer to a . . . or to a spectre, either! What the
morals of a spectre could be, Schomberg had no idea.
Something dreadful, no doubt. Compassion certainly
had no place in them. As to the ape—well, everybody
knew what an ape was. It had no morals. Nothing
could be more hopeless.

Outwardly, however, having picked up the cigar
which he had laid aside to get the drink, with his thick
fingers, one of them ornamented by a gold ring, Schomberg smoked with moody composure. Facing him,
Ricardo blinked slowly for a time, then closed his eyes
altogether, with the placidity of the domestic cat dozing
on the hearth-rug. In another moment he opened
them very wide, and seemed surprised to see Schomberg
there.

"You're having a very slack time to-day, aren't
you?" he observed. "But then this whole town is
confoundedly slack, anyhow; and I've never faced such
a slack party at a table before. Come eleven o'clock,
they begin to talk of breaking up. What's the matter
with them? Want to go to bed so early, or what?"

"I reckon you don't lose a fortune by their wanting
to go to bed," said Schomberg, with sombre sarcasm.

"No," admitted Ricardo, with a grin that stretched

his thin mouth from ear to ear, giving a sudden glimpse of his white teeth. "Only, you see, when I once start, I would play for nuts, for parched peas, for any rubbish. I would play them for their souls. But these Dutchmen aren't any good. They never seem to get warmed up properly, win or lose. I've tried them both ways, too. Hang them for a beggarly, bloodless lot of animated cucumbers!"

"And if anything out of the way was to happen, they would be just as cool in locking you and your gentleman up," Schomberg snarled unpleasantly.

"Indeed!" said Ricardo slowly, taking Schomberg's measure with his eyes. "And what about you?"

"You talk mighty big," burst out the hotel-keeper.

"You talk of ranging all over the world, and doing great things, and taking fortune by the scruff of the neck, but here you stick at this miserable business!"

"It isn't much of a lay—that's a fact," admitted Ricardo unexpectedly.

Schomberg was red in the face with audacity.

"I call it paltry," he spluttered.

"That's how it looks. Can't call it anything else." Ricardo seemed to be in an accommodating mood. "I should be ashamed of it myself, only you see the governor is subject to fits——"

"Fits!" Schomberg cried out, but in a low tone. "You don't say so!" He exulted inwardly, as if this disclosure had in some way diminished the difficulty of the situation. "Fits! That's a serious thing, isn't it? You ought to take him to the civil hospital—a lovely place."

Ricardo nodded slightly, with a faint grin.

"Serious enough. Regular fits of laziness, I call them. Now and then he lays down on me like this, and there's no moving him. If you think I like it, you're a long way out. Generally speaking, I can talk him over. I know how to deal with a gentleman. I am no daily-bread slave. But when he has said, 'Martin, I am bored,' then look out! There's nothing to do but to shut up, confound it!"

Schomberg, very much cast down, had listened open-mouthed.

"What's the cause of it?" he asked. "Why is he like this? I don't understand."

"I think I do," said Ricardo. "A gentleman, you know, is not such a simple person as you or I; and not so easy to manage, either. If only I had something to lever him out with!"

"What do you mean, to lever him out with?" muttered Schomberg hopelessly.

Ricardo was impatient with this denseness.

"Don't you understand English? Look here! I couldn't make this billiard table move an inch if I talked to it from now till the end of days—could I? Well, the governor is like that, too, when the fits are on him. He's bored. Nothing's worth while, nothing's good enough, that's mere sense. But if I saw a capstan bar lying about here, I would soon manage to shift that billiard table of yours a good many inches. And that's all there is to it."

He rose noiselessly, stretched himself, supple and stealthy, with curious sideways movements of his head and unexpected elongations of his thick body, glanced out of the corners of his eyes in the direction of the door, and finally leaned back against the table, folding his arms on his breast comfortably, in a completely human attitude.

"That's another thing you can tell a gentleman by —his freakishness. A gentleman ain't accountable to nobody, any more than a tramp on the roads. He ain't got to keep time. The governor got like this once in a one-horse Mexican pueblo* on the uplands, away from everywhere. He lay all day long in a dark room————"

"Drunk?" This word escaped Schomberg by inadvertence, at which he became frightened. But the devoted secretary seemed to find it natural.

"No, that never comes on together with this kind of fit. He just lay there full length on a mat, while a ragged, bare-legged boy that he had picked up in the street sat in the *patio*, between two oleanders near the open door of his room, strumming on a guitar and singing *tristes** to him from morning to night. You know *tristes*—twang, twang, twang, aouh, hoo! Chroo, yah!"

Schomberg uplifted his hands in distress. This tribute seemed to flatter Ricardo. His mouth twitched grimly.

"Like that—enough to give colic to an ostrich, eh? Awful. Well, there was a cook there who loved me—an old fat, negro woman with spectacles. I used to hide in the kitchen and turn her to, to make me *dulces* —sweet things, you know, mostly eggs and sugar—to pass the time away. I am like a kid for sweet things. And, by the way, why don't you ever have a pudding at your tablydott, Mr. Schomberg? Nothing but fruit, morning, noon, and night. Sickening! What do you think a fellow is—a wasp?"

Schomberg disregarded the injured tone.

"And how long did that fit, as you call it, last?" he asked anxiously.

"Weeks, months, years, centuries, it seemed to me," returned Mr. Ricardo with feeling. "Of an evening the governor would stroll out into the *sala* and fritter his life away playing cards with the *juez** of the place—a little Dago with a pair of black whiskers—ekarty,* you know, a quick French game, for small change. And the *comandante*,* a one-eyed, half-Indian, flat-nosed ruffian and I, we had to stand around and bet on their hands. It was awful!"

"Awful," echoed Schomberg, in a Teutonic throaty tone of despair. "Look here, I need your rooms."

"To be sure. I have been thinking that for some time past," said Ricardo indifferently.

"I was mad when I listened to you. This must end!"

"I think you are mad yet," said Ricardo, not even unfolding his arms or shifting his attitude an inch. He lowered his voice to add: "And if I thought you had been to the police, I would tell Pedro to catch you round the waist and break your fat neck by jerking your head backward—*snap!* I saw him do it to a big buck nigger who was flourishing a razor in front of the governor. It can be done. You hear a low crack, that's all—and the man drops down like a limp rag."

Not even Ricardo's head, slightly inclined on the left shoulder, had moved; but when he ceased the greenish irises which had been staring out of doors glided into the corners of his eyes nearest to Schomberg and stayed there with a coyly voluptuous expression.

VIII

Schomberg felt desperation, that lamentable substitute for courage, ooze out of him. It was not so much the threat of death as the weirdly circumstantial manner of its declaration which affected him. A mere "I'll murder you," however ferocious in tone and earnest in purpose, he could have faced; but before this novel mode of speech and procedure, his imagination being very sensitive to the unusual, he collapsed as if indeed his moral neck had been broken—snap!

"Go to the police? Of course not. Never dreamed of it. Too late now. I've let myself be mixed up in this. You got my consent while I wasn't myself. I explained it to you at the time."

Ricardo's eyes glided gently off Schomberg to stare far away.

"Ay! Some trouble with a girl. But that's nothing to us."

"Naturally. What I say is, what's the good of all that savage talk to me?" A bright argument occurred to him. "It's out of proportion; for even if I were fool enough to go to the police now, there's nothing serious to complain about. It would only mean deportation for you. They would put you on board the first west-bound steamer to Singapore." He had become animated. "Out of this to the devil," he added between his teeth for his own private satisfaction.

Ricardo made no comment, and gave no sign of having heard a single word. This discouraged Schomberg, who had looked up hopefully.

"Why do you want to stick here?" he cried. "It can't pay you people to fool around like this. Didn't you worry just now about moving your governor? Well, the police would move him for you; and from Singapore you can go on to the east coast of Africa."

"I'll be hanged if the fellow isn't up to that silly trick!" was Ricardo's comment, spoken in an ominous tone which recalled Schomberg to the realities of his position.

"No! No!" he protested. "It's a manner of speaking. Of course I wouldn't."

"I think that trouble about the girl has really muddled your brains, Mr. Schomberg. Believe me, you had better part friends with us; for, deportation or no deportation, you'll be seeing one of us turning up before long to pay you off for any nasty dodge you may be hatching in that fat head of yours."

"*Gott im Himmel!*"* groaned Schomberg. "Will nothing move him out? Will he stop here immer— I mean always? Suppose I were to make it worth your while, couldn't you——"

"No," Ricardo interrupted. "I couldn't, unless I had something to lever him out with. I've told you that before."

"An inducement?" muttered Schomberg.

"Ay. The east coast of Africa isn't good enough. He told me the other day that it will have to wait till he is ready for it; and he may not be ready for a long time, because the east coast can't run away, and no one is likely to run off with it."

These remarks, whether considered as truisms or as depicting Mr. Jones's mental state, were distinctly discouraging to the long-suffering Schomberg; but there is truth in the well-known saying that places the darkest hour before the dawn. The sound of words, apart from the context, has its power; and these two words, "run off," had a special affinity to the hotel-keeper's haunting idea. It was always present in his brain, and now it came forward evoked by a purely fortuitous expression. No, nobody could run off with a continent; but Heyst had run off with the girl!

Ricardo could have had no conception of the cause of Schomberg's changed expression. Yet it was noticeable enough to interest him so much that he stopped the careless swinging of his leg and said, looking at the hotel-keeper:

"There's not much use arguing against that sort of talk—is there?"

Schomberg was not listening.

"I could put you on another track," he said slowly, and stopped, as if suddenly choked by an unholy emotion of intense eagerness combined with fear of failure. Ricardo waited, attentive, yet not without a certain contempt.

"On the track of a man!" Schomberg uttered convulsively, and paused again, consulting his rage and his conscience.

"The man in the moon, eh?" suggested Ricardo, in a jeering murmur.

Schomberg shook his head.

"It would be nearly as safe to rook him as if he were the man in the moon. You go and try. It isn't so very far."

He reflected. These men were thieves and murderers as well as gamblers. Their fitness for purposes of vengeance was appallingly complete. But he preferred not to think of it in detail. He put it to himself summarily that he would be paying Heyst out and would, at the same time, relieve himself of these men's oppression. He had only to let loose his natural gift for talking scandalously about his fellow creatures. And in this case his great practice in it was assisted by hate, which, like love, has an eloquence of its own. With the utmost ease he portrayed for Ricardo, now seriously attentive, a Heyst fattened by years of private and public rapines, the murderer of Morrison, the swindler of many share-holders, a wonderful mixture of craft and impudence, of deep purposes and simple wiles, of mystery and futility. In this exercise of his natural function Schomberg revived, the colour coming back to his face, loquacious, florid, eager, his manliness set off by the military bearing.

"That's the exact story. He was seen hanging about this part of the world for years, spying into everybody's business; but I am the only one who has seen through him from the first—contemptible, double-faced, stick-at-nothing, dangerous fellow."

"Dangerous, is he?"

Schomberg came to himself at the sound of Ricardo's voice.

"Well, you know what I mean," he said uneasily. "A lying, circumventing, soft-spoken, polite, stuck-up rascal. Nothing open about him."

Mr. Ricardo had slipped off the table, and was prowling about the room in an oblique, noiseless manner. He flashed a grin at Schomberg in passing, and a snarling:

"Ah! H'm!"

"Well, what more dangerous do you want?" argued Schomberg. "He's in no way a fighting man, I believe," he added negligently.

"And you say he has been living alone there?"

"Like the man in the moon," answered Schomberg readily. "There's no one that cares a rap what becomes of him. He has been lying low, you understand, after bagging all that plunder."

"Plunder, eh? Why didn't he go home with it?" inquired Ricardo.

The henchman of "plain Mr. Jones" was beginning to think that this was something worth looking into. And he was pursuing truth in the manner of men of sounder morality and purer intentions than his own; that is he pursued it in the light of his own experience and prejudices. For facts, whatever their origin (and God only knows where they come from), can be only tested by our own particular suspicions. Ricardo was suspicious all round. Schomberg, such is the tonic power of recovered self-esteem, Schomberg retorted fearlessly:

"Go home? Why don't *you* go home? To hear your talk, you must have made a pretty considerable pile going round winning people's money. You ought to be ready by this time."

Ricardo stopped to look at Schomberg with surprise.

"You think yourself very clever, don't you?" he said.

Schomberg just then was so conscious of being clever that the snarling irony left him unmoved. There was positively a smile in his noble Teutonic beard, the first smile for weeks. He was in a felicitous vein.

"How do you know that he wasn't thinking of going home? As a matter of fact, he was on his way home."

"And how do I know that you are not amusing yourself by spinning out a blamed fairy tale?" interrupted Ricardo roughly. "I wonder at myself listening to the silly rot!"

Schomberg received this turn of temper unmoved. He did not require to be very subtly observant to notice that he had managed to arouse some sort of feeling, perhaps of greed, in Ricardo's breast.

"You won't believe me? Well! You can ask anybody that comes here if that—that Swede hadn't got as far as this house on his way home. Why should he turn up here if not for that? You ask anybody."

"Ask, indeed!" returned the other. "Catch me asking at large about a man I mean to drop on! Such jobs must be done on the quiet—or not at all."

The peculiar intonation of the last phrase touched the nape of Schomberg's neck with a chill. He cleared his throat slightly and looked away as though he had heard something indelicate. Then, with a jump as it were:

"Of course he didn't tell me. Is it likely? But haven't I got eyes? Haven't I got my common sense to tell me? I can see through people. By the same token, he called on the Tesmans. Why did he call on the Tesmans two days running, eh? You don't know? You can't tell?"

He waited complacently till Ricardo had finished swearing quite openly at him for a confounded chatterer, and then went on:

"A fellow doesn't go to a counting-house in business hours for a chat about the weather, two days running. Then why? To close his account with them one day, and to get his money out the next! Clear, what?"

Ricardo, with his trick of looking one way and moving another, approached Schomberg slowly.

"To get his money?" he purred.

"*Gewiss*,"* snapped Schomberg with impatient superiority. "What else? That is, only the money he had with the Tesmans. What he has buried or put away on the island, devil only knows. When you think of the lot of hard cash that passed through that man's hands, for wages and stores and all that—and he's just a cunning thief, I tell you." Ricardo's hard stare discomposed the hotel-keeper, and he added in an embarrassed tone: "I mean a common, sneaking thief—no account at all. And he calls himself a Swedish baron, too! Tfui!"

"He's a baron, is he? That foreign nobility ain't much," commented Mr. Ricardo seriously. "And then what? He hung about here."

"Yes, he hung about," said Schomberg, making a wry mouth. "He—hung about. That's it. Hung——"

His voice died out. Curiosity was depicted in Ricardo's countenance.

"Just like that; for nothing? And then turned about and went back to that island again?"

"And went back to that island again," Schomberg echoed lifelessly, fixing his gaze on the floor.

"What's the matter with you?" asked Ricardo with genuine surprise. "What is it?"

Schomberg, without looking up, made an impatient gesture. His face was crimson, and he kept it lowered. Ricardo went back to the point.

"Well, but how do you account for it? What was his reason? What did he go back to the island for?"

"Honeymoon!" spat out Schomberg viciously.

Perfectly still, his eyes downcast, he suddenly, with no preliminary stir, hit the table with his fist a blow which caused the utterly unprepared Ricardo to leap aside. And only then did Schomberg look up with a dull, resentful expression.

Ricardo stared hard for a moment, spun on his heel, walked to the end of the room, came back smartly and muttered a profound "Ay! Ay!" above Schomberg's rigid head. That the hotel-keeper was capable of a great moral effort was proved by a gradual return of his severe, Lieutenant-of-the-Reserve manner.

"Ay, ay!" repeated Ricardo more deliberately than before, and as if after a further survey of the circumstances. "I wish I hadn't asked you, or that you had told me a lie. It don't suit me to know that there's a woman mixed up in this affair. What's she like? It's the girl you——"

"Leave off!" muttered Schomberg, utterly pitiful behind his stiff military front.

"Ay, ay!" Ricardo ejaculated for the third time, more and more enlightened and perplexed. "Can't bear to talk about it—so bad as that? And yet I would bet she isn't a miracle to look at."

Schomberg made a gesture as if he didn't know, as if he didn't care. Then he squared his shoulders and frowned at vacancy.

"Swedish baron—h'm!" Ricardo continued meditatively. "I believe the governor would think that business worth looking up, quite, if I put it to him properly. The governor likes a duel, if you will call it so; but I don't know a man that can stand up to him on the square. Have you ever seen a cat play with a mouse? It's a pretty sight."

Ricardo, with his voluptuously gleaming eyes and the coy expression, looked so much like a cat that Schomberg would have felt all the alarm of a mouse if other feelings had not had complete possession of his breast.

"There are no lies between you and me," he said, more steadily than he thought he could speak.

"What's the good now? He funks women. In that Mexican pueblo where we lay grounded on our beef-bones, so to speak, I used to go to dances of an evening. The girls there would ask me if the English *caballero**in the *posada**was a monk in disguise, or if he had taken a vow to the *sanctissima madre**not to speak to a woman, or whether—— You can imagine what fairly free-spoken girls will ask when they come to the point of not caring what they say; and it used to vex me. Yes, the governor funks facing women."

"One woman?" interjected Schomberg in guttural tones.

"One may be more awkward to deal with than two, or two hundred, for that matter. In a place that's full of women you needn't look at them unless you like; but if you go into a room where there is only one woman, young or old, pretty or ugly, you have got to face her. And, unless you are after her, then—the governor is right enough—she's in the way."

"Why notice them?" muttered Schomberg. "What can they do?"

"Make a noise, if nothing else," opined Mr. Ricardo curtly, with the distaste of a man whose path is a path of silence; for indeed, nothing is more odious than a noise when one is engaged in a weighty and absorbing card game. "Noise, noise, my friend," he went on forcibly; "confounded screeching about something or other, and I like it no more than the governor does. But with the governor there's something else besides. He can't stand them at all."

He paused to reflect on this psychological phenomenon, and as no philosopher was at hand to tell him that there is no strong sentiment without some terror, as there is no real religion without a little fetichism, he emitted his own conclusion, which surely could not go to the root of the matter.

"I'm hanged if I don't think they are to him what liquor is to me. Brandy—pah!"

He made a disgusted face, and produced a genuine shudder. Schomberg listened to him in wonder. It looked as if the very scoundrelism of that—that Swede would protect him; the spoil of his iniquity standing between the thief and the retribution.

"That's so, old buck." Ricardo broke the silence after contemplating Schomberg's mute dejection with a sort of sympathy. "I don't think this trick will work."

"But that's silly," whispered the man deprived of the vengeance which he had seemed already to hold in his hand, by a mysterious and exasperating idiosyncrasy.

"Don't you set yourself to judge a gentleman." Ricardo without anger administered a moody rebuke. "Even I can't understand the governor thoroughly. And I am an Englishman and his follower. No; I don't think I care to put it before him, sick as I am of staying here."

Ricardo could not be more sick of staying than Schomberg was of seeing him stay. Schomberg believed so firmly in the reality of Heyst as created by his own power of false inferences, of his hate, of his love of scandal, that he could not contain a stifled cry of conviction as sincere as most of our convictions, the disguised servants of our passions, can appear at a supreme moment.

"It would have been like going to pick up a nugget of a thousand pounds, or two or three times as much, for all I know. No trouble, no——"

"The petticoat's the trouble," Ricardo struck in.

He had resumed his noiseless, feline, oblique prowling, in which an observer would have detected a new character of excitement, such as a wild animal of the cat species, anxious to make a spring, might betray. Schomberg saw nothing. It would probably have cheered his drooping spirits; but in a general way he preferred not to look at Ricardo. Ricardo, however, with one of his slanting, gliding, restless glances, observed the bitter smile on Schomberg's bearded lips—the unmistakable smile of ruined hopes.

"You are a pretty unforgiving sort of chap," he said,

stopping for a moment with an air of interest. "Hang me if I ever saw anybody look so disappointed! I bet you would send black plague to that island if you only knew how—eh, what? Plague too good for them? Ha, ha, ha!"

He bent down to stare at Schomberg who sat unstirring with stony eyes and set features, and apparently deaf to the rasping derision of that laughter so close to his red fleshy ear.

"Black plague too good for them, ha, ha!" Ricardo pressed the point on the tormented hotel-keeper. Schomberg kept his eyes down obstinately.

"I don't wish any harm to the girl," he muttered.

"But she did bolt from you? A fair bilk? Come!"

"Devil only knows what that villainous Swede had done to her—what he promised her, how he frightened her. She couldn't have cared for him, I know." Schomberg's vanity clung to the belief in some atrocious, extraordinary means of seduction employed by Heyst. "Look how he bewitched that poor Morrison," he murmured.

"Ah, Morrison—got all his money, what?"

"Yes—and his life."

"Terrible fellow, that Swedish baron! How is one to get at him?"

Schomberg exploded.

"Three against one! Are you shy? Do you want me to give you a letter of introduction?"

"You ought to look at yourself in a glass," Ricardo said quietly. "Dash me if you don't get a stroke of some kind presently. And this is the fellow who says women can do nothing! That one will do for you, unless you manage to forget her."

"I wish I could," Schomberg admitted earnestly. "And it's all the doing of that Swede. I don't get enough sleep, Mr. Ricardo. And then, to finish me off, you gentlemen turn up . . . as if I hadn't enough worry."

"That's done you good," suggested the secretary with ironic seriousness. "Takes your mind off that silly trouble. At your age too."

He checked himself, as if in pity, and changing his tone:

"I would really like to oblige you while doing a stroke of business at the same time."

"A good stroke," insisted Schomberg, as if it were mechanically. In his simplicity he was not able to give up the idea which had entered his head. An idea must be driven out by another idea, and with Schomberg ideas were rare and therefore tenacious. "Minted gold," he murmured with a sort of anguish.

Such an expressive combination of words was not without effect on Ricardo. Both these men were amenable to the influence of verbal suggestions. The secretary of "plain Mr. Jones" sighed and murmured:

"Yes. But how is one to get at it?"

"Being three to one," said Schomberg, "I suppose you could get it for the asking."

"One would think the fellow lived next door," Ricardo growled impatiently. "Hang it all, can't you understand a plain question? I have asked you the way."

Schomberg seemed to revive.

"The way?"

The torpor of deceived hopes underlying his superficial changes of mood had been pricked by these words which seemed pointed with purpose.

"The way is over the water, of course," said the hotel-keeper. "For people like you, three days in a good, big boat is nothing. It's no more than a little outing, a bit of a change. At this season the Java Sea* is a pond. I have an excellent, safe boat—a ship's life-boat—carry thirty, let alone three, and a child could handle her. You wouldn't get a wet face at this time of the year. You might call it a pleasure-trip."

"And yet, having this boat, you didn't go after her yourself—or after him? Well, you are a fine fellow*for a disappointed lover."

Schomberg gave a start at the suggestion.

"I am not three men," he said sulkily, as the shortest answer of the several he could have given.

"Oh, I know your sort," Ricardo let fall negligently. "You are like most people—or perhaps just a little more peaceable than the rest of the buying and selling gang that bosses this rotten show. Well, well, you respectable citizen," he went on, "let us go thoroughly into the matter."

When Schomberg had been made to understand that Mr. Jones's henchman was ready to discuss, in his own words, "this boat of yours, with courses and distances," and such concrete matters of no good augury to that villainous Swede, he recovered his soldierly bearing, squared his shoulders, and asked in his military manner:

"You wish, then, to proceed with the business?"

Ricardo nodded. He had a great mind to, he said. A gentleman had to be humoured as much as possible; but he must be managed, too, on occasions, for his own good. And it was the business of the right sort of "follower" to know the proper time and the proper methods of that delicate part of his duty. Having exposed this theory Ricardo proceeded to the application.

"I've never actually lied to him," he said, "and I ain't going to now. I shall just say nothing about the girl.

He will have to get over the shock the best he can. Hang it all! Too much humouring won't do here."

"Funny thing," Schomberg observed crisply.

"Is it? Ay, you wouldn't mind taking a woman by the throat in some dark corner and nobody by, I bet!"

Ricardo's dreadful, vicious, cat-like readiness to get his claws out at any moment startled Schomberg as usual. But it was provoking too.

"And you?" he defended himself. "Don't you want me to believe you are up to anything?"

"I, my boy? Oh, yes. I am not that gentleman; neither are you. Take 'em by the throat or chuck 'em under the chin is all one to me—almost," affirmed Ricardo, with something obscurely ironical in his complacency. "Now, as to this business. A three days' jaunt in a good boat isn't a thing to frighten people like us. You are right, so far; but there are other details."

Schomberg was ready enough to enter into details. He explained that he had a small plantation, with a fairly habitable hut on it, on Madura. He proposed that his guest should start from town in his boat, as if going for an excursion to that rural spot. The custom-house people on the quay were used to see his boat go off on such trips.

From Madura, after some repose and on a convenient day, Mr. Jones and party would make the real start. It would all be plain sailing. Schomberg undertook to provision the boat. The greatest hardship the voyagers need apprehend would be a mild shower of rain. At that season of the year there were no serious thunderstorms.

Schomberg's heart began to thump as he saw himself nearing his vengeance. His speech was thick but persuasive.

"No risk at all—none whatever!"

Ricardo dismissed these assurances of safety with an impatient gesture. He was thinking of other risks.

"The getting away from here is all right; but we may be sighted at sea, and that may bring awkwardness later on. A ship's boat with three white men in her, knocking about out of sight of land, is bound to make talk. Are we likely to be seen on our way?"

"No, unless by native craft," said Schomberg.

Ricardo nodded, satisfied. Both these white men looked on native life as a mere play of shadows. A play of shadows the dominant race could walk through unaffected and disregarded in the pursuit of its incomprehensible aims and needs. No. Native craft did not count, of course. It was an empty, solitary part of the sea, Schomberg expounded further. Only the Ternate mail-boat crossed that region about the 8th of every month, regularly—nowhere near the island, though. Rigid, his voice hoarse, his heart thumping, his mind concentrated on the success of his plan, the hotel-keeper multiplied words, as if to keep as many of them as possible between himself and the murderous aspect of his purpose.

"So, if you gentlemen depart from my plantation quietly at sunset on the 8th—always best to make a start at night, with a land breeze—it's a hundred to one —what am I saying?—it's a thousand to one that no human eye will see you on the passage. All you've got to do is to keep her heading northeast for, say, fifty hours; perhaps not quite so long. There will always be draft enough to keep a boat moving; you may reckon on that; and then——"

The muscles about his waist quivered under his clothes with eagerness, with impatience, and with something like apprehension, the true nature of which was

not clear to him. And he did not want to investigate it.
Ricardo regarded him steadily, with those dry eyes
of his shining more like polished stones than living
tissue.

"And then what?" he asked.

"And then—why, you will astonish *der herr baron*
—ha, ha!"

Schomberg seemed to force the words and the laugh
out of himself in a hoarse bass.

"And you believe he has all that plunder by him?"
asked Ricardo, rather perfunctorily, because the fact
seemed to him extremely probable when looked at all
round by his acute mind.

Schomberg raised his hands and lowered them slowly.

"How can it be otherwise? He was going home,
he was on his way, in this hotel. Ask people. Was
it likely he would leave it behind him?"

Ricardo was thoughtful. Then, suddenly raising his
head, he remarked:

"Steer northeast for fifty hours, eh? That's not much
of a sailing direction. I've heard of a port being missed
before on better information. Can't you say what sort
of landfall a fellow may expect? But I suppose you
have never seen that island yourself."

Schomberg admitted that he had not seen it, in a tone
in which a man congratulates himself on having escaped
the contamination of an unsavoury experience. No,
certainly not. He had never had any business to call
him there. But what of that? He could give Mr.
Ricardo as good a sea-mark as anybody need wish for.
He laughed nervously. Miss it! He defied any one
that came within forty miles of it to miss the retreat of
that villainous Swede.

"What do you think of a pillar of smoke by day and a
loom of fire at night?* There's a volcano in full blast

near that island—enough to guide almost a blind man. What more do you want? An active volcano to steer by!"

These last words he roared out exultingly, then jumped up and glared. The door to the left of the bar had swung open, and Mrs. Schomberg, dressed for duty, stood facing him down the whole length of the room. She clung to the handle for a moment, then came in and glided to her place, where she sat down to stare straight before her, as usual.

PART III

TROPICAL nature had been kind to the failure of the commercial enterprise. The desolation of the headquarters of the Tropical Belt Coal Company had been screened from the side of the sea; from the side where prying eyes—if any were sufficiently interested, either in malice or in sorrow—could have noted the decaying bones of that once sanguine enterprise.

Heyst had been sitting among the bones buried so kindly in the grass of two wet seasons' growth. The silence of his surroundings, broken only by such sounds as a distant roll of thunder, the lash of rain through the foliage of some big trees, the noise of the wind tossing the leaves of the forest, and of the short seas breaking against the shore, favoured rather than hindered his solitary meditation.

A meditation is always—in a white man, at least— more or less an interrogative exercise. Heyst meditated in simple terms on the mystery of his actions; and he answered himself with the honest reflection:

"There must be a lot of the original Adam in me, after all."

He reflected, too, with the sense of making a discovery, that this primeval ancestor is not easily suppressed. The oldest voice in the world is just the one that never ceases to speak. If anybody could have silenced its imperative echoes, it should have been Heyst's father, with his contemptuous, inflexible negation of all effort; but apparently he could not. There was in the son a lot of that first ancestor who, as soon

as he could uplift his muddy frame from the celestial
mould, started inspecting and naming the animals of
that paradise which he was so soon to lose.*

Action*—the first thought, or perhaps the first impulse, on earth! The barbed hook, baited with the
illusion of progress, to bring out of the lightless void
the shoals of unnumbered generations!

"And I, the son of my father, have been caught too,
like the silliest fish of them all," Heyst said to himself.

He suffered. He was hurt by the sight of his own
life, which ought to have been a masterpiece of aloofness. He remembered always his last evening with his
father. He remembered the thin features, the great
mass of white hair, and the ivory complexion. A five-
branched candlestick stood on a little table by the
side of the easy chair. They had been talking a long
time. The noises of the street had died out one by one,
till at last, in the moonlight, the London houses began
to look like the tombs of an unvisited, unhonoured,
cemetery of hopes.

He had listened. Then, after a silence, he had asked
—for he was really young then:

"Is there no guidance?"

His father was in an unexpectedly soft mood on that
night, when the moon swam in a cloudless sky over the
begrimed shadows of the town.

"You still believe in something, then?" he said in a
clear voice, which had been growing feeble of late.
"You believe in flesh and blood, perhaps? A full and
equable contempt would soon do away with that, too.
But since you have not attained to it, I advise you to
cultivate that form of contempt which is called pity.*
It is perhaps the least difficult—always remembering
that you, too, if you are anything, are as pitiful as the
rest, yet never expecting any pity for yourself."

"What is one to do, then?" sighed the young man, regarding his father, rigid in the high-backed chair.

"Look on—make no sound," were the last words of the man who had spent his life in blowing blasts upon a terrible trumpet which had filled heaven and earth with ruins, while mankind went on its way unheeding.

That very night he died in his bed, so quietly that they found him in his usual attitude of sleep, lying on his side, one hand under his cheek, and his knees slightly bent. He had not even straightened his legs.

His son buried the silenced destroyer of systems, of hopes, of beliefs. He observed that the death of that bitter contemner of life did not trouble the flow of life's stream, where men and women go by thick as dust, revolving and jostling one another like figures cut out of cork and weighted with lead just sufficiently to keep them in their proudly upright posture.

After the funeral, Heyst sat alone, in the dusk, and his meditation took the form of a definite vision of the stream, of the fatuously jostling, nodding, spinning figures hurried irresistibly along, and giving no sign of being aware that the voice on the bank had been suddenly silenced. . . . Yes. A few obituary notices generally insignificant and some grossly abusive. The son had read them all with mournful detachment.

"This is the hate and rage of their fear," he thought to himself, "and also of wounded vanity. They shriek their little shriek as they fly past. I suppose I ought to hate him too. . . ."

He became aware of his eyes being wet. It was not that the man was his father. For him it was purely a matter of hearsay which could not in itself cause this emotion. No! It was because he had looked at him so long that he missed him so much. The dead man had kept him on the bank by his side. And now Heyst

felt acutely that he was alone on the bank of the stream.
In his pride he determined not to enter it.

A few slow tears rolled down his face. The rooms,
filling with shadows, seemed haunted by a melancholy,
uneasy presence which could not express itself. The
young man got up with a strange sense of making way
for something impalpable that claimed possession, went
out of the house, and locked the door. A fortnight
later he started on his travels—to "look on and never
make a sound."

The elder Heyst had left behind him a little money
and a certain quantity of movable objects, such as books,
tables, chairs, and pictures, which might have complained of heartless desertion after many years of faithful service; for there is a soul in things. Heyst, our
Heyst, had often thought of them, reproachful and
mute, shrouded and locked up in those rooms, far away
in London with the sounds of the street reaching them
faintly, and sometimes a little sunshine, when the blinds
were pulled up and the windows opened from time to
time in pursuance of his original instructions and later
reminders. It seemed as if in his conception of a world
not worth touching, and perhaps not substantial enough
to grasp, these objects familiar to his childhood and his
youth and associated with the memory of an old man,
were the only realities, something having an absolute
existence. He would never have them sold, or even
moved from the places they occupied when he looked
upon them last. When he was advised from London
that his lease had expired, and that the house, with
some others as like it as two peas, was to be demolished,
he was surprisingly distressed.

He had entered by then the broad, human path of in-
consistencies. Already the Tropical Belt Coal Company was in existence. He sent instructions to have

some of the things sent out to him at Samburan, just
as any ordinary, credulous person would have done.
They came, torn out from their long repose—a lot
of books, some chairs and tables, his father's portrait
in oils, which surprised Heyst by its air of youth, because he remembered his father as a much older man;
a lot of small objects, such as candlesticks, inkstands,
and statuettes from his father's study, which surprised
him because they looked so old and so much worn.

The manager of the Tropical Belt Coal Company, un-
packing them on the verandah in the shade besieged by a
fierce sunshine, must have felt like a remorseful apostate
before these relics. He handled them tenderly; and it
was perhaps their presence there which attached him to
the island when he woke up to the failure of his apostasy.
Whatever the decisive reason, Heyst had remained
where another would have been glad to be off. The excellent Davidson had discovered the fact without dis-
covering the reason, and took a humane interest in
Heyst's strange existence, while at the same time his
native delicacy kept him from intruding on the other's
whim of solitude. He could not possibly guess that
Heyst, alone on the island, felt neither more nor less
lonely than in any other place, desert or populous.
Davidson's concern was, if one may express it so, the
danger of spiritual starvation; but this was a spirit
which had renounced all outside nourishment, and was
sustaining itself proudly on its own contempt of the
usual coarse aliments which life offers to the common
appetites of men.

Neither was Heyst's body in danger of starvation, as
Schomberg had so confidently asserted. At the beginning of the company's operations the island had been
provisioned in a manner which had outlasted the need.
Heyst did not need to fear hunger; and his very loneli-

ness had not been without some alleviation. Of the
crowd of imported Chinese labourers, one at least had
remained in Samburan, solitary and strange, like a
swallow left behind at the migrating season of his tribe.

Wang was not a common coolie. He had been a servant to white men before. The agreement between
him and Heyst consisted in the exchange of a few words
on the day when the last batch of the mine coolies was
leaving Samburan. Heyst, leaning over the balustrade
of the verandah, was looking on, as calm in appearance
as though he had never departed from the doctrine that
this world, for the wise, is nothing but an amusing
spectacle. Wang came round the house, and standing
below, raised up his yellow, thin face.

"All finish?" he asked.

Heyst nodded slightly from above, glancing towards
the jetty. A crowd of blue-clad figures with yellow
faces and calves was being hustled down into the boats
of the chartered steamer lying well out, like a painted
ship on a painted sea; painted in crude colours, without
shadows, without feeling, with brutal precision.

"You had better hurry up if you don't want to be left
behind."

But the Chinaman did not move.

"Me stop," he declared. Heyst looked down at him
for the first time.

"You want to stop here?"

"Yes."

"What were you? What was your work here?"

"Mess-loom boy."

"Do you want to stay with me here as my boy?" inquired Heyst, surprised.

The Chinaman unexpectedly put on a deprecatory expression, and said, after a marked pause:

"Can do."

"You needn't," said Heyst, "unless you like.   I propose to stay on here—it may be for a very long time.   I have no power to make you go if you wish to remain, but I don't see why you should."

"Catchee one piecee wife," remarked Wang unemotionally, and marched off, turning his back on the wharf and the great world beyond, represented by the steamer waiting for her boats.

Heyst learned presently that Wang had persuaded one of the women of the Alfuro*village, on the west shore of the island, beyond the central ridge, to come over to live with him in a remote part of the company's clearing. It was a curious case, inasmuch as the Alfuros, having been frightened by the sudden invasion of Chinamen, had blocked the path over the ridge by felling a few trees, and had kept strictly on their own side.   The coolies, as a body, mistrusting the manifest mildness of these harmless fisher-folk, had kept to their lines, without attempting to cross the island.   Wang was the brilliant exception.   He must have been uncommonly fascinating, in a way that was not apparent to Heyst, or else uncommonly persuasive.   The woman's services to Heyst were limited to the fact that she had anchored Wang to the spot by her charms, which remained unknown to the white man, because she never came near the houses.   The couple lived at the edge of the forest, and she could sometimes be seen gazing towards the bungalow shading her eyes with her hand. Even from a distance she appeared to be a shy, wild creature, and Heyst, anxious not to try her primitive nerves unduly, scrupulously avoided that side of the clearing in his strolls.

The day—or rather the first night—after his hermit life began, he was aware of vague sounds of revelry in that direction.   Emboldened by the departure of the

invading strangers, some Alfuros, the woman's friends
and relations, had ventured over the ridge to attend
something in the nature of a wedding feast. Wang
had invited them. But this was the only occasion
when any sound louder than the buzzing of insects
had troubled the profound silence of the clearing. The
natives were never invited again. Wang not only knew
how to live according to conventional proprieties, but
had strong personal views as to the manner of arranging his domestic existence. After a time Heyst perceived that Wang had annexed all the keys. Any
key left lying about vanished after Wang had passed
that way. Subsequently some of them—those that
did not belong to the storerooms and the empty
bungalows, and could not be regarded as the common
property of this community of two—were returned to
Heyst, tied in a bunch with a piece of string. He
found them one morning lying by the side of his
plate. He had not been inconvenienced by their absence, because he never locked up anything in the way
of drawers and boxes. Heyst said nothing. Wang
also said nothing. Perhaps he had always been
a taciturn man; perhaps he was influenced by the genius
of the locality, which was certainly that of silence. Till
Heyst and Morrison had landed in Black Diamond
Bay, and named it, that side of Samburan had hardly
ever heard the sound of human speech. It was easy
to be taciturn with Heyst, who had plunged himself
into an abyss of meditation over books, and remained
in it till the shadow of Wang falling across the page,
and the sound of a rough, low voice uttering the Malay
word "*makan*,"*would force him to climb out to a meal.

Wang in his native province in China might have been
an aggressively, sensitively genial person; but in Samburan he had clothed himself in a mysterious stolidity

and did not seem to resent not being spoken to except
in single words, at a rate which did not average half
a dozen per day. And he gave no more than he got.
It is to be presumed that if he suffered constraint, he
made up for it with the Alfuro woman. He always
went back to her at the first fall of dusk, vanishing from
the bungalow suddenly at his hour, like a sort of topsy-
turvy, day-hunting Chinese ghost with a white jacket
and a pigtail. Presently, giving way to a Chinaman's
ruling passion, he could be observed breaking the ground
near his hut, between the mighty stumps of felled
trees, with a miner's pickaxe. After a time, he discovered a rusty but serviceable spade in one of the
empty storerooms, and it is to be supposed that he got
on famously; but nothing of it could be seen, because
he went to the trouble of pulling to pieces one of the
company's sheds in order to get materials for making
a high and very close fence round his patch, as if the
growing of vegetables were a patented process, or an
awful and holy mystery entrusted to the keeping of his
race.

Heyst, following from a distance the progress of
Wang's gardening and of these precautions—there was
nothing else to look at—was amused at the thought
that he, in his own person, represented the market
for its produce. The Chinaman had found several
packets of seeds in the storerooms, and had surrendered
to an irresistible impulse to put them into the ground.
He would make his master pay for the vegetables
which he was raising to satisfy his instinct. And, looking silently at the silent Wang going about his work in
the bungalow in his unhasty, steady way, Heyst envied
the Chinaman's obedience to his instincts, the powerful
simplicity of purpose which made his existence appear
almost automatic in the mysterious precision of its facts.

II

DURING his master's absence at Sourabaya, Wang had busied himself with the ground immediately in front of the principal bungalow. Emerging from the fringe of grass growing across the shore end of the coal-jetty, Heyst beheld a broad, clear space, black and level, with only one or two clumps of charred twigs, where the flame had swept from the front of his house to the nearest trees of the forest.

"You took the risk of firing the grass?" Heyst asked.

Wang nodded. Hanging on the arm of the white man before whom he stood was the girl called Alma; but neither from the Chinaman's eyes nor from his expression could any one have guessed that he was in the slightest degree aware of the fact.

"He has been tidying the place in this labour-saving way," explained Heyst, without looking at the girl, whose hand rested on his forearm. "He's the whole establishment, you see. I told you I hadn't even a dog to keep me company here."

Wang had marched off towards the wharf.

"He's like those waiters in that place," she said. That place was Schomberg's hotel.

"One Chinaman looks very much like another," Heyst remarked. "We shall find it useful to have him here. This is the house."

They faced, at some distance, the six shallow steps leading up to the verandah. The girl had abandoned Heyst's arm.

"This is the house," he repeated.

She did not offer to budge away from his side, but stood staring fixedly at the steps, as if they had been something unique and impracticable. He waited a little, but she did not move.

"Don't you want to go in?" he asked, without turning his head to look at her. "The sun's too heavy to stand about here." He tried to overcome a sort of fear, a sort of impatient faintness, and his voice sounded rough. "You had better go in," he concluded.

They both moved then, but at the foot of the stairs Heyst stopped, while the girl went on rapidly, as if nothing could stop her now. She crossed the verandah swiftly, and entered the twilight of the big central room opening upon it, and then the deeper twilight of the room beyond. She stood still in the dusk, in which her dazzled eyes could scarcely make out the forms of objects, and sighed a sigh of relief. The impression of the sunlight, of sea and sky, remained with her like a memory of a painful trial gone through—done with at last!

Meanwhile Heyst had walked back slowly towards the jetty; but he did not get so far as that. The practical and automatic Wang had got hold of one of the little trucks that had been used for running baskets of coal alongside ships. He appeared pushing it before him, loaded lightly with Heyst's bag and the bundle of the girl's belongings, wrapped in Mrs. Schomberg's shawl. Heyst turned about and walked by the side of the rusty rails on which the truck ran. Opposite the house Wang stopped, lifted the bag to his shoulder, balanced it carefully, and then took the bundle in his hand.

"Leave those things on the table in the big room—understand?"

"Me savee," grunted Wang, moving off.

Heyst watched the Chinaman disappear from the

verandah. It was not till he had seen Wang come out
that he himself entered the twilight of the big room.
By that time Wang was out of sight at the back of the
house, but by no means out of hearing. The Chinaman
could hear the voice of him who, when there were many
people there, was generally referred to as "Number
One." Wang was not. able to understand the words,
but the tone interested him.

"Where are you?" cried Number One.

Then Wang heard, much more faint, a voice he had
never heard before—a novel impression which he acknowledged by cocking his head slightly to one side.

"I am here—out of the sun."

The new voice sounded remote and uncertain. Wang
heard nothing more, though he waited for some time,
very still, the top of his shaven poll exactly level with
the floor of the back verandah. His face meanwhile
preserved an inscrutable immobility. Suddenly he
stooped to pick up the lid of a deal candle-box which
was lying on the ground by his foot. Breaking it up
with his fingers, he directed his steps towards the cook-
shed, where, squatting on his heels, he proceeded to
kindle a small fire under a very sooty kettle, possibly
to make tea. Wang had some knowledge of the more
superficial rites and ceremonies of white men's existence, otherwise so enigmatically remote to his mind,
and containing unexpected possibilities of good and evil,
which had to be watched for with prudence and care.

III

THAT morning, as on all the others of the full tale
of mornings since his return with the girl to Samburan,
Heyst came out on the verandah and spread his elbows
on the railing, in an easy attitude of proprietorship.
The bulk of the central ridge of the island cut off the
bungalow from sunrises, whether glorious or cloudy,
angry or serene. The dwellers therein were debarred
from reading early the fortune of the new-born day.
It sprang upon them in its fulness with a swift retreat
of the great shadow when the sun, clearing the ridge,
looked down, hot and dry, with a devouring glare like
the eye of an enemy. But Heyst, once the Number
One of this locality, while it was comparatively teeming
with mankind, appreciated the prolongation of early
coolness, the subdued, lingering half light, the faint
ghost of the departed night, the fragrance of its dewy,
dark soul captured for a moment longer between the
great glow of the sky and the intense blaze of the uncovered sea.

It was naturally difficult for Heyst to keep his mind
from dwelling on the nature and consequences of this,
his latest departure from the part of an unconcerned
spectator. Yet he had retained enough of his wrecked
philosophy to prevent him from asking himself consciously how it would end. But at the same time he
could not help being temperamentally, from long habit
and from set purpose, a spectator still, perhaps a little
less naïve but (as he discovered with some surprise)
not much more far-sighted than the common run of

men. Like the rest of us who act, all he could say to himself, with a somewhat affected grimness, was:

"We shall see!"

This mood of grim doubt intruded on him only when he was alone. There were not many such moments in his day now; and he did not like them when they came. On this morning he had no time to grow uneasy. Alma came out to join him long before the sun, rising above the Samburan ridge, swept the cool shadow of the early morning and the remnant of the night's coolness clear off the roof under which they had dwelt for more than three months already. She came out as on other mornings. He had heard her light footsteps in the big room—the room where he had unpacked the cases from London; the room now lined with the backs of books halfway up on its three sides. Above the cases the fine matting met the ceiling of tightly stretched white calico. In the dusk and coolness nothing gleamed except the gilt frame of the portrait of Heyst's father, signed by a famous painter, lonely in the middle of a wall.

Heyst did not turn round.

"Do you know what I was thinking of?" he asked.

"No," she said. Her tone betrayed always a shade of anxiety, as though she were never certain how a conversation with him would end. She leaned on the guard-rail by his side.

"No," she repeated. "What was it?" She waited. Then, rather with reluctance than shyness, she asked: "Were you thinking of me?"

"I was wondering when you would come out," said Heyst still without looking at the girl—to whom, after several experimental essays in combining detached letters and loose syllables, he had given the name of Lena*.

She remarked after a pause:

"I was not very far from you."

"Apparently you were not near enough for me."

"You could have called if you wanted me," she said. "And I wasn't so long doing my hair."

"Apparently it was too long for me."

"Well, you were thinking of me, anyhow. I am glad of it. Do you know, it seems to me, somehow, that if you were to stop thinking of me I shouldn't be in the world at all!"

He turned round and looked at her. She often said things which surprised him. A vague smile faded away on her lips before his scrutiny.

"What is it?" he asked. "Is it a reproach?"

"A reproach! Why, how could it be?" she defended herself.

"Well, what did it mean?" he insisted.

"What I said—just what I said. Why aren't you fair?"

"Ah, this at least is a reproach!"

She coloured to the roots of her hair.

"It looks as if you were trying to make out that I am disagreeable," she murmured. "Am I? You will make me afraid to open my mouth presently. I shall end by believing I am no good."

Her head drooped a little. He looked at her smooth, low brow, the faintly coloured cheeks, and the red lips parted slightly, with the gleam of her teeth within.

"And then I *won't* be any good," she added with conviction. "That I won't! I can only be what you think I am."

He made a slight movement. She put her hand on his arm, without raising her head, and went on, her voice animated in the stillness of her body:

"It is so. It couldn't be any other way with a girl

like me and a man like you. Here we are, we two alone,
and I can't even tell where we are."

"A very well-known spot of the globe," Heyst uttered
gently. "There must have been at least fifty thousand
circulars issued at the time—a hundred and fifty thousand, more likely. My friend was looking after that,
and his ideas were large and his belief very strong. Of
us two it was he who had the faith. A hundred and fifty
thousand, certainly."

"What is it you mean?" she asked in a low tone.

"What should I find fault with you for?" Heyst
went on. "For being amiable, good, gracious—and
pretty?"

A silence fell. Then she said:

"It's all right that you should think that of me.
There's no one here to think anything of us, good or
bad."

The rare timbre of her voice gave a special value to
what she uttered. The indefinable emotion which
certain intonations gave him, he was aware, was more
physical than moral. Every time she spoke to him
she seemed to abandon to him something of herself—
something excessively subtle and inexpressible, to
which he was infinitely sensible, which he would have
missed horribly if she were to go away. While he was
looking into her eyes she raised her bare forearm, out
of the short sleeve, and held it in the air till he noticed
it and hastened to pose his great bronze moustaches on
the whiteness of the skin. Then they went in.

Wang immediately appeared in front, and, squatting
on his heels, began to potter mysteriously about some
plants at the foot of the verandah. When Heyst and the
girl came out again, the Chinaman had gone in his
peculiar manner, which suggested vanishing out of existence rather than out of sight, a process of evaporation

rather than of movement. They descended the steps, looking at each other, and started off smartly across the cleared ground; but they were not ten yards away when, without perceptible stir or sound, Wang materialized inside the empty room. The Chinaman stood still with roaming eyes, examining the walls as if for signs, for inscriptions; exploring the floor as if for pit-falls, for dropped coins. Then he cocked his head slightly at the profile of Heyst's father, pen in hand above a white sheet of paper on a crimson tablecloth; and, moving forward noiselessly, began to clear away the breakfast things.

Though he proceeded without haste, the unerring pre-cision of his movements, the absolute soundlessness of the operation, gave it something of the quality of a con-juring trick. And, the trick having been performed, Wang vanished from the scene, to materialise presently in front of the house. He materialised walking away from it, with no visible or guessable intention; but at the end of some ten paces he stopped, made a half turn, and put his hand up to shade his eyes. The sun had topped the grey ridge of Samburan. The great morn-ing shadow was gone; and far away in the devouring sunshine Wang was in time to see Number One and the woman, two remote white specks against the sombre line of the forest. In a moment they vanished. With the smallest display of action, Wang also vanished from the sunlight of the clearing.

Heyst and Lena entered the shade of the forest path which crossed the island, and which, near its highest point, had been blocked by felled trees. But their in-tention was not to go so far. After keeping to the path for some distance, they left it at a point where the forest was bare of undergrowth, and the trees, festooned with creepers, stood clear of one another in the gloom of their

own making. Here and there great splashes of light
lay on the ground. They moved, silent in the great
stillness, breathing the calmness, the infinite isolation,
the repose of a slumber without dreams. They emerged
at the upper limit of vegetation, among some rocks;
and in a depression of the sharp slope, like a small platform, they turned about and looked from on high over
the sea, lonely, its colour effaced by sunshine, its horizon
a heat mist, a mere unsubstantial shimmer in the pale
and blinding infinity overhung by the darker blaze of
the sky.

"It makes my head swim," the girl murmured, shutting her eyes and putting her hand on his shoulder.

Heyst, gazing fixedly to the southward, exclaimed:
"Sail ho!"

A moment of silence ensued.

"It must be very far away," he went on. "I don't
think you could see it. Some native craft making
for the Moluccas,* probably. Come, we mustn't stay
here."

With his arm round her waist, he led her down a little
distance, and they settled themselves in the shade; she,
seated on the ground, he a little lower, reclining at her
feet.

"You don't like to look at the sea from up there?"
he said after a time.

She shook her head. That empty space was to her
the abomination of desolation. But she only said again:
"It makes my head swim."

"Too big?" he inquired.

"Too lonely. It makes my heart sink, too," she
added in a low voice, as if confessing a secret.

"I am afraid," said Heyst, "that you would be justified in reproaching me for these sensations. But what
would you have?"

His tone was playful, but his eyes, directed at her face, were serious. She protested.

"I am not feeling lonely with you—not a bit. It is only when we come up to that place, and I look at all that water and all that light——"

"We will never come here again, then," he interrupted her.

She remained silent for a while, returning his gaze till he removed it.

"It seems as if everything that there is had gone under," she said.

"Reminds you of the story of the deluge," muttered the man, stretched at her feet and looking at them. "Are you frightened at it?"

"I should be rather frightened to be left behind alone. When I say, *I*, of course I mean we."

"Do you?" . . . Heyst remained silent for a while. "The vision of a world destroyed," he mused aloud. "Would you be sorry for it?"

"I should be sorry for the happy people in it," she said simply.

His gaze travelled up her figure and reached her face, where he seemed to detect the veiled glow of intelligence, as one gets a glimpse of the sun through the clouds.

"I should have thought it's they specially who ought to have been congratulated. Don't you?"

"Oh, yes—I understand what you mean; but there were forty days before it was all over."

"You seem to be in possession of all the details."

Heyst spoke just to say something rather than to gaze at her in silence. She was not looking at him.

"Sunday school," she murmured. "I went regularly from the time I was eight till I was thirteen. We lodged in the north of London, off Kingsland Road. It wasn't

a bad time. Father was earning good money then. The
woman of the house used to pack me off in the afternoon
with her own girls. She was a good woman. Her husband was in the post-office. Sorter or something. Such
a quiet man. He used to go off after supper for night
duty, sometimes. Then one day they had a row, and
broke up the home. I remember I cried when we had to
pack up all of a sudden and go into other lodgings. I
never knew what it was, though——"

"The deluge," muttered Heyst absently.

He felt intensely aware of her personality, as if this
were the first moment of leisure he had found to look at
her since they had come together. The peculiar timbre
of her voice, with its modulations of audacity and sadness, would have given interest to the most inane chatter. But she was no chatterer. She was rather silent,
with a capacity for immobility, an upright stillness, as
when resting on the concert platform between the
musical numbers, her feet crossed, her hands reposing
on her lap. But in the intimacy of their life her grey,
unabashed gaze forced upon him the sensation of something inexplicable reposing within her; stupidity or
inspiration, weakness or force—or simply an abysmal
emptiness, reserving itself even in the moments of complete surrender.

During a long pause she did not look at him. Then
suddenly, as if the word "deluge" had stuck in her
mind, she asked, looking up at the cloudless sky:

"Does it ever rain here?"

"There is a season when it rains almost every day,"
said Heyst, surprised. "There are also thunderstorms.
We had once a mud-shower."

"Mud-shower?"

"Our neighbour there was shooting up ashes. He
sometimes clears his red-hot gullet like that; and a

thunderstorm came along at the same time. It was very
messy; but our neighbour is generally well behaved—
just smokes quietly, as he did that day when I first
showed you the smudge in the sky from the schooner's
deck. He's a good-natured, lazy fellow of a volcano."

"I saw a mountain smoking like that before," she
said, staring at the slender stem of a tree-fern some
dozen feet in front of her. "It wasn't very long after
we left England—some few days, though. I was so ill at
first that I lost count of days. A smoking mountain—I
can't think how they called it."

"Vesuvius,* perhaps," suggested Heyst.

"That's the name."

"I saw it, too, years, ages ago," said Heyst.

"On your way here?"

"No, long before I ever thought of coming into this
part of the world. I was yet a boy."

She turned and looked at him attentively, as if seeking to discover some trace of that boyhood in the mature
face of the man with the hair thin at the top and the
long, thick moustaches. Heyst stood the frank examination with a playful smile, hiding the profound effect
these veiled grey eyes produced—whether on his heart
or on his nerves, whether sensuous or spiritual, tender
or irritating, he was unable to say.

"Well, princess of Samburan," he said at last, "have
I found favour in your sight?"*

She seemed to wake up, and shook her head.

"I was thinking," she murmured very low.

"Thought, action—so many snares! If you begin to
think you will be unhappy."

"I wasn't thinking of myself," she declared with a
simplicity which took Heyst aback somewhat.

"On the lips of a moralist this would sound like a
rebuke," he said, half seriously; "but I won't suspect

you of being one. Moralists and I haven't been friends for many years."

She had listened with an air of attention.

"I understood you had no friends," she said. "I am pleased that there's nobody to find fault with you for what you have done. I like to think that I am in no one's way."

Heyst would have said something, but she did not give him time. Unconscious of the movement he made she went on:

"What I was thinking to myself was, why are you here?"

Heyst let himself sink on his elbow again.

"If by 'you' you mean 'we'—well, you know why we are here."

She bent her gaze down at him.

"No, it isn't that. I meant before—all that time before you came across me and guessed at once that I was in trouble, with no one to turn to. And you know it was desperate trouble too."

Her voice fell on the last words, as if she would end there; but there was something so expectant in Heyst's attitude as he sat at her feet, looking up at her steadily, that she continued, after drawing a short, quick breath:

"It was, really. I told you I had been worried before by bad fellows. It made me unhappy, disturbed —angry, too. But oh, how I hated, hated, *hated* that man!"

"That man" was the florid Schomberg with the military bearing, benefactor of white men ("decent food to eat in decent company")—mature victim of belated passion. The girl shuddered. The characteristic harmoniousness of her face became, as it were, decomposed for an instant. Heyst was startled.

"Why think of it now?" he cried.

"It's because I was cornered that time. It wasn't as before. It was worse, ever so much. I wished I could die of my fright;—and yet it's only now that I begin to understand what a horror it might have been. Yes, only now, since we——"

Heyst stirred a little.

"Came here," he finished.

Her tenseness relaxed, her flushed face went gradually back to its normal tint.

"Yes," she said indifferently, but at the same time she gave him a stealthy glance of passionate appreciation; and then her face took on a melancholy cast, her whole figure drooped imperceptibly. "But you were coming back here anyhow?" she asked.

"Yes. I was only waiting for Davidson. Yes, I was coming back here, to these ruins—to Wang, who perhaps did not expect to see me again. It's impossible to guess at the way that Chinaman draws his conclusions, and how he looks upon one."

"Don't talk about him. He makes me feel uncomfortable. Talk about yourself."

"About myself? I see you are still busy with the mystery of my existence here; but it isn't at all mysterious. Primarily the man with the quill pen in his hand in that picture you so often look at is responsible for my existence. He is also responsible for what my existence is, or rather has been. He was a great man in his way. I don't know much of his history. I suppose he began like other people; took fine words for good, ringing coin and noble ideals for valuable banknotes. He was a great master of both, himself, by the way. Later he discovered—how am I to explain it to you? Suppose the world were a factory and all mankind workmen in it. Well, he discovered that the wages were not good enough. That they were paid in counterfeit money."

"I see!" the girl said slowly.

"Do you?"

Heyst, who had been speaking as if to himself, looked up curiously.

"It wasn't a new discovery, but he brought his capacity for scorn to bear on it. It was immense. It ought to have withered this globe. I don't know how many minds he convinced. But my mind was very young then, and youth I suppose can be easily seduced —even by a negation. He was very ruthless, and yet he was not without pity. He dominated me without difficulty. A heartless man could not have done so. Even to fools he was not utterly merciless. He could be indignant, but he was too great for flouts and jeers. What he said was not meant for the crowd; it could not be; and I was flattered to find myself among the elect. They read his books, but I have heard his living word. It was irresistible. It was as if that mind were taking me into its confidence, giving me a special insight into its mastery of despair. Mistake, no doubt. There is something of my father in every man who lives long enough. But they don't say anything. They can't. They wouldn't know how, or perhaps, they wouldn't speak if they could. Man on this earth is an unforeseen accident* which does not stand close investigation. However, that particular man died as quietly as a child goes to sleep. But, after listening to him, I could not take my soul down into the street to fight there. I started off to wander about, an independent spectator —if that is possible."

For a long time the girl's grey eyes had been watching his face. She discovered that, addressing her, he was really talking to himself. Heyst looked up, caught sight

of her as it were, and caught himself up, with a low laugh
and a change of tone.

"All this does not tell you why I ever came here.
Why, indeed? It's like prying into inscrutable mysteries which are not worth scrutinising. A man drifts.
The most successful men have drifted into their suc-
cesses. I don't want to tell you that this is a success.
You wouldn't believe me if I did. It isn't; neither is
it the ruinous failure it looks. It proves nothing, unless perhaps some hidden weakness in my character—
and even that is not certain."

He looked fixedly at her, and with such grave eyes
that she felt obliged to smile faintly at him, since she
did not understand what he meant. Her smile was
reflected, still fainter, on his lips.

"This does not advance you much in your inquiry,"
he went on. "And in truth your question is unanswer-
able; but facts have a certain positive value, and I will
tell you a fact. One day I met a cornered man. I use
the word because it expresses the man's situation exactly, and because you just used it yourself. You know
what that means?"

"What do you say?" she whispered, astounded. "A
man!"

Heyst laughed at her wondering eyes.

"No! No! I mean in his own way."

"I knew very well it couldn't be anything like that,"
she observed under her breath.

"I won't bother you with the story. It was a custom-
house affair, strange as it may sound to you. He would
have preferred to be killed outright—that is, to have his
soul despatched to another world, rather than to be robbed of his substance, his very insignificant substance,
in this. I saw that he believed in another world because, being cornered, as I have told you, he went

down on his knees and prayed. What do you think of that?"

Heyst paused. She looked at him earnestly.

"You didn't make fun of him for that?" she said.

Heyst made a brusque movement of protest.

"My dear girl, I am not a ruffian," he cried. Then, returning to his usual tone: "I didn't even have to conceal a smile. Somehow it didn't look a smiling matter. No, it was not funny; it was rather pathetic; he was so representative of all the past victims of the Great Joke.* But it is by folly alone that the world moves, and so it is a respectable thing upon the whole. And besides, he was what one would call a good man. I don't mean especially because he had offered up a prayer. No! He was really a decent fellow, he was quite unfitted for this world, he was a failure, a good man cornered—a sight for the gods; for no decent mortal cares to look at that sort." A thought seemed to occur to him. He turned his face to the girl. "And you, who have been cornered too—did you think of offering a prayer?"

Neither her eyes nor a single one of her features moved the least bit. She only let fall the words:

"I am not what they call a good girl."*

"That sounds evasive," said Heyst after a short silence. "Well, the good fellow did pray and after he had confessed to it I was struck by the comicality of the situation. No, don't misunderstand me—I am not alluding to his act, of course. And even the idea of Eternity, Infinity, Omnipotence, being called upon to defeat the conspiracy of two miserable Portuguese half-castes did not move my mirth. From the point of view of the supplicant, the danger to be conjured was something like the end of the world, or worse. No! What captivated my fancy was that I, Axel Heyst, the most detached of creatures in this earthly captivity, the veriest tramp on this earth, an indifferent stroller going through the world's bustle—that I should have been there to step into the situation of an agent of Providence. *I*, a man of universal scorn and unbelief. . . ."

"You are putting it on," she interrupted in her seductive voice, with a coaxing intonation.

"No. I am like that, born or fashioned, or both. I am not for nothing the son of my father, of that man in the painting. I am he, all but the genius. And there is even less in me than I make out, because the very scorn is falling away from me year after year. I have never been so amused as by that episode in which I was suddenly called to act such an incredible part. For a moment I enjoyed it greatly. It got him out of his corner, you know."

"You saved a man for fun—is that what you mean? Just for fun?"

"Why this tone of suspicion?" remonstrated Heyst. "I suppose the sight of this particular distress was disagreeable to me. What you call fun came afterward, when it dawned on me that I was for him a walking, breathing, incarnate proof of the efficacy of prayer. I was a little fascinated by it—and then, could I have argued with him? You don't argue against such evidence, and besides it would have looked as if I had wanted to claim all the merit. Already his gratitude was simply frightful. Funny position, wasn't it? The boredom came later, when we lived together on board his ship. I had, in a moment of inadvertence, created for myself a tie. How to define it precisely I don't know. One gets attached in a way to people one has done something for. But is that friendship? I am not sure what it was. I only know that he who forms a tie is lost. The germ of corruption has entered into his soul."

Heyst's tone was light, with the flavour of playfulness which seasoned all his speeches and seemed to be of the very essence of his thoughts. The girl he had come across, of whom he had possessed himself, to whose presence he was not yet accustomed, with whom he did not yet know how to live; that human being so near and still so strange, gave him a greater sense of his own reality than he had ever known in all his life.

IV

WITH her knees drawn up, Lena rested her elbows on them and held her head in both her hands.

"Are you tired of sitting here?" Heyst asked.

An almost imperceptible negative movement of the head was all the answer she made.

"Why are you looking so serious?" he pursued, and immediately thought that habitual seriousness, in the long run, was much more bearable than constant gaiety. "However, this expression suits you exceedingly," he added, not diplomatically, but because, by the tendency of his taste, it was a true statement. "And as long as I can be certain that it is not boredom which gives you this severe air, I am willing to sit here and look at you till you are ready to go."

And this was true. He was still under the fresh sortilege of their common life, the surprise of novelty, the flattered vanity of his possession of this woman; for a man must feel that, unless he has ceased to be masculine. Her eyes moved in his direction, rested on him, then returned to their stare into the deeper gloom at the foot of the straight tree-trunks, whose spreading crowns were slowly withdrawing their shade. The warm air stirred slightly about her motionless head. She would not look at him, from some obscure fear of betraying herself. She felt in her innermost depths an irresistible desire to give herself up to him more completely, by some act of absolute sacrifice. This was something of which he did not seem to have an idea. He was a strange being without needs. She felt his eyes fixed upon her; and as he kept silent, she said uneasily—for she didn't know what his silences might mean:

"And so you lived with that friend—that good man?"

"Excellent fellow," Heyst responded, with a readiness that she did not expect. "But it was a weakness on my part. I really didn't want to, only he wouldn't let me off, and I couldn't explain. He was the sort of man to whom you can't explain anything. He was extremely sensitive, and it would have been a tigerish thing to do to mangle his delicate feelings by the sort of plain speaking that would have been necessary. His mind was like a white-walled, pure chamber, furnished with, say, six straw-bottomed chairs, and he was always placing and displacing them in various combinations. But they were always the same chairs. He was extremely easy to live with; but then he got hold of this coal idea—or, rather, the idea got hold of him. It entered into that scantily furnished chamber of which I have just spoken, and sat on all the chairs. There was no dislodging it, you know! It was going to make his fortune, my fortune, everybody's fortune. In past years, in moments of doubt that will come to a man determined to remain free from absurdities of existence, I often asked myself, with a momentary dread, in what way would life try to get hold of me? And this was the way! He got it into his head that he could do nothing without me. And was I now, he asked me, to spurn and ruin him? Well, one morning —I wonder if he had gone down on his knees to pray that night!—one morning I gave in."

Heyst tugged violently at a tuft of dried grass, and cast it away from him with a nervous gesture.

"I gave in," he repeated.

Looking towards him with a movement of her eyes

only, the girl noticed the strong feeling on his face
with that intense interest which his person awakened
in her mind and in her heart. But it soon passed
away, leaving only a moody expression.

"It's difficult to resist where nothing matters," he
observed. "And perhaps there is a grain of freakishness in my nature. It amused me to go about uttering
silly, commonplace phrases. I was never so well
thought of in the islands till I began to jabber commercial gibberish like the veriest idiot. Upon my word,
I believe that I was actually respected for a time. I
was as grave as an owl over it; I had to be loyal to the
man. I have been from first to last, completely,
utterly loyal to the best of my ability. I thought he
understood something about coal. And if I had been
aware that he knew nothing of it, as in fact he didn't,
well—I don't know what I could have done to stop him.
In one way or another I should have had to be loyal.
Truth, work, ambition, love itself, may be only count-
ers in the lamentable or despicable game of life, but
when one takes a hand one must play the game. No,
the shade of Morrison needn't haunt me. What's
the matter? I say, Lena, why are you staring like
that? Do you feel ill?"

Heyst made as if to get on his feet. The girl extended her arm to arrest him, and he remained staring
in a sitting posture, propped on one arm, observing
her indefinable expression of anxiety, as if she were
unable to draw breath.

"What has come to you?" he insisted, feeling
strangely unwilling to move, to touch her.

"Nothing." She swallowed painfully. "Of course
it can't be. What name did you say? I didn't hear
it properly."

"Name?" repeated Heyst dazedly. "I only mentioned Morrison. It's the name of that man of whom I've been speaking. What of it?"

"And you mean to say that he was your friend?"

"You have heard enough to judge for yourself. You know as much of our connection as I know myself. The people in this part of the world went by appearances, and called us friends, as far as I can remember. Appearances—what more, what better can you ask for? In fact you can't have better. You can't have anything else."

"You are trying to confuse me with your talk," she cried. "You can't make fun of this."

"Can't? Well, no, I can't. It's a pity. Perhaps it would have been the best way," said Heyst, in a tone which for him could be called gloomy. "Unless one could forget the silly business altogether." His faint playfulness of manner and speech returned, like a habit one has schooled oneself into, even before his forehead had cleared completely. "But why are you looking so hard at me? Oh, I don't object, and I shall try not to flinch. Your eyes——"

He was looking straight into them, and as a matter of fact had forgotten all about the late Morrison at that moment.

"No," he exclaimed suddenly. "What an impenetrable girl you are, Lena, with those grey eyes of yours! Windows of the soul, as some poet has said. The fellow must have been a glazier by vocation. Well, nature has provided excellently for the shyness of your soul."

When he ceased speaking, the girl came to herself with a catch of her breath. He heard her voice, the varied charm of which he thought he knew so well, saying with an unfamiliar intonation:

"And that partner of yours is dead?"

"Morrison? Oh, yes, as I've told you, he——"

"You never told me."

"Didn't I? I thought I did; or, rather, I thought you must know. It seems impossible that anybody with whom I speak should not know that Morrison is dead."

She lowered her eyelids, and Heyst was startled by something like an expression of horror on her face.

"Morrison!" she whispered in an appalled tone. "Morrison!" Her head drooped. Unable to see her features, Heyst could tell from her voice that for some reason or other she was profoundly moved by the syllables of that unromantic name. A thought flashed through his head—could she have known Morrison? But the mere difference of their origins made it wildly improbable.

"This is very extraordinary!" he said. "Have you ever heard the name before?"

Her head moved quickly several times in tiny affirmative nods, as if she could not trust herself to speak, or even to look at him. She was biting her lower lip.

"Did you ever know anybody of that name?" he asked.

The girl answered by a negative sign; and then at last she spoke, jerkily, as if forcing herself against some doubt or fear. She had heard of that very man, she told Heyst.

"Impossible!" he said positively. "You are mistaken. You couldn't have heard of him. It's——"

He stopped short, with the thought that to talk like this was perfectly useless; that one doesn't argue against thin air.

"But I did hear of him; only I didn't know then, I couldn't guess, that it was your partner they were talking about."

"Talking about my partner?" repeated Heyst slowly.

"No." Her mind seemed almost as bewildered, as

full of incredulity, as his. "No. They were talking of you, really; only I didn't know it."

"Who were they?" Heyst raised his voice. "Who was talking of me? Talking where?"

With the first question he had lifted himself from his reclining position; at the last he was on his knees before her, their heads on a level.

"Why, in that town, in that hotel. Where else could it have been?" she said.

The idea of being talked about was always novel to Heyst's simplified conception of himself. For a moment he was as much surprised as if he had believed himself to be a mere gliding shadow among men. Besides, he had in him a half-unconscious notion that he was above the level of island gossip.

"But you said first that it was of Morrison they talked," he remarked to the girl, sinking on his heels, and no longer much interested. "Strange that you should have the opportunity to hear any talk at all! I was rather under the impression that you never saw anybody belonging to the town except from the platform."

"You forget that I was not living with the other girls," she said. "After meals they used to go back to the Pavilion, but I had to stay in the hotel and do my sewing, or what not, in the room where they talked."

"I didn't think of that. By the by, you never told me who *they* were."

"Why, that horrible red-faced beast," she said, with all the energy of disgust which the mere thought of the hotel-keeper provoked in her.

"Oh, Schomberg!" Heyst murmured carelessly.

"He talked to the boss—to Zangiacomo, I mean. I had to sit there. That devil-woman sometimes wouldn't let me go away. I mean Mrs. Zangiacomo."

"I guessed," murmured Heyst. "She liked to torment you in a variety of ways. But it is really strange that the hotel-keeper should talk of Morrison to Zangiacomo. As far as I can remember he saw very little of Morrison professionally. He knew many others much better."

The girl shuddered slightly.

"That was the only name I ever overheard. I would get as far away from them as I could, to the other end of the room; but when that beast started shouting, I could not help hearing. I wish I had never heard anything. If I had got up and gone out of the room I don't suppose the woman would have killed me for it; but she would have rowed me in a nasty way. She would have threatened me and called me names. That sort, when they know you are helpless, there's nothing to stop them. I don't know how it is, but bad people, real bad people that you can see are bad, they get over me somehow. It's the way they set about downing one. I am afraid of wickedness."

Heyst watched the changing expressions of her face. He encouraged her, profoundly sympathetic, a little amused.

"I quite understand. You needn't apologize for your great delicacy in the perception of inhuman evil. I am a little like you."

"I am not very plucky," she said.

"Well! I don't know myself what I would do, what countenance I would have before a creature which would strike me as being the evil incarnate. Don't you be ashamed."

She sighed, looked up with her pale, candid gaze and a timid expression of her face, and murmured:

"You don't seem to want to know what he was saying."

"About poor Morrison? It couldn't have been anything bad, for the poor fellow was innocence itself. And then, you know, he is dead, and nothing can possibly matter to him now."

"But I tell you that it was of *you* he was talking!" she cried. "He was saying that Morrison's partner first got all there was to get out of him, and then, and then—well, as good as murdered him—sent him out to die somewhere!"

"You believe that of me?" said Heyst, after a moment of perfect silence.

"I didn't know it had anything to do with you. Schomberg was talking of some Swede. How was I to know? It was only when you began telling me about how you came here——"

"And now you have my version." Heyst forced himself to speak quietly. "So that's how the business looked from outside!" he muttered.

"I remember him saying that everybody in these parts knew the story," the girl added breathlessly.

"Strange that it should hurt me!" mused Heyst to himself; "yet it does. I seem to be as much of a fool as those everybodies who know the story—and no doubt believe it. Can you remember any more?" he addressed the girl in a grimly polite tone. "I've often heard of the moral advantages of seeing oneself as others see one. Let us investigate further. Can't you recall something else that everybody knows?"

"Oh! Don't laugh!" she cried.

"Did I laugh? I assure you I was not aware of it. I won't ask you whether you believe the hotel-keeper's version. Surely you must know the value of human judgment."

She unclasped her hands, moved them slightly, and twined her fingers as before. Protest? Assent? Was there to be nothing more? He was relieved when she spoke in that warm and wonderful voice which in itself comforted and fascinated one's heart, which made her lovable.

"I heard this before you and I ever spoke to each other. It went out of my memory afterwards. Everything went out of my memory then; and I was glad of it. It was a fresh start for me, with you—and you know it. I wish I had forgotten who I was—that would have been best; and I very nearly did forget."

He was moved by the vibrating quality of the last words. She seemed to be talking low of some wonderful enchantment, in mysterious terms of special significance. He thought that if she only could talk to him in some unknown tongue, she would enslave him altogether by the sheer beauty of the sound, suggesting infinite depths of wisdom and feeling.

"But," she went on, "the name stuck in my head, it seems; and when you mentioned it——"

"It broke the spell," muttered Heyst in angry disappointment, as if he had been deceived in some hope.

The girl, from her position a little above him, surveyed with still eyes the abstracted silence of the man on whom she now depended with a completeness of which she had not been vividly conscious before, because, till then, she had never felt herself swinging between the abysses of earth and heaven* in the hollow of his arm. What if he should grow weary of the burden.

"And, moreover, nobody had ever believed that tale!"

Heyst came out with an abrupt burst of sound which made her open her steady eyes wider, with an effect of immense surprise. It was a purely mechanical effect, because she was nether surprised nor puzzled. In fact, she could understand him better then than at any moment since she first set eyes on him.

He laughed scornfully.

"What am I thinking of?" he cried. "As if it could matter to me what anybody had ever said or believed, from the beginning of the world till the crack of doom!"

"I never heard you laugh till to-day," she observed. "This is the second time."

He scrambled to his feet and towered above her.

"That's because, when one's heart has been broken into in the way you have broken into mine, all sorts of weaknesses are free to enter—shame, anger, stupid indignations, stupid fears—stupid laughter, too. I wonder what interpretation you are putting on it?"

"It wasn't gay, certainly," she said. "But why are you angry with me? Are you sorry you took me away from those beasts? I told you who I was. You could see it."

"Heavens!" he muttered. He had regained his command of himself. "I assure you I could see much more than you could tell me. I could see quite a lot that you don't even suspect yet; but you can't be seen quite through."

He sank to the ground by her side and took her hand. She asked gently:

"What more do you want from me?"

He made no sound for a time.

"The impossible, I suppose," he said very low, as one makes a confidence, and pressing the hand he grasped.

It did not return the pressure. He shook his head as if to drive away the thought of this, and added in a louder, light tone:

"Nothing less. And it isn't because I think little of what I've got already. Oh, no! It is because I think so much of this possession of mine that I can't have it complete enough. I know it's unreasonable. You can't hold back anything—now."

"Indeed I couldn't," she whispered, letting her hand lie passive in his tight grasp. "I only wish I could give you something more, or better, or whatever it is you want."

He was touched by the sincere accent of these simple words.

"I tell you what you can do—you can tell me whether you would have gone with me like this if you had known of whom that abominable idiot of a hotel-keeper was speaking. A murderer—no less!"

"But I didn't know you at all then," she cried. "And I had the sense to understand what he was saying. It wasn't murder, really. I never thought it was."

"What made him invent such an atrocity?" Heyst exclaimed. "He seems a stupid animal. He *is* stupid. How did he manage to hatch that pretty tale? Have I a particularly vile countenance? Is black selfishness written all over my face? Or is that sort of thing so universally human that it might be said of anybody?"

"It wasn't murder," she insisted earnestly.

"I know. I understand. It was worse. As to killing a man, which would be a comparatively decent thing to do, well—I have never done that."

"Why should you do it?" she asked in a frightened voice.

"My dear girl, you don't know the sort of life I have been leading in unexplored countries, in the wilds; it's difficult to give you an idea. There are men who haven't been in such tight places as I have found myself in who have had to—to shed blood, as the saying is. Even the wilds hold prizes which tempt some people; but I had no schemes, no plans—and not even great firmness of mind to make me unduly obstinate. I was simply moving on, while the others, perhaps, were going somewhere. An indifference as to roads and purposes makes one meeker, as it were. And I may say truly, too, that I never did care, I won't say for life—I had scorned what people call by that name from the first—but for being alive. I don't know if that is what men call courage, but I doubt it very much."

"You! You have no courage?" she protested.

"I really don't know. Not the sort that always itches for a weapon, for I have never been anxious to use one in the quarrels that a man gets into in the most innocent way, sometimes. The differences for which men murder each other are, like everything else they do, the most contemptible, the most pitiful things to look back upon. No, I've never killed a man or loved a woman—not even in my thoughts, not even in my dreams."

He raised her hand to his lips, and let them rest on it for a space, during which she moved a little closer to him. After the lingering kiss he did not relinquish his hold.

"To slay, to love—the greatest enterprises of life upon a man! And I have no experience of either. You must forgive me anything that may have appeared to you awkward in my behaviour, inexpressive in my speeches, untimely in my silences."

He moved uneasily, a little disappointed by her attitude, but indulgent to it, and feeling, in this moment of perfect quietness, that in holding her surrendered hand he had found a closer communion than they had ever achieved before. But even then there still lingered in him a sense of incompleteness not altogether overcome—which, it seemed, nothing ever would overcome—the fatal imperfection of all the gifts of life, which makes of them a delusion and a snare.

All of a sudden he squeezed her hand angrily. His

delicately playful equanimity, the product of kindness and scorn, had perished with the loss of his bitter liberty.

"Not murder, you say! I should think not. But when you led me to talk just now, when the name turned up, when you understood that it was of me that these things had been said, you showed a strange emotion. I could see it."

"I was a bit startled," she said.

"At the baseness of my conduct?" he asked.

"I wouldn't judge you; not for anything."

"Really?"

"It would be as if I dared to judge everything that there is." With her other hand she made a gesture that seemed to embrace in one movement the earth and the heaven. "I wouldn't do such a thing."

Then came a silence, broken at last by Heyst:

"I! I! do a deadly wrong to my poor Morrison!" he cried. "I, who could not bear to hurt his feelings! I, who respected his very madness! Yes, this madness, the wreck of which you can see lying about the jetty of Diamond Bay. What else could I do? He insisted on regarding me as his saviour; he was always restraining the eternal obligation on the tip of his tongue, till I was burning with shame at his gratitude. What could I do? He was going to repay me with this infernal coal, and I had to join him as one joins a child's game in a nursery. One would no more have thought of humiliating him than one would think of humiliating a child. What's the use of talking of all this! Of course, the people here could not understand the truth of our relation to each other. But what business of theirs was it? Kill old Morrison! Well, it is less criminal, less base—I am not saying it is less difficult—to kill a man than to cheat him in that way. You understand that?"

She nodded slightly, but more than once and with evident conviction. His eyes rested on her, inquisitive, ready for tenderness.

"But it was neither one nor the other," he went on. "Then, why your emotion? All you confess is that you wouldn't judge me."

She turned upon him her veiled, unseeing grey eyes in which nothing of her wonder could be read.

"I said I couldn't," she whispered.

"But you thought that there was no smoke without fire!" The playfulness of tone hardly concealed his irritation. "What power there must be in words, only imperfectly heard—for you did not listen with particular care, did you? What were they? What evil effort of invention drove them into that idiot's mouth out of his lying throat? If you were to try to remember, they would perhaps convince me, too."

"I didn't listen," she protested. "What was it to me what they said of anybody? He was saying that there never were such loving friends to look at as you two; then, when you got all you wanted out of him and got thoroughly tired of him, too, you kicked him out to go home and die."

Indignation, with an undercurrent of some other feeling, rang in these quoted words, uttered in her pure and enchanting voice. She ceased abruptly and lowered her long, dark lashes, as if mortally weary, sick at heart.

"Of course, why shouldn't you get tired of that or any other—company? You aren't like any one else and—and the thought of it made me unhappy suddenly; but indeed, I did not believe anything bad of you. I——"

A brusque movement of his arm, flinging her hand away, stopped her short. Heyst had again lost control of himself. He would have shouted, if shouting had been in his character.

"No, this earth must be the appointed hatching planet of calumny enough to furnish the whole universe! I feel a disgust at my own person, as if I had tumbled into some filthy hole. Pah! And you—all you can say is that you won't judge me; that you———"

She raised her head at this attack, though indeed he had not turned to her.

"I don't believe anything bad of you," she repeated. "I couldn't."

He made a gesture as if to say:

"That's sufficient."

In his soul and in his body he experienced a nervous reaction from tenderness. All at once, without transition, he detested her. But only for a moment. He remembered that she was pretty, and, more, that she had a special grace in the intimacy of life. She had the secret of individuality which excites—and escapes.

He jumped up and began to walk to and fro. Presently his hidden fury fell into dust within him, like a crazy structure, leaving behind emptiness, desolation, regret. His resentment was not against the girl, but against life itself—that commonest of snares, in which he felt himself caught, seeing clearly the plot of plots and unconsoled by the lucidity of his mind.

He swerved and, stepping up to her, sank to the ground by her side. Before she could make a movement, or even turn her head his way, he took her in his arms and kissed her lips. He tasted on them the bitterness of a tear fallen there. He had never seen her cry. It was like another appeal to his tenderness—a new seduction. The girl glanced round, moved suddenly away, and averted her face. With her hand she signed imperiously to him to leave her alone—a command which Heyst did not obey.

WHEN she opened her eyes at last and sat up, Heyst scrambled quickly to his feet and went to pick up her cork helmet, which had rolled a little way off. Meanwhile she busied herself in doing up her hair, plaited on the top of her head in two heavy, dark tresses, which had come loose. He tendered her the helmet in silence, and waited as if unwilling to hear the sound of his own voice.

"We had better go down now," he suggested in a low tone.

He extended his hand to help her up. He had the intention to smile, but abandoned it at the nearer sight of her still face, in which was depicted the infinite lassitude of her soul. On their way to regain the forest path they had to pass through the spot from which the view of the sea could be obtained. The flaming abyss of emptiness, the liquid, undulating glare, the tragic brutality of the light, made her long for the friendly night, with its stars stilled by an austere spell; for the velvety dark sky and the mysterious great shadow of the sea, conveying peace to the day-weary heart. She put her hand to her eyes. Behind her back Heyst spoke gently.

"Let us get on, Lena."

She walked ahead in silence. Heyst remarked that they had never been out before during the hottest hours. It would do her no good, he feared. This solicitude pleased and soothed her. She felt more and more like herself—a poor London girl playing in an orchestra, and snatched out from the humiliations, the squalid dangers of a miserable existence, by a man like whom there was not, there could not be, another in this world. She felt this with elation, with uneasiness, with an intimate pride—and with a peculiar sinking of the heart.

"I am not easily knocked out by any such thing as heat," she said decisively.

"Yes, but I don't forget that you're not a tropical bird."

"You weren't born in these parts, either," she returned.

"No, and perhaps I haven't even your physique. I am a transplanted being. Transplanted! I ought to call myself uprooted—an unnatural state of existence; but a man is supposed to stand anything."

She looked back at him and received a smile. He told her to keep in the shelter of the forest path, which was very still and close, full of heat if free from glare. Now and then they had glimpses of the company's old clearing blazing with light, in which the black stumps of trees stood charred, without shadows, miserable and sinister. They crossed the open in a direct line for the bungalow. On the verandah they fancied they had a glimpse of a vanishing Wang, though the girl was not at all sure that she had seen anything move. Heyst had no doubts.

"Wang has been looking out for us. We are late."

"Was he? I thought I saw something white for a moment, and then I did not see it any more."

"That's it—he vanishes. It's a very remarkable gift in that Chinaman."

"Are they all like that?" she asked with naïve curiosity and uneasiness.

"Not in such perfection," said Heyst, amused.

He noticed with approval that she was not heated by

the walk. The drops of perspiration on her forehead were like dew on the cool, white petal of a flower. He looked at her figure of grace and strength, solid and supple, with an ever-growing appreciation.

"Go in and rest yourself for a quarter of an hour; and then Mr. Wang will give us something to eat," he said.

They had found the table laid. When they came together again and sat down to it, Wang materialised without a sound, unheard, uncalled, and did his office. Which being accomplished, at a given moment he was not.

A great silence brooded over Samburan—the silence of the great heat that seems pregnant with fatal issues, like the silence of ardent thought. Heyst remained alone in the big room. The girl seeing him take up a book, had retreated to her chamber. Heyst sat down under his father's portrait; and the abominable calumny crept back into his recollection. The taste of it came on his lips, nauseating and corrosive like some kinds of poison. He was tempted to spit on the floor, naïvely, in sheer unsophisticated disgust of the physical sensation. He shook his head, surprised at himself. He was not used to receive his intellectual impressions in that way—reflected in movements of carnal emotion. He stirred impatiently in his chair, and raised the book to his eyes with both hands. It was one of his father's. He opened it haphazard, and his eyes fell on the middle of the page. The elder Heyst had written of everything in many books—of space and of time, of animals and of stars; analysing ideas and actions, the laughter and the frowns of men, and the grimaces of their agony. The son read, shrinking into himself, composing his face as if under the author's eye, with a vivid consciousness of the portrait on his right hand, a little above his head; a wonderful presence in its heavy frame on the flimsy wall of mats, looking exiled and at home, out of place and masterful, in the painted immobility of profile.

And Heyst, the son, read:

Of the stratagems of life the most cruel is the consolation of love—the most subtle, too; for the desire is the bed of dreams.*

He turned the pages of the little volume, "Storm and Dust," glancing here and there at the broken text of reflections, maxims, short phrases, enigmatical sometimes and sometimes eloquent. It seemed to him that he was hearing his father's voice, speaking and ceasing to speak again. Startled at first, he ended by finding a charm in the illusion. He abandoned himself to the half-belief that something of his father dwelt yet on earth—a ghostly voice, audible to the ear of his own flesh and blood. With what strange serenity, mingled with terrors, had that man considered the universal nothingness! He had plunged into it headlong, perhaps to render death, the answer that faced one at every inquiry, more supportable.

Heyst stirred, and the ghostly voice ceased; but his eyes followed the words on the last page of the book:

Men of tormented conscience, or of a criminal imagination, are aware of much that minds of a peaceful, resigned cast do not even suspect. It is not poets alone who dare descend into the abyss of infernal regions, or even who dream of such a descent. The most inexpressive of human beings must have said to himself, at one time or another: "Anything but this!" . . . .

We all have our instants of clairvoyance. They are not very helpful. The character of the scheme does not permit that or anything else to be helpful. Properly speaking its character, judged by the standards established by its victims, is infamous. It excuses every violence of protest and at the same time never fails to crush it, just as it crushes the blindest assent. The so-called wickedness must be, like the so-called virtue, its own reward—to be anything at all . . . .

Clairvoyance or no clairvoyance, men love their captivity. To the unknown force of negation they prefer the miserably tumbled bed of their servitude. Man alone can give one the disgust of pity;* yet I find it easier to believe in the misfortune of mankind than in its wickedness.

These were the last words. Heyst lowered the book to his knees. Lena's voice spoke above his drooping head:

"You sit there as if you were unhappy."

"I thought you were asleep," he said.

"I was lying down, right enough, but I never closed my eyes."

"The rest would have done you good after our walk. Didn't you try?"

"I was lying down, I tell you, but sleep I couldn't."

"And you made no sound! What want of sincerity! Or did you want to be alone for a time?"

"I—alone!" she murmured.

He noticed her eyeing the book, and got up to put it back in the bookcase. When he turned round, he saw that she had dropped into the chair—it was the one she always used—and looked as if her strength had suddenly gone from her, leaving her only her youth, which seemed very pathetic, very much at his mercy. He moved quickly towards the chair.

"Tired, are you? It's my fault, taking you up so high and keeping you out so long. Such a windless day, too!"

She watched his concern, her pose languid, her eyes raised to him, but as unreadable as ever. He avoided looking into them for that very reason. He forgot himself in the contemplation of those passive arms, of these defenceless lips, and—yes, one had to go back to them —of these wide-open eyes. Something wild in their grey stare made him think of sea-birds in the cold murkiness of high latitudes. He started when she spoke, all the charm of physical intimacy revealed suddenly in that voice.

"You should try to love me!" she said.

He made a movement of astonishment.

"Try!" he muttered. "But it seems to me——" He broke off, saying to himself that if he loved her, he had never told her so in so many words. Simple words! They died on his lips. "What makes you say that?" he asked.

She lowered her eyelids and turned her head a little.

"I have done nothing," she said in a low voice. "It's you who have been good, helpful and tender to me. Perhaps you love me for that—just for that; or perhaps you love me for company, and because—well! But sometimes it seems to me that you can never love me for myself, only for myself, as people do love each other when it is to be for ever." Her head drooped. "For ever," she breathed out again; then, still more faintly, she added an entreating: "Do try!"

These last words went straight to his heart—the sound of them more than the sense. He did not know what to say, either from want of practice in dealing with women or simply from his innate honesty of thought. All his defences were broken now. Life had him fairly by the throat. But he managed a smile, though she was not looking at him; yes, he did manage it—the well-known Heyst smile of playful courtesy, so familiar to all sorts and conditions of men in the islands.

"My dear Lena," he said, "it looks as if you were trying to pick a very unnecessary quarrel with me—of all people!"

She made no movement. With his elbows spread out he was twisting the ends of his long moustaches, very masculine and perplexed, enveloped in the atmosphere of femininity as in a cloud, suspecting pitfalls, and as if afraid to move.

"I must admit, though," he added, "that there is no one else; and I suppose a certain amount of quarrelling is necessary for existence in this world."

That girl, seated in her chair in graceful quietude, was to him like a script in an unknown language, or even more simply mysterious: like any writing to the illiterate. As far as women went he was altogether uninstructed and he had not the gift of intuition which is fostered in the days of youth by dreams and visions, exercises of the heart fitting it for the encounters of a world in which love itself rests as much on antagonism as on attraction. His mental attitude was that of a man looking this way and that on a piece of writing which he is unable to decipher, but which may be big with some revelation. He didn't know what to say. All he found to add was:

"I don't even understand what I have done or left undone to distress you like this."

He stopped, struck afresh by the physical and moral sense of the imperfections of their relations—a sense which made him desire her constant nearness, before his eyes, under his hand, and which, when she was out of his sight, made her so vague, so elusive and illusory, a promise that could not be embraced and held.

"No! I don't see clearly what you mean. Is your mind turned towards the future?" he interpellated her with marked playfulness, because he was ashamed to let such a word pass his lips. But all his cherished negations were falling off him one by one.

"Because if it is so there is nothing easier than to dismiss it. In our future, as in what people call the other life, there is nothing to be frightened of."

She raised her eyes to him; and if nature had formed

them to express anything else but blank candour he
would have learned how terrified she was by his talk
and the fact that her sinking heart loved him more desperately than ever. He smiled at her.

"Dismiss all thought of it," he insisted. "Surely you
don't suspect after what I have heard from you, that I
am anxious to return to mankind. I! I! murder my
poor Morrison! It's possible that I may be really
capable of that which they say I have done. The point
is that I haven't done it. But it is an unpleasant subject to me. I ought to be ashamed to confess it—but it
is! Let us forget it. There's that in you, Lena, which
can console me for worse things, for uglier passages.
And if we forget, there are no voices here to remind us."

She had raised her head before he paused.

"Nothing can break in on us here," he went on and
as if there had been an appeal or a provocation in her
upward glance, he bent down and took her under the
arms, raising her straight out of the chair into a sudden
and close embrace. Her alacrity to respond, which
made her seem as light as a feather, warmed his heart
at that moment more than closer caresses had done
before. He had not expected that ready impulse
towards himself which had been dormant in her passive
attitude. He had just felt the clasp of her arms round
his neck, when, with a slight exclamation—"He's here!"
—she disengaged herself and bolted away into her room.

VI

HEYST was astounded. Looking all round, as if to take the whole room to witness of this outrage, he became aware of Wang materialised in the doorway. The intrusion was as surprising as anything could be, in view of the strict regularity with which Wang made himself visible. Heyst was tempted to laugh at first. This practical comment on his affirmation that nothing could break in on them relieved the strain of his feelings. He was a little vexed, too. The Chinaman preserved a profound silence.

"What do you want?" asked Heyst sternly.

"Boat out there," said the Chinaman.

"Where? What do you mean? Boat adrift in the straits?"

Some subtle change in Wang's bearing suggested his being out of breath; but he did not pant, and his voice was steady.

"No—row."

It was Heyst now who was startled and raised his voice.

"Malay man, eh?"

Wang made a slight negative movement with his head.

"Do you hear, Lena?" Heyst called out. "Wang says there is a boat in sight—somewhere near, apparently. Where's that boat, Wang?"

"Round the point," said Wang, leaping into Malay unexpectedly, and in a loud voice. "White men—three."

"So close as that?" exclaimed Heyst, moving out on the verandah followed by Wang. "White men? Impossible!"

Over the clearing the shadows were already lengthening. The sun hung low; a ruddy glare lay on the burnt black patch in front of the bungalow, and slanted on the ground between the straight, tall, mast-like trees soaring a hundred feet or more without a branch. The growth of bushes cut off all view of the jetty from the verandah. Far away to the right Wang's hut, or rather its dark roof of mats, could be seen above the bamboo fence which insured the privacy of the Alfuro woman. The Chinaman looked that way swiftly. Heyst paused, and then stepped back a pace into the room.

"White men, Lena, apparently. What are you doing?"

"I am just bathing my eyes a little," the girl's voice said from the inner room.

"Oh, yes; all right!"

"Do you want me?"

"No. You had better—I am going down to the jetty. Yes, you had better stay in. What an extraordinary thing!"

It was so extraordinary that nobody could possibly appreciate how extraordinary it was but himself. His mind was full of mere exclamations, while his feet were carrying him in the direction of the jetty. He followed the line of the rails, escorted by Wang.

"Where were you when you first saw the boat?" he asked over his shoulder.

Wang explained in Malay that he had gone to the shore end of the wharf, to get a few lumps of coal from the big heap, when, happening to raise his eyes from the ground, he saw the boat—a white man boat, not a canoe. He had good eyes. He had seen the boat, with the men at the oars; and here Wang made a particular gesture over his eyes, as if his vision had received a blow. He had turned at once and run to the house to report.

"No mistake, eh?" said Heyst, moving on. At the very outer edge of the belt he stopped short. Wang halted behind him on the path, till the voice of Number One called him sharply forward into the open. He obeyed.

"Where's that boat?" asked Heyst forcibly. "I say —where is it?"

Nothing whatever was to be seen between the point and the jetty. The stretch of Diamond Bay was like a piece of purple shadow, lustrous and empty, while beyond the land, the open sea lay blue and opaque under the sun. Heyst's eyes swept all over the offing till they met, far off, the dark cone of the volcano, with its faint plume of smoke broadening and vanishing everlastingly at the top, without altering its shape in the glowing transparency of the evening.

"The fellow has been dreaming," he muttered to himself.

He looked hard at the Chinaman. Wang seemed turned into stone. Suddenly, as if he had received a shock, he started, flung his arm out with a pointing forefinger, and made guttural noises to the effect that there, there, there, he had seen a boat.

It was very uncanny. Heyst thought of some strange hallucination. Unlikely enough; but that a boat with three men in it should have sunk between the point and the jetty, suddenly, like a stone, without leaving as much on the surface as a floating oar, was still more unlikely. The theory of a phantom boat would have been more credible than that.

"Confound it!" he muttered to himself.

He was unpleasantly affected by this mystery; but now a simple explanation occurred to him. He stepped hastily out on the wharf. The boat, if it had existed and had retreated, could perhaps be seen from the far end of the long jetty.

Nothing was to be seen. Heyst let his eyes roam idly over the sea. He was so absorbed in his perplexity that a hollow sound, as of somebody tumbling about in a boat, with a clatter of oars and spars, failed to make him move for a moment. When his mind seized its meaning, he had no difficulty in locating the sound. It had come from below—from under the jetty!

He ran back for a dozen yards or so, and then looked over. His sight plunged straight into the stern-sheets of a big boat, the greater part of which was hidden from him by the planking of the jetty. His eyes fell on the thin back of a man doubled up over the tiller in a queer, uncomfortable attitude of drooping sorrow. Another man, more directly below Heyst, sprawled on his back from gunwale to gunwale, half off the after thwart, his head lower than his feet. This second man glared wildly upward, and struggled to raise himself, but to all appearance was much too drunk to succeed. The visible part of the boat contained also a flat, leather trunk, on which the first man's long legs were tucked up nervelessly. A large earthenware jar, with its wide mouth uncorked, rolled out on the bottom-boards from under the sprawling man.

Heyst had never been so much astonished in his life. He stared dumbly at the strange boat's crew. From the first he was positive that these men were not sailors. They wore the white drill suit of tropical civilisation; but their apparition in a boat Heyst could not connect with anything plausible. The civilisation of the tropics could have had nothing to do with it. It was more like those myths, current in Polynesia, of amazing strangers, who arrive at an island, gods or demons, bringing good or evil to the innocence of the inhabitants—gifts of unknown things, words never heard before.

Heyst noticed a cork helmet floating alongside the boat, evidently fallen from the head of the man doubled over the tiller, who displayed a dark, bony poll. An oar, too, had been knocked overboard, probably by the sprawling man, who was still struggling between the thwarts. By this time Heyst regarded the visitation no longer with surprise, but with the sustained attention demanded by a difficult problem. With one foot posed on the string-piece, and leaning on his raised knee, he was taking in everything. The sprawling man rolled off the thwart, collapsed, and, most unexpectedly, got on his feet. He swayed dizzily, spreading his arms out, and uttered faintly a hoarse, dreamy "Hallo!" His upturned face was swollen, red, peeling all over the nose and cheeks. His stare was irrational. Heyst perceived stains of dried blood all over the front of his dirty white coat, and also on one sleeve.

"What's the matter? Are you wounded?"

The other glanced down, reeled—one of his feet was inside a large pith hat—and, recovering himself, let out a dismal, grating sound in the manner of a grim laugh.

"Blood—not mine. Thirst's the matter. Exhausted's the matter. Done up. Drink, man! Give us water!"

Thirst was in the very tone of his words, alternating a broken croak and a faint, throaty rustle which just reached Heyst's ears. The man in the boat raised his hands to be helped up on the jetty, whispering:

"I tried. I am too weak. I tumbled down."

Wang was coming along the jetty slowly, with intent, straining eyes.

"Run back and bring a crowbar here. There's one lying by the coal-heap," Heyst shouted to him.

The man standing in the boat sat down on the thwart behind him. A horrible coughing laugh came through his swollen lips.

"Crowbar? What's that for?" he mumbled, and his head dropped on his chest mournfully.

Meantime Heyst, as if he had forgotten the boat, started kicking hard at a large brass tap projecting above the planks. To accommodate ships that came for coal and happened to need water as well, a stream had been tapped in the interior and an iron pipe led along the jetty. It terminated with a curved end almost exactly where the strangers' boat had been driven between the piles; but the tap was set fast.

"Hurry up!" Heyst yelled to the Chinaman, who was running with the crowbar in his hand.

Heyst snatched it from him and, obtaining a leverage against the string-piece, wrung the stiff tap round with a mighty jerk.

"I hope that pipe hasn't got choked!" he muttered to himself anxiously.

It hadn't; but it did not yield a strong gush. The sound of a thin stream, partly breaking on the gunwale of the boat and partly splashing alongside, became at once audible. It was greeted by a cry of inarticulate and savage joy. Heyst knelt on the string-piece and peered down. The man who had spoken was already holding his open mouth under the bright trickle. Water ran over his eyelids and over his nose, gurgled down his throat, flowed over his chin. Then some obstruction in the pipe gave way, and a sudden thick jet broke on his face. In a moment his shoulders were soaked, the front of his coat inundated; he streamed and dripped; water ran into his pockets, down his legs, into his shoes;

but he had clutched the end of the pipe, and, hanging on with both hands, swallowed, spluttered, choked, snorted with the noises of a swimmer. Suddenly a curious dull roar reached Heyst's ears. Something hairy and black flew from under the jetty. A dishevelled head, coming on like a cannon-ball, took the man at the pipe in flank, with enough force to tear his grip loose and fling him headlong into the stern-sheets. He fell upon the folded legs of the man at the tiller, who, roused by the commotion in the boat, was sitting up, silent, rigid, and very much like a corpse. His eyes were but two black patches, and his teeth glistened with a death's head grin between his retracted lips, no thicker than blackish parchment glued over the gums.

From him Heyst's eyes wandered to the creature who had replaced the first man at the end of the water-pipe. Enormous brown paws clutched it savagely; the wild, big head hung back, and in a face covered with a wet mass of hair there gaped crookedly a wide mouth full of fangs. The water filled it, welled up in hoarse coughs, ran down on each side of the jaws and down the hairy throat, soaked the black pelt of the enormous chest, naked under a torn check shirt, heaving convulsively with a play of massive muscles carved in red mahogany.

As soon as the first man had recovered the breath knocked out of him by the irresistible charge, a scream of mad cursing issued from the stern-sheets. With a rigid, angular crooking of the elbow, the man at the tiller put his hand back to his hip.

"Don't shoot him, sir!" yelled the first man. "Wait! Let me have that tiller. I will teach him to shove himself in front of a *caballero!*"

Martin Ricardo flourished the heavy piece of wood, leaped forward with astonishing vigour, and brought it down on Pedro's head with a crash that resounded all over the quiet sweep of Black Diamond Bay. A crimson patch appeared on the matted hair; red veins appeared in the water flowing all over his face, and it dripped in rosy drops off his head. But the man hung on. Not till a second furious blow descended did the hairy paws let go their grip and the squirming body sink limply. Before it could touch the bottom-boards, a tremendous kick in the ribs from Ricardo's foot shifted it forward out of sight, whence came the noise of a heavy thud, a clatter of spars, and a pitiful grunt. Ricardo stooped to look under the jetty.

"Aha, dog! This will teach you to keep back where you belong, you murdering brute, you slaughtering savage, you! You infidel, you robber of churches! Next time I will rip you open from neck to heel, you carrion-eater! *Esclavo!*"*

He backed a little and straightened himself up.

"I don't mean it really," he remarked to Heyst, whose steady eyes met his from above. He ran aft briskly.

"Come along, sir. It's your turn. I oughtn't to have drunk first. 'S truth, I forgot myself! A gentleman like you will overlook that, I know." As he made these apologies, Ricardo extended his hand. "Let me steady you, sir."

Slowly Mr. Jones unfolded himself in all his slenderness, rocked, staggered, and caught Ricardo's shoulder. His henchman assisted him to the pipe, which went on gushing a clear stream of water, sparkling exceedingly against the black piles and the gloom under the jetty.

"Catch hold, sir," Ricardo advised solicitously. "All right?"

He stepped back, and, while Mr. Jones revelled in the abundance of water, he addressed himself to Heyst with a sort of justificatory speech, the tone of which, reflecting his feelings, partook of purring and spitting.

They had been thirty hours tugging at the oars, he explained, and they had been more than forty hours without water, except that the night before they had licked the dew off the gunwales.

Ricardo did not explain to Heyst how it happened. At that precise moment he had no explanation ready for the man on the wharf, who, he guessed, must be wondering much more at the presence of his visitors than at their plight.

VII

THE explanation lay in the two simple facts that the
light winds and strong currents of the Java Sea had
drifted the boat about until they partly lost their bearings; and that by some extraordinary mistake one of
the two jars put into the boat by Schomberg's man contained salt water. Ricardo tried to put some pathos
into his tones. Pulling for thirty hours with eighteen-
foot oars! And the sun! Ricardo relieved his feelings
by cursing the sun. They had felt their hearts and
lungs shrivel within them. And then, as if all that
hadn't been trouble enough, he complained bitterly,
he had had to waste his fainting strength in beating
their servant about the head with a stretcher. The
fool had wanted to drink sea water, and wouldn't listen
to reason. There was no stopping him otherwise.
It was better to beat him into insensibility than to
have him go crazy in the boat, and to be obliged to
shoot him. The preventive, administered with enough
force to brain an elephant, boasted Ricardo, had to be
applied on two occasions—the second time all but in
sight of the jetty.

"You have seen the beauty," Ricardo went on ex-
pansively, hiding his lack of some sort of probable story
under this loquacity. "I had to hammer him away
from the spout. Opened afresh all the old broken
spots on his head. You saw how hard I had to hit.
He has no restraint, no restraint at all. If it wasn't
that he can be made useful in one way or another, I
would just as soon have let the governor shoot him."

He smiled up at Heyst in his peculiar lip-retracting manner, and added by way of afterthought:

"That's what will happen to him in the end, if he doesn't learn to restrain himself. But I've taught him to mind his manners for a while, anyhow!"

And again he addressed his quick grin up to the man on the wharf. His round eyes had never left Heyst's face ever since he began to deliver his account of the voyage.

"So that's how he looks!" Ricardo was saying to himself.

He had not expected Heyst to be like this. He had formed for himself a conception containing the helpful suggestion of a vulnerable point. These solitary men were often tipplers. But no!—this was not a drinking man's face; nor could he detect the weakness of alarm, or even the weakness of surprise, on these features, in these steady eyes.

"We were too far gone to climb out," Ricardo went on. "I heard you walking along, though. I thought I shouted; I tried to. You didn't hear me shout?"

Heyst made an almost imperceptible negative sign, which the greedy eyes of Ricardo—greedy for all signs —did not miss.

"Throat too parched. We didn't even care to whisper to each other lately. Thirst chokes one. We might have died there under this wharf before you found us."

"I couldn't think where you had gone to." Heyst was heard at last, addressing directly the newcomers from the sea. "You were seen as soon as you cleared that point."

"We were seen, eh?" grunted Mr. Ricardo. "We pulled like machines—daren't stop. The governor sat at the tiller, but he couldn't speak to us. She drove in between the piles till she hit something, and we all

tumbled off the thwarts as if we had been drunk.
Drunk—ha, ha! Too dry, by George! We fetched
in here with the very last of our strength, and no mistake. Another mile would have done for us. When
I heard your footsteps above, I tried to get up, and I
fell down."

"That was the first sound I heard," said Heyst.

Mr. Jones, the front of his soiled white tunic soaked
and plastered against his breast-bone, staggered away
from the water-pipe. Steadying himself on Ricardo's
shoulder, he drew a long breath, raised his dripping head,
and produced a smile of ghastly amiability, which was
lost upon the thoughtful Heyst. Behind his back the
sun, touching the water, was like a disc of iron cooled
to a dull red glow, ready to start rolling round the circular steel plate of the sea, which, under the darkening
sky, looked more solid than the high ridge of Samburan;
more solid than the point, whose long outlined slope
melted into its own unfathomable shadow blurring
the dim sheen on the bay. The forceful stream from
the pipe broke like shattered glass on the boat's gunwale.
Its loud, fitful, and persistent splashing revealed the
depth of the world's silence.

"Great notion, to lead the water out here," pronounced Ricardo appreciatively.

Water was life. He felt now as if he could run a mile,
scale a ten-foot wall, sing a song. Only a few minutes
ago he was next door to a corpse, done up, unable to
stand, to lift a hand; unable to groan. A drop of water
had done that miracle.

"Didn't you feel life itself running and soaking into
you, sir?" he asked his principal, with deferential but
forced vivacity.

Without a word, Mr. Jones stepped off the thwart and
sat down in the stern-sheets.

"Isn't that man of yours bleeding to death in the bows under there?" inquired Heyst.

Ricardo ceased his ecstasies over the life-giving water and answered in a tone of innocence:

"He? You may call him a man, but his hide is a jolly sight tougher than the toughest alligator he ever skinned in the good old days. You don't know how much he can stand: I do. We have tried him long time ago. *Olà*, there! Pedro! Pedro!" he yelled, with a force of lung testifying to the regenerative virtues of water.

A weak "*Señor?*" came from under the wharf.

"What did I tell you?" said Ricardo triumphantly. "Nothing can hurt him. He's all right. But, I say, the boat's getting swamped. Can't you turn this water off before you sink her under us? She's half full already."

At a sign from Heyst, Wang hammered at the brass tap on the wharf, then stood behind Number One, crowbar in hand, motionless as before. Ricardo was perhaps not so certain of Pedro's toughness as he affirmed; for he stooped, peering under the wharf, then moved forward out of sight. The gush of water, ceasing suddenly, made a silence which became complete when the after-trickle stopped. Afar, the sun was reduced to a red spark, glowing very low in the breathless immensity of twilight. Purple gleams lingered on the water all round the boat. The spectral figure in the stern-sheets spoke in a languid tone:

"That—er—companion—er—secretary of mine is a queer chap. I am afraid we aren't presenting ourselves in a very favourable light."

Heyst listened. It was the conventional voice of an educated man, only strangely lifeless. But more strange yet was this concern for appearances, expressed, he did not know, whether in jest or in earnest. Earnestness was hardly to be supposed under the circumstances, and no one had ever jested in such dead tones. It was something which could not be answered, and Heyst said nothing. The other went on:

"Travelling as I do, I find a man of his sort extremely useful. He has his little weaknesses, no doubt."

"Indeed!" Heyst was provoked into speaking. "Weakness of the arm is not one of them; neither is an exaggerated humanity, as far as I can judge."

"Defects of temper," explained Mr. Jones from the stern-sheets.

The subject of this dialogue, coming out just then from under the wharf into the visible part of the boat, made himself heard in his own defence, in a voice full of life, and with nothing languid in his manner. On the contrary, it was brisk, almost jocose. He begged pardon for contradicting. He was never out of temper with "our Pedro." The fellow was a Dago of immense strength and of no sense whatever. This combination made him dangerous, and he had to be treated accordingly, in a manner which he could understand. Reasoning was beyond him.

"And so"—Ricardo addressed Heyst with animation—"you mustn't be surprised if———"

"I assure you," Heyst interrupted, "that my wonder at your arrival in your boat here is so great that it leaves no room for minor astonishments. But hadn't you better land?"

"That's the talk, sir!" Ricardo began to bustle about the boat, talking all the time. Finding himself unable to "size up" this man, he was inclined to credit him with extraordinary powers of penetration, which, it seemed to him, would be favoured by silence. Also, he feared some pointblank question. He had no ready-

made story to tell.   He and his patron had put off considering that rather important detail too long.   For the
last two days, the horrors of thirst, coming on them
unexpectedly, had prevented consultation.   They had
had to pull for dear life.   But the man on the wharf,
were he in league with the devil himself, would pay for
all their sufferings, thought Ricardo with an unholy
joy.

   Meantime, splashing in the water which covered the
bottom-boards, Ricardo congratulated himself aloud on
the luggage being out of the way of the wet.   He had
piled it up forward.   He had roughly tied up Pedro's
head.   Pedro had nothing to grumble about.   On the
contrary, he ought to be mighty thankful to him,
Ricardo, for being alive at all.

   "Well, now, let me give you a leg up, sir," he said
cheerily to his motionless principal in the stern-sheets.
"All our troubles are over—for a time, anyhow.   Ain't
it luck to find a white man on this island?   I would have
just as soon expected to meet an angel from heaven—
eh, Mr. Jones?   Now then—ready, sir?   One, two,
three, up you go!"

   Helped from below by Ricardo, and from above by
the man more unexpected than an angel, Mr. Jones
scrambled up and stood on the wharf by the side of
Heyst.   He swayed like a reed.   The night descending
on Samburan turned into dense shadow the point of
land and the wharf itself, and gave a dark solidity to
the unshimmering water extending to the last faint
trace of light away to the west.   Heyst stared at the
guests whom the renounced world had sent him thus
at the end of the day.   The only other vestige of light
left on earth lurked in the hollows of the thin man's
eyes.   They gleamed, mobile and languidly evasive.
The eyelids fluttered.

"You are feeling weak," said Heyst.

"For the moment, a little," confessed the other.

With loud panting, Ricardo scrambled on his hands and knees upon the wharf, energetic and unaided. He rose up at Heyst's elbow and stamped his foot on the planks, with a sharp, provocative, double beat, such as is heard sometimes in fencing-schools before the adversaries engage their foils. Not that the renegade seaman Ricardo knew anything of fencing. What he called "shooting-irons" were his weapons, or the still less aristocratic knife, such as was even then ingeniously strapped to his leg. He thought of it, at that moment. A swift stooping motion, then, on the recovery, a ripping blow, a shove off the wharf, and no noise except a splash in the water that would scarcely disturb the silence. Heyst would have no time for a cry. It would be quick and neat, and immensely in accord with Ricardo's humour. But he repressed this gust of savagery. The job was not such a simple one. This piece had to be played to another tune, and in much slower time. He returned to his note of talkative simplicity.

"Ay; and I too don't feel as strong as I thought I was when the first drink set me up. Great wonder-worker water is! And to get it right here on the spot! It was heaven—hey, sir?"

Mr. Jones, being directly addressed, took up his part in the concerted piece:

"Really, when I saw a wharf on what might have been an uninhabited island, I couldn't believe my eyes. I doubted its existence. I thought it was a delusion, till the boat actually drove between the piles, as you see her lying now."

While he was speaking faintly, in a voice which did not seem to belong to the earth, his henchman, in extremely loud and terrestrial accents, was fussing about

v.—13

their belongings in the boat, addressing himself to
Pedro:

"Come, now—pass up the dunnage* there! Move
yourself, *hombre*, or I'll have to get down again and give
you a tap on those bandages of yours, you growling bear,
you!"

"Ah! You didn't believe in the reality of the wharf?"
Heyst was saying to Mr. Jones.

"You ought to kiss my hands!"

Ricardo caught hold of an ancient Gladstone bag and
swung it on the wharf with a thump.

"Yes! You ought to burn a candle before me as
they do before the saints in your country. No saint
has ever done so much for you as I have, you ungrateful
vagabond. Now then! Up you get."

Helped by the talkative Ricardo, Pedro scrambled
up on the wharf, where he remained for some time on
all fours, swinging to and fro his shaggy head tied up in
white rags. Then he got up clumsily, like a bulky
animal in the dusk, balancing itself on its hind
legs.

Mr. Jones began to explain languidly to Heyst that
they were in a pretty bad state that morning, when they
caught sight of the smoke of the volcano. It nerved
them to make an effort for their lives. Soon afterwards
they made out the island.

"I had just wits enough left in my baked brain to
alter the direction of the boat," the ghostly voice went
on. "As to finding assistance, a wharf, a white man—
nobody would have dreamed of it. Simply preposterous!"

"That's what I thought when my Chinaman came
and told me he had seen a boat with white men pulling
up," said Heyst.

"Most extraordinary luck," interjected Ricardo,

standing by anxiously attentive to every word. "Seems a dream," he added. "A lovely dream!"*

A silence fell on that group of three, as if every one had become afraid to speak, in an obscure sense of an impending crisis. Pedro on one side of them and Wang on the other had the air of watchful spectators. A few stars had come out pursuing the ebbing twilight. A light draught of air, tepid enough in the thickening twilight after the scorching day, struck a chill into Mr. Jones in his soaked clothes.

"I may infer, then, that there is a settlement of white people here?" he murmured, shivering visibly.

Heyst roused himself.

"Oh, abandoned, abandoned. I am alone here—practically alone; but several empty houses are still standing. No lack of accommodation. We may just as well—here, Wang, go back to the shore and run the trolley out here."

The last words having been spoken in Malay, he explained courteously that he had given directions for the transport of the luggage. Wang had melted into the night in his soundless manner.

"My word! Rails laid down and all," exclaimed Ricardo softly, in a tone of admiration. "Well, I never!"

"We were working a coal-mine here," said the late manager of the Tropical Belt Coal Company. "These are only the ghosts of things that have been."

Mr. Jones's teeth were suddenly started chattering by another faint puff of wind, a mere sigh from the west, where Venus cast her rays on the dark edge of the horizon, like a bright lamp hung above the grave of the sun.

"We might be moving on," proposed Heyst. "The Chinaman and that—ah—ungrateful servant of yours, with the broken head, can load the things and come along after us."

The suggestion was accepted without words. Moving towards the shore, the three men met the trolley, a mere metallic rustle which whisked past them, the shadowy Wang running noiselessly behind. Only the sound of their footsteps accompanied them. It was a long time since so many footsteps had rung together on that jetty. Before they stepped on to the path trodden through the grass, Heyst said:

"I am prevented from offering you a share of my own quarters." The distant courtliness of this beginning arrested the other two suddenly, as if amazed by some manifest incongruity. "I should regret it more," he went on, "if I were not in a position to give you the choice of those empty bungalows for a temporary home."

He turned round and plunged into the narrow track, the two others following in single file.

"Queer start!" Ricardo took the opportunity for whispering, as he fell behind Mr. Jones, who swayed in the gloom, enclosed by the stalks of tropical grass, almost as slender as a stalk of grass himself.

In this order they emerged into the open space kept clear of vegetation by Wang's judicious system of periodical firing. The shapes of buildings, unlighted, high-roofed, looked mysteriously extensive and featureless against the increasing glitter of the stars. Heyst was pleased at the absence of light in his bungalow. It looked as uninhabited as the others. He continued to lead the way, inclining to the right. His equable voice was heard:

"This one would be the best. It was our counting-house. There is some furniture in it yet. I am pretty certain that you'll find a couple of camp bedsteads in one of the rooms."

The high-pitched roof of the bungalow towered up very close, eclipsing the sky.

"Here we are. Three steps. As you see, there's a wide verandah. Sorry to keep you waiting for a moment; the door is locked, I think."

He was heard trying it. Then he leaned against the rail, saying:

"Wang will get the keys."

The others waited, two vague shapes nearly mingled together in the darkness of the verandah, from which issued a sudden chattering of Mr. Jones's teeth, directly suppressed, and a slight shuffle of Ricardo's feet. Their guide and host, his back against the rail, seemed to have forgotten their existence. Suddenly he moved, and murmured:

"Ah, here's the trolley."

Then he raised his voice in Malay, and was answered, "*Ya tuan,*" from an indistinct group that could be made out in the direction of the track.

"I have sent Wang for the key and a light," he said, in a voice that came out without any particular direction—a peculiarity which disconcerted Ricardo.

Wang did not tarry long on his mission. Very soon from the distant recesses of obscurity appeared the swinging lantern he carried. It cast a fugitive ray on the arrested trolley with the uncouth figure of the wild Pedro drooping over the load; then it moved towards the bungalow and ascended the stairs. After working at the stiff lock, Wang applied his shoulder to the door. It came open with explosive suddenness, as if in a passion at being thus disturbed after two years' repose. From the dark slope of a tall stand-up writing-desk a forgotten, solitary sheet of paper flew up and settled gracefully on the floor.

Wang and Pedro came and went through the offended

door, bringing the things off the trolley, one flitting swiftly in and out, the other staggering heavily. Later, directed by a few quiet words from Number One, Wang made several journeys with the lantern to the store-rooms, bringing in blankets, provisions in tins, coffee, sugar, and a packet of candles. He lighted one, and stuck it on the ledge of the stand-up desk. Meantime Pedro, being introduced to some kindling-wood and a bundle of dry sticks, had busied himself outside in lighting a fire, on which he placed a ready-filled kettle handed to him by Wang impassively, at arm's length, as if across a chasm. Having received the thanks of his guests, Heyst wished them good-night and withdrew, leaving them to their repose.

VIII

HEYST walked away slowly. There was still no light
in his bungalow, and he thought that perhaps it was
just as well. By this time he was much less perturbed.
Wang had preceded him with the lantern, as if in a hurry
to get away from the two white men and their hairy attendant. The light was not dancing along any more; it
was standing perfectly still by the steps of the verandah.

Heyst, glancing back casually, saw behind him still
another light,—the light of the strangers' open fire. A
black, uncouth form, stooping over it monstrously,
staggered away into the outlying shadows. The kettle
had boiled, probably.

With that weird vision of something questionably
human impressed upon his senses, Heyst moved on a
pace or two. What could the people be who had such
a creature for their familiar attendant? He stopped.
The vague apprehension of a distant future, in which
he saw Lena unavoidably separated from him by profound and subtle differences; the sceptical carelessness
which had accompanied every one of his attempts at
action, like a secret reserve of his soul, fell away from
him. He no longer belonged to himself. There was a
call far more imperious and august. He came up to
the bungalow, and, at the very limit of the lantern's
light, on the top step, he saw her feet and the bottom
part of her dress. The rest of her person was suggested
dimly as high as her waist. She sat on a chair, and the
gloom of the low eaves descended upon her head and
shoulders. She didn't stir.

"You haven't gone to sleep here?" he asked.

"Oh, no! I was waiting for you—in the dark."

Heyst, on the top step, leaned against a wooden pillar, after moving the lantern to one side.

"I have been thinking that it is just as well you had no light. But wasn't it dull for you to sit in the dark?"

"I don't need a light to think of you." Her charming voice gave a value to this banal answer, which had also the merit of truth. Heyst laughed a little, and said that he had had a curious experience. She made no remark. He tried to figure to himself the outlines of her easy pose. A spot of dim light here and there hinted at the unfailing grace of attitude which was one of her natural possessions.

She had thought of him, but not in connection with the strangers. She had admired him from the first; she had been attracted by his warm voice, his gentle eye, but she had felt him too wonderfully difficult to know. He had given to life a savour, a movement, a promise mingled with menaces, which she had not suspected were to be found in it—or, at any rate, not by a girl wedded to misery as she was. She said to herself that she must not be irritated because he seemed too self-contained, and as if shut up in a world of his own. When he took her in his arms, she felt that his embrace had a great and compelling force, that he was moved deeply, and that perhaps he would not get tired of her so very soon. She thought that he had opened to her the feelings of delicate joy, that the very uneasiness he caused her was delicious in its sadness, and that she would try to hold him as long as she could—till her fainting arms, her sinking soul, could cling to him no more.

"Wang's not here, of course?" Heyst said suddenly. She answered as if in her sleep.

"He put this light down here without stopping, and ran."

"Ran, did he? H'm! Well, it's considerably later than his usual time to go home to his Alfuro wife; but to be seen running is a sort of degradation for Wang, who has mastered the art of vanishing. Do you think he was startled out of his perfection by something?"

"Why should he be startled?"

Her voice remained dreamy, a little uncertain.

"I have been startled," Heyst said.

She was not listening to him. The lantern at their feet threw the shadows of her face upward. Her eyes glistened, as if frightened and attentive, above a lighted chin and a very white throat.

"Upon my word," mused Heyst, "now that I don't see them, I can hardly believe that those fellows exist!"

"And what about me?" she asked, so swiftly that he made a movement like somebody pounced upon from an ambush. "When you don't see me, do you believe that I exist?"

"Exist? Most charmingly! My dear Lena, you don't know your own advantages. Why, your voice alone would be enough to make you unforgettable!"

"Oh, I didn't mean forgetting in that way. I dare say if I were to die you would remember me right enough. And what good would that be to anybody? It's while I am alive that I want——"

Heyst stood by her chair, a stalwart figure imperfectly lighted. The broad shoulders, the martial face that was like a disguise of his disarmed soul, were lost in the gloom above the plane of light in which his feet were planted. He suffered from a trouble with which she had nothing to do. She had no general conception of the conditions of the existence he had offered to her.

Drawn into its peculiar stagnation she remained un-related to it because of her ignorance.

For instance, she could never perceive the prodigious improbability of the arrival of that boat. She did not seem to be thinking of it. Perhaps she had already forgotten the fact herself. And Heyst resolved suddenly to say nothing more of it. It was not that he shrank from alarming her. Not feeling anything definite himself he could not imagine a precise effect being produced on her by any amount of explanation. There is a quality in events which is apprehended differently by different minds or even by the same mind at different times. Any man living at all consciously knows that embarrassing truth. Heyst was aware that this visit could bode nothing pleasant. In his present soured temper towards all mankind he looked upon it as a visitation of a particularly offensive kind.

He glanced along the verandah in the direction of the other bungalow. The fire of sticks in front of it had gone out. No faint glow of embers, not the slightest thread of light in that direction, hinted at the presence of strangers. The darker shapes in the obscurity, the dead silence, betrayed nothing of that strange intrusion. The peace of Samburan asserted itself as on any other night. Everything was as before, except—Heyst became aware of it suddenly—that for a whole minute, perhaps, with his hand on the back of the girl's chair and within a foot of her person, he had lost the sense of her existence, for the first time since he had brought her over to share this invincible, this undefiled peace. He picked up the lantern, and the act made a silent stir all along the verandah. A spoke of shadow swung swiftly across her face, and the strong light rested on the immobility of her features, as of a woman looking at a vision. Her eyes were still, her lips serious. Her dress, open at the neck, stirred slightly to her even breathing.

"We had better go in, Lena," suggested Heyst, very low, as if breaking a spell cautiously.

She rose without a word. Heyst followed her indoors. As they passed through the living-room, he left the lantern burning on the centre table.

IX

THAT night the girl woke up, for the first time in her new experience, with the sensation of having been abandoned to her own devices. She woke up from a painful dream of separation brought about in a way which she could not understand, and missed the relief of the waking instant. The desolate feeling of being alone persisted. She was really alone. A night-light made it plain enough in the dim, mysterious manner of a dream; but this was reality. It startled her exceedingly.

In a moment she was at the curtain that hung in the doorway, and raised it with a steady hand. The conditions of their life in Samburan would have made peeping absurd; nor was such a thing in her character. This was not a movement of curiosity, but of downright alarm—the continued distress and fear of the dream. The night could not have been very far advanced. The light in the lantern was burning strongly, striping the floor and walls of the room with thick black bands. She hardly knew whether she expected to see Heyst or not; but she saw him at once, standing by the table in his sleeping-suit, his back to the doorway. She stepped in noiselessly with her bare feet, and let the curtain fall behind her. Something characteristic in Heyst's attitude made her say, almost in a whisper:

"You are looking for something."

He could not have heard her before; but he didn't start at the unexpected whisper. He only pushed the drawer of the table in and, without even looking over his shoulder, asked quietly, accepting her presence as if he had been aware of all her movements:

"I say, are you certain that Wang didn't go through this room this evening?"

"Wang? When?"

"After leaving the lantern, I mean."

"Oh, no. He ran on. I watched him."

"Or before, perhaps—while I was with these boat people? Do you know? Can you tell?"

"I hardly think so. I came out as the sun went down, and sat outside till you came back to me."

"He could have popped in for an instant through the back verandah."

"I heard nothing in here," she said. "What is the matter?"

"Naturally you wouldn't hear. He can be as quiet as a shadow, when he likes. I believe he could steal the pillows from under our heads. He might have been here ten minutes ago."

"What woke you up? Was it a noise?"

"Can't say that. Generally one can't tell; but is it likely, Lena? You are, I believe, the lighter sleeper of us two. A noise loud enough to wake me up would have awakened you, too. I tried to be as quiet as I could. What roused you?"

"I don't know—a dream, perhaps. I woke up crying."

"What was the dream?"

Heyst, with one hand resting on the table, had turned in her direction, his round, uncovered head set on a fighter's muscular neck. She left his question unanswered, as if she had not heard it.

"What is it you have missed?" she asked in her turn, very grave.

Her dark hair, drawn smoothly back, was done in

two thick tresses for the night.   Heyst noticed the good
form of her brow, the dignity of its width, its unshin-
ing whiteness.   It was a sculptural forehead.   He had
a moment of acute appreciation intruding upon another
order of thoughts.   It was as if there could be no end
of his discoveries about that girl, at the most incongruous moments.

   She had on nothing but a hand-woven cotton sarong
—one of Heyst's few purchases, years ago, in Celebes,
where they are made.   He had forgotten all about it
till she came, and then had found it at the bottom of an
old sandalwood trunk dating back to pre-Morrison days.
She had quickly learned to wind it up under her armpits
with a safe twist, as Malay village girls do when going
down to bathe in a river.   Her shoulders and arms were
bare; one of her tresses, hanging forward, looked almost
black against the white skin.   As she was taller than
the average Malay woman, the sarong ended a good way
above her ankles.   She stood poised firmly, halfway
between the table and the curtained doorway, the in-
steps of her bare feet gleaming like marble on the over-
shadowed matting of the floor.   The fall of her lighted
shoulders, the strong and fine modelling of her arms
hanging down her sides, her immobility, too, had something statuesque, the charm of art tense with life.
She was not very big—Heyst used to think of her, at
first, as "that poor little girl"—but revealed free from
the shabby banality of a white platform dress, in the
simple drapery of the sarong, there was that in her form
and in the proportions of her body which suggested a
reduction from a heroic size.

   She moved forward a step.

   "What is it you have missed?" she asked again.

   Heyst turned his back altogether on the table.   The
black spokes of darkness over the floor and the walls,

joining up on the ceiling in a path of shadow, were like the bars of a cage about them. It was his turn to ignore a question.

"You woke up in a fright, you say?" he said.

She walked up to him, exotic yet familiar, with her white woman's face and shoulders above the Malay sarong, as if it were an airy disguise; but her expression was serious.

"No!" she replied. "It was distress, rather. You see, you weren't there, and I couldn't tell why you had gone away from me. A nasty dream—the first I've had, too, since——"

"You don't believe in dreams, do you?" asked Heyst.

"I once knew a woman who did. Leastwise, she used to tell people what dreams meant, for a shilling."

"Would you go now and ask her what this dream means?" inquired Heyst jocularly.

"She lived in Camberwell. She was a nasty old thing!"

Heyst laughed a little uneasily.

"Dreams are madness, my dear. It's things that happen in the waking world, while one is asleep, that one would be glad to know the meaning of."

"You have missed something out of this drawer," she said positively.

"This or some other. I have looked into every single one of them and come back to this again, as people do. It's difficult to believe the evidence of my own senses; but it isn't there. Now, Lena, are you sure that you didn't——"

"I have touched nothing in the house but what you have given me."

"Lena!" he cried.

He was painfully affected by this disclaimer of a charge which he had not made. It was what a servant might have said—an inferior open to suspicion—or, at any rate, a stranger. He was angry at being so wretchedly misunderstood; disenchanted at her not being instinctively aware of the place he had secretly given her in his thoughts.

"After all," he said to himself, "we are strangers to each other."

And then he felt sorry for her. He spoke calmly:

"I was about to say, are you sure you have no reason to think that the Chinaman has been in this room to-night?"

"You suspect him?" she asked, knitting her eyebrows.

"There is no one else to suspect. You may call it a certitude."

"You don't want to tell me what it is?" she inquired, in the equable tone in which one takes a fact into account.

Heyst only smiled faintly.

"Nothing very precious, as far as value goes," he replied.

"I thought it might have been money," she said.

"Money!" exclaimed Heyst, as if the suggestion had been altogether preposterous. She was so visibly surprised that he hastened to add: "Of course, there is some money in the house—there, in that writing-desk, the drawer on the left. It's not locked. You can pull it right out. There is a recess, and the board at the back pivots; a very simple hiding-place, when you know the way to it. I discovered it by accident, and I keep our store of sovereigns in there. The treasure, my dear, is not big enough to require a cavern."

He paused, laughed very low, and returned her steady stare.

"The loose silver, some guilders and dollars, I have always kept in that unlocked left drawer. I have no doubt Wang knows what there is in it; but he isn't a thief, and that's why I—no, Lena, what I've missed is not gold or jewels; and that's what makes the fact interesting—which the theft of money cannot be."

She took a long breath, relieved to hear that it was not money. A great curiosity was depicted on her face, but she refrained from pressing him with questions. She only gave him one of her deep-gleaming smiles.

"It isn't me, so it must be Wang. You ought to make him give it back to you."

Heyst said nothing to that naïve and practical suggestion, for the object that he missed from the drawer was his revolver.

It was a heavy weapon which he had owned for many years and had never used in his life. Ever since the London furniture had arrived in Samburan, it had been reposing in the drawer of the table. The real dangers of life, for him, were not those which could be repelled by swords or bullets. On the other hand, neither his manner nor his appearance looked sufficiently inoffensive to expose him to light-minded aggression.

He could not have explained what had induced him to go to the drawer in the middle of the night. He had started up suddenly—which was very unusual with him. He had found himself sitting up and extremely wide awake all at once, with the girl reposing by his side, lying with her face away from him, a vague, characteristically feminine form in the dim light. She was perfectly still.

At that season of the year there were no mosquitoes in Samburan, and the sides of the mosquito net were looped up. Heyst swung his feet to the floor, and found himself standing there, almost before he had become aware of his intention to get up. Why he did this he did not know. He didn't wish to wake her up, and the

slight creak of the broad bedstead had sounded very
loud to him. He turned round apprehensively and
waited for her to move; but she did not stir. While he
looked at her, he had a vision of himself lying there too,
also fast asleep, and—it occurred to him for the first
time in his life—very defenceless. This quite novel
impression of the dangers of slumber made him think
suddenly of his revolver. He left the bedroom with
noiseless footsteps. The lightness of the curtain he had
to lift as he passed out, and the outer door, wide open
on the blackness of the verandah—for the roof eaves
came down low, shutting out the starlight—gave him
a sense of having been dangerously exposed, he could
not have said to what. He pulled the drawer open.
Its emptiness cut his train of self-communion short.
He murmured to the assertive fact:

"Impossible! Somewhere else!"

He tried to remember where he had put the thing;
but those provoked whispers of memory were not en-
couraging. Foraging in every receptacle and nook big
enough to contain a revolver, he came slowly to the conclusion that it was not in that room. Neither was it in
the other. The whole bungalow consisted of the two
rooms and a profuse allowance of verandah all round.
Heyst stepped out on the verandah.

"It's Wang, beyond a doubt," he thought, staring
into the night. "He has got hold of it for some reason."

There was nothing to prevent that ghostly Chinaman
from materialising suddenly at the foot of the stairs, or
anywhere, at any moment, and toppling him over with
a dead sure shot. The danger was so irremediable that
it was not worth worrying about, any more than the
general precariousness of human life. Heyst speculated
on this added risk. How long had he had been at the
mercy of a slender yellow finger on the trigger? That

is, if that was the fellow's reason for purloining the revolver.

"Shoot and inherit," thought Heyst. "Very simple!" Yet there was in his mind a marked reluctance to regard the domesticated grower of vegetables in the light of a murderer.

"No, it wasn't that. For Wang could have done it any time this last twelve months or more."

Heyst's mind had worked on the assumption that Wang had possessed himself of the revolver during his own absence from Samburan; but at that period of his speculation his point of view changed. It struck him with the force of manifest certitude that the revolver had been taken only late in the day, or on that very night. Wang, of course—— But why? So there had been no danger in the past. It was all ahead.

"He has me at his mercy now," thought Heyst, without particular excitement.

The sentiment he experienced was curiosity. He forgot himself in it; it was as if he were considering somebody else's strange predicament. But even that sort of interest was dying out when, looking to his left, he saw the accustomed shapes of the other bungalows looming in the night, and remembered the arrival of the thirsty company in the boat. Wang would hardly risk such a crime in the presence of other white men. It was a peculiar instance of the "safety in numbers" principle, which somehow was not much to Heyst's taste.

He went in gloomily, and stood over the empty drawer in deep and unsatisfactory thought. He had just made up his mind that he must breathe nothing of this to the girl, when he heard her voice behind him. She had taken him by surprise, but he resisted the impulse to turn round at once under the impression that

she might read his trouble in his face. Yes, she had
taken him by surprise; and for that reason the conversation which began was not exactly as he would have
conducted it if he had been prepared for her pointblank
question. He ought to have said at once: "I've
missed nothing." It was a deplorable thing that he
should have let it come so far as to have her ask what
it was he missed. He closed the conversation by saying
lightly:

"It's an object of very small value. Don't worry
about it—it isn't worth while. The best you can do is
to go and lie down again, Lena."

Reluctant she turned away, and only in the doorway
asked:

"And you?"

"I think I shall smoke a cheroot on the verandah. I
don't feel sleepy for the moment."

"Well, don't be long."

He made no answer. She saw him standing there,
very still, with a frown on his brow, and slowly dropped
the curtain.

Heyst did really light a cheroot before going out
again on the verandah. He glanced up from under the
low eaves, to see by the stars how the night went on.
It was going very slowly. Why it should have irked
him he did not know; for he had nothing to expect from
the dawn; but everything round him had become unreasonable, unsettled, and vaguely urgent, laying him
under an obligation, but giving him no line of action.
He felt contemptuously irritated with the situation.
The outer world had broken upon him; and he did not
know what wrong he had done to bring this on himself,
any more than he knew what he had done to provoke
the horrible calumny about his treatment of poor
Morrison. For he could not forget this. It had reached

the ears of one who needed to have the most perfect confidence in the rectitude of his conduct.

"And she only half disbelieves it," he thought, with hopeless humiliation.

This moral stab in the back seemed to have taken some of his strength from him, as a physical wound would have done. He had no desire to do anything—neither to bring Wang to terms in the matter of the revolver nor to find out from the strangers who they were, and how their predicament had come about. He flung his glowing cigar away into the night. But Samburan was no longer a solitude wherein he could indulge in all his moods. The fiery parabolic trail the cast-out stump traced in the air was seen from another verandah at a distance of some twenty yards. It was noted as a symptom of importance by an observer with his faculties greedy for signs, and in a state of alertness tense enough almost to hear the grass grow.

X

THE observer was Martin Ricardo. To him life was not a matter of passive renunciation, but of a particularly active warfare. He was not mistrustful of it, he was not disgusted with it, still less was he inclined to be suspicious of its disenchantments; but he was vividly aware that it held many possibilities of failure. Though very far from being a pessimist, he was not a man of foolish illusions. He did not like failure; not only because of its unpleasant and dangerous consequences, but also because of its damaging effect upon his own appreciation of Martin Ricardo. And this was a special job, of his own contriving, and of considerable novelty. It was not, so to speak, in his usual line of business—except, perhaps, from a moral standpoint, about which he was not likely to trouble his head. For these reasons Martin Ricardo was unable to sleep.

Mr. Jones, after repeated shivering fits, and after drinking much hot tea, had apparently fallen into deep slumber. He had very peremptorily discouraged attempts at conversation on the part of his faithful follower. Ricardo listened to his regular breathing. It was all very well for the governor. He looked upon it as a sort of sport. A gentleman naturally would. But this ticklish and important job had to be pulled off at all costs, both for honour and for safety. Ricardo rose quietly, and made his way on the verandah. He could not lie still. He wanted to go out for air; and he had a feeling that by the force of his eagerness even

the darkness and the silence could be made to yield
something to his eyes and ears.

He noted the stars, and stepped back again into the
dense darkness. He resisted the growing impulse to go
out and steal toward the other bungalow. It would
have been madness to start prowling in the dark on unknown ground. And for what end? Unless to relieve
the oppression. Immobility lay on his limbs like a
leaden garment. And yet he was unwilling to give up.
He persisted in his objectless vigil. The man of the
island was keeping quiet.

It was at that moment that Ricardo's eyes caught the
vanishing red trail of light made by the cigar—a startling revelation of the man's wakefulness. He could not
suppress a low "Hallo!" and began to sidle along
towards the door, with his shoulders rubbing the wall. For
all he knew, the man might have been out in front by
this time, observing the verandah. As a matter of fact,
after flinging away the cheroot, Heyst had gone indoors
with the feeling of a man who gives up an unprofitable
occupation. But Ricardo fancied he could hear faint
footfalls on the open ground, and dodged quickly into
the room. There he drew breath, and meditated for a
while. His next step was to feel for the matches on
the tall desk, and to light the candle. He had to com-
municate to his governor views and reflections of such
importance that it was absolutely necessary for him
to watch their effect on the very countenance of the
hearer. At first he had thought that these matters
could have waited till daylight; but Heyst's wakefulness,
disclosed in that startling way, made him feel suddenly
certain that there could be no sleep for him that night.

He said as much to his governor. When the little
dagger-like flame had done its best to dispel the darkness, Mr. Jones was to be seen reposing on a camp bed-

stead, in a distant part of the room. A railway rug
concealed his spare form up to his very head, which
rested on the other railway rug rolled up for a pillow.
Ricardo plumped himself down cross-legged on the
floor, very close to the low bedstead; so that Mr. Jones
—who perhaps had not been so very profoundly asleep
—on opening his eyes found them conveniently levelled
at the face of his secretary.

"Eh? What is it you say? No sleep for you to-
night? But why can't you let *me* sleep? Confound
your fussiness!"

"Because that there fellow can't sleep—that's why.
Dash me if he hasn't been doing a think just now!
What business has he to think in the middle of the
night?"

"How do you know?"

"He was out, sir—up in the middle of the night. My
own eyes saw it."

"But how do you know that he was up to think?"
inquired Mr. Jones. "It might have been anything
—toothache, for instance. And you may have dreamed
it for all I know. Didn't you try to sleep?"

"No, sir. I didn't even try to go to sleep."

Ricardo informed his patron of his vigil on the verandah, and of the revelation which put an end to it.
He concluded that a man up with a cigar in the middle
of the night must be doing a think.

Mr. Jones raised himself on his elbow. This sign of
interest comforted his faithful henchman.

"Seems to me it's time we did a little think ourselves,"
added Ricardo, with more assurance. Long as they had
been together the moods of his governor were still a
source of anxiety to his simple soul.

"You are always making a fuss," remarked Mr.
Jones, in a tolerant tone.

"Ay, but not for nothing, am I? You can't say that, sir. Mine may not be a gentleman's way of looking round a thing, but it isn't a fool's way, either. You've admitted that much yourself at odd times."

Ricardo was growing warmly argumentative. Mr. Jones interrupted him without heat.

"You haven't roused me to talk about yourself, I presume."

"No, sir." Ricardo remained silent for a minute, with the tip of his tongue caught between his teeth. "I don't think I could tell you anything about myself that you don't know," he continued. There was a sort of amused satisfaction in his tone which changed completely as he went on. "It's that man, over there, that's got to be talked over. I don't like him!"

He failed to observe the flicker of a ghastly smile on his governor's lips.

"Don't you?" murmured Mr. Jones, whose face, as he reclined on his elbow, was on a level with the top of his follower's head.

"No, sir," said Ricardo emphatically. The candle from the other side of the room threw his monstrous black shadow on the wall. "He—I don't know how to say it—he isn't hearty-like."

Mr. Jones agreed languidly in his own manner:

"He seems to be a very self-possessed man."

"Ay, that's it. Self——" Ricardo choked with indignation. "I would soon let out some of his self-possession through a hole between his ribs, if this weren't a special job!"

Mr. Jones had been making his own reflections, for he asked:

"Do you think he is suspicious?"

"I don't see very well what he can be suspicious of," pondered Ricardo. "Yet there he was, doing a think.

And what could be the object of it? What made him get out of his bed in the middle of the night? 'Tain't fleas, surely."

"Bad conscience, perhaps," suggested Mr. Jones jocularly.

His faithful secretary suffered from irritation, and did not see the joke. In a fretful tone he declared that there was no such thing as conscience. There was such a thing as funk; but there was nothing to make that fellow funky in any special way. He admitted, however, that the man might have been uneasy at the arrival of strangers, because of all that plunder of his put away somewhere.

Ricardo glanced here and there, as if he were afraid of being overheard by the heavy shadows cast by the dim light all over the room. His patron, very quiet, spoke in a calm whisper:

"And perhaps that hotel-keeper has been lying to you about him. He may be a very poor devil indeed."

Ricardo shook his head slightly. The Schombergian theory of Heyst had become in him a profound conviction, which he had absorbed as naturally as a sponge takes up water. His patron's doubts were a wanton denying of what was self-evident; but Ricardo's voice remained as before, a soft purring with a snarling undertone.

"I am sup-prised at you, sir! It's the very way them tame ones—the common 'yporcrits of the world—get on. When it comes to plunder drifting under one's very nose, there's not one of them that would keep his hands off. And I don't blame them. It's the way they do it that sets my back up. Just look at the story of how he got rid of that pal of his! Send a man home to croak of a cold on the chest—that's one of your tame tricks. And d'you mean to say, sir, that a man that's

up to it wouldn't bag whatever he could lay his hands
on in his 'yporcritical way? What was all that coal
business? Tame citizen dodge; 'yporcrisy—nothing
else. No, no, sir! The thing is to 'xtract it from him
as neatly as possible. That's the job; and it isn't
so simple as it looks. I reckon you have looked at it
all round, sir, before you took up the notion of this
trip."

"No." Mr. Jones was hardly audible, staring far
away from his couch. "I didn't think about it much.
I was bored."

"Ay, that you were—bad. I was feeling pretty
desperate that afternoon when that bearded softy of
a landlord got talking to me about this fellow here.
Quite accidentally, it was. Well, sir, here we are after
a mighty narrow squeak. I feel all limp yet; but never
mind—his swag will pay for the lot!"

"He's all alone here," remarked Mr. Jones in a hollow
murmur.

"Ye-es, in a way. Yes, alone enough. Yes, you
may say he is."

"There's that Chinaman, though."

"Ay, there's the Chink," assented Ricardo rather
absentmindedly.

He was debating in his mind the advisability of
making a clean breast of his knowledge of the girl's existence. Finally he concluded he wouldn't. The enterprise was difficult enough without complicating it with
an upset to the sensibilities of the gentleman with whom
he had the honour of being associated. Let the discovery come of itself, he thought, and then he could
swear that he had known nothing of that offensive
presence.

He did not need to lie. He had only to hold his
tongue.

"Yes," he muttered reflectively, "there's that Chink, certainly."

At bottom, he felt a certain ambiguous respect for his governor's exaggerated dislike of women, as if that horror of feminine presence were a sort of depraved morality; but still morality, since he counted it as an advantage. It prevented many undesirable complications. He did not pretend to understand it. He did not even try to investigate this idiosyncrasy of his chief. All he knew was that he himself was differently inclined, and that it did not make him any happier or safer. He did not know how it would have acted if he had been knocking about the world on his own. Luckily he was a subordinate, not a wage-slave but a follower—which was a restraint. Yes! The other sort of disposition simplified matters in general; it wasn't to be gainsaid. But it was clear that it could also complicate them—as in this most important and, in Ricardo's view, already sufficiently delicate case. And the worst of it was that one could not tell exactly in what precise manner it would act.

It was unnatural, he thought somewhat peevishly. How was one to reckon up the unnatural? There were no rules for that. The faithful henchman of plain Mr. Jones, foreseeing many difficulties of a material order, decided to keep the girl out of the governor's knowledge; out of his sight, too, for as long a time as it could be managed. That, alas, seemed to be at most a matter of a few hours; whereas Ricardo feared that to get the affair properly going would take some days. Once well started, he was not afraid of his gentleman failing him. As is often the case with lawless natures, Ricardo's faith in any given individual was of a simple, unquestioning character. For man must have some support in life.

Cross-legged, his head drooping a little and perfectly still, he might have been meditating in a bonze-like attitude upon the sacred syllable "Om." It was a striking illustration of the untruth of appearances, for his contempt for the world was of a severely practical kind. There was nothing oriental about Ricardo but the amazing quietness of his pose. Mr. Jones was also very quiet. He had let his head sink on the rolled-up rug, and lay stretched out on his side with his back to the light. In that position the shadows gathered in the cavities of his eyes made them look perfectly empty. When he spoke, his ghostly voice had only to travel a few inches straight into Ricardo's left ear.

"Why don't you say something, now that you've got me awake?"

"I wonder if you were sleeping as sound as you are trying to make out, sir," said the unmoved Ricardo.

"I wonder," repeated Mr. Jones. "At any rate, I was resting quietly."

"Come, sir!" Ricardo's whisper was alarmed. "You don't mean to say you're going to be bored?"

"No."

"Quite right!" The secretary was very much relieved. "There's no occasion to be, I can tell you, sir," he whispered earnestly. "Anything but that! If I didn't say anything for a bit, it ain't because there isn't plenty to talk about. Ay, more than enough."

"What's the matter with you?" breathed out his patron. "Are you going to turn pessimist?"

"Me turn? No, sir! I ain't of those that turn. You may call me hard names, if you like, but you know very well that I ain't a croaker." Ricardo changed his tone. "If I said nothing for a while, it was because I was meditating over the Chink, sir."

"You were? Waste of time, my Martin. A Chinaman is unfathomable."

Ricardo admitted that this might be so. Anyhow, a Chink was neither here nor there, as a general thing, unfathomable as he might be; but a Swedish baron wasn't—couldn't be! The woods were full of such barons.

"I don't know that he is so tame," was Mr. Jones's remark, in a sepulchral undertone.

"How do you mean, sir? He ain't a rabbit, of course. You couldn't hypnotise him, as I saw you do to more than one Dago, and other kinds of tame citizens, when it came to the point of holding them down to a game."

"Don't you reckon on that," murmured plain Mr. Jones seriously.

"No, sir, I don't; though you have a wonderful power of the eye. It's a fact."

"I have a wonderful patience," remarked Mr. Jones drily.

A dim smile flitted over the lips of the faithful Ricardo who never raised his head.

"I don't want to try you too much, sir; but this is like no other job we ever turned our minds to."

"Perhaps not. At any rate let us think so."

A weariness with the monotony of life was reflected in the tone of this qualified assent. It jarred on the nerves of the sanguine Ricardo.

"Let us think of the way to go to work," he retorted a little impatiently. "He's a deep one. Just look at the way he treated that chum of his. Did you ever hear of anything so low? And the artfulness of the beast— the dirty, tame artfulness!"

"Don't you start moralising, Martin," said Mr. Jones warningly. "As far as I can make out the story that German hotel-keeper told you, it seems to show a certain amount of character; and independence from common feelings which is not usual. It's very remarkable, if true."

"Ay, ay! Very remarkable. It's mighty low down, all the same," muttered Ricardo obstinately. "I must say I am glad to think he will be paid off for it in a way that'll surprise him!"

The tip of his tongue appeared lively for an instant, as if trying for the taste of that ferocious retribution on his compressed lips. For Ricardo was sincere in his indignation before the elementary principle of loyalty to a chum violated in cold blood, slowly, in a patient duplicity of years. There are standards in villainy as in virtue, and the act as he pictured it to himself acquired an additional horror from the slow pace of that treachery so atrocious and so tame. But he understood too the educated judgment of his governor, a gentleman looking on all this with the privileged detachment of a cultivated mind, of an elevated personality.

"Ay, he's deep—he's artful," he mumbled between his sharp teeth.

"Confound you!" Mr. Jones's calm whisper crept into his ear. "Come to the point."

Obedient, the secretary shook off his thoughtfulness. There was a similarity of mind between these two—one the outcast of his vices, the other inspired by a spirit of scornful defiance, the aggressiveness of a beast of prey looking upon all the tame creatures of the earth as its natural victims. Both were astute enough, however, and both were aware that they had plunged into this adventure without a sufficient scrutiny of detail. The figure of a lonely man far from all assistance had loomed up largely, fascinating and defenceless in the middle of the sea, filling the whole field of their vision. There had not seemed to be any need for thinking. As Schomberg had been saying: "Three to one."

But it did not look so simple now in the face of that solitude which was like an armour for this man. The feeling voiced by the henchman in his own way—"We don't seem much forwarder now we are here"—was acknowledged by the silence of the patron. It was easy enough to rip a fellow up or drill a hole in him, whether he was alone or not, Ricardo reflected in low, confidential tones, but——

"He isn't alone," Mr. Jones said faintly, in his attitude of a man composed for sleep. "Don't forget that Chinaman." Ricardo started slightly.

"Oh, ay—the Chink!"

Ricardo had been on the point of confessing about the girl; but no! He wanted his governor to be unperturbed and steady. Vague thoughts, which he hardly dared to look in the face, were stirring in his brain in connection with that girl. She couldn't be much account, he thought. She could be frightened. And there were also other possibilities. The Chink, however, could be considered openly.

"What I was thinking about it, sir," he went on earnestly, "is this—here we've got a man. He's nothing. If he won't be good, he can be made quiet. That's easy. But then there's his plunder. He doesn't carry it in his pocket."

"I hope not," breathed Mr. Jones.

"Same here. It's too big, we know; but if he were alone, he would not feel worried about it overmuch—I mean the safety of the pieces. He would just put the lot into any box or drawer that was handy."

"Would he?"

"Yes, sir. He would keep it under his eye, as it were. Why not? It is natural. A fellow doesn't put his swag underground, unless there's a very good reason for it."

"A very good reason, eh?"

"Yes, sir. What do you think a fellow is—a mole?"

From his experience, Ricardo declared that man was not a burrowing beast. Even the misers very seldom buried their hoard, unless for exceptional reasons. In the given situation of a man alone on an island, the company of a Chink was a very good reason. Drawers would not be safe, nor boxes, either, from a prying, slant-eyed Chink. No, sir; unless a safe—a proper office safe. But the safe was there in the room.

"Is there a safe in this room? I didn't notice it," whispered Mr. Jones.

That was because the thing was painted white, like the walls of the room; and besides, it was tucked away in the shadows of a corner. Mr. Jones had been too tired to observe anything on his first coming ashore; but Ricardo had very soon spotted the characteristic form. He only wished he could believe that the plunder of treachery, duplicity, and all the moral abominations of Heyst had been there. But no; the blamed thing was open.

"It might have been there at one time or another," he commented gloomily, "but it isn't there now."

"The man did not elect to live in this house," remarked Mr. Jones. "And by the by, what could he have meant by speaking of circumstances which prevented him lodging us in the other bungalow? You remember what he said, Martin? Sounded cryptic."

Martin, who remembered and understood the phrase as directly motived by the existence of the girl, waited a little before saying:

"Some of his artfulness, sir; and not the worst of it either. That manner of his to us, this asking no questions, is some more of his artfulness. A man's bound to be curious, and he is; yet he goes on as if he didn't care. He does care—or else what was he doing up with a cigar in the middle of the night, doing a think? I don't like it!"

"He may be outside, observing the light here, and saying the very same thing to himself of our own wakefulness," gravely suggested Ricardo's governor.

"He may be, sir; but this is too important to be talked over in the dark. And the light is all right. It can be accounted for. There's a light in this bungalow in the middle of the night because—why, because you are not well. Not well, sir—that's what's the matter; and you will have to act up to it."

This consideration had suddenly occurred to the faithful henchman, in the light of a felicitous expedient to keep his governor and the girl apart as long as possible. Mr. Jones received the suggestion without the slightest stir, even in the deep sockets of his eyes, where a steady, faint gleam was the only thing telling of life and attention in his attenuated body. But Ricardo, as soon as he had enunciated his happy thought, perceived in it other possibilities more to the point and of greater practical advantage.

"With your looks, sir, it will be easy enough," he went on evenly, as if no silence had intervened, always respectful, but frank, with perfect simplicity of purpose. "All you've got to do is just to lie down quietly. I noticed him looking sort of surprised at you on the wharf, sir."

At these words, a naïve tribute to the aspect of his physique, even more suggestive of the grave than of the sick-bed, a fold appeared on that side of the governor's face which was exposed to the dim light—a deep, shadowy, semicircular fold from the side of the nose to

bottom of the chin—a silent smile. By a side glance
Ricardo had noted this play of feature. He smiled, too,
appreciative, encouraged.

"And you as hard as nails all the time," he went on.
"Hang me if anybody would believe you aren't sick, if
I were to swear myself black in the face! Give us a day
or two to look into matters and size up that 'yporcrit."

Ricardo's eyes remained fixed on his crossed shins.
The chief, in his lifeless accents, approved.

"Perhaps it would be a good idea."

"The Chink, he's nothing. He can be made quiet
any time."

One of Ricardo's hands, reposing palm upwards on his
folded legs, made a swift thrusting gesture, repeated by
the enormous darting shadow of an arm very low on the
wall. It broke the spell of perfect stillness in the room.
The secretary eyed moodily the wall from which the
shadow had gone. Anybody could be made quiet, he
pointed out. It was not anything that the Chink could
do; no, it was the effect that his company must have
produced on the conduct of the doomed man. A man!
What was a man? A Swedish baron could be ripped up,
or else holed by a shot, as easily as any other creature;
but that was exactly what was to be avoided, till one
knew where he had hidden his plunder.

"I shouldn't think it would be some sort of hole in
his bungalow," argued Ricardo with real anxiety.

No. A house can be burnt—set on fire accidentally,
or on purpose, while a man's sleep. Under the house—
or in some crack, cranny, or crevice? Something told
him it wasn't that. The anguish of mental effort con-
tracted Ricardo's brow. The skin of his head seemed
to move in this travail of vain and tormenting supposi-
tions.

"What did you think a fellow is, sir—a baby?" he

said, in answer to Mr. Jones's objections. "I am trying
to find out what I would do myself. He wouldn't be
likely to be cleverer than I am."

"And what do you know about yourself?"

Mr. Jones seemed to watch his follower's perplexities
with amusement concealed in a death-like composure.

Ricardo disregarded the question. The material
vision of the spoil absorbed all his faculties. A great
vision! He seemed to see it. A few small canvas bags
tied up with thin cord, their distended rotundity showing the inside pressure of the disk-like forms of coins—
gold, solid, heavy, eminently portable. Perhaps steel
cash-boxes with a chased design on the covers; or perhaps a black and brass box with a handle on the top,
and full of goodness knows what. Bank notes? Why
not? The fellow had been going home; so it was surely
something worth going home with.

"And he may have put it anywhere outside—anywhere!" cried Ricardo in a deadened voice. "In the
forest——"

That was it! A temporary darkness replaced the
dim light of the room. The darkness of the forest at
night, and in it the gleam of a lantern, by which a figure
is digging at the foot of a tree-trunk. As likely as not,
another figure holding that lantern—ha, feminine! The
girl!

The prudent Ricardo stifled a picturesque and pro-
fane exclamation, partly joy, partly dismay. Had the
girl been trusted or mistrusted by that man? Whatever
it was, it was bound to be wholly! With women there
could be no half-measures. He could not imagine a
fellow half-trusting a woman in that intimate relation
to himself, and in those particular circumstances of con-
quest and loneliness where no confidences could appear
dangerous since, apparently, there could be no one she

could give him away to. Moreover in nine cases out
of ten, the woman would be trusted. But, trusted or
mistrusted, was her presence a favourable or unfavour-
able condition of the problem? That was the question!

The temptation to consult his chief, to talk over the
weighty fact and get his opinion on it, was great indeed.
Ricardo resisted it; but the agony of his solitary mental
conflict was extremely sharp. A woman in a problem
is an incalculable quantity, even if you have something
to go upon in forming your guess. How much more
so when you haven't even once caught sight of her.

Swift as were his mental processes, he felt that a
longer silence was inadvisable. He hastened to speak:

"And do you see us, sir, you and I, with a couple
of spades having to tackle this whole confounded
island?"

He allowed himself a slight movement of the arm.
The shadow enlarged it into a sweeping gesture.

"This seems rather discouraging, Martin," murmured
the unmoved governor.

"We mustn't be discouraged—that's all," retorted
his henchman. "And after what we had to go through
in that boat too! Why it would be——"

He couldn't find the qualifying words. Very calm,
faithful, and yet astute, he expressed his new-born hopes
darkly.

"Something's sure to turn up to give us a hint; only
this job can't be rushed. You may depend on me to
pick up the least little bit of a hint; but you, sir—you've
got to play him very gently. For the rest you can trust
me."

"Yes; but I ask myself what *you* are trusting
to."

"Our luck," said the faithful Ricardo. "Don't

say a word against that. It might spoil the run of
it."

"You are a superstitious beggar. No, I won't say
anything against it."

"That's right, sir. Don't you even think lightly of
it. Luck's not to be played with."

"Yes, luck's a delicate thing," assented Mr. Jones
in a dreamy whisper.

A short silence ensued, which Ricardo ended in a discreet and tentative voice.

"Talking of luck, I suppose he could be made to take
a hand with you, sir—two-handed picket* or ekarty,*
you being seedy and keeping indoors—just to pass the
time. For all we know, he may be one of them hot
ones once they start——"

"Is it likely?" came coldly from the principal.
"Considering what we know of his history—say with
his partner."

"True, sir. He's a cold-blooded beast; a cold-
blooded, inhuman——"

"And I'll tell you another thing that isn't likely. He
would not be likely to let himself be stripped bare. We
haven't to do with a young fool that can be led on by
chaff or flattery, and in the end simply over-awed. This
is a calculating man."

Ricardo recognised that clearly. What he had in
his mind was something on a small scale, just to keep
the enemy busy while he, Ricardo, had time to nose
around a bit.

"You could even lose a little money to him, sir," he
suggested.

"I could."

Ricardo was thoughtful for a moment.

"He strikes me, too, as the sort of man to start
prancing when one didn't expect it. What do you think,

sir? Is he a man that would prance? That is, if
something startled him. More likely to prance than
to run—what?"

The answer came at once, because Mr. Jones understood the peculiar idiom of his faithful follower.

"Oh, without doubt! Without doubt!"

"It does me good to hear that you think so. He's
a prancing beast, and so we mustn't startle him—not
till I have located the stuff. Afterwards——"

Ricardo paused, sinister in the stillness of his pose.
Suddenly he got up with a swift movement and gazed
down at his chief in moody abstraction. Mr. Jones
did not stir.

"There's one thing that's worrying me," began
Ricardo in a subdued voice.

"Only one?" was the faint comment from the motionless body on the bedstead.

"I mean more than all the others put together."

"That's grave news."

"Ay, grave enough. It's this—how do you feel in yourself, sir? Are you likely to get bored? I know them fits
come on you suddenly; but surely you can tell——"

"Martin, you are an ass."

The moody face of the secretary brightened up.

"Really, sir? Well, I am quite content to be on
these terms—I mean as long as you don't get bored. It
wouldn't do, sir."

For coolness, Ricardo had thrown open his shirt and
rolled up his sleeves. He moved stealthily across the
room, bare-footed, towards the candle, the shadow of
his head and shoulders growing bigger behind him on
the opposite wall, to which the face of plain Mr. Jones
was turned. With a feline movement, Ricardo glanced
over his shoulder at the thin back of the spectre reposing
on the bed, and then blew out the candle.

"In fact, I am rather amused, Martin," Mr. Jones said in the dark.

He heard the sound of a slapped thigh and the jubilant exclamation of his henchman:

"Good! That's the way to talk, sir!"

PART IV

PART IV

I

RICARDO advanced prudently by short darts from one tree-trunk to another, more in the manner of a squirrel than a cat. The sun had risen some time before. Already the sparkle of open sea was encroaching rapidly on the dark, cool, early-morning blue of Diamond Bay; but the deep dusk lingered yet under the mighty pillars of the forest, between which the secretary dodged.

He was watching Number One's bungalow with an animal-like patience, if with a very human complexity of purpose. This was the second morning of such watching. The first one had not been rewarded by success. Well, strictly speaking, there was no hurry.

The sun, swinging above the ridge all at once, inundated with light the space of burnt grass in front of Ricardo and the face of the bungalow, on which his eyes were fixed, leaving only the one dark spot of the doorway. To his right, to his left, and behind him, splashes of gold appeared in the deep shade of the forest, thinning the gloom under the ragged roof of leaves.

This was not a very favourable circumstance for Ricardo's purpose. He did not wish to be detected in his patient occupation. For what he was watching for was a sight of the girl—that girl! Just a glimpse across the burnt patch to see what she was like. He had excellent eyes, and the distance was not so great. He would be able to distinguish her face quite easily if she only came out on the verandah; and she was bound to do that sooner or later. He was confident that he could form some opinion about her—which, he felt, was very necessary, before venturing on some steps to get in touch with her behind that Swedish baron's back. His theoretical view of the girl was such that he was quite prepared, on the strength of that distant examination, to show himself discreetly—perhaps even make a sign. It all depended on his reading of the face. She couldn't be much. He knew that sort!

By protruding his head a little he commanded, through the foliage of a festooning creeper, a view of the three bungalows, irregularly disposed along a flat curve. Over the verandah rail of the farthermost one hung a dark rug of a tartan pattern, amazingly conspicuous. Ricardo could see the very checks. A brisk fire of sticks was burning on the ground in front of the steps, and in the sunlight the thin, fluttering flame had paled almost to invisibility—a mere rosy stir under a faint wreath of smoke. He could see the white bandage on the head of Pedro bending over it, and the wisps of black hair sticking up weirdly. He had wound that bandage himself, after breaking that shaggy and enormous head. The creature balanced it like a load, staggering towards the steps. Ricardo could see a small, long-handled saucepan at the end of a great hairy paw.

Yes, he could see all that there was to be seen, far and near. Excellent eyes! The only thing they could not penetrate was the dark oblong of the doorway on the verandah under the low eaves of the bungalow's roof. And that was vexing. It was an outrage. Ricardo was easily outraged. Surely she would come out presently! Why didn't she? Surely the fellow did not tie her up to the bed-post before leaving the house!

Nothing appeared. Ricardo was as still as the leafy cables of creepers depending in a convenient curtain from the mighty limb sixty feet above his head. His very eyelids were still, and this unblinking watchfulness gave him the dreamy air of a cat posed on a hearth-rug contemplating the fire. Was he dreaming? There, in plain sight, he had before him a white, blouse-like jacket, short blue trousers, a pair of bare yellow calves, a pigtail, long and slender——

"The confounded Chink!" he muttered, astounded.

He was not conscious of having looked away; and yet right there, in the middle of the picture, without having come round the right-hand corner or the left-hand corner of the house, without falling from the sky or surging up from the ground, Wang had become visible, as large as life, and engaged in the young-ladyish occupation of picking flowers. Step by step, stooping repeatedly over the flower-beds at the foot of the verandah, the startlingly materialised Chinaman passed off the scene in a very commonplace manner, by going up the steps and disappearing in the darkness of the doorway.

Only then the yellow eyes of Martin Ricardo lost their intent fixity. He understood that it was time for him to be moving. That bunch of flowers going into the house in the hand of a Chinaman was for the breakfast-table. What else could it be for?

"I'll give you flowers!" he muttered threateningly. "You wait!"

Another moment, just for a glance towards the Jones bungalow, whence he expected Heyst to issue on his way to that breakfast so offensively decorated, and Ricardo began his retreat. His impulse, his desire, was for a rush into the open, face to face with the ap-pointed victim, for what he called a "ripping up," vis-ualised greedily, and always with the swift preliminary stooping movement on his part—the forerunner of certain death to his adversary. This was his impulse;

and as it was, so to speak, constitutional, it was extremely difficult to resist when his blood was up. What could be more trying than to have to skulk and dodge and restrain oneself, mentally and physically, when one's blood was up? Mr. Secretary Ricardo began his retreat from his post of observation behind a tree opposite Heyst's bungalow, using great care to remain unseen. His proceedings were made easier by the declivity of the ground, which sloped sharply down to the water's edge. There, his feet feeling the warmth of the island's rocky foundation already heated by the sun, through the thin soles of his straw slippers he was, as it were, sunk out of sight of the houses. A short scramble of some twenty feet brought him up again to the upper level, at the place where the jetty had its root in the shore. He leaned his back against one of the lofty uprights which still held up the company's sign-board above the mound of derelict coal. Nobody could have guessed how much his blood was up. To contain himself he folded his arms tightly on his breast.

Ricardo was not used to a prolonged effort of self-control. His craft, his artfulness, felt themselves always at the mercy of his nature, which was truly feral and only held in subjection by the influence of the "governor," the prestige of a gentleman. It had its cunning too, but it was being almost too severely tried since the feral solution of a growl and a spring was forbidden by the problem. Ricardo dared not venture out on the cleared ground. He dared not.

"If I meet the beggar," he thought, "I don't know what I mayn't do. I daren't trust myself."

What exasperated him just now was his inability to understand Heyst. Ricardo was human enough to suffer from the discovery of his limitations. No, he

couldn't size Heyst up. He could kill him with extreme ease—a growl and a spring—but that was forbidden! However, he could not remain indefinitely
under the funereal blackboard.

"I must make a move," he thought.

He moved on, his head swimming a little with the
repressed desire of violence, and came out openly in
front of the bungalows, as if he had just been down to
the jetty to look at the boat. The sunshine enveloped
him, very brilliant, very still, very hot. The three
buildings faced him. The one with the rug on the
balustrade was the most distant; next to it was the
empty bungalow; the nearest, with the flower-beds
at the foot of its verandah, contained that bothersome
girl, who had managed so provokingly to keep herself
invisible. That was why Ricardo's eyes lingered on
that building. The girl would surely be easier to
"size up" than Heyst. A sight of her, a mere glimpse,
would have been something to go by, a step nearer to
the goal—the first real move, in fact. Ricardo saw
no other move. And any time she might appear on
that verandah!

She did not appear; but, like a concealed magnet, she
exercised her attraction. As he went on, he deviated
towards the bungalow. Though his movements were
deliberate, his feral instincts had such sway that if
he had met Heyst walking towards him, he would have
had to satisfy his need of violence. But he saw nobody.
Wang was at the back of the house, keeping the coffee
hot against Number One's return for breakfast. Even
the simian Pedro was out of sight, no doubt crouching
on the doorstep, his red little eyes fastened with animal-
like devotion on Mr. Jones, who was in discourse with
Heyst in the other bungalow—the conversation of an
evil spectre with a disarmed man, watched by an ape.

His will having very little to do with it, Ricardo, darting swift glances in all directions, found himself at the steps of the Heyst bungalow. Once there, falling under an uncontrollable force of attraction, he mounted them with a savage and stealthy action of his limbs, and paused for a moment under the eaves to listen to the silence. Presently he advanced over the threshold one leg—it seemed to stretch itself, like a limb of india-rubber—planted his foot within, brought up the other swiftly, and stood inside the room, turning his head from side to side. To his eyes, brought in there from the dazzling sunshine, all was gloom for a moment. His pupils, like a cat's, dilating swiftly, he distinguished an enormous quantity of books. He was amazed; and he was put off, too. He was vexed in his astonishment. He had meant to note the aspect and nature of things, and hoped to draw some useful inference, some hint as to the man. But what guess could one make out of a multitude of books? He didn't know what to think; and he formulated his bewilderment in the mental exclamation:

"What the devil has this fellow been trying to set up here—a school?"

He gave a prolonged stare to the portrait of Heyst's father, that severe profile ignoring the vanities of this earth. His eyes gleamed sideways at the heavy silver candlesticks—signs of opulence. He prowled as a stray cat entering a strange place might have done; for if Ricardo had not Wang's miraculous gift of materialising and vanishing, rather than coming and going, he could be nearly as noiseless in his less elusive movements. He noted the back door standing just ajar; and all the time his slightly pointed ears, at the utmost stretch of watchfulness, kept in touch with the profound silence outside enveloping the absolute stillness of the house.

He had not been in the room two minutes when it occurred to him that he must be alone in the bungalow. The woman, most likely, had sneaked out, and was walking about somewhere in the grounds at the back. She had been probably ordered to keep out of sight. Why? Because the fellow mistrusted his guests; or was it because he mistrusted *her?*

Ricardo reflected that from a certain point of view it amounted nearly to the same thing. He remembered Schomberg's story. He felt that running away with somebody only to get clear of that beastly, tame, hotel-keeper's attentions, was no proof of hopeless infatuation. She could be got in touch with.

His moustaches stirred. For some time he had been looking at a closed door. He would peep into that other room, and perhaps see something more informing than a confounded lot of books. As he crossed over, he thought recklessly:

"If the beggar comes in suddenly, and starts to prance, I'll rip him up and be done with it!"

He laid his hand on the handle, and felt the door come unlatched. Before he pulled it open, he listened again to the silence. He felt it all about him, complete, without a flaw.

The necessity of prudence had exasperated his self-restraint. A mood of ferocity woke up in him, and, as always at such times, he became physically aware of the sheeted knife strapped to his leg. He pulled at the door with fierce curiosity. It came open without a squeak of hinge, without a rustle, with no sound at all; and he found himself glaring at the opaque surface of some rough blue stuff, like serge. A curtain was fitted inside, heavy enough and long enough not to stir.

A curtain! This unforeseen veil, baffling his curiosity, checked his brusqueness. He did not fling it aside with an impatient movement; he only looked at it closely, as if its texture had to be examined before his hand could touch such stuff. In this interval of hesitation he seemed to detect a flaw in the perfection of the silence, the faintest possible rustle, which his ears caught and instantly, in the effort of conscious listening, lost again. No! Everything was still inside and outside the house, only he had no longer the sense of being alone there.

When he put out his hand towards the motionless folds it was with extreme caution, and merely to push the stuff aside a little, advancing his head at the same time to peep within. A moment of complete immobility ensued. Then, without anything else of him stirring, Ricardo's head shrank back on his shoulders, his arm descended slowly to his side. There was a woman in there. The very woman! Lighted dimly by the reflection of the outer glare, she loomed up strangely big and shadowy at the other end of the long, narrow room. With her back to the door, she was doing her hair with her bare arms uplifted. One of them gleamed pearly white; the other detached its perfect form in black against the unshuttered, uncurtained square window-hole. She was there, her fingers busy with her dark hair, utterly unconscious, exposed and defenceless—and tempting.

Ricardo drew back one foot and pressed his elbows close to his sides; his chest started heaving convulsively as if he were wrestling or running a race; his body began to sway gently back and forth. The self-restraint was at an end: his psychology must have its way. The instinct for the feral spring could no longer be denied. Ravish or kill—it was all one to him, as long as by the act he liberated the suffering soul of savagery repressed for so long. After a quick glance over his shoulder, which hunters of big game tell us no lion or tiger omits to give before charging home, Ricardo charged, head down, straight at the curtain. The stuff, tossed up violently by his rush, settled itself with a slow, floating descent into vertical folds, motionless, without a shudder even, in the still, warm air.

II

THE clock—which once upon a time had measured
the hours of philosophic meditation—could not have
ticked away more than five seconds when Wang
materialised within the living-room. His concern primarily was with the delayed breakfast, but at once his
slanting eyes became immovably fixed upon the unstirring curtain. For it was behind it that he had located
the strange, deadened scuffling sounds which filled the
empty room. The slanting eyes of his race could not
achieve a round, amazed stare; but they remained still,
dead still, and his impassive yellow face grew all at
once careworn and lean with the sudden strain of intense, doubtful, frightened watchfulness. Contrary
impulses swayed his body, rooted to the floor-mats.
He even went so far as to extend his hand towards the
curtain. He could not reach it, and he didn't make the
necessary step forward.

The mysterious struggle was going on with confused
thuds of bare feet, in a mute wrestling match, no human
sound, hiss, groan, murmur, or exclamation coming
through the curtain. A chair fell over, not with a
crash but lightly, as if just grazed, and a faint metallic
ring of the tin bath succeeded. Finally the tense
silence, as of two adversaries locked in a deadly grip,
was ended by the heavy, dull thump of a soft body flung
against the inner partition of planks. It seemed to
shake the whole bungalow. By that time, walking
backward, his eyes, his very throat, strained with
fearful excitement, his extended arm still pointing at

the curtain, Wang had disappeared through the back
door. Once out in the compound, he bolted round the
end of the house. Emerging innocently between the
two bungalows he lingered and lounged in the open,
where anybody issuing from any of the dwellings was
bound to see him—a self-possessed Chinaman idling
there, with nothing but perhaps an unserved breakfast
on his mind.

It was at this time that Wang made up his mind to
give up all connection with Number One, a man not
only disarmed but already half vanquished. Till that
morning he had had doubts as to his course of action, but
this overheard scuffle decided the question. Number
One was a doomed man—one of those beings whom it is
unlucky to help. Even as he walked in the open with a
fine air of unconcern, Wang wondered that no sound of
any sort was to be heard inside the house. For all he
knew, the white woman might have been scuffling
in there with an evil spirit, which had of course killed
her. For nothing visible came out of the house he
watched out of the slanting corner of his eye. The
sunshine and the silence outside the bungalow reigned
undisturbed.

But in the house the silence of the big room would not
have struck an acute ear as perfect. It was troubled by
a stir so faint that it could hardly be called a ghost of
whispering from behind the curtain.

Ricardo, feeling his throat with tender care, breathed
out admiringly:

"You have fingers like steel. Jimminy! You have
muscle like a giant!"

Luckily for Lena, Ricardo's onset had been so sudden
—she was winding her two heavy tresses round her head
—that she had no time to lower her arms. This, which
saved them from being pinned to her sides, gave her a

better chance to resist. His spring had nearly thrown her down. Luckily, again, she was standing so near the wall that, though she was driven against it headlong, yet the shock was not heavy enough to knock all the breath out of her body. On the contrary, it helped her first instinctive attempt to drive her assailant backward.

After the first gasp of a surprise that was really too overpowering for a cry, she was never in doubt of the nature of the danger. She defended herself in the full, clear knowledge of it, from the force of instinct which is the true source of every great display of energy, and with a determination which could hardly have been expected from a girl who, cornered in a dim corridor by the red-faced, stammering Schomberg, had trembled with shame, disgust, and fear; had drooped, terrified, before mere words spluttered out odiously by a man who had never in his life laid his big paw on her.

This new enemy's attack was simple, straightforward violence. It was not the slimy, underhand plotting to deliver her up like a slave, which had sickened her heart and had made her feel in her loneliness that her oppressors were too many for her. She was no longer alone in the world now. She resisted without a moment of faltering, because she was no longer deprived of moral support; because she was a human being who counted; because she was no longer defending herself for herself alone; because of the faith that had been born in her—the faith in the man of her destiny, and perhaps in the Heaven which had sent him so wonderfully to cross her path.

She had defended herself principally by maintaining a desperate, murderous clutch on Ricardo's windpipe, till she felt a sudden relaxation of the terrific hug in which he stupidly and ineffectually persisted to hold her. Then with a supreme effort of her arms and of her suddenly raised knee, she sent him flying against the partition. The cedar-wood chest stood in the way, and Ricardo, with a thump which boomed hollow through the whole bungalow, fell on it in a sitting posture, half strangled, and exhausted not so much by the efforts as by the emotions of the struggle.

With the recoil of her exerted strength, she too reeled, staggered back, and sat on the edge of the bed. Out of breath, but calm and unabashed, she busied herself in readjusting under her arms the brown and yellow figured Celebes sarong, the tuck of which had come undone during the fight. Then, folding her bare arms tightly on her breast, she leaned forward on her crossed legs, determined and without fear.

Ricardo, leaning forward too, his nervous force gone, crestfallen like a beast of prey that has missed its spring, met her big grey eyes looking at him—wide open, observing, mysterious—from under the dark arches of her courageous eyebrows. Their faces were not a foot apart. He ceased feeling about his aching throat and dropped the palms of his hands heavily on his knees. He was not looking at her bare shoulders, at her strong arms; he was looking down at the floor. He had lost one of his straw slippers. A chair with a white dress on it had been overturned. These, with splashes of water on the floor out of a brusquely misplaced sponge-bath, were the only traces of the struggle.

Ricardo swallowed twice consciously, as if to make sure of his throat, before he spoke again:

"All right. I never meant to hurt you—though I am no joker when it comes to it."

He pulled up the leg of his pyjamas to exhibit the strapped knife. She glanced at it without moving her head, and murmured, with scornful bitterness:

"Ah, yes—with that thing stuck in my side. In no other way."

He shook his head with a shamefaced smile.

"Listen! I am quiet now. Straight—I am. I don't need to explain why—you know how it is. And I can see, now, this wasn't the way with you."

She made no sound. Her still, upward gaze had a patient mournfulness which troubled him like a suggestion of an inconceivable depth. He added doubtfully:

"You are not going to make a noise about this silly try of mine?"

She moved her head the least bit.

"Jee-miny! You are a wonder," he murmured earnestly, relieved more than she could have guessed.

Of course, if she had attempted to run out, he would have stuck the knife between her shoulders, to stop her screaming; but all the fat would have been in the fire, the business utterly spoiled, and the rage of the governor—especially when he learned the cause—boundless. A woman that does not make a noise after an attempt of that kind has tacitly condoned the offence. Ricardo had no small vanities. But clearly, if she would pass it over like this, then he could not be so utterly repugnant to her. He felt flattered. And she didn't seem afraid of him either. He already felt almost tender towards the girl—that plucky, fine girl who had not tried to run screaming from him.

"We shall be friends yet. I don't give you up. Don't think it. Friends as friends can be!" he whispered confidently. "Jee-miny! You aren't a tame one. Neither am I. You will find that out before long."

He could not know that if she had not run out, it was because that morning, under the stress of growing uneasiness at the presence of the incomprehensible visi-

tors, Heyst had confessed to her that it was his revolver
he had been looking for in the night; that it was gone;
that he was a disarmed, defenceless man. She had
hardly comprehended the meaning of his confession.
Now she understood better what it meant. The
effort of her self-control, her stillness, impressed Ricardo.
Suddenly she spoke:

"What are you after?"

He did not raise his eyes. His hands reposing on
his knees, his drooping head, something reflective in his
pose, suggested the weariness of a simple soul, the
fatigue of a mental rather than physical contest. He
answered the direct question by a direct statement, as if
he were too tired to dissemble:

"After the swag."

The word was strange to her. The veiled ardour of
her grey gaze from under the dark eyebrows never left
Ricardo's face.

"A swag?" she murmured quietly. "What's that?"

"Why, swag, plunder—what your gentleman has
been pinching right and left for years—the pieces.
Don't you know? This!"

Without looking up, he made the motion of counting
money into the palm of his hand. She lowered her eyes
slightly to observe this bit of pantomime, but returned
them to his face at once. Then, in a mere breath:

"How do you know anything about him?" she asked,
concealing her puzzled alarm. "What has it got to do
with you?"

"Everything," was Ricardo's concise answer, in a
low, emphatic whisper. He reflected that this girl was
really his best hope. Out of the unfaded impression
of past violence there was growing the sort of sentiment
which prevents a man from being indifferent to a woman
he has once held in his arms—if even against her will—

and still more so if she has pardoned the outrage. It
becomes then a sort of bond. He felt positively the
need to confide in her—a subtle trait of masculinity,
this, almost physical, need of trust which can exist
side by side with the most brutal readiness of suspicion.

"It's a game of grab—see?" he went on, with a new
inflection of intimacy in his murmur. He was looking
straight at her now. "That fat, tame slug of a gin-
slinger; Schomberg, put us up to it."

So strong is the impression of helpless and persecuted
misery, that the girl who had fought down a savage
assault without faltering could not completely repress a
shudder at the mere sound of the abhorred name.

Ricardo became more rapid and confidential:

"He wants to pay him off—pay both of you, at that; so
he told me. He was hot after you. He would have given
all he had into those hands of yours that have nearly
strangled me. But you couldn't, eh? Nohow—what?"
He paused. "So, rather than—you followed a gentleman?"

He noticed a slight movement of her head and spoke
quickly.

"Same here—rather than be a wage-slave. Only
these foreigners aren't to be trusted. You're too good
for him. A man that will rob his best chum!" She
raised her head. He went on, well pleased with his
progress, whispering hurriedly: "Yes. I know all about
him. So you may guess how he's likely to treat a
woman after a bit!"

He did not know that he was striking terror into her
breast now. Still the grey eyes remained fixed on him
unmovably watchful, as if sleepy, under the white forehead. She was beginning to understand. His words
conveyed a definite, dreadful meaning to her mind,

which he proceeded to enlighten further in a convinced murmur.

"You and I are made to understand each other. Born alike, bred alike, I guess. You are not tame. Same here! You have been chucked out into this rotten world of 'yporcrits. Same here!"

Her stillness, her appalled stillness, wore to him an air of fascinated attention. He asked abruptly:

"Where is it?"

She made an effort to breathe out:

"Where's what?"

His tone expressed excited secrecy.

"The swag—plunder—pieces. It's a game of grab. We must have it; but it isn't easy, and so you will have to lend a hand. Come! Is it kept in the house?"

As often with women, her wits were sharpened by the very terror of the glimpsed menace. She shook her head negatively.

"No."

"Sure?"

"Sure," she said.

"Ay! Thought so. Does your gentleman trust you?"

Again she shook her head.

"Blamed 'yporcrit," he said feelingly, and then reflected: "He's one of the tame ones, ain't he?"

"You had better find out for yourself," she said.

"You trust me. I don't want to die before you and I have made friends." This was said with a strange air of feline gallantry. Then, tentatively: "But he could be brought to trust you, couldn't he?"

"Trust me?" she said, in a tone which bordered on despair, but which he mistook for derision.

"Stand in with us," he urged. "Give the chuck to all this blamed 'yporcrisy. Perhaps, without being trusted, you have managed to find out something already, eh?"

"Perhaps I have," she uttered with lips that seemed to her to be freezing fast.

Ricardo now looked at her calm face with something like respect. He was even a little awed by her stillness, by her economy of words. Womanlike, she felt the effect she had produced, the effect of knowing much and of keeping all her knowledge in reserve. So far, somehow, this had come about of itself. Thus encouraged, directed in the way of duplicity, the refuge of the weak, she made a heroically conscious effort and forced her stiff, cold lips into a smile.

Duplicity—the refuge of the weak and the cowardly, but of the disarmed, too! Nothing stood between the enchanted dream of her existence and a cruel catastrophe but her duplicity. It seemed to her that the man sitting there before her was an unavoidable presence, which had attended all her life. He was the embodied evil of the world. She was not ashamed of her duplicity. With a woman's frank courage, as soon as she saw that opening she threw herself into it without reserve, with only one doubt—that of her own strength. She was appalled by the situation; but already all her aroused femininity, understanding that whether Heyst loved her or not she loved him, and feeling that she had brought this on his head, faced the danger with a passionate desire to defend her own.

III

To Ricardo the girl had been so unforeseen that he was unable to bring upon her the light of his critical faculties. Her smile appeared to him full of promise. He had not expected her to be what she was. Who, from the talk he had heard, could expect to meet a girl like this? She was a blooming miracle, he said to himself, familiarly, yet with a tinge of respect. She was no meat for the likes of that tame, respectable gin-slinger. Ricardo grew hot with indignation. Her courage, her physical strength, demonstrated at the cost of his discomfiture, commanded his sympathy. He felt himself drawn to her by the proofs of her amazing spirit. Such a girl! She had a strong soul; and her reflective disposition to throw over her connection proved that she was no hypocrite.

"Is your gentleman a good shot?" he said, looking down on the floor again, as if indifferent.

She hardly understood the phrase; but in its form it suggested some accomplishment. It was safe to whisper an affirmative.

"Yes."

"Mine, too—and better than good," Ricardo murmured, and then, in a confidential burst: "I am not so good at it, but I carry a pretty deadly thing about me, all the same!"

He tapped his leg. She was past the stage of shudders now. Stiff all over, unable even to move her eyes, she felt an awful mental tension which was like blank forgetfulness. Ricardo tried to influence her in his own way.

"And my gentleman is not the sort that would drop me. He ain't no foreigner; whereas you, with your baron, you don't know what's before you—or, rather, being a woman, you know only too well. Much better not to wait for the chuck. Pile in with us and get your share—of the plunder, I mean. You have some notion about it already."

She felt that if she as much as hinted by word or sign that there was no such thing on the island, Heyst's life wouldn't be worth half an hour's purchase; but all power of combining words had vanished in the tension of her mind. Words themselves were too difficult to think of—all except the word "yes." The saving word! She whispered it with not a feature of her face moving. To Ricardo the faint and concise sound proved a cool, reserved assent, more worth having from that amazing mistress of herself than a thousand words from any other woman. He thought with exultation that he had come upon one in a million—in ten millions! His whisper became frankly entreating.

"That's good! Now all you've got to do is to make sure where he keeps his swag. Only do be quick about it! I can't stand much longer this crawling-on-the-stomach business so as not to scare your gentleman. What do you think a fellow is—a reptile?"

She stared without seeing any one, as a person in the night sits staring and listening to deadly sounds, to evil incantations. And always in her head there was that tension of the mind trying to get hold of something, of a saving idea which seemed to be so near and could not be captured. Suddenly she seized it. Yes—she had to get that man out of the house. At that very moment, raised outside, not very near, but heard distinctly, Heyst's voice uttered the words:

"Have you been looking out for me, Wang?"

It was for her like a flash of lightning framed in the darkness which had beset her on all sides, showing a deadly precipice right under her feet. With a convulsive movement she sat up straight, but had no power to rise. Ricardo, on the contrary, was on his feet on the instant, as noiseless as a cat. His yellow eyes gleamed, gliding here and there; but he, too, seemed unable to make another movement. Only his moustaches stirred visibly, like the feelers of some animal.

Wang's answer, "*Ya tuan,*"*was heard by the two in the room, but more faintly. Then Heyst again:

"All right! You may bring the coffee in. Mem Putih* out in the room yet?"

To this question Wang made no answer.

Ricardo's and the girl's eyes met, utterly without expression, all their faculties being absorbed in listening for the first sound of Heyst's footsteps, for any sound outside which would mean that Ricardo's retreat was cut off. Both understood perfectly well that Wang must have gone round the house, and that he was now at the back, making it impossible for Ricardo to slip out unseen that way before Heyst came in at the front.

A darkling shade settled on the face of the devoted secretary. Here was the business utterly spoiled! It was the gloom of anger, and even of apprehension. He would perhaps have made a dash for it through the back door, if Heyst had not been heard ascending the front steps. He climbed them slowly, very slowly, like a man who is discouraged or weary—or simply thoughtful; and Ricardo had a mental vision of his face, with its martial moustaches, the lofty forehead, the impassive features, and the quiet, meditative eyes. Trapped! Confound it! After all, perhaps the governor was right. Women had to be shunned. Fooling with this one had apparently ruined the whole business.

For, trapped as he was, he might just as well kill, since, anyhow, to be seen was to be unmasked. But he was too fair-minded to be angry with the girl.

Heyst had paused on the verandah, or in the very doorway.

"I shall be shot down like a dog if I ain't quick," Ricardo muttered excitedly to the girl.

He stooped to get hold of his knife; and the next moment would have hurled himself out through the curtain, nearly as prompt and fully as deadly to Heyst as an unexpected thunderbolt. The feel more than the strength of the girl's hand, clutching at his shoulder, checked him. He swung round, crouching with a yellow upward glare. Ah! Was she turning against him?

He would have stuck his knife into the hollow of her bare throat if he had not seen her other hand pointing to the window. It was a long opening, high up, close under the ceiling almost, with a single pivoting shutter.

While he was still looking at it, she moved noiselessly away, picked up the overturned chair, and placed it under the wall. Then she looked round; but he didn't need to be beckoned to. In two long, tiptoeing strides he was at her side.

"Be quick!" she gasped.

He seized her hand and wrung it with all the force of his dumb gratitude, as a man does to a chum when there is no time for words. Then he mounted the chair. Ricardo was short—too short to get over without a noisy scramble. He hesitated an instant; she, watchful, bore rigidly on the seat with her beautiful bare arms, while, light and sure, he used the back of the chair as a ladder. The masses of her brown hair fell all about her face.

Footsteps resounded in the next room, and Heyst's voice, not very loud, called her by name.

"Lena!"

"Yes! In a minute," she answered with a particular intonation which she knew would prevent Heyst from coming in at once.

When she looked up, Ricardo had vanished, letting himself down outside so lightly that she had not heard the slightest noise. She stood up then, bewildered, frightened, as if awakened from a drugged sleep, with heavy, downcast, unseeing eyes, her fortitude tired out, her imagination as if dead within her and unable to keep her fear alive.

Heyst moved about aimlessly in the other room. This sound roused her exhausted wits. At once she began to think, hear, see; and what she saw—or rather recognized, for her eyes had been resting on it all the time— was Ricardo's straw slipper, lost in the scuffle, lying near the bath. She had just time to step forward and plant her foot on it when the curtain shook, and, pushed aside, disclosed Heyst in the doorway.

Out of the appeased enchantment of the senses she had found with him, like a sort of bewitched state, his danger brought a sensation of warmth to her breast. She felt something stir in there, something profound, like a new sort of life.

The room was in partial darkness, Ricardo having accidentally swung the pivoted shutter as he went out of the window. Heyst peered from the doorway.

"Why, you haven't done your hair yet," he said.

"I won't stop to do it now. I sha'n't be long," she replied steadily, and remained still, feeling Ricardo's slipper under the sole of her foot.

Heyst, with a movement of retreat, let the curtain drop slowly. On the instant she stooped for the slipper, and, with it in her hand, spun round wildly, looking for some hiding-place; but there was no such spot in the

bare room. The chest, the leather trunk, a dress or
two of hers hanging on pegs—there was no place where
the merest hazard might not guide Heyst's hand at any
moment. Her wildly roaming eyes were caught by the
half-closed window. She ran to it, and by raising herself on her toes was able to reach the shutter with her
fingertips. She pushed it square, stole back to the
middle of the room, and, turning about, swung her arm,
regulating the force of the throw so as not to let the
slipper fly too far out and hit the edge of the over-
hanging eaves. It was a task of the nicest judgment
for the muscles of those round arms, still quivering
from the deadly wrestle with a man, for that brain,
tense with the excitement of the situation and for the
unstrung nerves flickering darkness before her eyes.
At last the slipper left her hand. As soon as it passed
the opening, it was out of her sight. She listened.
She did not hear it strike anything; it just vanished,
as if it had wings to fly on through the air. Not a
sound! It had gone clear.

Her valiant arms hanging close against her side, she
stood as if turned into stone. A faint whistle reached
her ears. The forgetful Ricardo, becoming very much
aware of his loss, had been hanging about in great
anxiety, which was relieved by the appearance of the
slipper flying from under the eaves; and now, thoughtfully, he had ventured a whistle to put her mind at ease.

Suddenly the girl reeled forward. She saved herself
from a fall only by embracing with both arms one of
the tall, roughly carved posts holding the mosquito net
above the bed. For a long time she clung to it, with
her forehead leaning against the wood. One side of her
loosened sarong had slipped down as low as her hip. The
long brown tresses of her hair fell in lank wisps, as if
wet, almost black against her white body. Her un-

covered flank, damp with the sweat of anguish and
fatigue, gleamed coldly with the immobility of polished
marble in the hot, diffused light falling through the
window above her head—a dim reflection of the consuming, passionate blaze of sunshine outside, all aquiver
with the effort to set the earth on fire, to burn it to ashes.

IV

HEYST, seated at the table with his chin on his breast, raised his head at the faint rustle of Lena's dress. He was startled by the dead pallor of her cheeks, by something lifeless in her eyes, which looked at him strangely, without recognition. But to his anxious inquiries she answered reassuringly that there was nothing the matter with her, really. She had felt giddy on rising. She had even had a moment of faintness, after her bath. She had to sit down to wait for it to pass. This had made her late dressing.

"I didn't try to do my hair. I didn't want to keep you waiting any longer," she said.

He was unwilling to press her with questions about her health, since she seemed to make light of this indisposition. She had not done her hair, but she had brushed it, and had tied it with a ribbon behind. With her forehead uncovered, she looked very young, almost a child, a careworn child; a child with something on its mind.

What surprised Heyst was the non-appearance of Wang. The Chinaman had always materialised at the precise moment of his service, neither too soon nor too late. This time the usual miracle failed. What was the meaning of this?

Heyst raised his voice—a thing he disliked doing. It was promptly answered from the compound:

"*Ada tuan!*"*

Lena, leaning on her elbow, with her eyes on her plate, did not seem to hear anything. When Wang entered

with a tray, his narrow eyes, tilted inward by the prominence of salient cheekbones, kept her under stealthy
observation all the time. Neither the one nor the other
of that white couple paid the slightest attention to him
and he withdrew without having heard them exchange
a single word. He squatted on his heels on the back
verandah. His Chinaman's mind, very clear but not
far-reaching, was made up according to the plain reason
of things, such as it appeared to him in the light of his
simple feeling for self-preservation, untrammelled by
any notions of romantic honour or tender conscience.
His yellow hands, lightly clasped, hung idly between his
knees. The graves of Wang's ancestors were far away,
his parents were dead, his elder brother was a soldier
in the yamen*of some Mandarin away in Formosa.* No
one near by had a claim on his veneration or his obedience. He had been for years a labouring, restless
vagabond. His only tie in the world was the Alfuro
woman, in exchange for whom he had given away some
considerable part of his hard-earned substance; and his
duty, in reason, could be to no one but himself.

The scuffle behind the curtain was a thing of bad
augury for that Number One for whom the Chinaman
had neither love nor dislike. He had been awed enough
by that development to hang back with the coffee-pot
till at last the white man was induced to call him in.
Wang went in with curiosity. Certainly, the white
woman looked as if she had been wrestling with a spirit,
which had managed to tear half her blood out of her
before letting her go. As to the man, Wang had long
looked upon him as being in some sort bewitched; and
now he was doomed. He heard their voices in the room.
Heyst was urging the girl to go and lie down again. He
was extremely concerned. She had eaten nothing.

"The best thing for you. You really must!"

She sat listless, shaking her head from time to time
negatively, as if nothing could be any good. But he
insisted; she saw the beginning of wonder in his eyes,
and suddenly gave way.

"Perhaps I had better."

She did not want to arouse his wonder, which would
lead him straight to suspicion. He must not suspect!

Already, with the consciousness of her love for this
man, of that something rapturous and profound going
beyond the mere embrace, there was born in her a
woman's innate mistrust of masculinity, of that seductive strength allied to an absurd, delicate shrinking
from the recognition of the naked necessity of facts,
which never yet frightened a woman worthy of the
name. She had no plan; but her mind, quieted down
somewhat by the very effort to preserve outward composure for his sake, perceived that her behaviour had
secured, at any rate, a short period of safety. Perhaps
because of the similarity of their miserable origin in
the dregs of mankind, she had understood Ricardo
perfectly. He would keep quiet for a time now. In
this momentarily soothing certitude her bodily fatigue
asserted itself, the more overpoweringly since its cause
was not so much the demand on her strength as the
awful suddenness of the stress she had had to meet.
She would have tried to overcome it from the mere instinct of resistance, if it had not been for Heyst's alter-
nate pleadings and commands. Before this eminently
masculine fussing she felt the woman's need to give way,
the sweetness of surrender.

"I will do anything you like," she said.

Getting up, she was surprised by a wave of languid
weakness that came over her, embracing and enveloping
her like warm water, with a noise in her ears as of a
breaking sea.

"You must help me along," she added quickly.

While he put his arm round her waist—not by any means an uncommon thing for him to do—she found a special satisfaction in the feeling of being thus sustained. She abandoned all her weight to that encircling and protecting pressure, while a thrill went through her at the sudden thought that it was she who would have to protect him, to be the defender of a man who was strong enough to lift her bodily, as he was doing even then in his two arms. For Heyst had done this as soon as they had crept through the doorway of the room. He thought it was quicker and simpler to carry her the last step or two. He had grown really too anxious to be aware of the effort. He lifted her high and deposited her on the bed, as one lays a child on its side in a cot. Then he sat down on the edge, masking his concern with a smile which obtained no response from the dreamy immobility of her eyes. But she sought his hand, seized it eagerly; and while she was pressing it with all the force of which she was capable, the sleep she needed overtook her suddenly, overwhelmingly, as it overtakes a child in a cot, with her lips parted for a safe, endearing word which she had thought of but had no time to utter.

The usual flaming silence brooded over Samburan.

"What in the world is this new mystery?" murmured Heyst to himself, contemplating her deep slumber.

It was so deep, this enchanted sleep, that when some time afterward he gently tried to open her fingers and free his hand, he succeeded without provoking the slightest stir.

"There is some very simple explanation, no doubt," he thought, as he stole out into the living-room.

Absent-mindedly he pulled a book out of the top shelf, and sat down with it; but even after he had opened it on his knee, and had been staring at the pages for a time, he had not the slightest idea of what it was about. He stared and stared at the crowded, parallel lines. It was only when, raising his eyes for no particular reason, he saw Wang standing motionless on the other side of the table, that he regained complete control of his faculties.

"Oh, yes," he said, as if suddenly reminded of a forgotten appointment of a not particularly welcome sort.

He waited a little, and then, with reluctant curiosity, forced himself to ask the silent Wang what he had to say. He had some idea that the matter of the vanished revolver would come up at last; but the guttural sounds which proceeded from the Chinaman did not refer to that delicate subject. His speech was concerned with cups, saucers, plates, forks, and knives. All these things had been put away in the cupboards on the back verandah, where they belonged, perfectly clean, "all plopel." Heyst wondered at the scrupulosity of a man who was about to abandon him; for he was not surprised to hear Wang conclude the account of his stewardship with the words:

"Me go now."

"Oh! You go now?" said Heyst, leaning back, his book on his knees.

"Yes. Me no likee. One man, two man, thlee man—no can do! Me go now."

"What's frightening you away like this?" asked Heyst, while through his mind flashed the hope that something enlightening might come from that being so unlike himself, taking contact with the world with a simplicity and directness of which his own mind was not capable. "Why?" he went on. "You are used to white men. You know them well."

"Yes. Me savee them," assented Wang inscrutably. "Me savee plenty."

All that he really knew was his own mind. He had made it up to withdraw himself and the Alfuro woman from the uncertainties of the relations which were going to establish themselves between those white men. It was Pedro who had been the first cause of Wang's suspicion and fear. The Chinaman had seen wild men. He had penetrated, in the train of a Chinese pedlar, up one or two of the Bornean rivers into the country of the Dyaks.* He had also been in the interior of Mindanao,* where there are people who live in trees*— savages, no better than animals; but a hairy brute like Pedro, with his great fangs and ferocious growls, was altogether beyond his conception of anything that could be looked upon as human. The strong impression made on him by Pedro was the prime inducement which had led Wang to purloin the revolver. Reflection on the general situation, and on the insecurity of Number One, came later, after he had obtained possession of the revolver and of the box of cartridges out of the table drawer in the living-room.

"Oh, you savee plenty about white men," Heyst went on in a slightly bantering tone, after a moment of silent reflection in which he had confessed to himself that the recovery of the revolver was not to be thought of, either by persuasion or by some more forcible means. "You speak in that fashion, but you are frightened of those white men over there!"

"Me no flightened," protested Wang raucously, throwing up his head—which gave to his throat a more strained, anxious appearance than ever. "Me no likee," he added in a quieter tone. "Me velly sick."

He put his hand over the region under the breast-bone.

"That," said Heyst, serenely positive, "belong one piecee lie. That isn't proper man-talk at all. And after stealing my revolver, too!"

He had suddenly decided to speak about it, because this frankness could not make the situation much worse than it was. He did not suppose for a moment that Wang had the revolver anywhere about his person; and after having thought the matter over, he had arrived at the conclusion that the Chinaman never meant to use the weapon against him. After a slight start, because the direct charge had taken him unawares, Wang tore open the front of his jacket with a convulsive show of indignation.

"No hab got. Look see!" he mouthed in pretended anger.

He slapped his bare chest violently; he uncovered his very ribs, all astir with the panting of outraged virtue; his smooth stomach heaved with indignation. He started his wide blue breeches flapping about his yellow calves. Heyst watched him quietly.

"I never said you had it on you," he observed, without raising his voice; "but the revolver is gone from where I kept it."

"Me no savee levolvel," Wang said obstinately.

The book lying open on Heyst's knee slipped suddenly and he made a sharp movement to catch it up. Wang was unable to see the reason of this because of the table, and leaped away from what seemed to him a threatening symptom. When Heyst looked up, the Chinaman was already at the door facing the room, not frightened, but alert.

"What's the matter?" asked Heyst.

Wang nodded his shaven head significantly at the curtain closing the doorway of the bedroom.

"Me no likee," he repeated.

"What the devil do you mean?" Heyst was genuinely amazed. "Don't like what?"

Wang pointed a long, lemon-coloured finger at the motionless folds.

"Two," he said.

"Two what? I don't understand."

"Suppose you savee, you no like that fashion. Me savee plenty. Me go now."

Heyst had risen from his chair, but Wang kept his ground in the doorway for a little while longer. His almond-shaped eyes imparted to his face an expression of soft and sentimental melancholy. The muscles of his throat moved visibly while he uttered a distinct and guttural "Good-bye," and vanished from Number One's sight.

The Chinaman's departure altered the situation. Heyst reflected on what would be best to do in view of that fact. For a long time he hesitated; then, shrugging his shoulders wearily, he walked out on the verandah, down the steps, and continued at a steady gait, with a thoughtful mien, in the direction of his guests' bungalow. He wanted to make an important communication to them, and he had no other object—least of all to give them the shock of a surprise call. Nevertheless, their brutish henchman not being on watch, it was Heyst's fate to startle Mr. Jones and his secretary by his sudden appearance in the doorway. Their conversation must have been very interesting to prevent them from hearing the visitor's approach. In the dim room—the shutters were kept constantly closed against the heat—Heyst saw them start apart. It was Mr. Jones who spoke!

"Ah, here you are again! Come in, come in!"

Heyst, taking his hat off in the doorway, entered the room.

V

Waking up suddenly, Lena looked, without raising her head from the pillow, at the room in which she was alone. She got up quickly, as if to counteract the awful sinking of her heart by the vigorous use of her limbs. But this sinking was only momentary. Mistress of herself from pride, from love, from necessity, and also because of a woman's vanity in self-sacrifice, she met Heyst, returning from the strangers' bungalow, with a clear glance and a smile.

The smile he managed to answer; but, noticing that he avoided her eyes, she composed her lips and lowered her gaze. For the same reason she hastened to speak to him in a tone of indifference, which she put on without effort, as if she had grown adept in duplicity since sunrise.

"You have been over there again?"

"I have. I thought—but you had better know first that we have lost Wang for good."

She repeated "For good?" as if she had not understood.

"For good or evil—I shouldn't know which if you were to ask me. He has dismissed himself. He's gone."

"You expected him to go, though, didn't you?"

Heyst sat down on the other side of the table.

"Yes. I expected it as soon as I discovered that he had annexed my revolver. He says he hasn't taken it. That's of course. A Chinaman would not see the sense of confessing under any circumstances. To deny

any charge is a principle of right conduct; but he hardly
expected to be believed. He was a little enigmatic at
the last, Lena. He startled me."

Heyst paused. The girl seemed absorbed in her own
thoughts.

"He startled me," repeated Heyst. She noted the
anxiety in his tone, and turned her head slightly to look
at him across the table.

"It must have been something—to startle *you*," she
said. In the depth of her parted lips, like a ripe pome-
granate, there was a gleam of white teeth.

"It was only a single word—and some of his gestures.
He had been making a good deal of noise. I wonder
we didn't wake you up. How soundly you can sleep!
I say, do you feel all right now?"

"As fresh as can be," she said, treating him to another
deep gleam of a smile. "I heard no noise, and I'm
glad of it. The way he talks in his harsh voice frightens
me. I don't like all these foreign people."

"It was just before he went away—bolted out, I
should say. He nodded and pointed at the curtain
of our room. He knew you were there, of course. He
seemed to think—he seemed to try to give me to understand that you were in special—well, danger. You
know how he talks."

She said nothing; she made no sound, only the faint
tinge of colour ebbed out of her cheek.

"Yes," Heyst went on. "He seemed to try to warn
me. That must have been it. Did he imagine I had
forgotten your existence? The only word he said was
'two.' It sounded so, at least. Yes, 'two'—and that
he didn't like it."

"What does that mean?" she whispered.

"We know what the word two means, don't we, Lena?
We are two. Never were such a lonely two out of the

world, my dear! He might have tried to remind me
that he himself has a woman to look after. Why are
you so pale, Lena?"

"Am I pale?" she asked negligently.

"You are." Heyst was really anxious.

"Well, it isn't from fright," she protested truthfully.

Indeed, what she felt was a sort of horror which left
her absolutely in the full possession of all her faculties;
more difficult to bear, perhaps, for that reason, but not
paralysing to her fortitude.

Heyst in his turn smiled at her.

"I really don't know that there is any reason to be
frightened."

"I mean I am not frightened for myself."

"I believe you are very plucky," he said. The colour
had returned to her face. "I," continued Heyst, "am
so rebellious to outward impressions that I can't say
that much about myself. I don't react with sufficient
distinctness." He changed his tone. "You know I
went to see those men first thing this morning."

"I know. Be careful!" she murmured.

"I wonder how one can be careful! I had a long
talk with—but I don't believe you have seen them. One
of them is a fantastically thin, long person, apparently
ailing; I shouldn't wonder if he were really so. He
makes rather a point of it in a mysterious manner. I
imagine he must have suffered from tropical fevers, but
not so much as he tries to make out. He's what people
would call a gentleman. He seemed on the point of
volunteering a tale of his adventures—for which I didn't
ask him—but remarked that it was a long story; some
other time, perhaps.

"'I suppose you would like to know who I am?' he
asked me.

"I told him I would leave it to him, in a tone which,

between gentlemen, could have left no doubt in his mind. He raised himself on his elbow—he was lying down on the camp-bed—and said:

"'I am he who is——'"*

Lena seemed not to be listening; but when Heyst paused, she turned her head quickly to him. He took it for a movement of inquiry, but in this he was wrong. A great vagueness enveloped her impressions, but all her energy was concentrated on the struggle that she wanted to take upon herself, in a great exaltation of love and self-sacrifice, which is woman's sublime faculty; altogether on herself, every bit of it, leaving him nothing, not even the knowledge of what she did, if that were possible. She would have liked to lock him up by some stratagem. Had she known of some means to put him to sleep for days she would have used incantations or philtres without misgivings. He seemed to her too good for such contacts, and not sufficiently equipped. This last feeling had nothing to do with the material fact of the revolver being stolen. She could hardly appreciate that fact at its full value.

Observing her eyes fixed and as if sightless—for the concentration on her purpose took all expression out of them—Heyst imagined it to be the effect of a great mental effort.

"No use asking me what he meant, Lena; I don't know, and I did not ask him. The gentleman, as I have told you before, seems devoted to mystification. I said nothing, and he laid down his head again on the bundle of rugs he uses for a pillow. He affects a state of great weakness, but I suspect that he's perfectly capable of leaping to his feet if he likes. Having been ejected, he said, from his proper social sphere because he had refused to conform to certain usual conventions, he was a rebel now, and was coming and going up and down the earth.* As I really did not want to listen to all this nonsense, I told him that I had heard that sort of story about somebody else before. His grin is really ghastly. He confessed that I was very far from the sort of man he expected to meet. Then he said:

"'As to me, I am no blacker than the gentleman you are thinking of, and I have neither more nor less determination.'"

Heyst looked across the table at Lena. Propped on her elbows, and holding her head in both hands, she moved it a little with an air of understanding.

"Nothing could be plainer, eh?" said Heyst grimly. "Unless, indeed, this is his idea of a pleasant joke; for, when he finished speaking, he burst into a long, loud laugh. I didn't join him!"

"I wish you had," she breathed out.

"I didn't join him. It did not occur to me. I am not much of a diplomatist. It would probably have been wise; for, indeed, I believe he had said more than he meant to say, and was trying to take it back by this affected jocularity. Yet, when one thinks of it, diplomacy without force in the background is but a rotten reed to lean upon. And I don't know whether I could have done it if I had thought of it. I don't know. It would have been against the grain. Could I have done it? I have lived too long within myself, watching the mere shadows and shades of life. To deceive a man on some issue which could be decided quicker by his destruction while one is disarmed, helpless, without even the power to run away—no! *That* seems to me too degrading. And yet I have you here! I have your very existence in my keeping. What do you say, Lena? Would I be capable of throwing you to the lions to save my dignity?"

She got up, walked quickly round the table, posed

herself on his knees lightly, throwing one arm round his neck, and whispered in his ear:

"You may, if you like. And may be that's the only way I would consent to leave you. For something like that. If it were something no bigger than your little finger."

She gave him a light kiss on the lips and was gone before he could detain her. She regained her seat and propped her elbows again on the table. It was hard to believe that she had moved from the spot at all. The fleeting weight of her body on his knees, the hug round his neck, the whisper in his ear, the kiss on his lips, might have been the unsubstantial sensations of a dream invading the reality of waking life; a sort of charming mirage in the barren aridity of his thoughts. He hesitated to speak till she said, business-like:

"Well. And what then?"

Heyst gave a start.

"Oh, yes. I didn't join him. I let him have his laugh out by himself. He was shaking all over, like a merry skeleton, under a cotton sheet he was covered with—I believe in order to conceal the revolver that he had in his right hand. I didn't see it, but I have a distinct impression it was there in his fist. As he had not been looking at me for some time, but staring into a certain part of the room, I turned my head and saw a hairy, wild sort of creature which they take about with them, squatting on its heels in the angle of the walls behind me. He wasn't there when I came in. I didn't like the notion of that watchful monster behind my back. If I had been less at their mercy, I should certainly have changed my position. As things are now, to move would have been a mere weakness. So I remained where I was. The gentleman on the bed said he could assure me of one thing; and that was that his presence here was no more morally reprehensible than mine.

"'We pursue the same ends,' he said, 'only perhaps I pursue them with more openness than you—with more simplicity.'

"That's what he said," Heyst went on, after looking at Lena in a sort of inquiring silence. "I asked him if he knew beforehand that I was living here; but he only gave me a ghastly grin. I didn't press him for an answer, Lena. I thought I had better not."

On her smooth forehead a ray of light always seemed to rest. Her loose hair, parted in the middle, covered the hands sustaining her head. She seemed spellbound by the interest of the narrative. Heyst did not pause long. He managed to continue his relation smoothly enough, beginning afresh with a piece of comment.

"He would have lied impudently—and I detest being told a lie. It makes me uncomfortable. It's pretty clear that I am not fitted for the affairs of the wide world. But I did not want him to think that I accepted his presence too meekly; so I said that his comings or goings on the earth were none of my business, of course, except that I had a natural curiosity to know when he would find it convenient to resume them.

"He asked me to look at the state he was in. Had I been all alone here, as they think I am, I should have laughed at him. But not being alone—I say, Lena, you are sure you haven't shown yourself where you could be seen?"

"Certain," she said promptly.

He looked relieved.

"You understand, Lena, that when I ask you to keep so strictly out of sight, it is because you are not for them to look at—to talk about. My poor Lena! I can't help that feeling. Do you understand it?"

She moved her head slightly in a manner that was neither affirmative nor negative.

"People will have to see me some day," she said.

"I wonder how long it will be possible for you to keep out of sight!" murmured Heyst thoughtfully. He bent over the table. "Let me finish telling you. I asked him pointblank what it was he wanted with me; he appeared extremely unwilling to come to the point. It was not really so pressing as all that, he said. His secretary, who was in fact his partner, was not present, having gone down to the wharf to look at their boat. Finally the fellow proposed that he should put off a certain communication he had to make till the day after to-morrow. I agreed; but I also told him that I was not at all anxious to hear it. I had no conception in what way his affairs could concern me.

"'Ah, Mr. Heyst,' he said, 'you and I have much more in common than you think.'"

Heyst struck the table with his fist unexpectedly.

"It was a jeer; I am sure it was!"

He seemed ashamed of this outburst and smiled faintly into the motionless eyes of the girl.

"What could I have done—even if I had had my pockets full of revolvers?"

She made an appreciative sign.

"Killing's a sin, sure enough," she murmured.

"I went away," Heyst continued. "I left him there, lying on his side with his eyes shut. When I got back here, I found you looking ill. What was it, Lena? You did give me a scare! Then I had the interview with Wang while you rested. You were sleeping quietly. I sat here to consider all these things calmly, to try to penetrate their inner meaning and their outward bearing. It struck me that the two days we have before us have the character of a sort of truce. The more I thought of it, the more I felt that this was tacitly understood between Jones and myself. It was to our advantage, if anything can be of advantage to people caught so completely unawares as we are. Wang was gone. He, at any rate, had declared himself, but as I did not know what he might take it into his head to do, I thought I had better warn these people that I was no longer responsible for the Chinaman. I did not want Mr. Wang making some move which would precipitate the action against us. Do you see my point of view?"

She made a sign that she did. All her soul was wrapped in her passionate determination, in an exalted belief in herself—in the contemplation of her amazing opportunity to win the certitude, the eternity, of that man's love.

"I never saw two men," Heyst was saying, "more affected by a piece of information than Jones and his secretary, who was back in the bungalow by then. They had not heard me come up. I told them I was sorry to intrude.

"'Not at all! Not at all,' said Jones.

"The secretary backed away into a corner and watched me like a wary cat. In fact, they both were visibly on their guard.

"'I am come,' I told them, 'to let you know that my servant has deserted—gone off.'

"At first they looked at each other as if they had not understood what I was saying; but very soon they seemed quite concerned.

"'You mean to say your Chink's cleared out?' said Ricardo, coming forward from his corner. 'Like this—all at once? What did he do it for?'

"I said that a Chinaman had always a simple and precise reason for what he did, but that to get such a reason out of him was not so easy. All he had told me, I said, was that he 'didn't like.'

"They looked extremely disturbed at this. Didn't like what, they wanted to know.

"'The looks of you and your party,' I told Jones.

"'Nonsense!' he cried out; and immediately Ricardo, the short man, struck in.

"'Told you *that?* What did he take you for, sir—an infant? Or do you take us for kids?—meaning no offence. Come, I bet you will tell us next that you've missed something.'

"'I didn't mean to tell you anything of the sort,' I said, 'but as a matter of fact it is so.'

"He slapped his thigh.

"'Thought so. What do you think of this trick, governor?'

"Jones made some sort of sign to him, and then that extraordinary cat-faced associate proposed that he and their servant should come out and help me to catch or kill the Chink.

"My object, I said, was not to get assistance. I did not intend to chase the Chinaman. I had come only to warn them that he was armed, and that he really objected to their presence on the island. I wanted them to understand that I was not responsible for anything that might happen.

"'Do you mean to tell us,' asked Ricardo, 'that there is a crazy Chink with a six-shooter broke loose on this island, and that you don't care?'

"Strangely enough, they did not seem to believe my story. They were exchanging significant looks all the time. Ricardo stole up close to his principal; they had a confabulation together, and then something happened which I did not expect. It's rather awkward, too.

"Since I would not have their assistance to get hold of the Chink and recover my property, the least they could do was to send me their servant. It was Jones who said that, and Ricardo backed up the idea.

"'Yes, yes—let our Pedro cook for all hands in your compound. He isn't so bad as he looks. That's what we will do!'

"He bustled out of the room to the verandah, and let out an air-splitting whistle for their Pedro. Having heard the brute's answering howl, Ricardo ran back into the room.

"'Yes, Mr. Heyst. This will do capitally, Mr. Heyst. You just direct him to do whatever you are accustomed to have done for you in the way of attendance. See?'

"Lena, I confess to you that I was taken completely by surprise. I had not expected anything of the sort. I don't know what I expected. I am so anxious about you that I can't keep away from these infernal scoundrels. And only two months ago I would not have cared. I would have defied their scoundrelism as much as I have scorned all the other intrusions of life. But now I have you! You stole into my life, and——"

Heyst drew a deep breath. The girl gave him a quick, wide-eyed glance.

"Ah! That's what you are thinking of—that you have me!"

It was impossible to read the thoughts veiled by her steady grey eyes, to penetrate the meaning of her silences, her words, and even her embraces. He used to come out of her very arms with the feeling of a baffled man.

"If I haven't you, if you are not here, then where are you?" cried Heyst. "You understand me very well!"

She shook her head a little. Her red lips, at which he

looked now, her lips as fascinating as the voice that
came out of them, uttered the words:

"I hear what you say; but what does it mean?"

"It means that I could lie and perhaps cringe for
your sake."

"No! No! Don't you ever do that," she said in
haste, while her eyes glistened suddenly. "You would
hate me for it afterwards!"

"Hate you?" repeated Heyst, who had recalled his
polite manner. "No! You needn't consider the ex-
tremity of the improbable—as yet. But I will confess
to you that I—how shall I call it?—that I dissembled.
First I dissembled my dismay at the unforeseen result
of my idiotic diplomacy. Do you understand, my
dear girl?"

It was evident that she did not understand the word.
Heyst produced his playful smile, which contrasted
oddly with the worried character of his whole expression.
His temples seemed to have sunk in, his face looked a
little leaner.

"A diplomatic statement, Lena, is a statement of
which everything is true but the sentiment which seems
to prompt it. I have never been diplomatic in my
relation with mankind—not from regard for its feelings,
but from a certain regard for my own. Diplomacy
doesn't go well with consistent contempt. I cared little
for life and still less for death."

"Don't talk like that!"

"I dissembled my extreme longing to take these wandering scoundrels by their throats," he went on. "I
have only two hands—I wish I had a hundred to defend
you—and there were three throats. By that time their
Pedro was in the room too. Had he seen me engaged
with their two throats, he would have been at mine
like a fierce dog, or any other savage and faithful brute.

I had no difficulty in dissembling my longing for the vulgar, stupid, and hopeless argument of fight. I remarked that I really did not want a servant. I couldn't think of depriving them of their man's services; but they would not hear me. They had made up their minds.

"'We shall send him over at once,' Ricardo said, 'to start cooking dinner for everybody. I hope you won't mind me coming to eat it with you in your bungalow; and we will send the governor's dinner over to him here.'

"I could do nothing but hold my tongue or bring on a quarrel—some manifestation of their dark purpose, which we have no means to resist. Of course, you may remain invisible this evening; but with that atrocious brute prowling all the time at the back of the house, how long can your presence be concealed from these men?"

Heyst's distress could be felt in his silence. The girl's head, sustained by her hands buried in the thick masses of her hair, had a perfect immobility.

"You are certain you have not been seen so far?" he asked suddenly.

The motionless head spoke.

"How can I be certain? You told me you wanted me to keep out of the way. I kept out of the way. I didn't ask your reason. I thought you didn't want people to know that you had a girl like me about you."

"What? Ashamed?" cried Heyst.

"It isn't what's right, perhaps—I mean for you— is it?"

Heyst lifted his hands, reproachfully courteous.

"I look upon it as so very much right that I couldn't bear the idea of any other than sympathetic, respectful eyes resting on you. I disliked and mistrusted these fellows from the first. Didn't you understand?"

"Yes; I did keep out of sight," she said.

A silence fell. At last Heyst stirred slightly.

"All this is of very little importance now," he said with a sigh. "This is a question of something infinitely worse than mere looks and thoughts, however base and contemptible. As I have told you, I met Ricardo's suggestions by silence. As I was turning away he said:

"'If you happen to have the key of that storeroom of yours on you, Mr. Heyst, you may just as well let me have it; I will give it to our Pedro.'

"I had it on me, and I tendered it to him without speaking. The hairy creature was at the door by then, and caught the key, which Ricardo threw to him, better than any trained ape could have done. I came away. All the time I had been thinking anxiously of you, whom I had left asleep, alone here, and apparently ill."

Heyst interrupted himself, with a listening turn of his head. He had heard the faint sound of sticks being snapped in the compound. He rose and crossed the room to look out of the back door.

"And here the creature is," he said, returning to the table. "Here he is, already attending to the fire. Oh, my dear Lena!"

She had followed him with her eyes. She watched him go out on the front verandah cautiously. He lowered stealthily a couple of screens that hung between the columns, and remained outside very still, as if interested by something on the open ground. Meantime she had risen in her turn, to take a peep into the compound. Heyst, glancing over his shoulder, saw her returning to her seat. He beckoned to her, and she continued to move, crossing the shady room, pure and bright in her white dress, her hair loose, with some-

thing of a sleep-walker in her unhurried motion, in her
extended hand, in the sightless effect of her grey eyes
luminous in the half light. He had never seen such
an expression in her face before. It had dreaminess
in it, intense attention, and something like sternness.
Arrested in the doorway by Heyst's extended arm, she
seemed to wake up, flushed faintly—and this flush,
passing off, carried away with it the strange transfigur-
ing mood. With a courageous gesture she pushed
back the heavy masses of her hair. The light clung
to her forehead. Her delicate nostrils quivered.
Heyst seized her arm and whispered excitedly:

"Slip out here, quickly! The screens will conceal
you. Only you must mind the stair-space. They are
actually out—I mean the other two. You had better
see them before you——"

She made a barely perceptible movement of recoil,
checked at once, and stood still. Heyst released her
arm.

"Yes, perhaps I had better," she said with unnatural
deliberation, and stepped out on the verandah to stand
close by his side.

Together, one on each side of the screen, they peeped
between the edge of the canvas and the verandah-post
entwined with creepers. A great heat ascended from
the sun-smitten ground, in an ever-rising wave, as if
from some secret store of earth's fiery heart; for the sky
was growing cooler already, and the sun had declined
sufficiently for the shadows of Mr. Jones and his henchman to be projected towards the bungalow side by
side—one infinitely slender, the other short and
broad.

The two visitors stood still and gazed. To keep
up the fiction of his invalidism, Mr. Jones, the gentleman, leaned on the arm of Ricardo, the secretary,

the top of whose hat just came up to his governor's
shoulder.

"Do you see them?" Heyst whispered into the
girl's ear. "Here they are, the envoys of the outer
world.* Here they are before you—evil intelligence,
instinctive savagery, arm in arm. The brute force is
at the back. A trio of fitting envoys perhaps—but
what about the welcome? Suppose I were armed, could
I shoot those two down where they stand? Could I?"

Without moving her head, the girl felt for Heyst's
hand, pressed it, and thereafter did not let it go. He
continued, bitterly playful:

"I don't know. I don't think so. There is a strain
in me which lays me under an insensate obligation to
avoid even the appearance of murder. I have never
pulled a trigger or lifted my hand on a man, even in
self-defence."

The suddenly tightened grip of her hand checked
him.

"They are making a move," she murmured.

"Can they be thinking of coming here?" Heyst
wondered anxiously.

"No, they aren't coming this way," she said; and
there was another pause. "They are going back to
their house," she reported finally.

After watching them a little longer, she let go Heyst's
hand and moved away from the screen. He followed
her into the room.

"You have seen them now," he began. "Think
what it was to me to see them land in the dusk, fantasms
from the sea—apparitions, chimæras!* And they
persist. That's the worst of it—they persist. They
have no right to be—but they are. They ought to
have aroused my fury. But I have refined everything
away by this time—anger, indignation, scorn itself.

Nothing's left but disgust. Since you have told me of that abominable calumny, it has become immense—it extends even to myself." He looked up at her.

"But luckily I have you. And if only Wang had not carried off that miserable revolver—yes, Lena, here we are, we two!"

She put both her hands on his shoulders and looked straight into his eyes. He returned her penetrating gaze. It baffled him. He could not pierce the grey veil of her eyes; but the sadness of her voice thrilled him profoundly.

"You are not reproaching me?" she asked slowly.

"Reproach? What a word between us! It could only be myself—but the mention of Wang has given me an idea. I have been, not exactly cringing, not exactly lying, but still dissembling. You have been hiding yourself, to please me, but still you have been hiding. All this is very dignified. Why shouldn't we try begging now? A noble art! Yes, Lena, we must go out together. I couldn't think of leaving you alone, and I must—yes, I must speak to Wang. We shall go and seek that man, who knows what he wants and how to secure what he wants. We will go at once!"

"Wait till I put my hair up," she agreed instantly, and vanished behind the curtain.

When the curtain had fallen behind her, she turned her head back with an expression of infinite and tender concern for him—for him whom she could never hope to understand, and whom she was afraid she could never satisfy; as if her passion were of a hopelessly lower quality, unable to appease some exalted and delicate desire of his superior soul. In a couple of minutes she reappeared. They left the house by the door of the compound, and passed within three feet of the thunderstruck Pedro, without even looking in

his direction. He rose from stooping over a fire of
sticks, and, balancing himself clumsily, uncovered his
enormous fangs in gaping astonishment. Then suddenly he set off rolling on his bandy legs to impart to
his masters the astonishing discovery of a woman.

VI

As LUCK would have it, Ricardo was lounging alone on the verandah of the former counting-house. He scented some new development at once, and ran down to meet the trotting, bear-like figure. The deep, growling noises it made, though they had only a very remote resemblance to the Spanish language, or indeed to any sort of human speech, were from long practice quite intelligible to Mr. Jones's secretary. Ricardo was rather surprised. He had imagined that the girl would continue to keep out of sight. That line apparently was given up. He did not mistrust her. How could he? Indeed, he could not think of her existence calmly.

He tried to keep her image out of his mind so that he should be able to use its powers with some approach to that coolness which the complex nature of the situation demanded from him, both for his own sake and as the faithful follower of plain Mr. Jones, gentleman.

He collected his wits and thought. This was a change of policy, probably on the part of Heyst. If so, what could it mean? A deep fellow! Unless it was her doing; in which case—h'm—all right! Must be. She would know what she was doing. Before him Pedro, lifting his feet alternately, swayed to and fro sideways—his usual attitude of expectation. His little red eyes, lost in the mass of hair, were motionless. Ricardo stared into them with calculated contempt and said in a rough, angry voice:

"Woman! Of course there is. We know that with-

out you!" He gave the tame monster a push. "Git!
*Vamos!** Waddle! Get back and cook the dinner!
Which way did they go, then?"

Pedro extended a huge, hairy forearm to show the
direction, and went off on his bandy legs. Advancing
a few steps, Ricardo was just in time to see, above some
bushes, two white helmets moving side by side in the
clearing. They disappeared. Now that he had managed to keep Pedro from informing the governor that
there was a woman on the island, he could indulge in
speculation as to the movements of these people. His
attitude towards Mr. Jones had undergone a spiritual
change, of which he himself was not yet fully aware.

That morning, before tiffin, after his escape from the
Heyst bungalow, completed in such an inspiring way by
the recovery of the slipper, Ricardo had made his way
to their allotted house, reeling as he ran, his head in a
whirl. He was wildly excited by visions of inconceivable promise. He waited to compose himself before
he dared to meet the governor. On entering the room,
he found Mr. Jones sitting on the camp bedstead like
a tailor on his board, cross-legged, his long back against
the wall.

"I say, sir! You aren't going to tell me you are
bored?"

"Bored? No! Where the devil have you been all
this time?"

"Observing—watching—nosing around. What else?
I knew you had company. Have you talked freely,
sir?"

"Yes, I have," muttered Mr. Jones.

"Not downright plain, sir?"

"No. I wished you had been here. You loaf all
the morning, and now you come in out of breath.
What's the matter?"

"I haven't been wasting my time out there," said Ricardo. "Nothing's the matter. I—I—might have hurried a bit." He was in truth still panting; only it was not with running, but with the tumult of thoughts and sensations long repressed, which had been set free by the adventure of the morning. He was almost distracted by them now. He forgot himself in the maze of possibilities threatening and inspiring. "And so you had a long talk?" he said, to gain time.

"Confound you! The sun hasn't affected your head, has it? Why are you staring at me like a basilisk?"*

"Beg pardon, sir. Wasn't aware I stared," Ricardo apologised good-humouredly. "The sun might well affect a thicker skull than mine. It blazes. Phew! What do you think a fellow is, sir—a salamander?"*

"You ought to have been here," observed Mr. Jones.

"Did the beast give any signs of wanting to prance?" asked Ricardo quickly, with absolutely genuine anxiety. "It wouldn't do, sir. You must play him easy for at least a couple of days, sir. I have a plan. I have a notion that I can find out a lot in a couple of days."

"You have? In what way?"

"Why, by watching," Ricardo answered slowly.

Mr. Jones grunted.

"Nothing new, that. Watch, eh? Why not pray a little, too?"*

"Ha, ha, ha! That's a good one," burst out the secretary, fixing Mr. Jones with mirthless eyes.

The latter dropped the subject indolently.

"Oh, you may be certain of at least two days," he said.

Ricardo recovered himself. His eyes gleamed voluptuously.

"We'll pull this off yet—clean—whole—right through, if you will only trust me, sir."

"I am trusting you right enough," said Mr. Jones. "It's your interest, too."

And, indeed, Ricardo was truthful enough in his statement. He did absolutely believe in success now. But he couldn't tell his governor that he had intelligences in the enemy's camp. It wouldn't do to tell him of the girl. Devil only knew what he would do if he learned there was a woman about. And how could he begin to tell of it? He couldn't confess his sudden escapade.

"We'll pull it off, sir," he said, with perfectly acted cheerfulness. He experienced gusts of awful joy expanding in his heart and hot like a fanned flame.

"We must," pronounced Mr. Jones. "This thing, Martin, is not like our other tries. I have a peculiar feeling about this. It's a different thing. It's a sort of test."

Ricardo was impressed by the governor's manner; for the first time a hint of passion could be detected in him. But also a word he used, the word "test," had struck him as particularly significant somehow. It was the last word uttered during that morning's conversation. Immediately afterwards Ricardo went out of the room. It was impossible for him to keep still. An elation in which an extraordinary softness mingled with savage triumph would not allow it. It prevented his thinking, also. He walked up and down the verandah far into the afternoon, eyeing the other bungalow at every turn. It gave no sign of being inhabited. Once or twice he stopped dead short and looked down at his left slipper. Each time he chuckled audibly. His restlessness kept on increasing till at last it frightened him. He caught hold of the balustrade of the verandah and stood still, smiling not at his thoughts but at the strong sense of life within him. He abandoned himself to it carelessly, even recklessly. He

cared for no one, friend or enemy. At that moment
Mr. Jones called him by name from within. A shadow
fell on the secretary's face.

"Here, sir," he answered; but it was a moment before
he could make up his mind to go in.

He found his governor on his feet. Mr. Jones was
tired of lying down when there was no necessity for it.
His slender form, gliding about the room, came to a
standstill.

"I've been thinking, Martin, of something you suggested. At the time it did not strike me as practical;
but on reflection it seems to me that to propose a game
is as good a way as any to let him understand that the
time has come to disgorge. It's less—how should I
say?—vulgar. He will know what it means. It's
not a bad form to give to the business—which in itself
is crude, Martin, crude."

"Want to spare his feelings?" jeered the secretary
in such a bitter tone that Mr. Jones was really surprised.

"Why, it was your own notion, confound you!"

"Who says it wasn't?" retorted Ricardo sulkily.
"But I am fairly sick of this crawling. No! No! Get
the exact bearings of his swag and then a rip up. That's
plenty good enough for him."

His passions being thoroughly aroused, a thirst for
blood was allied in him with a thirst for tenderness—
yes, tenderness. A sort of anxious, melting sensation
pervaded and softened his heart when he thought of
that girl—one of his own sort. And at the same time
jealousy started gnawing at his breast as the image
of Heyst intruded itself on his fierce anticipation of bliss.

"The crudeness of your ferocity is positively gross,
Martin," Mr. Jones said disdainfully. "You don't
even understand my purpose. I mean to have some

sport out of him. Just try to imagine the atmosphere of the game—the fellow handling the cards—the agonising mockery of it! Oh, I shall appreciate this greatly. Yes, let him lose his money instead of being forced to hand it over. You, of course, would shoot him at once, but I shall enjoy the refinement and the jest of it. He's a man of the best society. I've been hounded out of my sphere by people very much like that fellow. How enraged and humiliated he will be! I promise myself some exquisite moments while watching his play."

"Ay, and suppose he suddenly starts prancing! He may not appreciate the fun."

"I mean you to be present," Mr. Jones remarked calmly.

"Well, as long as I am free to plug him or rip him up whenever I think the time has come, you are welcome to your bit of sport, sir. I sha'n't spoil it."

VII

It was at this precise moment of their conversation that Heyst had intruded on Mr. Jones and his secretary with his warning about Wang, as he had related to Lena. When he left them, the two looked at each other in wondering silence. Mr. Jones was the first to break it.

"I say, Martin!"

"Yes, sir."

"What does this mean?"

"It's some move. Blame me if I can understand!"

"Too deep for you?" Mr. Jones inquired drily.

"It's nothing but some of his infernal impudence," growled the secretary. "You don't believe all that about the Chink, do you sir? 'Tain't true."

"It isn't necessary for it to be true to have a meaning for us. It's the why of his coming to tell us this tale that's important."

"Do you think he made it up to frighten us?" asked Ricardo.

Mr. Jones scowled at him thoughtfully.

"The man looked worried," he muttered, as if to himself. "Suppose that Chinaman has really stolen his money! The man looked very worried."

"Nothing but his artfulness, sir," protested Ricardo earnestly, for the idea was too disconcerting to entertain. "Is it likely that he would have trusted a Chink with enough knowledge to make it possible?" he argued warmly. "Why, it's the very thing that he would keep close about. There's something else there. Ay, but what?"

"Ha, ha, ha!" Mr. Jones let out a ghostly, squeaky laugh. "I've never been placed in such a ridiculous position before," he went on, with a sepulchral equanimity of tone. "It's you, Martin, who dragged me into it. However, it's my fault too. I ought to—but I was really too bored to use my brain, and yours is not to be trusted. You are a hothead!"

A blasphemous exclamation of grief escaped from Ricardo. Not to be trusted! Hothead! He was almost tearful.

"Haven't I heard you, sir, saying more than twenty times since we got fired out from Manila*that we should want a lot of capital to work the East Coast*with? You were always telling me that to prime properly all them officials and Portuguese scallawags we should have to lose heavily at first. Weren't you always worrying about some means of getting hold of a good lot of cash? It wasn't to be got hold of by allowing yourself to become bored in that rotten Dutch town and playing a twopenny game with confounded beggarly bank-clerks and such like. Well, I've brought you here, where there is cash to be got—and a big lot, to a moral," he added through his set teeth.

Silence fell. Each of them was staring into a different corner of the room. Suddenly, with a slight stamp of his foot, Mr. Jones made for the door. Ricardo caught him up outside.

"Put your arm through mine, sir," he begged him gently but firmly. "No use giving the game away. An invalid may well come out for a breath of fresh air after the sun's gone down a bit. That's it, sir. But where do you want to go? Why did you come out, sir?"

Mr. Jones stopped short.

"I hardly know myself," he confessed in a hollow mutter, staring intently at the Number One bungalow.

"It's quite irrational," he declared in a still lower tone.

"Better go in, sir," suggested Ricardo. "What's that? Those screens weren't down before. He's spying from behind them now, I bet—the dodging, artful plotting beast!"

"Why not go over there and see if we can't get to the bottom of this game?" was the unexpected proposal uttered by Mr. Jones. "He will have to talk to us."

Ricardo repressed a start of dismay, but for a moment could not speak. He only pressed the governor's hand to his side instinctively.

"No, sir. What could you say? Do you expect to get to the bottom of his lies? How could you make him talk? It isn't time yet to come to grips with that gent. You don't think I would hang back, do you? His Chink, of course, I'll shoot like a dog the moment I catch sight of him; but as to that Mr. Blasted Heyst, the time isn't yet. My head's cooler just now than yours. Let's go in again. Why, we are exposed here. Suppose he took it into his head to let off a gun on us! He's an unaccountable, 'yporcritical skunk."

Allowing himself to be persuaded, Mr. Jones returned to his seclusion. The secretary, however, remained on the verandah—for the purpose, he said, of seeing whether that Chink wasn't sneaking around; in which case he proposed to take a long shot at the galoot and chance the consequences. His real reason was that he wanted to be alone, away from the governor's deep-sunk eyes. He felt a sentimental desire to indulge his fancies in solitude. A great change had come over Mr. Ricardo since that morning. A whole side of him which from prudence, from necessity, from loyalty, had been kept dormant, was aroused now, colouring his thoughts and disturbing his mental poise by the vision of such staggering consequences as, for instance, the possibility of an active conflict with his governor. The appearance of the monstrous Pedro with his news drew Ricardo out of a feeling of dreaminess wrapped up in a sense of impending trouble. A woman? Yes, there was one; and it made all the difference. After driving away Pedro, and watching the white helmets of Heyst and Lena vanish among the bushes he stood lost in meditation.

"Where could they be off to like this?" he mentally asked himself.

The answer found by his speculative faculties on their utmost stretch was—to meet that Chink. For in the desertion of Wang Ricardo did not believe. It was a lying yarn, the organic part of a dangerous plot. Heyst had gone to combine some fresh move. But then Ricardo felt sure that the girl was with him—the girl full of pluck, full of sense, full of understanding; an ally of his own kind!

He went indoors briskly. Mr. Jones had resumed his cross-legged pose at the head of the bed, with his back against the wall.

"Anything new?"

"No, sir."

Ricardo walked about the room as if he had no care in the world. He hummed snatches of song. Mr. Jones raised his waspish eyebrows at the sound. The secretary got down on his knees before an old leather trunk, and, rummaging in there, brought out a small looking-glass. He fell to examining his physiognomy in it with silent absorption.

"I think I'll shave," he decided, getting up.

He gave a sidelong glance to the governor, and repeated it several times during the operation, which did not take long, and even afterwards, when, after putting away the implements, he resumed his walking, humming more snatches of unknown songs. Mr. Jones preserved a complete immobility, his thin lips compressed, his eyes veiled. His face was like a carving.

"So you would like to try your hand at cards with that skunk, sir?" said Ricardo, stopping suddenly and rubbing his hands.

Mr. Jones gave no sign of having heard anything.

"Well, why not? Why shouldn't he have the experience? You remember in that Mexican town—what's its name?—the robber fellow they caught in the mountains and condemned to be shot? He played cards half the night with the jailer and the sheriff. Well, this fellow is condemned, too. He must give you your game. Hang it all, a gentleman ought to have some little relaxation! And you have been uncommonly patient, sir."

"You are uncommonly volatile all of a sudden," Mr. Jones remarked in a bored voice. "What's come to you?"

The secretary hummed for a while, and then said:

"I'll try to get him over here for you to-night, after dinner. If I ain't here myself, don't you worry, sir. I shall be doing a bit of nosing round—see?"

"I see," sneered Mr. Jones languidly. "But what do *you* expect to see in the dark?"

Ricardo made no answer, and after another turn or two slipped out of the room. He no longer felt comfortable alone with the governor.

VIII

Meantime Heyst and Lena, walking rather fast, approached Wang's hut. Asking the girl to wait, Heyst ascended the little ladder of bamboos giving access to the door. It was as he had expected. The smoky interior was empty, except for a big chest of sandalwood too heavy for hurried removal. Its lid was thrown up, but whatever it might have contained was no longer there. All Wang's possessions were gone. Without tarrying in the hut, Heyst came back to the girl, who asked no questions, with her strange air of knowing or understanding everything.

"Let us push on," he said.

He went ahead, the rustle of her white skirt following him into the shades of the forest, along the path of their usual walk. Though the air lay heavy between straight denuded trunks, the sunlit patches moved on the ground, and raising her eyes Lena saw far above her head the flutter of the leaves, the surface shudder on the mighty limbs extended horizontally in the perfect immobility of patience. Twice Heyst looked over his shoulder at her. Behind the readiness of her answering smile there was a fund of devoted, concentrated passion, burning with the hope of a more perfect satisfaction. They passed the spot where it was their practice to turn towards the barren summit of the central hill. Heyst held steadily on his way towards the upper limit of the forest. The moment they left its shelter, a breeze enveloped them, and a great cloud, racing over the sun, threw a peculiar sombre tint over everything. Heyst pointed up a precipitous, rugged path clinging to the side of the hill. It ended in a barricade of felled trees, a primitively conceived obstacle which must have cost much labour to erect at just that spot.

"This," Heyst explained in his urbane tone, "is a barrier against the march of civilisation. The poor folk over there did not like it, as it appeared to them in the shape of my company—a great step forward, as some people used to call it with mistaken confidence. The advanced foot has been drawn back, but the barricade remains."

They went on climbing slowly. The cloud had driven over, leaving an added brightness on the face of the world.

"It's a very ridiculous thing," Heyst went on; "but then it is the product of honest fear—fear of the unknown, of the incomprehensible. It's pathetic, too, in a way. And I heartily wish, Lena, that we were on the other side of it."

"Oh, stop, stop!" she cried, seizing his arm.

The face of the barricade they were approaching had been piled up with a lot of fresh-cut branches. The leaves were still green. A gentle breeze, sweeping over the top, stirred them a little; but what had startled the girl was the discovery of several spear-blades protruding from the mass of foliage. She had made them out suddenly. They did not gleam, but she saw them with extreme distinctness, very still, very vicious to look at.

"You had better let me go forward alone, Lena," said Heyst.

She tugged persistently at his arm, but after a time, during which he never ceased to look smilingly into her terrified eyes, he ended by disengaging himself.

"It's a sign rather than a demonstration," he argued

persuasively. "Just wait here a moment. I promise not to approach near enough to be stabbed."

As in a nightmare she watched Heyst go up the few yards of the path as if he never meant to stop; and she heard his voice, like voices heard in dreams, shouting unknown words in an unearthly tone. Heyst was only demanding to see Wang. He was not kept waiting very long. Recovering from the first flurry of her fright, Lena noticed a commotion in the green top-dressing of the barricade. She exhaled a sigh of relief when the spear-blades retreated out of sight, sliding inward—the horrible things! In a spot facing Heyst a pair of yellow hands parted the leaves, and a face filled the small opening—a face with very noticeable eyes. It was Wang's face, of course, with no suggestion of a body belonging to it, like those cardboard faces at which she remembered gazing as a child in the window of a certain dim shop kept by a mysterious little man in Kingsland Road.* Only this face, instead of mere holes, had eyes which blinked. She could see the beating of the eyelids. The hands on each side of the face, keeping the boughs apart, also did not look as if they belonged to any real body. One of them was holding a revolver—a weapon which she recognised merely by intuition, never having seen such an object before.

She leaned her shoulders against the rock of the perpendicular hillside and kept her eyes on Heyst, with comparative composure, since the spears were not menacing him any longer. Beyond the rigid and motionless back he presented to her, she saw Wang's unreal cardboard face moving its thin lips and grimacing artificially. She was too far down the path to hear the dialogue, carried on in an ordinary voice. She waited patiently for its end. Her shoulders felt the warmth of the rock; now and then a whiff of cooler air seemed to slip down upon her head from above; the ravine at her feet, choked full of vegetation, emitted the faint, drowsy hum of insect life. Everything was very quiet. She failed to notice the exact moment when Wang's head vanished from the foliage, taking the unreal hands away with it. To her horror, the spear-blades came gliding slowly out. The very hair on her head stirred; but before she had time to cry out, Heyst, who seemed rooted to the ground, turned round abruptly and began to move towards her. His great moustaches did not quite hide an ugly but irresolute smile; and when he had come down near enough to touch her, he burst out into a harsh laugh:

"Ha, ha, ha!"

She looked at him, uncomprehending. He cut short his laugh and said curtly:

"We had better go down as we came."

She followed him into the forest. The advance of the afternoon had filled it with gloom. Far away a slant of light between the trees closed the view. All was dark beyond. Heyst stopped.

"No reason to hurry, Lena," he said in his ordinary, serenely polite tones. "We return unsuccessful. I suppose you know, or at least can guess, what was my object in coming up there?"

"No, I can't guess, dear," she said, and smiled, noticing with emotion that his breast was heaving as if he had been out of breath. Nevertheless, he tried to command his speech, pausing only a little between the words.

"No? I went up to find Wang. I went up"—he gasped again here, but this was for the last time—"I made you come with me because I didn't like to leave you unprotected in the proximity of those fellows." Suddenly he snatched his cork helmet off his head and dashed it on the ground. "No!" he cried roughly. "All this is too unreal altogether. It isn't to be borne! I can't protect you! I haven't the power."

He glared at her for a moment, then hastened after his hat, which had bounded away to some distance. He came back looking at her face, which was very white.

"I ought to beg your pardon for these antics," he said, adjusting his hat. "A movement of childish petulance! Indeed, I feel very much like a child in my ignorance, in my powerlessness, in my want of resource, in everything except in the dreadful consciousness of some evil hanging over your head—yours!"

"It's you they are after," she murmured.

"No doubt, but unfortunately——"

"Unfortunately—what?"

"Unfortunately, I have not succeeded with Wang," he said. "I failed to move his Celestial* heart—that is, if there is such a thing. He told me with horrible Chinese reasonableness that he could not let us pass the barrier, because we should be pursued. He doesn't like fights. He gave me to understand that he would shoot me with my own revolver without any sort of compunction, rather than risk a rude and distasteful contest with the strange barbarians for my sake. He has preached to the villagers. They respect him. He is the most remarkable man they have ever seen, and their kinsman by marriage. They understand his policy. And anyway only women and children and a few old fellows are left in the village. This is the season when the men are away in trading vessels. But it would have been all the same. None of them have a taste for fighting— and with white men too! They are peaceable, kindly folk and would have seen me shot with extreme satisfaction. Wang seemed to think my insistence—for I insisted, you know—very stupid and tactless. But a drowning man clutches at straws. We were talking in such Malay as we are both equal to.

"'Your fears are foolish,' I said to him.

"'Foolish? Of course I am foolish,' he replied. 'If I were a wise man, I would be a merchant with a big hong in Singapore, instead of being a mine coolie turned houseboy. But if you don't go away in time, I will shoot you before it grows too dark to take aim. Not till then, Number One, but I will do it then. Now —finish!'

"'All right,' I said. 'Finish as far as I am concerned; but you can have no objections to the *mem putih* coming over to stay with the Orang Kaya's women for a few days. I will make a present in silver for it.' Orang Kaya is the head man of the village, Lena," added Heyst.

She looked at him in astonishment.

"You wanted me to go to that village of savages?" she gasped. "You wanted me to leave you?"

"It would have given me a freer hand."

Heyst stretched out his hands and looked at them for a moment, then let them fall by his side. Indignation was expressed more in the curve of her lips than in her clear eyes, which never wavered.

"I believe Wang laughed," he went on. "He made a noise like a turkey-cock."

"'That would be worse than anything,' he told me.

"I was taken aback. I pointed out to him that he was talking nonsense. It could not make any difference to his security where you were, because the evil men, as he calls them, did not know of your existence. I did not lie exactly, Lena, though I did stretch the truth till it cracked; but the fellow seems to have an uncanny insight. He shook his head. He assured me they knew all about you. He made a horrible grimace at me."

"It doesn't matter," said the girl. "I didn't want —I would not have gone."

Heyst raised his eyes.

"Wonderful intuition! As I continued to press him, Wang made that very remark about you. When he smiles, his face looks like a conceited death's head. It was his very last remark—that you wouldn't want to. I went away then."

She leaned back against a tree. Heyst faced her in the same attitude of leisure, as if they had done with time and all the other concerns of the earth. Suddenly, high above their heads, the roof of leaves whispered at them tumultuously and then ceased.

"That was a strange notion of yours, to send me away," she said. "Send me away? What for? Yes, what for?"

"You seem indignant," he remarked listlessly.

"To these savages, too!" she pursued. "And you think I would have gone? You can do what you like with me—but not that, not that!"

Heyst looked into the dim aisles of the forest. Everything was so still now that the very ground on which they stood seemed to exhale silence into the shade.

"Why be indignant?" he remonstrated. "It has not happened. I gave up pleading with Wang. Here we are, repulsed! Not only without power to resist the evil, but unable to make terms for ourselves with the worthy envoys, the envoys extraordinary of the world we thought we had done with for years and years. And that's bad, Lena, very bad."

"It's funny," she said thoughtfully. "Bad? I suppose it is. I don't know that it is. But do you? Do you? You talk as if you didn't believe in it."

She gazed at him earnestly.

"Do I? Ah! That's it. I don't know how to talk. I have managed to refine everything away. I've said to the Earth that bore me: 'I am I and you are a shadow.' And, by Jove, it is so! But it appears that such words cannot be uttered with impunity. Here I am on a Shadow inhabited by Shades. How helpless a man is against the Shades! How is one to intimidate, persuade, resist, assert oneself against them? I have lost all belief in realities. . . . Lena, give me your hand."

She looked at him surprised, uncomprehending.

"Your hand," he cried.

She obeyed; he seized it with avidity as if eager to raise it to his lips, but halfway up released his grasp. They looked at each other for a time.

"What's the matter, dear?" she whispered timidly.

"Neither force nor conviction," Heyst muttered wearily to himself. "How am I to meet this charmingly simple problem?"

"I am sorry," she murmured.

"And so am I," he confessed quickly. "And the bitterest of this humiliation is its complete uselessness—which I feel, I feel!"

She had never before seen him give such signs of feeling. Across his ghastly face the long moustaches flamed in the shade. He spoke suddenly:

"I wonder if I could find enough courage to creep among them in the night, with a knife, and cut their throats one after another, as they slept! I wonder——"

She was frightened by his unwonted appearance more than by the words in his mouth, and said earnestly:

"Don't you try to do such a thing! Don't you think of it!"

"I don't possess anything bigger than a penknife. As to thinking of it, Lena, there's no saying what one

may think of. I don't think. Something in me thinks
—something foreign to my nature. What is the
matter?"

He noticed her parted lips, and the peculiar stare in
her eyes, which had wandered from his face.

"There's somebody after us. I saw something white
moving," she cried.

Heyst did not turn his head; he only glanced at her
outstretched arm.

"No doubt we are followed; we are watched."

"I don't see anything now," she said.

"And it does not matter," Heyst went on in his
ordinary voice. "Here we are in the forest. I have
neither strength nor persuasion. Indeed, it's extremely difficult to be eloquent before a Chinaman's
head stuck at one out of a lot of brushwood. But
can we wander among these big trees indefinitely? Is
this a refuge? No! What else is left to us? I did
think for a moment of the mine; but even there we
could not remain very long. And then that gallery
is not safe. The props were too weak to begin with.
Ants have been at work there—ants after the men. A
death-trap, at best. One can die but once, but there
are many manners of death."

The girl glanced about fearfully, in search of the
watcher or follower whom she had glimpsed once
among the trees; but if he existed, he had concealed
himself. Nothing met her eyes but the deepening
shadows of the short vistas between the living columns
of the still roof of leaves. She looked at the man beside her expectantly, tenderly, with suppressed affright
and a sort of awed wonder.

"I have also thought of these people's boat," Heyst
went on. "We could get into that, and—only they
have taken everything out of her. I have seen her oars

and mast in a corner of their room. To shove off in an empty boat would be nothing but a desperate expedient, supposing even that she would drift out a good distance between the islands before the morning. It would only be a complicated manner of committing suicide—to be found dead in a boat, dead from sun and thirst. A sea mystery. I wonder who would find us! Davidson, perhaps; but Davidson passed westward ten days ago. I watched him steaming past one early morning, from the jetty."

"You never told me," she said.

"He must have been looking at me through his big binoculars. Perhaps, if I had raised my arm—but what did we want with Davidson then, you and I? He won't be back this way for three weeks or more, Lena. I wish I had raised my arm that morning."

"What would have been the good of it?" she sighed out.

"What good? No good, of course. We had no forebodings. This seemed to be an inexpugnable refuge, where we could live untroubled and learn to know each other."

"It's perhaps in trouble that people get to know each other," she suggested.

"Perhaps," he said indifferently. "At any rate, we would not have gone away from here with him; though I believe he would have come in eagerly enough, and ready for any service he could render. It's that fat man's nature—a delightful fellow. You would not come on the wharf that time I sent the shawl back to Mrs. Schomberg through him. He has never seen you."

"I didn't know that you wanted anybody ever to see me," she said.

He had folded his arms on his breast and hung his head.

"And I did not know that you cared to be seen as yet. A misunderstanding evidently. An honourable misunderstanding. But it does not matter now."

He raised his head after a silence.

"How gloomy this forest has grown! Yet surely the sun cannot have set already."

She looked round; and as if her eyes had just been opened, she perceived the shades of the forest surrounding her, not so much with gloom, but with a sullen, dumb, menacing hostility. Her heart sank in the engulfing stillness; at that moment she felt the nearness of death breathing on her and on the man with her. If there had been a sudden stir of leaves, the crack of a dry branch, the faintest rustle, she would have screamed aloud. But she shook off the unworthy weakness. Such as she was, a fiddle-scraping girl picked up on the very threshold of infamy, she would try to rise above herself, triumphant and humble; and then happiness would burst on her like a torrent, flinging at her feet the man whom she loved.

Heyst stirred slightly.

"We had better be getting back, Lena, since we can't stay all night in the woods—or anywhere else, for that matter. We are the slaves of this infernal surprise which has been sprung on us by—shall I say fate?—your fate, or mine."

It was the man who had broken the silence, but it was the woman who led the way. At the very edge of the forest she stopped, concealed by a tree. He joined her cautiously.

"What is it? What do you see, Lena?" he whispered.

She said that it was only a thought that had come into her head. She hesitated for a moment, giving him over her shoulder a shining gleam of her grey eyes. She wanted to know whether this trouble, this danger, this evil, whatever it was, finding them out in their retreat, was not a sort of punishment.

"Punishment?" repeated Heyst. He could not understand what she meant. When she explained, he was still more surprised. "A sort of retribution from an angry Heaven?" he said in wonder. "On us? What on earth for?"

He saw her pale face darken in the dusk. She had blushed. Her whispering flowed very fast. It was the way they lived together—that wasn't right, was it? It was a guilty life. For she had not been forced into it, driven, scared into it. No, no—she had come to him of her own free will, with her whole soul yearning unlawfully.

He was so profoundly touched that he could not speak for a moment. To conceal his trouble, he assumed his best Heystian manner.

"What? Are our visitors then messengers of morality, avengers of righteousness, agents of Providence? That's certainly an original view. How flattered they would be if they could hear you!"

"Now you are making fun of me," she said in a subdued voice which broke suddenly.

"Are you conscious of sin?" Heyst asked gravely. She made no answer. "For I am not," he added; "before Heaven, I am not!"

"You! You are different. Woman is the tempter. You took me up from pity. I threw myself at you."

"Oh, you exaggerate, you exaggerate. It was not so bad as that," he said playfully, keeping his voice steady with an effort.

He considered himself a dead man already, yet forced to pretend that he was alive for her sake, for her defence. He regretted that he had no Heaven to which he could recommend this fair, palpitating handful of ashes

and dust—warm, living, sentient, his own—and
exposed helplessly to insult, outrage, degradation, and
infinite misery of the body.

She had averted her face from him and was still.   He
suddenly seized her passive hand.

"You will have it so?" he said.   "Yes? Well, let
us then hope for mercy together."

She shook her head without looking at him, like an
abashed child.

"Remember," he went on incorrigible with his delicate raillery, "that hope is a Christian virtue, and surely
you can't want all the mercy for yourself."

Before their eyes the bungalow across the cleared
ground stood bathed in a sinister light.   An unexpected
chill gust of wind made a noise in the tree-tops.   She
snatched her hand away and stepped out into the open;
but before she had advanced more than three yards,
she stood still and pointed to the west.

"Oh, look there!" she exclaimed.

Beyond the headland of Diamond Bay, lying black
on a purple sea, great masses of cloud stood piled up
and bathed in a mist of blood.   A crimson crack like
an open wound zigzagged between them, with a piece
of dark red sun showing at the bottom.   Heyst cast
an indifferent glance at the ill-omened chaos of the sky.

"Thunderstorm making up.   We shall hear it all
night, but it won't visit us, probably.   The clouds
generally gather round the volcano."

She was not listening to him.   Her eyes reflected
the sombre and violent hues of the sunset.

"That does not look much like a sign of mercy," she
said slowly, as if to herself, and hurried on, followed by
Heyst.   Suddenly she stopped.   "I don't care.   I
would do more yet!   And some day you'll forgive me.
You'll have to forgive me!"

IX

STUMBLING up the steps, as if suddenly exhausted, Lena entered the room and let herself fall on the nearest chair. Before following her, Heyst took a survey of the surroundings from the verandah. It was a complete solitude. There was nothing in the aspect of this familiar scene to tell him that he and the girl were not as completely alone as they had been in the early days of their common life on this abandoned spot, with only Wang discreetly materialising from time to time and the uncomplaining memory of Morrison to keep them company.

After the cold gust of wind there was an absolute stillness of the air. The thunder-charged mass hung unbroken beyond the low, ink-black headland, darkening the twilight. By contrast, the sky at the zenith displayed pellucid clearness, the sheen of a delicate glass bubble which the merest movement of air might shatter. A little to the left, between the black masses of the headland and of the forest, the volcano, a feather of smoke by day and a cigar-glow at night, took its first fiery expanding breath of the evening. Above it a reddish star came out like an expelled spark from the fiery bosom of the earth, enchanted into permanency by the mysterious spell of frozen spaces.

In front of Heyst the forest, already full of the deepest shades, stood like a wall. But he lingered, watching its edge, especially where it ended at the line of bushes, masking the land end of the jetty. Since the girl had spoken of catching a glimpse of something white among

the trees, he believed pretty firmly that they had been
followed in their excursion up the mountain by Mr.
Jones's secretary. No doubt the fellow had watched
them out of the forest, and now, unless he took the
trouble to go back some distance and fetch a considerable circuit inland over the clearing, he was bound to
walk out into the open space before the bungalows.
Heyst did, indeed, imagine at one time some movement between the trees, lost as soon as perceived. He
stared patiently, but nothing more happened. After
all, why should he trouble about these people's actions?
Why this stupid concern for the preliminaries, since,
when the issue was joined, it would find him disarmed
and shrinking from the ugliness and degradation of
it?

He turned and entered the room. Deep dusk reigned
in there already. Lena, near the door, did not move or
speak. The sheen of the white tablecloth was very obtrusive. The brute these two vagabonds had tamed
had entered on its service while Heyst and Lena were
away. The table was laid. Heyst walked up and
down the room several times. The girl remained without sound or movement on the chair. But when Heyst,
placing the two silver candelabra on the table, struck
a match to light the candles, she got up suddenly
and went into the bedroom. She came out again
almost immediately, having taken off her hat. Heyst
looked at her over his shoulder.

"What's the good of shirking the evil hour? I've
lighted these candles for a sign of our return. After
all, we might not have been watched—while returning,
I mean. Of course we were seen leaving the house."

The girl sat down again. The great wealth of her
hair looked very dark above her colourless face. She
raised her eyes, glis╌ ╌ning softly in the light with a sort

of unreadable appeal, with a strange effect of unseeing innocence.

"Yes," said Heyst across the table, the fingertips of one hand resting on the immaculate cloth. "A creature with an antediluvian lower jaw, hairy like a mastodon, and formed like a prehistoric ape, has laid this table. Are you awake, Lena? Am I? I would pinch myself, only I know that nothing would do away with this dream. Three covers. You know it is the shorter of the two who's coming—the gentleman who, in the play of his shoulders as he walks, and in his facial structure, recalls a jaguar. Ah, you don't know what a jaguar is? But you have had a good look at these two. It's the short one, you know, who's to be our guest."

She made a sign with her head that she knew. Heyst's insistence brought Ricardo vividly before her mental vision. A sudden languor, like the physical echo of her struggle with the man, paralysed all her limbs. She lay still in the chair, feeling very frightened at this phenomenon—ready to pray aloud for strength.

Heyst had started to pace the room.

"Our guest! There is a proverb—in Russia, I believe —that when a guest enters the house, God enters the house. The sacred virtue of hospitality! But it leads one into trouble as well as any other."

The girl unexpectedly got up from the chair, swaying her supple figure and stretching her arms above her head. He stopped to look at her curiously, paused, and then went on:

"I venture to think that God has nothing to do with such a hospitality and with such a guest!"

She had jumped to her feet to react against the numbness, to discover whether her body would obey her will. It did. She could stand up, and she could move her

arms freely. Though no physiologist, she concluded
that all that sudden numbness was in her head, not in
her limbs. Her fears assuaged, she thanked God for
it mentally, and to Heyst murmured a protest:

"Oh, yes! He's got to do with everything—every
little thing. Nothing can happen——"

"Yes," he said hastily, "one of the two sparrows*
can't be struck to the ground—you are thinking of
that." The habitual playful smile faded on the kindly
lips under the martial moustache. "Ah, you remember
what you have been told—as a child—on Sundays."

"Yes, I do remember." She sank into the chair
again. "It was the only decent bit of time I ever had
when I was a kid, with our landlady's two girls, you
know."

"I wonder, Lena," Heyst said, with a return of his
urbane playfulness, "whether you are just a little child,
or whether you represent something as old as the
world."

She surprised Heyst by saying dreamily:

"Well—and what about you?"

"I? I date later—much later? I can't call myself a
child, but I am so recent that I may call myself a man
of the last hour—or is it the hour before last? I have
been out of it so long that I am not certain how far the
hands of the clock have moved since—since——"

He glanced at the portrait of his father, exactly above
the head of the girl, and as it were ignoring her in its
painted austerity of feeling. He did not finish the
sentence; but he did not remain silent for long.

"Only what must be avoided are fallacious inferences,
my dear Lena—especially at this hour."

"Now you are making fun of me again," she said
without looking up.

"Am I?" he cried. "Making fun? No, giving

warning. Hang it all, whatever truth people told you in the old days, there is also this one—that sparrows do fall to the ground, that they are brought down to the ground. This is no vain assertion, but a fact. That's why"—again his tone changed, while he picked up a table knife and let it fall disdainfully—"that's why I wish these wretched round knives had some edge on them. Absolute rubbish—neither edge, point, nor substance. I believe one of these forks would make a better weapon at a pinch. But can I go about with a fork in my pocket?" He gnashed his teeth with a rage very real, and yet comic.

"There used to be a carver here, but it was broken and thrown away a long time ago. Nothing much to carve here. It would have made a noble weapon, no doubt; but——"

He stopped. The girl sat very quiet, with downcast eyes. As he kept silent for some time, she looked up and said thoughtfully:

"Yes, a knife—it's a knife that you would want, wouldn't you, in case, in case——"

He shrugged his shoulders.

"There must be a crowbar or two in the sheds; but I have given up all the keys together. And then, do you see me walking about with a crowbar in my hand? Ha, ha! And besides, that edifying sight alone might start the trouble for all I know. In truth, why has it not started yet?"

"Perhaps they are afraid of you," she whispered, looking down again.

"By Jove, it looks like it," he assented meditatively. "They do seem to hang back for some reason. Is that reason prudence, or downright fear, or perhaps the leisurely method of certitude?"

Out in the black night, not very far from the bungalow, resounded a loud and prolonged whistle. Lena's hands grasped the sides of the chair, but she made no movement. Heyst started, and turned his face away from the door.

The startling sound had died away.

"Whistles, yells, omens, signals, portents—what do they matter?" he said. "But what about that crowbar? Suppose I had it! Could I stand in ambush at the side of the door—this door—and smash the first protruding head, scatter blood and brains over the floor, over these walls, and then run stealthily to the other door to do the same thing—and repeat the performance for a third time, perhaps? Could I? On suspicion, without compunction, with a calm and determined purpose? No, it is not in me. I date too late. Would you like to see me attempt this thing while that mysterious prestige of mine lasts—or their not less mysterious hesitation?"

"No, no!" she whispered ardently, as if compelled to speak by his eyes fixed on her face. "No, it's a knife you want to defend yourself with—to defend—there will be time——"

"And who knows if it isn't really my duty?" he began again, as if he had not heard her disjointed words at all. "It may be—my duty to you, to myself. For why should I put up with the humiliation of their secret menaces? Do you know what the world would say?"

He emitted a low laugh, which struck her with terror. She would have got up, but he stooped so low over her that she could not move without first pushing him away.

"It would say, Lena, that I—that Swede—after luring my friend and partner to his death from mere greed of money, have murdered these unoffending shipwrecked strangers from sheer funk. That would be

the story whispered—perhaps shouted—certainly
spread out, and believed—and *believed*, my dear Lena!"

"Who would believe such awful things?"

"Perhaps you wouldn't—not at first, at any rate;
but the power of calumny grows with time. It's in-
sidious and penetrating. It can even destroy one's
faith in oneself—dry-rot the soul."

All at once her eyes leaped to the door and remained
fixed, stony, a little enlarged. Turning his head, Heyst
beheld the figure of Ricardo framed in the doorway. For
a moment none of the three moved; then, looking from
the newcomer to the girl in the chair, Heyst formulated
a sardonic introduction.

"Mr. Ricardo, my dear."

Her head drooped a little. Ricardo's hand went up
to his moustache. His voice exploded in the room.

"At your service, ma'am!"

He stepped in, taking his hat off with a flourish, and
dropping it carelessly on a chair near the door.

"At your service," he repeated, in quite another tone.
"I was made aware there was a lady about, by that
Pedro of ours; only I didn't know I should have the
privilege of seeing you to-night, ma'am."

Lena and Heyst looked at him covertly, but he, with a
vague gaze avoiding them both, looked at nothing, seem-
ing to pursue some point in space.

"Had a pleasant walk?" he asked suddenly.

"Yes. And you?" returned Heyst, who had managed to catch his glance.

"I? I haven't been a yard away from the governor
this afternoon till I started for here." The genuineness
of the accent surprised Heyst, without convincing him of
the truth of the words. "Why do you ask?" pursued
Ricardo with every inflexion of perfect candour.

"You might have wished to explore the island a,

little," said Heyst, studying the man, who, to render
him justice, did not try to free his captured gaze. "I
may remind you that it wouldn't be a perfectly safe
proceeding."

Ricardo presented a picture of innocence.

"Oh, yes!—meaning that Chink that has run away
from you. He ain't much!"

"He has a revolver," observed Heyst meaningly.

"Well, and you have a revolver, too," Mr. Ricardo
argued unexpectedly. "I don't worry myself about
that."

"I? That's different. I am not afraid of you,"
Heyst made answer after a short pause.

"Of me?"

"Of all of you."

"You have a queer way of putting things," began
Ricardo.

At that moment the door on the compound side of
the house came open with some noise, and Pedro entered, pressing the edge of a loaded tray to his breast.
His big, hairy head rolled a little, his feet fell in front
of each other with a short, hard thump on the floor.
The arrival changed the current of Ricardo's thought,
perhaps, but certainly of his speech.

"You heard me whistling a little while ago outside?
That was to give him a hint, as I came along, that it
was time to bring in the dinner; and here it is."

Lena rose and passed to the right of Ricardo, who
lowered his glance for a moment. They sat down at
the table. The enormous gorilla back of Pedro swayed
out through the door.

"Extraordinary strong brute, ma'am," said Ricardo.
He had a propensity to talk about "his Pedro," as
some men will talk of their dog. "He ain't pretty,
though. No, he ain't pretty. And he has got to be

kept under. I am his keeper, as it might be. The governor don't trouble his head much about dee-tails. All that's left to Martin. Martin, that's me, ma'am."

Heyst saw the girl's eyes turn towards Mr. Jones's secretary and rest blankly on his face. Ricardo, however, looked vaguely into space, and, with faint flickers of a smile about his lips, made conversation indefatigably against the silence of his entertainers. He boasted largely of his long association with Mr. Jones—over four years now, he said. Then, glancing rapidly at Heyst:

"You can see at once he's a gentleman, can't you?"

"You people," Heyst said, his habitual playful intonation tinged with gloom, "are divorced from all reality in my eyes."

Ricardo received this speech as if he had been expecting to hear those very words, or else did not mind at all what Heyst might say. He muttered an absent-minded "Ay, ay," played with a bit of biscuit, sighed, and said, with a peculiar stare which did not seem to carry any distance, but to stop short at a point in the air very near his face:

"Anybody can see at once *you* are one. You and the governor ought to understand each other. He expects to see you to-night. The governor isn't well, and we've got to think of getting away from here."

While saying these words he turned himself full towards Lena, but without any marked expression. Leaning back with folded arms, the girl stared before her as if she had been alone in the room. But under that aspect of almost vacant unconcern the perils and emotion that had entered into her life warmed her heart, exalted her mind with a sense of an inconceivable intensity of existence.

"Really? Thinking of going away from here?" Heyst murmured.

"The best of friends must part," Ricardo pronounced slowly. "And, as long as they part friends, there's no harm done. We two are used to be on the move. You, I understand, prefer to stick in one place."

It was obvious that all this was being said merely for the sake of talking, and that Ricardo's mind was concentrated on some purpose unconnected with the words that were coming out of his mouth.

"I should like to know," Heyst asked with incisive politeness, "how you have come to understand this or anything else about me? As far as I can remember, I've made you no confidences."

Ricardo, gazing comfortably into space out of the back of his chair—for some time all three had given up any pretence of eating—answered abstractedly:

"Any fellow might have guessed it." He sat up suddenly, and uncovered all his teeth in a grin of extraordinary ferocity, which was belied by the persistent amiability of his tone. "The governor will be the man to tell you something about that. I wish you would say you would see my governor. He's the one who does all our talking. Let me take you to him this evening. He ain't at all well; and he can't make up his mind to go away without having a talk with you."

Heyst, looking up, met Lena's eyes. Their expression of candour seemed to hide some struggling intention. Her head, he fancied, had made an imperceptible affirmative movement. Why? What reason could she have? Was it the prompting of some obscure instinct? Or was it simply a delusion of his own senses? But in this strange complication invading the quietude of his life, in his state of doubt and disdain and almost of despair with which he looked at himself, he would let even a delusive appearance guide him through a darkness so dense that it made for indifference.

"Well, suppose I *do* say so."

Ricardo did not conceal his satisfaction, which for a moment interested Heyst.

"It can't be my life they are after," he said to himself. "What good could it be to them?"

He looked across the table at the girl. What did it matter whether she had nodded or not? As always when looking into her unconscious eyes, he tasted something like the dregs of tender pity. He had decided to go. Her nod, imaginary or not imaginary, advice or illusion, had tipped the scale. He reflected that Ricardo's invitation could scarcely be anything in the nature of a trap. It would have been too absurd. Why carry subtly into a trap someone already bound hand and foot, as it were?

All this time he had been looking fixedly at the girl he called Lena. In the submissive quietness of her being, which had been her attitude ever since they had begun their life on the island, she remained as secret as ever. Heyst got up abruptly, with a smile of such enigmatic and despairing character that Mr. Secretary Ricardo, whose abstract gaze had an all-round efficiency, made a slight crouching start, as if to dive under the table for his leg-knife—a start that was repressed as soon as begun. He had expected Heyst to spring on him or draw a revolver, because he created for himself a vision of him in his own image. Instead of doing either of these obvious things, Heyst walked across the room, opened the door, and put his head through it to look out into the compound.

As soon as his back was turned, Ricardo's hand sought the girl's arm under the table. He was not looking at her, but she felt the groping, nervous touch of his search, felt suddenly the grip of his fingers above her wrist. He leaned forward a little; still he dared

not look at her. His hard stare remained fastened on
Heyst's back. In an extremely low hiss, his fixed
idea of argument found expression scathingly:

"See! He's no good. He's not the man for you!"

He glanced at her at last. Her lips moved a little,
and he was awed by that movement without a sound.
Next instant the hard grasp of his fingers vanished from
her arm. Heyst had shut the door. On his way back
to the table, he crossed the path of the girl they had
called Alma*—she didn't know why—also Magdalen*,
whose mind had remained so long in doubt as to the
reason of her own existence. She no longer wondered
at that bitter riddle, since her heart found its solution
in a blinding, hot glow of passionate purpose.

X

SHE passed by Heyst as if she had indeed been blinded by some secret, lurid, and consuming glare into which she was about to enter. The curtain of the bedroom door fell behind her into rigid folds. Ricardo's vacant gaze seemed to be watching the dancing flight of a fly in mid air.

"Extra dark outside, ain't it?" he muttered.

"Not so dark but that I could see that man of yours prowling about there," said Heyst in measured tones.

"What—Pedro? He's scarcely a man, you know; or else I wouldn't be so fond of him as I am."

"Very well. Let's call him your worthy associate."

"Ay! Worthy enough for what we want of him. A great stand-by is Peter in a scrimmage. A growl and a bite—oh, my! And you don't want him about?"

"I don't."

"You want him out of the way?" insisted Ricardo with an affectation of incredulity which Heyst accepted calmly, though the air in the room seemed to grow more oppressive with every word spoken.

"That's it. I do want him out of the way." He forced himself to speak equably.

"Lor'! That's no great matter. Pedro's not much use here. The business my governor's after can be settled by ten minutes' rational talk with—with another gentleman. Quiet talk!"

He looked up suddenly with hard, phosphorescent eyes. Heyst didn't move a muscle. Ricardo congratulated himself on having left his revolver behind.

He was so exasperated that he didn't know what he might have done. He said at last:

"You want poor, harmless Peter out of the way before you let me take you to see the governor—is that it?"

"Yes, that is it."

"H'm! One can see," Ricardo said with hidden venom, "that you are a gentleman; but all that gentlemanly fancifulness is apt to turn sour on a plain man's stomach. However—you'll have to pardon me."

He put his fingers into his mouth and let out a whistle which seemed to drive a thin, sharp shaft of air solidly against one's nearest ear-drum. Though he greatly enjoyed Heyst's involuntary grimace, he sat perfectly stolid waiting for the effect of the call.

It brought Pedro in with an extraordinary, uncouth, primeval impetuosity. The door flew open with a clatter, and the wild figure it disclosed seemed anxious to devastate the room in leaps and bounds; but Ricardo raised his open palm, and the creature came in quietly. His enormous half-closed paws swung to and fro a little in front of his bowed trunk as he walked. Ricardo looked on truculently.

"You go to the boat—understand? Go now!"

The little red eyes of the tame monster blinked with painful attention in the mass of hair.

"Well? Why don't you get? Forgot human speech, eh? Don't you know any longer what a boat is?"

"*Si*—boat," the creature stammered out doubtfully.

"Well, go there—the boat at the jetty. March off to it and sit there, lie down there, do anything but go to sleep there—till you hear my call, and then fly here. Them's your orders. March! Get, *vamos!** No, not that way—out through the front door. No sulks!"

Pedro obeyed with uncouth alacrity. When he had

gone, the gleam of pitiless savagery went out of Ricardo's yellow eyes, and his physiognomy took on, for the first time that evening, the expression of a domestic cat which is being noticed.

"You can watch him right into the bushes, if you like. Too dark, eh? Why not go with him to the very spot, then?"

Heyst made a gesture of vague protest.

"There's nothing to assure me that he will stay there. I have no doubt of his going; but it's an act without a guarantee."

"There you are!" Ricardo shrugged his shoulders philosophically. "Can't be helped. Short of shooting our Pedro, nobody can make absolutely sure of his staying in the same place longer than he has a mind to; but I tell you, he lives in holy terror of my temper. That's why I put on my sudden-death air when I talk to him. And yet I wouldn't shoot him—not I, unless in such a fit of rage as would make a man shoot his favourite dog. Look here, sir! This deal is on the square. I didn't tip him a wink to do anything else. He won't budge from the jetty. Are you coming along now, sir?"

A short silence ensued. Ricardo's jaws were working ominously under his skin. His eyes glided voluptuously here and there, cruel and dreamy. Heyst checked a sudden movement, reflected for a while, then said:

"You must wait a little."

"Wait a little! Wait a little! What does he think a fellow is—a graven image?" grumbled Ricardo half audibly.

Heyst went into the bedroom, and shut the door after him with a bang. Coming from the light, he could not see a thing in there at first; yet he received the impres-

sion of the girl getting up from the floor. On the less
opaque darkness of the shutter-hole, her head detached
itself suddenly, very faint, a mere hint of a round, dark
shape without a face.

"I am going, Lena. I am going to confront these
scoundrels." He was surprised to feel two arms falling
on his shoulders. "I thought that you——" he began.

"Yes, yes!" the girl whispered hastily.

She neither clung to him, nor yet did she try to draw
him to her. Her hands grasped his shoulders, and she
seemed to him to be staring into his face in the dark.
And now he could see something of her face, too—an
oval without features—and faintly distinguish her
person, in the blackness, a form without definite lines.

"You have a black dress here, haven't you, Lena?"
he asked, speaking rapidly, and so low that she could
just hear him.

"Yes—an old thing."

"Very good. Put it on at once."

"But why?"

"Not for mourning!" There was something per-
emptory in the slightly ironic murmur. "Can you find
it and get into it in the dark?"

She could. She would try. He waited, very still.
He could imagine her movements over there at the far
end of the room; but his eyes, accustomed now to the
darkness, had lost her completely. When she spoke,
her voice surprised him by its nearness. She had done
what he had told her to do, and had approached him,
invisible.

"Good! Where's that piece of purple veil I've seen
lying about?" he asked.

There was no answer, only a slight rustle.

"Where is it?" he repeated impatiently.

Her unexpected breath was on his cheek.

"In my hands."

"Capital! Listen, Lena. As soon as I leave the bungalow with that horrible scoundrel, you slip out at the back—instantly, lose no time!—and run round into the forest. That will be your time, while we are walking away, and I am sure he won't give me the slip. Run into the forest behind the fringe of bushes between the big trees. You will know, surely, how to find a place in full view of the front door. I fear for you; but in this black dress, with most of your face muffled up in that dark veil, I defy anybody to find you there before daylight. Wait in the forest till the table is pushed into full view of the doorway, and you see three candles out of four blown out and one relighted—or, should the lights be put out here while you watch them, wait till three candles are lighted and then two put out. At either of these signals run back as hard as you can, for it will mean that I am waiting for you here."

While he was speaking, the girl had sought and seized one of his hands. She did not press it; she held it loosely, as it were timidly, caressingly. It was no grasp; it was a mere contact, as if only to make sure that he was there, that he was real and no mere darker shadow in the obscurity. The warmth of her hand gave Heyst a strange, intimate sensation of all her person. He had to fight down a new sort of emotion, which almost unmanned him. He went on, whispering sternly:

"But if you see no such signals, don't let anything—fear, curiosity, despair, or hope—entice you back to this house; and with the first sign of the dawn steal away along the edge of the clearing till you strike the path. Wait no longer, because I shall probably be dead."

The murmur of the word "Never!" floated into his ear as if it had formed itself in the air.

"You know the path," he continued. "Make your
way to the barricade. Go to Wang—yes, to Wang. Let
nothing stop you!" It seemed to him that the girl's
hand trembled a little. "The worst he can do to you
is to shoot you; but he won't. I really think he won't,
if I am not there. Stay with the villagers, with the
wild people, and fear nothing. They will be more awed
by you than you can be frightened of them. Davidson's bound to turn up before very long. Keep a
look-out for a passing steamer. Think of some sort
of signal to call him."

She made no answer. The sense of the heavy,
brooding silence in the outside world seemed to enter
and fill the room—the oppressive infinity of it, without
breath, without light. It was as if the heart of hearts
had ceased to beat and the end of all things had come.

"Have you understood? You are to run out of the
house at once," Heyst whispered urgently.

She lifted his hand to her lips and let it go. He was
startled.

"Lena!" he cried out under his breath.

She was gone from his side. He dared not trust himself—no, not even to the extent of a tender word.

Turning to go out, he heard a thud somewhere in the
house. To open the door, he had first to lift the curtain; he did so with his face over his shoulder. The
merest trickle of light, coming through the keyhole
and one or two cracks, was enough for his eyes to see
her plainly, all black, down on her knees, with her head
and arms flung on the foot of the bed—all black in the
desolation of a mourning sinner. What was this? A
suspicion that there were everywhere more things than
he could understand crossed Heyst's mind. Her arm,
detached from the bed, motioned him away. He
obeyed, and went out, full of disquiet.

The curtain behind him had not ceased to tremble when she was up on her feet, close against it, listening for sounds, for words, in a stooping, tragic attitude of stealthy attention, one hand clutching at her breast as if to compress, to make less loud the beating of her heart. Heyst had caught Mr. Jones's secretary in the contemplation of his closed writing-desk. Ricardo might have been meditating how to break into it; but when he turned about suddenly, he showed so distorted a face that it made Heyst pause in wonder at the upturned whites of the eyes, which were blinking horribly, as if the man were inwardly convulsed.

"I thought you were never coming," Ricardo mumbled.

"I didn't know you were pressed for time. Even if your going away depends on this conversation, as you say, I doubt if you are the men to put to sea on such a night as this," said Heyst, motioning Ricardo to precede him out of the house.

With feline undulations of hip and shoulder, the secretary left the room at once. There was something cruel in the absolute dumbness of the night. The great cloud covering half the sky hung right against one, like an enormous curtain hiding menacing preparations of violence. As the feet of the two men touched the ground, a rumble came from behind it, preceded by a swift, mysterious gleam of light on the waters of the bay.

"Ha!" said Ricardo. "It begins."

"It may be nothing in the end," observed Heyst, stepping along steadily.

"No! Let it come!" Ricardo said viciously. "I am in the humour for it!"

By the time the two men had reached the other bungalow, the far-off, modulated rumble growled incessantly, while pale lightning in waves of cold fire flooded and ran off the island in rapid succession. Ricardo, unexpectedly, dashed ahead up the steps and put his head through the doorway.

"Here he is, governor! Keep him with you as long as you can—till you hear me whistle. I am on the track."

He flung these words into the room with inconceivable speed, and stood aside to let the visitor pass through the doorway; but he had to wait an appreciable moment, because Heyst, seeing his purpose, had scornfully slowed his pace. When Heyst entered the room it was with a smile, the Heyst smile, lurking under his martial moustache.

XI

Two candles were burning on the stand-up desk. Mr. Jones, tightly enfolded in an old but gorgeous blue silk dressing-gown, kept his elbows close against his sides and his hands deeply plunged into the extraordinarily deep pockets of the garment. The costume accentuated his emaciation. He resembled a painted pole leaning against the edge of the desk, with a dried head of dubious distinction* stuck on the top of it. Ricardo lounged in the doorway. Indifferent, in appearance, to what was going on, he was biding his time. At a given moment, between two flickers of lightning, he melted out of his frame into the outer air. His disappearance was observed on the instant by Mr. Jones, who abandoned his nonchalant immobility against the desk, and made a few steps calculated to put him between Heyst and the doorway.

"It's awfully close," he remarked.

Heyst, in the middle of the room, had made up his mind to speak plainly.

"We haven't met to talk about the weather. You favoured me earlier in the day with a rather cryptic phrase about yourself. 'I am he that is,'* you said. What does that mean?"

Mr. Jones, without looking at Heyst, continued his absent-minded movements till, attaining the desired position, he brought his shoulders with a thump against the wall near the door, and raised his head. In the emotion of the decisive moment his haggard face glistened with perspiration. Drops ran down his hollow

cheeks and almost blinded the spectral eyes in their
bony caverns.

"It means that I am a person to be reckoned with.
No—stop! Don't put your hand into your pocket—
don't."

His voice had a wild, unexpected shrillness. Heyst
started, and there ensued a moment of suspended animation, during which the thunder's deep bass muttered
distantly and the doorway to the right of Mr. Jones
flickered with bluish light. At last Heyst shrugged
his shoulders; he even looked at his hand. He didn't
put it in his pocket, however. Mr. Jones, glued against
the wall, watched him raise both his hands to the ends
of his horizontal moustaches, and answered the note
of interrogation in his steady eyes.

"A matter of prudence," said Mr. Jones in his natural
hollow tones, and with a face of deathlike composure.
"A man of your free life has surely perceived that.
You are a much talked-about man, Mr. Heyst—and
though as far as I understand, you are accustomed to
employ the subtler weapons of intelligence, still I can't
afford to take any risks of the cr—grosser methods.
I am not unscrupulous enough to be a match for you
in the use of intelligence; but I assure you, Mr. Heyst,
that in the other way you are no match for me. I
have you covered at this very moment. You have
been covered ever since you entered this room. Yes—
from my pocket."

During this harangue Heyst looked deliberately over
his shoulder, stepped back a pace, and sat down on the
end of the camp bedstead. Leaning his elbow on one
knee, he laid his cheek in the palm of his hand and
seemed to meditate on what he should say next. Mr.
Jones, planted against the wall, was obviously waiting
for some sort of overture. As nothing came, he re-

solved to speak himself; but he hesitated. For, though
he considered that the most difficult step had been
taken, he said to himself that every stage of progress
required great caution, lest the man, in Ricardo's phrase-
ology, should "start to prance"—which would be most
inconvenient. He fell back on a previous statement:

"And I am a person to be reckoned with."

The other man went on looking at the floor, as if he
were alone in the room. There was a pause.

"You have heard of me, then?" Heyst said at length,
looking up.

"I should think so! We have been staying at Schomberg's hotel."

"Schom——" Heyst choked on the word.

"What's the matter, Mr. Heyst?"

"Nothing. Nausea," Heyst said resignedly. He
resumed his former attitude of meditative indifference.
"What is this reckoning you are talking about?" he
asked after a time, in the quietest possible tone. "I
don't know you."

"It's obvious that we belong to the same—social
sphere," began Mr. Jones with languid irony. Inwardly
he was as watchful as he could be. "Something has
driven you out—the originality of your ideas, perhaps.
Or your tastes."

Mr. Jones indulged in one of his ghastly smiles. In
repose his features had a curious character of evil, exhausted austerity; but when he smiled, the whole mask
took on an unpleasantly infantile expression. A recru-
descence of the rolling thunder invaded the room loudly,
and passed into silence.

"You are not taking this very well," observed Mr.
Jones. This was what he said, but as a matter of fact
he thought that the business was shaping quite satis-
factorily. The man, he said to himself, had no stomach

for a fight. Aloud he continued: "Come! You can't expect to have it always your own way. You are a man of the world."

"And you?" Heyst interrupted him unexpectedly. "How do you define yourself?"

"I, my dear sir? In one way I am—yes, I am the world itself, come to pay you a visit. In another sense I am an outcast—almost an outlaw. If you prefer a less materialistic view, I am a sort of fate—the retribution that waits its time."

"I wish to goodness you were the commonest sort of ruffian!" said Heyst, raising his equable gaze to Mr. Jones. "One would be able to talk to you straight, then, and hope for some humanity. As it is——"

"I dislike violence and ferocity of every sort as much as you do," Mr. Jones declared, looking very languid as he leaned against the wall, but speaking fairly loud. "You can ask my Martin if it is not so. This, Mr. Heyst, is a soft age. It is also an age without prejudices. I've heard that you are free from them yourself. You mustn't be shocked if I tell you plainly that we are after your money—or I am, if you prefer to make me alone responsible. Pedro, of course, knows no more of it than any other animal would. Ricardo is of the faithful retainer class—absolutely identified with all my ideas, wishes, and even whims."

Mr. Jones pulled his left hand out of his pocket, got a handkerchief out of another, and began to wipe the perspiration from his forehead, neck and chin. The excitement from which he suffered made his breathing visible. In his long dressing-gown he had the air of a convalescent invalid who had imprudently overtaxed his strength. Heyst, broad-shouldered, robust, watched the operation from the end of the camp bedstead, very calm, his hands on his knees.

"And by the by," he asked, "where is he now, that henchman of yours? Breaking into my desk?"

"That would be crude. Still, crudeness is one of life's conditions." There was the slightest flavour of banter in the tone of Ricardo's governor. "Conceivable, but unlikely. Martin is a little crude; but you are not, Mr. Heyst. To tell you the truth, I don't know precisely where he is. He has been a little mysterious of late; but he has my confidence. No, don't get up, Mr. Heyst!"

The viciousness of his spectral face was indescribable. Heyst, who had moved a little, was surprised by the disclosure.

"It was not my intention," he said.

"Pray remain seated," Mr. Jones insisted in a languid voice, but with a very determined glitter in his black eye-caverns.

"If you were more observant," said Heyst with dispassionate contempt, "you would have known before I had been five minutes in the room that I had no weapon of any sort on me."

"Possibly; but pray keep your hands still. They are very well where they are. This is too big an affair for me to take any risks."

"Big? Too big?" Heyst repeated with genuine surprise. "Good Heavens! Whatever you are looking for, there's very little of it here—very little of anything."

"You would naturally say so, but that's not what we have heard," retorted Mr. Jones quickly, with a grin so ghastly that it was impossible to think it voluntary.

Heyst's face had grown very gloomy. He knitted his brows.

"What have you heard?" he asked.

"A lot, Mr. Heyst—a lot," affirmed Mr. Jones. He

was trying to recover his manner of languid superiority.
"We have heard, for instance, of a certain Mr. Morrison, once your partner."

Heyst could not repress a slight movement.

"Aha!" said Mr. Jones, with a sort of ghostly glee on
his face.

The muffled thunder resembled the echo of a distant
cannonade below the horizon, and the two men seemed
to be listening to it in sullen silence.

"This diabolical calumny will end in actually and
literally taking my life from me," thought Heyst.

Then, suddenly, he laughed. Portentously spectral,
Mr. Jones frowned at the sound.

"Laugh as much as you please," he said. "I, who
have been hounded out from society by a lot of highly
moral souls, can't see anything funny in that story.
But here we are, and you will now have to pay for your
fun, Mr. Heyst."

"You have heard a lot of ugly lies," observed Heyst.
"Take my word for it."

"You would say so, of course—very natural. As a
matter of fact, I haven't heard very much. Strictly
speaking, it was Martin. He collects information, and
so on. You don't suppose I would talk to that Schomberg animal more than I could help? It was Martin
whom he took into his confidence."

"The stupidity of that creature is so great that it
becomes formidable," Heyst said, as if speaking to himself.

Involuntarily, his mind turned to the girl, wandering
in the forest, alone and terrified. Would he ever see
her again? At that thought he nearly lost his self-
possession. But the idea that if she followed his instructions those men were not likely to find her, steadied
him a little. They did not know that the island had any

inhabitants; and he himself once disposed of, they would be too anxious to get away to waste time hunting for a vanished girl.

All this passed through Heyst's mind in a flash, as men think in moments of danger. He looked speculatively at Mr. Jones, who, of course, had never for a moment taken his eyes from his intended victim. And the conviction came to Heyst that this outlaw from the higher spheres was an absolutely hard and pitiless scoundrel.

Mr. Jones's voice made him start.

"It would be useless, for instance, to tell me that your Chinaman has run off with your money. A man living alone with a Chinaman on an island takes care to conceal property of that kind so well that the devil himself——"

"Certainly," Heyst muttered.

Again, with his left hand, Mr. Jones mopped his frontal bone, his stalk-like neck, his razor jaws, his fleshless chin. Again his voice faltered and his aspect became still more gruesomely malevolent, as of a wicked and pitiless corpse.

"I see what you mean," he cried, "but you mustn't put too much trust in your ingenuity. You don't strike me as a very ingenious person, Mr. Heyst. Neither am I. My talents lie another way. But Martin——"

"Who is now engaged in rifling my desk," interjected Heyst.

"I don't think so. What I was going to say is that Martin is much cleverer than a Chinaman. Do you believe in racial superiority, Mr. Heyst? I do, firmly. Martin is great at ferreting out such secrets as yours, for instance."

"Secrets like mine!" repeated Heyst bitterly. "Well, I wish him joy of all he can ferret out!"

"That's very kind of you," remarked Mr. Jones. He was beginning to be anxious for Martin's return. Of iron self-possession at the gaming-table, fearless in a sudden affray, he found that this rather special kind of work was telling on his nerves. "Keep still as you are!" he cried sharply.

"I've told you I am not armed," said Heyst, folding his arms on his breast.

"I am really inclined to believe that you are not," admitted Mr. Jones seriously. "Strange!" he mused aloud, the caverns of his eyes turned upon Heyst. Then briskly: "But my object is to keep you in this room. Don't provoke me, by some unguarded movement, to smash your knee or do something definite of that sort." He passed his tongue over his lips, which were dry and black, while his forehead glistened with moisture. "I don't know if it wouldn't be better to do it at once!"

"He who deliberates is lost,"*said Heyst with grave mockery.

Mr. Jones disregarded the remark. He had the air of communing with himself.

"Physically I am no match for you," he said slowly, his black gaze fixed upon the man sitting on the end of the bed. "You could spring——"

"Are you trying to frighten yourself?" asked Heyst abruptly. "You don't seem to have quite enough pluck for your business. Why don't you do it at once?"

Mr. Jones, taking violent offence, snorted like a savage skeleton.

"Strange as it may seem to you, it is because of my origin, my breeding, my traditions, my early associations, and such-like trifles. Not everybody can divest himself of the prejudices of a gentleman as easily as you have done, Mr. Heyst. But don't worry about my pluck. If you were to make a clean spring at me,

you would receive in mid air, so to speak, something
that would make you perfectly harmless by the time
you landed. No, don't misapprehend us, Mr. Heyst.
We are—er—adequate bandits; and we are after the
fruit of your labours as a—er—successful swindler.
It's the way of the world—gorge and disgorge!"

He leaned wearily the back of his head against the
wall. His vitality seemed exhausted. Even his sunken
eyelids drooped within the bony sockets. Only his thin,
waspish, beautifully pencilled eyebrows, drawn together
a little, suggested the will and the power to sting—
something vicious, unconquerable, and deadly.

"Fruits! Swindler!" repeated Heyst, without heat,
almost without contempt. "You are giving yourself
no end of trouble, you and your faithful henchman, to
crack an empty nut. There are no fruits here, as you
imagine. There are a few sovereigns, which you may
have if you like; and since you have called yourself a
bandit——"

"Yaas!" drawled Mr. Jones. "That, rather than a
swindler. Open warfare at least!"

"Very good! Only let me tell you that there were
never in the world two more deluded bandits—never!"

Heyst uttered these words with such energy that Mr.
Jones, stiffening up, seemed to become thinner and taller
in his metallic blue dressing-gown against the white-
washed wall.

"Fooled by a silly, rascally innkeeper!" Heyst went
on. "Talked over like a pair of children with a promise
of sweets!"

"I didn't talk with that disgusting animal," muttered
Mr. Jones sullenly; "but he convinced Martin, who is
no fool."

"I should think he wanted very much to be convinced," said Heyst, with the courteous intonation so

well known in the islands. "I don't want to disturb your touching trust in your—your follower, but he must be the most credulous brigand in existence. What do you imagine? If the story of my riches were ever so true, do you think Schomberg would have imparted it to you from sheer altruism?* Is that the way of the world, Mr. Jones?"

For a moment the lower jaw of Ricardo's gentleman dropped; but it came up with snap of scorn, and he said with spectral intensity:

"The beast is cowardly! He was frightened, and wanted to get rid of us, if you want to know, Mr. Heyst. I don't know that the material inducement was so very great, but I was bored, and we decided to accept the bribe. I don't regret it. All my life I have been seeking new impressions; and you have turned out to be something quite out of the common. Martin, of course, looks to the material results. He's simple—and faithful—and wonderfully acute."

"Ah, yes! He's on the track"—and now Heyst's speech had the character of politely grim raillery—"but not sufficiently on the track, as yet, to make it quite convenient to shoot me without more ado. Didn't Schomberg tell you precisely where I conceal the fruit of my rapines? Pah! Don't you know he would have told you anything, true or false, from a very clear motive? Revenge! Mad hate—the unclean idiot!"

Mr. Jones did not seem very much moved. On his right hand the doorway incessantly flickered with distant lightning, and the continuous rumble of thunder went on irritatingly, like the growl of an inarticulate giant muttering fatuously.

Heyst overcame his immense repugnance to allude to her whose image, cowering in the forest, was constantly before his eyes, with all the pathos and force of its appeal, august, pitiful, and almost holy to him. It was in a hurried, embarrassed manner that he went on:

"If it had not been for that girl whom he persecuted with his insane and odious passion, and who threw herself on my protection, he would never have—but you know well enough!"

"I *don't* know!" burst out Mr. Jones with amazing heat. "That hotel-keeper tried to talk to me once of some girl he had lost, but I told him I didn't want to hear any of his beastly women stories. It had something to do with you, had it?"

Heyst looked on serenely at this outburst, then lost his patience a little.

"What sort of comedy is this? You don't mean to say that you didn't know that I had—that there was a girl living with me here?"

One could see that the eyes of Mr. Jones had become fixed in the depths of their black holes by the gleam of white becoming steady there. The whole man seemed frozen still.

"Here! Here!" he screamed out twice. There was no mistaking his astonishment, his shocked incredulity —something like frightened disgust.

Heyst was disgusted also, but in another way. He too was incredulous. He regretted having mentioned the girl; but the thing was done, his repugnance had been overcome in the heat of his argument against the absurd bandit.

"Is it possible that you didn't know of that significant fact?" he inquired. "Of the only effective truth in the welter of silly lies that deceived you so easily?"

"No, I didn't!" Mr. Jones shouted. "But Martin did!" he added in a faint whisper, which Heyst's ears just caught and no more.

"I kept her out of sight as long as I could," said Heyst. "Perhaps, with your bringing up, traditions, and so on, you will understand my reason for it."

"He knew. He knew before!" Mr. Jones mourned in a hollow voice. "He knew of her from the first!"

Backed hard against the wall, he no longer watched Heyst. He had the air of a man who had seen an abyss yawning under his feet.

"If I want to kill him, this is my time,"* thought Heyst; but he did not move.

Next moment Mr. Jones jerked his head up, glaring with sardonic fury.

"I have a good mind to shoot you, you woman-ridden hermit, you man in the moon, that can't exist without—no, it won't be you that I'll shoot. It's the other woman-lover—the prevaricating, sly, low-class, amorous cuss! And he shaved—shaved under my very nose. I'll shoot him!"

"He's gone mad," thought Heyst, startled by the spectre's sudden fury.

He felt himself more in danger, nearer death, than ever since he had entered that room. An insane bandit is a deadly combination. He did not, could not know that Mr. Jones was quick-minded enough to see already the end of his reign over his excellent secretary's thoughts and feelings; the coming failure of Ricardo's fidelity. A woman had intervened! A woman, a girl, who apparently possessed the power to awaken men's disgusting folly. Her power had been proved in two instances already—the beastly innkeeper, and that man with moustaches, upon whom Mr. Jones, his deadly right hand twitching in his pocket, glared more in repulsion than in anger. The very object of the expedition was lost from view in his sudden and overwhelming sense of utter insecurity. And this

made Mr. Jones feel very savage; but not against the
man with the moustaches. Thus, while Heyst was
really feeling that his life was not worth two minutes'
purchase, he heard himself addressed with no affectation of languid impertinence, but with a burst of feverish
determination.

"Here! Let's call a truce!" said Mr. Jones.

Heyst's heart was too sick to allow him to smile.

"Have I been making war on you?" he asked wearily.
"How do you expect me to attach any meaning to your
words?" he went on. "You seem to be a morbid, sense-
less sort of bandit. We don't speak the same language.
If I were to tell you why I am here, talking to you, you
wouldn't believe me, because you would not understand
me. It certainly isn't the love of life, from which I
have divorced myself long ago—not sufficiently, perhaps; but if you are thinking of yours, then I repeat
to you that it has never been in danger from me. I
am unarmed."

Mr. Jones was biting his lower lip, in a deep meditation. It was only toward the last that he looked at
Heyst.

"Unarmed, eh?" Then he burst out violently: "I
tell you, a gentleman is no match for the common herd.
And yet one must make use of the brutes. Unarmed,
eh? And I suppose that creature is of the commonest
sort. You could hardly have got her out of a drawing-
room. Though they're all alike, for that matter. Unarmed! It's a pity. I am in much greater danger than
you are, or were—or I am much mistaken. But I am
not—I know my man!"

He lost his air of mental vacancy and broke out into
shrill exclamations. To Heyst they seemed madder
than anything that had gone before.

"On the track! On the scent!" he cried, forgetting

himself to the point of executing a dance of rage in the middle of the floor.

Heyst looked on, fascinated by this skeleton in a gay dressing-gown, jerkily agitated like a grotesque toy on the end of an invisible string. It became quiet suddenly.

"I might have smelt a rat! I always knew that this would be the danger." He changed suddenly to a confidential tone, fixing his sepulchral stare on Heyst. "And yet here I am, taken in by the fellow, like the veriest fool. I've been always on the watch for some such beastly influence, but here I am, fairly caught. He shaved himself right in front of me—and I never guessed!"

The shrill laugh, following on the low tone of secrecy, sounded so convincingly insane that Heyst got up as if moved by a spring. Mr. Jones stepped back two paces, but displayed no uneasiness.

"It's as clear as daylight!" he uttered mournfully, and fell silent.

Behind him the doorway flickered lividly, and the sound as of a naval action somewhere away on the horizon filled the breathless pause. Mr. Jones inclined his head on his shoulder. His mood had completely changed.

"What do you say, unarmed man? Shall we go and see what is detaining my trusted Martin so long? He asked me to keep you engaged in friendly conversation till he made a further examination of that track. Ha, ha, ha!"

"He is no doubt ransacking my house," said Heyst.

He was bewildered. It seemed to him that all this was an incomprehensible dream, or perhaps an elaborate other-world joke, contrived by that spectre in a gorgeous dressing-gown.

Mr. Jones looked at him with a horrible, cadaverous smile of inscrutable mockery, and pointed to the door. Heyst passed through it first. His feelings had become so blunted that he did not care how soon he was shot in the back.

"How oppressive the air is!" the voice of Mr. Jones said at his elbow. "This stupid storm gets on my nerves. I would welcome some rain, though it would be unpleasant to get wet. On the other hand, this exasperating thunder has the advantage of covering the sound of our approach. The lightning's not so convenient. Ah, your house is fully illuminated! My clever Martin is punishing your stock of candles. He belongs to the unceremonious classes, which are also unlovely, untrustworthy, and so on."

"I left the candles burning," said Heyst, "to save him trouble."

"You really believed he would go to your house?" asked Mr. Jones with genuine interest.

"I had that notion, strongly. I do believe he is there now."

"And you don't mind?"

"No!"

"You don't?" Mr. Jones stopped to wonder. "You are an extraordinary man," he said suspiciously, and moved on, touching elbows with Heyst.

In the latter's breast dwelt a deep silence, the complete silence of unused faculties. At this moment, by simply shouldering Mr. Jones, he could have thrown him down and put himself by a couple of leaps, beyond the certain aim of the revolver; but he did not even think of that. His very will seemed dead of weariness. He moved automatically, his head low, like a prisoner captured by the evil power of a masquerading skeleton out of a grave. Mr. Jones took charge of the direction. They fetched a wide sweep. The echoes of distant thunder seemed to dog their footsteps.

"By the by," said Mr. Jones, as if unable to restrain his curiosity, "aren't you anxious about that—ouch!—that fascinating creature to whom you owe whatever pleasure you can find in our visit?"

"I have placed her in safety," said Heyst. "I—I took good care of that."

Mr. Jones laid a hand on his arm.

"You have? Look! Is that what you mean?"

Heyst raised his head. In the flicker of lightning the desolation of the cleared ground on his left leaped out and sank into the night, together with the elusive forms of things distant, pale, unearthly. But in the brilliant square of the door he saw the girl—the woman he had longed to see once more—as if enthroned, with her hands on the arms of the chair. She was in black; her face was white, her head dreamily inclined on her breast. He saw her only as low as her knees. He saw her—there, in the room, alive with a sombre reality. It was no mocking vision. She was not in the forest—but there! She sat there in the chair, seemingly without strength, yet without fear, tenderly stooping.

"Can you understand their power?" whispered the hot breath of Mr. Jones into his ear. "Can there be a more disgusting spectacle? It's enough to make the earth detestable. She seems to have found her affinity. Move on closer. If I have to shoot you in the end, then perhaps you will die cured."

Heyst obeyed the pushing pressure of a revolver barrel between his shoulders. He felt it distinctly, but he did not feel the ground under his feet. They found the steps, without his being aware that he was ascending them—slowly, one by one. Doubt entered into him—a doubt of a new kind, formless, hideous. It seemed to

spread itself all over him, enter his limbs, and lodge
in his entrails. He stopped suddenly, with a thought
that he who experienced such a feeling had no business
to live—or perhaps was no longer living.

Everything—the bungalow, the forest, the open
ground—trembled incessantly; the earth, the sky itself,
shivered all the time, and the only thing immovable
in the shuddering universe was the interior of the lighted
room and the woman in black sitting in the light of the
eight candle-flames. They flung around her an intolerable brilliance which hurt his eyes, seemed to sear his
very brain with the radiation of infernal heat. It was
some time before his scorched eyes made out Ricardo
seated on the floor at some little distance, his back to
the doorway, but only partly so; one side of his upturned
face showing the absorbed, all-forgetful rapture of his
contemplation.

The grip of Mr. Jones's hard claw drew Heyst back a
little. In the roll of thunder, swelling and subsiding, he
whispered in his ear a sarcastic: "Of course!"

A great shame descended upon Heyst—the shame of
guilt, absurd and maddening. Mr. Jones drew him still
farther back into the darkness of the verandah.

"This is serious," he went on, distilling his ghostly
venom into Heyst's very ear. " I had to shut my eyes
many times to his little flings; but this is serious. He
has found his soul-mate. Mud souls, obscene and
cunning! Mud bodies, too—the mud of the gutter!
I tell you, we are no match for the vile populace. I,
even I, have been nearly caught. He asked me to detain you till he gave me the signal. It won't be you
that I'll have to shoot, but him. I wouldn't trust him
near me for five minutes after this!"

He shook Heyst's arm a little.

"If you had not happened to mention the creature,

we should both have been dead before morning. He would have stabbed you as you came down the steps after leaving me, and then he would have walked up to me and planted the same knife between my ribs. He has no prejudices. The viler the origin, the greater the freedom of these simple souls!"

He drew a cautious, hissing breath and added in an agitated murmur: "I can see right into his mind; I have been nearly caught napping by his cunning."

He stretched his neck to peer into the room from the side. Heyst, too, made a step forward, under the slight impulse of that slender hand clasping his arm with a thin, bony grasp.

"Behold!" the skeleton of the crazy bandit jabbered thinly into his ear in spectral fellowship. "Behold the simple Acis*kissing the sandals of the nymph, on the way to her lips, all forgetful, while the menacing fife of Polyphemus*already sounds close at hand—if he could only hear it! Stoop a little."

XII

On RETURNING to the Heyst bungalow, rapid as if on wings, Ricardo found Lena waiting for him. She was dressed in black; and at once his uplifting exultation was replaced by an awed and quivering patience before her white face, before the immobility of her reposeful pose, the more amazing to him who had encountered the strength of her limbs and the indomitable spirit in her body. She had come out after Heyst's departure, and had sat down under the portrait to wait for the return of the man of violence and death. While lifting the curtain, she felt the anguish of her disobedience to her lover, which was soothed by a feeling she had known before—a gentle flood of penetrating sweetness. She was not automatically obeying a momentary suggestion; she was under influences more deliberate, more vague, and of greater potency. She had been prompted, not by her will, but by a force that was outside of her and more worthy. She reckoned upon nothing definite; she had calculated nothing. She saw only her purpose of capturing death—savage, sudden, irresponsible death, prowling round the man who possessed her; death embodied in the knife ready to strike into his heart. No doubt it had been a sin to throw herself into his arms. With that inspiration that descends at times from above for the good or evil of our common mediocrity, she had a sense of having been for him only a violent and sincere choice of curiosity and pity— a thing that passes. She did not know him. If he were to go away from her and disappear, she would

utter no reproach, she would not resent it; for she would
hold in herself the impress of something most rare and
precious—his embraces made her own by her courage
in saving his life.

All she thought of—the essence of her tremors, her
flushes of heat, and her shudders of cold—was the question how to get hold of that knife, the mark and sign
of stalking death. A tremor of impatience to clutch
the frightful thing, glimpsed once and unforgettable,
agitated her hands.

The instinctive flinging forward of these hands stopped Ricardo dead short between the door and her chair,
with the ready obedience of a conquered man who can
bide his time. Her success disconcerted her. She listened to the man's impassioned transports of terrible
eulogy and even more awful declarations of love. She
was even able to meet his eyes, oblique, apt to glide
away, throwing feral gleams of desire.

"No!" he was saying, after a fiery outpouring of
words in which the most ferocious phrases of love were
mingled with wooing accents of entreaty. "I will have
no more of it! Don't you mistrust me. I am sober in
my talk. Feel how quietly my heart beats. Ten
times to-day when you, you, you, swam in my eye, I
thought it would burst one of my ribs or leap out of my
throat. It has knocked itself dead tired, waiting for
this evening, for this very minute. And now it can
do no more. Feel how quiet it is!"

He made a step forward, but she raised her clear
voice commandingly:

"No nearer!"

He stopped with a smile of imbecile worship on his
lips, and with the delighted obedience of a man who
could at any moment seize her in his hands and dash
her to the ground.

"Ah! If I had taken you by the throat this morning and had my way with you, I should never have known what you are. And now I do. You are a wonder! And so am I, in my way. I have nerve, and I have brains, too. We should have been lost many times but for me. I plan—I plot for my gentleman. Gentleman—pah! I am sick of him. And you are sick of yours, eh? You, you!"

He shook all over; he cooed at her a string of endearing names, obscene and tender, and then asked abruptly:

"Why don't you speak to me?"

"It's my part to listen," she said, giving him an inscrutable smile, with a flush on her cheek and her lips cold as ice.

"But you will answer me?"

"Yes," she said, her eyes dilated as if with sudden interest.

"Where's that plunder? Do you know?"

"No! Not yet."

"But there is plunder stowed somewhere that's worth having?"

"Yes, I think so. But who knows?" she added after a pause.

"And who cares?" he retorted recklessly. "I've had enough of this crawling on my belly. It's you who are my treasure. It's I who found you out where a gentleman had buried you to rot for his accursed pleasure!"

He looked behind him and all around for a seat, then turned to her his troubled eyes and dim smile.

"I am dog-tired," he said, and sat down on the floor. "I went tired this morning, since I came in here and started talking to you—as tired as if I had been pouring my life-blood here on these planks for you to dabble your white feet in."

Unmoved, she nodded at him thoughtfully. Woman-like, all her faculties remained concentrated on her heart's desire—on the knife—while the man went on babbling insanely at her feet, ingratiating and savage, almost crazy with elation. But he, too, was holding on to his purpose.

"For you! For you I will throw away money, lives —all the lives but mine! What you want is a man, a master that will let you put the heel of your shoe on his neck; not that skulker, who will get tired of you in a year—and you of him. And then what? You are not the one to sit still; neither am I. I live for myself, and you shall live for yourself, too—not for a Swedish baron. They make a convenience of people like you and me. A gentleman is better than an employer, but an equal partnership against all the 'yporcrits is the thing for you and me. We'll go on wandering the world over, you and I, both free and both true. You are no cage bird. We'll rove together, for we are of them that have no homes. We are born rovers!"

She listened to him with the utmost attention, as if any unexpected word might give her some sort of opening to get that dagger, that awful knife—to disarm murder itself, pleading for her love at her feet. Again she nodded at him thoughtfully, rousing a gleam in his yellow eyes, yearning devotedly upon her face. When he hitched himself a little closer, her soul had no movement of recoil. This had to be. Anything had to be which would bring the knife within her reach. He talked more confidentially now.

"We have met, and their time has come," he began, looking up into her eyes. "The partnership between me and my gentleman has to be ripped up. There's no room for him where we two are. Why, he would shoot

me like a dog! Don't you worry. This will settle it
not later than to-night!"

He tapped his folded leg below the knee, and was surprised, flattered, by the lighting up of her face, which
stooped towards him eagerly and remained expectant,
the lips girlishly parted, red in the pale face, and quivering in the quickened drawing of her breath.

"You marvel, you miracle, you man's luck and joy
—one in a million! No, the only one. You have
found your man in me," he whispered tremulously.
"Listen! They are having their last talk together;
for I'll do for your gentleman, too, by midnight!"

Without the slightest tremor she murmured, as
soon as the tightening of her breast had eased off and
the words would come:

"I wouldn't be in too much of a hurry—with
him."

The pause, the tone, had all the value of meditated
advice.

"Good, thrifty girl!" he laughed low, with a strange
feline gaiety, expressed by the undulating movement of
his shoulders and the sparkling snap of his oblique eyes.
"You are still thinking about the chance of that swag.
You'll make a good partner, that you will! And, I say,
what a decoy you will make! Jee-miny!"

He was carried away for a moment, but his face
darkened swiftly.

"No! No reprieve. What do you think a fellow
is—a scarecrow? All hat and clothes and no feeling,
no inside, no brain to make fancies for himself? No!"
he went on violently. "Never in his life will he go
again into that room of yours—never any more!"

A silence fell. He was gloomy with the torment of his
jealousy, and did not even look at her. She sat up and
slowly, gradually, bent lower and lower over him, as if

ready to fall into his arms. He looked up at last, and checked this droop unwittingly.

"Say! You, who are up to fighting a man with your bare hands, could you—eh?—could you manage to stick one with a thing like that knife of mine?"

She opened her eyes very wide and gave him a wild smile.

"How can I tell?" she whispered enchantingly. "Will you let me have a look at it?"

Without taking his eyes from her face, he pulled the knife out of its sheath—a short, broad, cruel, double-edged blade with a bone handle—and only then looked down at it.

"A good friend," he said simply. "Take it in your hand and feel the balance," he suggested.

At the moment when she bent forward to receive it from him, there was a flash of fire in her mysterious eyes—a red gleam in the white mist which wrapped the promptings and longings of her soul. She had done it! The very sting of death was in her hands; the venom of the viper in her paradise, extracted, safe in her possession—and the viper's head all but lying under her heel. Ricardo, stretched on the mats of the floor, crept closer and closer to the chair in which she sat.

All her thoughts were busy planning how to keep possession of that weapon which had seemed to have drawn into itself every danger and menace on the death-ridden earth. She said with a low laugh, the exultation in which he failed to recognize:

"I didn't think that you would ever trust me with that thing!"

"Why not?"

"For fear I should suddenly strike you with it."

"What for? For this morning's work? Oh, no! There's no spite in you for that. You forgave me. You

saved me. You got the better of me, too. And anyhow, what good would it be?"

"No, no good," she admitted.

In her heart she felt that she would not know how to
do it; that if it came to a struggle, she would have to
drop the dagger and fight with her hands.

"Listen. When we are going about the world together, you shall always call me husband. Do you
hear?"

"Yes," she said, bracing herself for the contest, in
whatever shape it was coming.

The knife was lying in her lap. She let it slip into
the fold of her dress, and laid her forearms with clasped
fingers over her knees, which she pressed desperately
together. The dreaded thing was out of sight at last.
She felt a dampness break out all over her.

"I am not going to hide you, like that good-for-
nothing, finicky, sneery gentleman. You shall be my
pride and my chum. Isn't that better than rotting
on an island for the pleasure of a gentleman, till he
gives you the chuck?"

"I'll be anything you like," she said.

In his intoxication he crept closer with every word
she uttered, with every movement she made.

"Give your foot," he begged in a timid murmur, and
in the full consciousness of his power.

Anything! Anything to keep murder quiet and disarmed till strength had returned to her limbs and she
could make up her mind what to do. Her fortitude
had been shaken by the very facility of success that
had come to her. She advanced her foot forward a
little from under the hem of her skirt; and he threw
himself on it greedily. She was not even aware of him.
She had thought of the forest, to which she had been
told to run. Yes, the forest—that was the place for

her to carry off the terrible spoil, the sting of vanquished
death. Ricardo, clasping her ankle, pressed his lips
time after time to the instep, muttering gasping words
that were like sobs, making little noises that resembled
the sounds of grief and distress. Unheard by them
both, the thunder growled distantly with angry modulations of its tremendous voice, while the world outside
shuddered incessantly around the dead stillness of the
room where the framed profile of Heyst's father looked
severely into space.

Suddenly Ricardo felt himself spurned by the foot
he had been cherishing—spurned with a push of such
violence into the very hollow of his throat that it swung
him back instantly into an upright position on his knees.
He read his danger in the stony eyes of the girl; and
in the very act of leaping to his feet he heard sharply,
detached on the comminatory voice of the storm, the
brief report of a shot which half stunned him, in the
manner of a blow. He turned his burning head, and
saw Heyst towering in the doorway. The thought
that the beggar had started to prance darted through
his mind. For a fraction of a second his distracted
eyes sought for his weapon all over the floor. He
couldn't see it.

"Stick him, you!" he called hoarsely to the girl, and
dashed headlong for the door of the compound.

While he thus obeyed the instinct of self-preservation,
his reason was telling him that he could not possibly
reach it alive. It flew open, however, with a crash,
before his launched weight, and instantly he swung it to
behind him. There, his shoulder leaning against it,
his hands clinging to the handle, dazed and alone in
the night full of shudders and muttered menaces, he
tried to pull himself together. He asked himself if
he had been shot at more than once. His shoulder

was wet with the blood trickling from his head. Feeling above his ear, he ascertained that it was only a graze, but the shock of the surprise had unmanned him for the moment.

What the deuce was the governor about, to let the beggar break loose like this? Or—was the governor dead, perhaps?

The silence within the room awed him. Of going back there could be no question.

"But she knows how to take care of herself," he muttered.

She had his knife. It was she now who was deadly, while he was disarmed, no good for the moment. He stole away from the door, staggering, the warm trickle running down his neck, to find out what had become of the governor and to provide himself with a firearm from the armoury in the trunks.

XIII

MR. JONES, after firing his shot over Heyst's shoulder, had thought it proper to dodge away. Like the spectre he was, he had noiselessly vanished from the verandah. Heyst stumbled into the room and looked around. All the objects in there—the books, the gleam of old silver familiar to him from boyhood, the very portrait on the wall—seemed shadowy, unsubstantial, the dumb accomplices of an amazing dream-plot ending in an illusory effect of awakening and the impossibility of ever closing his eyes again. With dread he forced himself to look at the girl. Still in the chair, she was leaning forward far over her knees, and had hidden her face in her hands. Heyst remembered Wang suddenly. How clear all this was—and how extremely amusing! Very.

She sat up a little, then leaned back, and taking her hands from her face, pressed both of them to her breast, as if moved to the heart by seeing him there looking at her with a black, horror-struck curiosity. He would have pitied her, if the triumphant expression of her face had not given him a shock which destroyed the balance of his feelings. She spoke with an accent of wild joy:

"I knew you would come back in time! You are safe now. I have done it! I would never, never have let him——" Her voice died out, while her eyes shone at him as when the sun breaks through a mist. "Never get it back. Oh, my beloved!"

He bowed his head gravely, and said in his polite, Heystian tone:

"No doubt you acted from instinct. Women have been provided with their own weapon. I was a disarmed man, I have been a disarmed man all my life as I see it now. You may glory in your resourcefulness and your profound knowledge of yourself; but I may say that the other attitude, suggestive of shame, had its charm. For you are full of charm!"

The exultation vanished from her face.

"You mustn't make fun of me now. I know no shame. I was thanking God with all my sinful heart for having been able to do it—for giving you to me in that way—oh, my beloved—all my own at last!"

He stared as if mad. Timidly she tried to excuse herself for disobeying his directions for her safety. Every modulation of her enchanting voice cut deep into his very breast, so that he could hardly understand the words for the sheer pain of it. He turned his back on her; but a sudden drop, an extraordinary faltering of her tone, made him spin round. On her white neck her pale head dropped as in a cruel drought a withered flower droops on its stalk. He caught his breath, looked at her closely, and seemed to read some awful intelligence in her eyes. At the moment when her eyelids fell as if smitten from above by an invisible power, he snatched her up bodily out of the chair, and disregarding an unexpected metallic clatter on the floor, carried her off into the other room. The limpness of her body frightened him. Laying her down on the bed, he ran out again, seized a four-branched candlestick on the table, and ran back, tearing down with a furious jerk the curtain that swung stupidly in his way; but after putting the candlestick on the table by the bed, he remained absolutely idle. There did not seem anything more for him to do. Holding his chin in his hand, he looked down intently at her still face.

"Has she been stabbed with this thing?" asked Davidson, whom suddenly he saw standing by his side and holding up Ricardo's dagger to his sight. Heyst uttered no word of recognition or surprise. He gave Davidson only a dumb look of unutterable awe; then, as if possessed with a sudden fury, started tearing open the front of the girl's dress. She remained insensible under his hands, and Heyst let out a groan which made Davidson shudder inwardly—the heavy plaint of a man who falls clubbed in the dark.

They stood side by side, looking mournfully at the little black hole made by Mr. Jones's bullet under the swelling breast of a dazzling and as it were sacred whiteness. It rose and fell slightly—so slightly that only the eyes of the lover could detect the faint stir of life. Heyst, calm and utterly unlike himself in the face, moving about noiselessly, prepared a wet cloth, and laid it on the insignificant wound, round which there was hardly a trace of blood to mar the charm, the fascination, of that mortal flesh.

Her eyelids fluttered. She looked drowsily about, serene, as if fatigued only by the exertions of her tremendous victory, capturing the very sting of death in the service of love. But her eyes became very wide awake when they caught sight of Ricardo's dagger, the spoil of vanquished death, which Davidson was still holding unconsciously.

"Give it to me!" she said. "It's mine."

Davidson put the symbol of her victory into her feeble hands extended to him with the innocent gesture of a child reaching eagerly for a toy.

"For you," she gasped, turning her eyes to Heyst. "Kill nobody."

"No," said Heyst, taking the dagger and laying it gently on her breast, while her hands fell powerless by her side.

The faint smile on her deep-cut lips waned, and her head sank deep into the pillow, taking on the majestic pallor and immobility of marble. But over the muscles, which seemed set in their transfigured beauty for ever, passed a slight and awful tremor. With an amazing strength she asked loudly:

"What's the matter with me?"

"You have been shot, dear Lena," Heyst said in a steady voice, while Davidson, at the question, turned away and leaned his forehead against the post of the foot of the bed.

"Shot? I did think, too, that something had struck me."

Over Samburin the thunder had ceased to growl at last, and the world of material forms shuddered no more under the emerging stars. The spirit of the girl which was passing away from under them clung to her triumph convinced of the reality of her victory over death.

"No more," she muttered. "There will be no more! Oh, my beloved," she cried weakly, "I've saved you! Why don't you take me into your arms and carry me out of this lonely place?"

Heyst bent low over her, cursing his fastidious soul, which even at that moment kept the true cry of love from his lips in its infernal mistrust of all life. He dared not touch her, and she had no longer the strength to throw her arms about his neck.

"Who else could have done this for you?" she whispered gloriously.

"No one in the world," he answered her in a murmur of unconcealed despair.

She tried to raise herself, but all she could do was to

lift her head a little from the pillow. With a terrified and gentle movement, Heyst hastened to slip his arm under her neck. She felt relieved at once of an intolerable weight, and was content to surrender to him the infinite weariness of her tremendous achievement. Exulting, she saw herself extended on the bed, in a black dress, and profoundly at peace; while, stooping over her with a kindly, playful smile, he was ready to lift her up in his firm arms and take her into the sanctuary of his innermost heart—for ever! The flush of rapture flooding her whole being broke out in a smile of innocent, girlish happiness; and with that divine radiance on her lips she breathed her last, triumphant, seeking for his glance in the shades of death.

XIV

"Yes, Excellency," said Davidson in his placid voice; "there are more dead in this affair—more white people, I mean—than have been killed in many of the battles of the last Achin war."*

Davidson was talking with an Excellency, because what was alluded to in conversation as "the mystery of Samburan" had caused such a sensation in the Archipelago that even those in the highest spheres were anxious to hear something at first hand. Davidson had been summoned to an audience. It was a high official on his tour.

"You knew the late Baron Heyst well?"

"The truth is that nobody out here can boast of having known him well," said Davidson. "He was a queer chap. I doubt if he himself knew how queer he was. But everybody was aware that I was keeping my eye on him in a friendly way. And that's how I got the warning which made me turn round in my tracks in the middle of my trip and steam back to Samburan, where, I am grieved to say, I arrived too late."

Without enlarging very much, Davidson explained to the attentive Excellency how a woman, the wife of a certain hotel-keeper named Schomberg, had overheard two card-sharping rascals making inquiries from her husband as to the exact position of the island. She caught only a few words referring to the neighbouring volcano, but these were enough to arouse her suspicions —"which," went on Davidson, "she imparted to me, your Excellency. They were only too well founded!"

"That was very clever of her," remarked the great man.

"She's much cleverer than people have any conception of," said Davidson.

But he refrained from disclosing to the Excellency the real cause which had sharpened Mrs. Schomberg's wits. The poor woman was in mortal terror of the girl being brought back within reach of her infatuated Wilhelm. Davidson only said that her agitation had impressed him; but he confessed that while going back, he began to have his doubts as to there being anything in it.

"I steamed into one of those silly thunderstorms that hang about the volcano, and had some trouble in making the island," narrated Davidson. "I had to grope my way dead slow into Diamond Bay. I don't suppose that anybody, even if looking out for me, could have heard me let go the anchor."

He admitted that he ought to have gone ashore at once; but everything was perfectly dark and absolutely quiet. He felt ashamed of his impulsiveness. What a fool he would have looked, waking up a man in the middle of the night just to ask him if he was all right! And then, the girl being there, he feared that Heyst would look upon his visit as an unwarrantable intrusion.

The first intimation he had of there being something wrong was a big white boat, adrift, with the dead body of a very hairy man inside, bumping against the bows of his steamer. Then indeed he lost no time in going ashore—alone, of course, from motives of delicacy.

"I arrived in time to see that poor girl die, as I have told your Excellency," pursued Davidson. "I won't tell you what a time I had with him afterwards. He talked to me. His father seems to have been a crank, and to have upset his head when he was young. He

was a queer chap. Practically the last words he said
to me, as we came out on the verandah, were:

"'Ah, Davidson, woe to the man whose heart has
not learned while young to hope, to love—and to put
its trust in life!'

"As we stood there, just before I left him, for he said
he wanted to be alone with his dead for a time, we heard
a snarly sort of voice near the bushes by the shore calling out:

"'Is that you, governor?'

"'Yes, it's me.'

"'Jeeminy! I thought the beggar had done for you.
He has started prancing and nearly had me. I have
been dodging around, looking for you ever since.'

"'Well, here I am,' suddenly screamed the other
voice, and then a shot rang out.

"'This time he has not missed him,' Heyst said to me
bitterly, and went back into the house.

"I returned on board as he had insisted I should
do. I didn't want to intrude on his grief. Later, about
five in the morning, some of my calashes came running to me, yelling that there was a fire ashore. I
landed at once, of course. The principal bungalow was
blazing. The heat drove us back. The other two
houses caught one after another like kindling-wood.
There was no going beyond the shore end of the jetty
till the afternoon."

Davidson sighed placidly.

"I suppose you are certain that Baron Heyst is dead?"

"He is—ashes, your Excellency," said Davidson,
wheezing a little; "he and the girl together. I suppose
he couldn't stand his thoughts before her dead body—
and fire purifies everything. That Chinaman of whom
I told your Excellency helped me to investigate next
day, when the embers got cooled a little. We found

enough to be sure. He's not a bad Chinaman. He told me that he had followed Heyst and the girl through the forest from pity, and partly out of curiosity. He watched the house till he saw Heyst go out, after dinner, and Ricardo come back alone. While he was dodging there, it occurred to him that he had better cast the boat adrift, for fear those scoundrels should come round by water and bombard the village from the sea with their revolvers and Winchesters. He judged that they were devils enough for anything. So he walked down the wharf quietly; and as he got into the boat, to cast her off, that hairy man who, it seems, was dozing in her, jumped up growling, and Wang shot him dead. Then he shoved the boat off as far as he could and went away."

There was a pause. Presently Davidson went on, in his tranquil manner:

"Let Heaven look after what has been purified. The wind and rain will take care of the ashes. The carcass of that follower, secretary, or whatever the unclean ruffian called himself, I left where it lay, to swell and rot in the sun. His principal had shot him neatly through the heart. Then, apparently, this Jones went down the wharf to look for the boat and for the hairy man. I suppose he tumbled into the water by accident —or perhaps not by accident. The boat and the man were gone, and the scoundrel saw himself all alone, his game clearly up, and fairly trapped. Who knows? The water's very clear there, and I could see him huddled up on the bottom between two piles, like a heap of bones in a blue silk bag, with only the head and the feet sticking out. Wang was very pleased when he discovered him. That made everything safe, he said, and he went at once over the hill to fetch his Alfuro woman back to the hut."

Davidson took out his handkerchief to wipe the perspiration off his forehead.

"And then, your Excellency, I went away. There was nothing to be done there."

"Clearly," assented the Excellency.

Davidson, thoughtful, seemed to weigh the matter in his mind, and then murmured with placid sadness:

"Nothing!"

October, 1912—May, 1914.

THE END

EXPLANATORY NOTES

I AM grateful to A. D. Nuttall for his help with the references to Schopenhauer and Nietzsche and to the Harry Ransom Humanities Research Center, University of Texas at Austin, for lending a microfilm of the MS of *Victory*.

Title-page. Comus: the lines from Milton's *Comus* are spoken by the Lady, ll. 206–8. They express a sense of mystification rather than terror; Circe's island is full of bewildering apparitions. The Lady has yet to encounter Comus himself, Circe's son, who will threaten her chastity. Presumably Lena is to be identified with the Lady (she is also to be identified with Miranda from Shakespeare's *The Tempest*, which in turn was one of the sources for *Comus*) and Ricardo with Comus. In this scheme Heyst becomes the Attendant Spirit (or a rather ineffectual Elder Brother).

3 *coal and diamonds*: at the great Kimberley diamond mine in South Africa, opened in the 1870s, diamonds had been mined by the use of shafts and tunnels, the process being drastically modernized and mechanized by the De Beers in 1889; this lends picturesque and dramatic reinforcement to the notion that coal and diamonds are alike.

Axel Heyst: In the manuscript the name is 'Augustus Berg' or 'Gustavus Berg'. On MS p. 21 (about p. 9 in the published text) we are told that the name 'was really either Bergström or Stromberg', and the narrator goes on: 'But I shall continue to call him Berg as we used to do amongst ourselves.' The first of these names, Bergström, strengthens *Victory's* links with *Lord Jim* by recalling the name of one of Jim's employers (Egström); the second is rather too close to 'Schomberg' to avoid confusion. By changing the name to 'Axel Heyst' Conrad arouses two sets of echoes: 'Heyst' rhymes with Christ, and the novel contains a number of hints suggesting that Heyst is to be seen as a Christ figure. Axel is the eponymous hero of the play by

Villiers de l'Isle-Adam, published in 1890, in which a young man detaches himself from life, preferring death to love.

liquidation: in the manuscript the narrator is given a rather awkwardly jocular personality, and here he says: 'I am truly distressed. I must apologise for the clumsiness of my proceeding. Here I begin as though I were going into chemistry and then I seem to be putting my foot into finances.'

5 *Samburan*: there is a 'Round Island' in Lampong Bay, South Sumatra, in the Admiralty charts that I have consulted (1870–90), but it is clearly in the wrong position to be a 'Samburan'. Heyst's island must be somewhere in the Java or Flores Seas, since its location is described as empty, shallow, and tepid, unlikely to be visited except by the mail boat from Sourabaya (Java) to Ternate (in the Moluccas). In the Admiralty charts there is a group of islands south-east of Celebes which might have caught Conrad's eye as a possible location for Heyst's island: they are described as 'quite unknown' and they include a circular island called Binongko which has a volcanic island, Wangi Wangi, to the north. The relationship between these two would correspond quite closely to the relationship between Heyst's island and its neighbouring volcano.

6 *Malacca*: north-east of Singapore on the coast of the Malay Peninsula; a British possession at this date (the dramatic date of the novel is about 1880).

à propos des bottes: casually, without a serious motive.

7 *Saigon (and the other names in Heyst's magic circle)*: see map.

Sourabaya: port on the island of Java (controlled for the last quarter of the nineteenth century by the Dutch, as was much of the Archipelago).

8 *proa*: usually 'prau', a native wooden sailing craft with mat sails. In *The Malay Archipelago*, a source of much of Conrad's information about the Archipelago (both here and in *Lord Jim*), Alfred Wallace describes long passages between the islands in native praus and praises the seaworthiness of these boats.

Goram: a small island, one of the Moluccas. Its people are described by Wallace as competent boatmen, racially different from the Malays, being black, primitive, heavy-featured, and curly haired (like the natives of New Guinea).

9   *chimaeras*: a chimaera is a fabulous creature from Greek mythology with a lion's head, a goat's body, and a serpent's tail.

Charles XII: (1682–1718) King of Sweden, a brilliant but unstable ruler, heavily influenced by his father; he became a foolhardy military leader whose refusᵣ' to compromise led to ultimate defeat by Peter the Great of Russia. His career offers several points of comparison with that of Heyst himself.

10   *Timor*: the northern part of this island was one of the few remaining Portuguese possessions in the Archipelago in the 1880s.

Delli: Portuguese-controlled port, 'pestilential' because, according to Wallace, it was surrounded by undrained swamps so that no European could escape malarial infection. Wallace is scathing about the incompetence of the Portuguese who had maladministered the place for three hundred years.

gunny-bag: bag made of (jute) sackcloth.

"one of us": a phrase which recurs like a refrain in *Lord Jim*. Here it means an officer of the merchant navy (which is also one of—the simplest of—its meanings in *Lord Jim*).

12   *millrei*: usually 'milrei', a Portuguese coin of moderate value (two shillings and threepence in English money in 1883). It is slightly puzzling that the milrei was worth *more* than the shilling, since Conrad's phrasing implies that it was worth less. In the MS the *millrei* is described as 'rather less than a farthing'.

20   *Schomberg*: appeared earlier in Conrad's fiction, in both *Lord Jim* and 'Falk'. In those narratives he was stupid but harmless, whereas in this novel he is vicious; Conrad has perhaps changed the character in response to British anti-German feeling in 1914–15.

Lieutenant of the Reserve: he claims to be a half-pay officer who would be recalled for active service (for Germany, of course) in the event of war. The suggestion here and elsewhere is that

Schomberg is lying and that the lie is part of his exaggerated (and vulnerable) pose of virility (see note to p. 96).

Bangkok: the site of Schomberg's hotel in *Lord Jim* and 'Falk'.

Sourabaya: see note to p. 7. In the manuscript Schomberg's hotel is at Samarang, not Sourabaya.

22 *Moluccas*: a group of islands to the west of New Guinea (under Dutch control).

Amboyna: port on the island of Ceram, off New Guinea.

27 *Davidson*: has appeared in an earlier story, 'Because of the Dollars'. There, as in this novel, he is profoundly good natured and somewhat incompetent. His act of mercy towards the child of a prostitute (Laughing Anne) causes his wife to leave him. Davidson in *Victory* shows no signs of being married, but he is clearly the same 'good Davidson' in command of a merchant vessel owned by a Chinaman who utterly trusts him.

32 *my poor father*: Heyst's father has prompted a great deal of critical discussion. The philosophy represented in his writings owes much to Schopenhauer's pessimism but also, at times, seems to echo phrases from Nietzsche's writings. Whether he had read them or not, Conrad would certainly have known from conversation about the ideas of both philosophers. A further source for Heyst senior is Franz Hueffer, the expatriate German music critic who was the father of Ford Madox Hueffer (later Ford). Hueffer had collaborated with Conrad from 1899–1909 and some aspects of Hueffer/Ford's complex and difficult personality can be felt in Heyst: the impeccably gentlemanly manner, the impulsive generosity, the administrative incompetence (Ford's *The English Review* had been as much of a disaster as Heyst's and Morrison's Tropical Coal Company) and, of course, the sense (which Ford shared with Conrad) of being an outsider when in the company of ordinary Englishmen.

33 *Java Sea*: see map and note to p. 5 above. Heyst's island must be in the Java or in the adjacent 'Flores' Sea, immediately to the East.

36 *cuirass*: breastplate (in a suit of armour).

 Officer-of-the-Reserve: see note to p. 20.

45 *eating her*: a striking instance of this narrator's detachment, this phrase also recalls—albeit faintly—the theme of cannibalism which has appeared earlier in Conrad's work in 'Heart of Darkness' and 'Falk'. Some of the natives of the islands (notably the Dyaks of Borneo) were cannibals and head-hunters.

47 *Schwein-Hund*: Schomberg's 'pig-dog' (p. 46) is a literal translation.

49 *grenadine*: sweet drink made of pomegranates or gooseberries.

 gharry: box-like carriage with small wheels; native transport, in which these two angry Germans will look ludicrous.

59 *joss*: Chinese idol (before which incense may be burnt: hence joss-stick).

62 *risk*: in this well-governed Dutch possession gambling without licence will inevitably be found out.

66 *ring of magic stillness*: atmospherically, rather than explicitly, suggesting *The Tempest*, references to which have been sensed by many readers of the novel; but they are never quite quotations.

75 *most charming accents*: in the manuscript Lena comments here that her own accent is 'Cockney, too'.

78 *well*: orchestra pit.

 music-hall: place of light entertainment for the working class.

82 *Geelvink Bay*: in north-eastern New Guinea.

88 *Alma* and *Magdalen*: the names signify two aspects of Lena. Alma is an Egyptian dancing-girl who performs for men's pleasure; Magdalen is a harlot restored to purity and elevated to sainthood by repentance and faith. In this scenario Heyst plays the role of Christ, clearly. Lena belongs to the Victorian dramatic tradition of the 'fallen woman'; she says later 'I am not what they call a good girl' (p. 198). At this point in the MS Conrad had not arrived at the name 'Magdalen' for Lena; she

says (MS p. 223): 'They call me Alma. I don't know why. Silly name. Margaret too.'

92 *blown away*: the contrast between the average man's 'warm mental fog' and Heyst's senior's 'cold blasts' closely resembles Schopenhauer's distinction between the man who is entangled in phenomena, entrapped in his own 'will' (by which Schopenhauer refers to all the desires including sexual desire), and the man of vision who can see the futility and horror of his own impulses and who takes the path of asceticism, of the 'denial of the will to live' (*The World as Will and Idea*, tr. R. B. Haldane and J. Kemp, 1883; Conrad would certainly have been aware of this translation and may have read it).

flesh and blood: one of the many references in the novel associating Heyst with Adam, here the association is with Milton's Adam rather than with the Adam of Genesis. In *Paradise Lost*, VIII, 452–90, while God is creating Eve out of one of Adam's ribs, Adam, asleep, dreams of her and wakes to find her 'such as I saw her in my dream'. Keats took this passage as a figure of the poetic imagination: 'The Imagination may be compared to Adam's dream—he awoke and found it truth' (letter to Bailey, 22 November 1817).

96 *the Franco–Prussian War*: (1870–1) a war which ended in defeat and humiliation for the French. The reference may indicate that Heyst was a temporary officer who was demobilized after the war and could find no other employment; this might be the basis of his claim to be a Lieutenant of the Reserve (see note to p. 20).

98 *Macassar*: a Dutch-controlled port on the large island of Celebes, between Borneo and New Guinea.

100 *Colombia*: Spanish-speaking republic in the north-west angle of the South American continent. Politically very unstable.

Manila: principal city of the Philippines (under Spanish, later under American, control).

103 *plain Mr. Jones*: in the MS here he is 'plain John Smith, gentleman'; he becomes 'Mr Jones' after he and his companions have reached Samburan.

105 *sticking point*: Lady Macbeth, 'screw your courage to the sticking-place', *Macbeth*, I. vii.

108 *Officer-of-the-Reserve*: see above, notes to pp. 20 and 96.

113 *Venezuela*: notoriously unstable South American republic; Conrad's knowledge of it was drawn largely from his friend R. B. Cunninghame Graham's *Vanished Arcadia*, which is a memoir of Graham's adventures in Venezuela.

115 *écarté*: card-game favoured by gamblers.

117 *shoulder*: in the MS this is followed by a cancelled scene, consisting largely of dialogue between 'Smith' (Jones) and Ricardo upstairs in Schomberg's hotel. The interest of this scene is that Ricardo is shown resenting 'Smith's' power over him; it prepares the reader for Ricardo's disobedience to his master on Samburan.

122 *jalousies*: slatted blinds.

125 *Gulf of Mexico*: name of the huge bay formed by the eastern seaboard of the southern United States and Mexico.

127 *Pall Mall*: fashionable London street, close to the royal palaces, known for its famous gentlemen's clubs.

West India Docks: the West India Docks cut across the top of the peninsula in East London formed by a loop in the Thames and known as the Isle of Dogs; a notoriously rough district, and a natural habitat for Ricardo.

dunnage: colloquial for luggage.

135 *hash-seller*: keeper of a cheap eating-house.

gin-slinger: a bartender (from the American drink, gin sling). Ricardo likes to use American slang.

147 *Sirop de Groseille*: red currant cordial.

151 *pueblo*: small town.

tristes: songs sung by a disappointed lover.

juez: the local magistrate (who obviously ought not to be gambling with Jones).

ekarty: écarté (see note to p. 115).

152 *comandante*: military officer.

154 *Gott im Himmel*: 'God in Heaven', a mild idiomatic expletive in German.

158 *Gewiss*: certainly.

160 *caballero*: gentleman.

posada: inn.

sanctissima madre: holy mother, the Virgin Mary.

165 *Java Sea*: shallow sea between Java and Sumatra to the south, Borneo and Celebes to the north. Schomberg's directions indicate that Samburan is either in the Java Sea or, as I believe, just beyond it to the West in the Flores Sea (see note to p. 5).

fine fellow: the awkwardness of the plotting is felt here; surely in reality Jones and Ricardo would not allow themselves to be used by Schomberg for his own purposes, particularly as they are fully aware that Schomberg is eager to get rid of them.

168 *pillar of smoke ... loom of fire*: Genesis 13:21: 'And the Lord went before them by day in a pillar of a cloud, to lead them by the way; and by night in a pillar of fire, to give them light.' I am puzzled by Conrad's 'loom'.

174 *paradise ... so soon to lose*: the most explicit of the Heyst/Adam parallels (see also second note to p. 92). The references here are to Milton and Genesis and Darwin, whom Conrad knew best through Alfred Wallace. Among the animals whom this second Adam names is, of course, Lena herself.

Action: used here in the same sense as Schopenhauer's 'will' in *The World as Will and Idea*. The man caught on the barbed hook of will, or action, is trapped, in Schopenhauer, in the world of phenomena or illusion and has lost his clarity of mind.

that form of contempt which is called pity: recalls Nietzsche, *Zarathustra*, vol. I: 'What is the greatest experience you can have? It is the hour of the greatest contempt. The hour in which your happiness, too, arouses your disgust, and even your reason and your virtue.' Compare notes to pp. 219 and 220.

179 *Alfuro*: the Alfuros are described by Wallace as an island people who resemble the people of Papua and New Guinea rather than the Malays (see *Goram*, note to p. 8).

180 *makan*: eat (i.e., a meal is ready).

186 *Lena*: she is now called 'Magdalen' rather than 'Margaret' in the MS, and the MS here gives rather more detail about the way in which Heyst arrived at 'Lena' by seeking an appropriate 'diminutive' for 'Magdalen'. Lena asks why she has been given this name and 'Berg' replies that it is a pet name given to 'many girls in Germany': presumably Conrad dropped this phrase because the novel was to be published when Britain was at war with Germany.

190 *Moluccas*: west of New Guinea. If Heyst's island is to be imagined to the south of the Moluccas this reinforces the notion that it is in the Flores Sea (see note to p. 5).

193 *Vesuvius*: volcano in the Bay of Naples.

  found favour in your sight?: Genesis 18:3. Abraham: 'Lord, if now I have found favour in thy sight, pass not away, I pray thee, from thy servant.'

196 *unforeseen accident*: Darwin's doctrine of natural selection reinforces the Schopenhaurian pessimism of Heyst's father.

198 *Great Joke*: a bleak phrase, uniting doctrines from Nietzsche, Schopenhauer, and Darwin: God is dead, destiny is cruel and capricious, man is a biological mistake.

  a good girl: see above, note to p. 88.

209 *the abysses of earth and heaven*: the imagery suggests the condition of Adam and Eve before they lose paradise in Milton's poem, but also Nietzsche's metaphor for the risks that man takes in living at all: 'Man is a rope, tied between beast and overman—a rope over an abyss' (*Zarathustra*, vol. I).

219 *bed of dreams*: compare Nietzsche: 'we would like to destroy the sting of the desires [. . .] yet the illusion of the phenomenon soon entangles us again [. . .] We cannot tear ourselves free' (*Zarathustra*, vol. I).

220   *disgust of pity*: see note on 'that form of contempt which is
      called pity', p. 174. Heyst's father combines Nietzschean
      disdain with Schopenhauerian self-hatred.

231   *Esclavo*: slave.

237   *wonder at your arrival*: an ironical echo of Miranda's innocent
      delight in the visitors to Prospero's island:

                                                    O, wonder!
      How many goodly creatures are there here!
      How beauteous mankind is! O brave new world
      That hath such people in't!
                                        (*The Tempest*, V. i. 182–5)

240   *dunnage*: see above, note to p. 127.

      hombre: man.

241   *a lovely dream*: Ferdinand, one of the invaders of Prospero's
      island whose innocence matches Miranda's, exclaims: 'My
      spirits, as in a dream, are all bound up' (*The Tempest*, I. ii.
      487). Prospero, in the most quoted lines of the play, extends
      the image: 'We are such stuff /As dreams are made on; and our
      little life/ Is rounded with a sleep' (IV. i. 156–8). Ricardo's
      exclamations bear the same kind of ironic relation to these
      lines as did Heyst's to Miranda's on p. 237 (see note to that
      page).

251   *a dream*: Lena's dream recalls Eve's dream in *Paradise Lost* (V,
      28–93) in which her temptation and fall are predicted. Lena is
      stronger than Milton's Eve—she resists Ricardo's tempt-
      tation—and more constant than Heyst, the second Adam, who
      will later believe that she is disloyal to him when she is in fact
      seeking to save him.

253   *dreams are madness*: in Milton's poem Adam also seeks to
      dismiss Eve's dream as unimportant:

      Evil into the mind of god or man
      May come and go, so unapproved, and leave
      No spot or blame behind
                                        (*Paradise Lost*, V, 117–19)

Heyst and Adam both believe that dreams have no bearing on the waking moral life: and they are both wrong.

276 *picket*: piquet, a card-game.

ekarty: écarté, see above, note to p. 115.

282 *three bungalows*: the manuscript of *Victory* is full of little drawings. Most of them are irrelevant doodles, but here there is a small plan of the disposition of the three bungalows 'irregularly disposed along a flat curve', enabling Conrad to work out precisely how much Ricardo is able to see.

286 *pointed ears*: suggesting that he is biologically degenerate. Donkin in *The Nigger of the 'Narcissus'* and Stevie in *The Secret Agent* also have pointed ears.

296 *gin-slinger*: see above, note to p. 135.

301 *ya tuan*: yes, sir. 'Tuan' can be the equivalent of 'Lord' as in *Lord Jim* but can equally be used as a normal polite form of address.

Mem Putih: the mistress (literally, the white madam).

306 *ada tuan*: I am here, sir.

307 *yamen*: or yamun, the official residence (and offices) of a mandarin.

Formosa: large island off the coast of China.

311 *Dyaks*: the natives of Borneo, known for head-hunting and piracy. Wang's fear of them is ignorant and superstitious: Alfred Wallace had reported the Dyaks were a people of intelligence and high moral character.

Mindanao: large island to the south of the Philippines.

people who live in trees: possibly orang-utans, 'man-apes'; this would be a more blatant instance of Wang's ignorance.

317 *"'I am he who is* ——'"': perhaps suggesting that Jones is Antichrist. Compare John 8:28: 'When ye have lifted up the Son of man, then shall ye know that I am he.'

318 *up and down the earth*: here Jones is compared with Satan, who is described as 'going to and fro in the earth' and 'walking up and down in it', Job 1:7.

329 *of the outer world* and *chimaeras* (see above, note to p. 9): these phrases evoke again, indirectly, *The Tempest*, with its persistent suggestions that the inhabitants of Prospero's island and its visitors are unreal—to each other.

333 *vamos*: go!

spiritual change: Ricardo's changing feelings about Jones parody Ferdinand's changing feelings about his father (whom he assumes dead) when Ariel sings that the drowned Alonso 'doth suffer a sea-change/Into something rich and strange' (*The Tempest*, I. ii. 398–9).

334 *basilisk*: legendary reptile hatched by a serpent from a cock's egg: its look is fatal.

salamander: mythical, lizard-like creature which can live in fire.

"Why not pray a little, too?" Jones should take this advice himself, since Ricardo has now turned against him. Mark 13:33: 'Take ye heed, watch and pray: for ye know not when the time is'.

339 *Manila*: see above, note to p. 100.

East Coast: i.e., of the Asiatic land mass.

345 *Kingsland Road*: a reminder of Lena's Cockney origins; an insalubrious area of East London.

347 *Celestial*: 'Celestial Empire' is a translation of one of the native names of China and thus, humorously, 'Celestial' means Chinaman.

359 *one of the two sparrows*: Matthew 10:29: 'Are not two sparrows sold for a farthing? and one of them shall not fall on the ground without your father.'

much later: i.e., he is part of the degeneration which was widely believed (partly under the influence of Darwin and Schopenhauer) to be overtaking the human race in the late nineteenth century.

361 *duty*: suggests Hamlet's dilatoriness in taking his revenge.

367 *Alma* and *Magdalen*: see above, notes to p. 88.

369 *vamos*: see note to p. 333.

373 *mourning sinner*: another point of contact with St Mary Magdalen, who in many depictions of the Deposition (or Pietà) is one of the women mourning Jesus. Presumably Lena's posture here expresses her anguish in the knowledge that she is forced to deceive Heyst in her attempt to save his life.

376 *dubious distinction*: recalls the heads on stakes surrounding Kurtz's bungalow at the inner station in *Heart of Darkness*.

'*I am he that is*': see p. 317 and note.

378 *social sphere*: recalls Gentleman Brown's claim to social kinship with Jim in *Lord Jim*. The *doppelgänger* pattern, present in *Lord Jim* and 'The Secret Sharer', is evoked here: Jones is to some extent Heyst's diabolical counterpart.

379 *the world itself*: in *The Tempest* Alonso, Sebastian, and Gonzalo, Ariel's 'three men of sin' are part of Destiny's 'instrument', the 'lower world', come to pay Prospero a visit.

383 "*He who deliberates is lost*": a proverb derived from Addison's *Cato*, IV. i:

When love once pleads admission to our hearts,
(In spite of all the virtue we can boast)
The woman that deliberates is lost.

385 *Schomberg ... altruism*: a reasonable question, probing a weakness of the plot.

new impressions: another thin patch; Jones's motivation for coming to Samburan is never quite satisfactory.

387 *this is my time*: recalls many of Hamlet's soliloquies in which he tries to persuade himself that he has reached the moment to act, e.g. 'Now might I do it pat' (III. 3. 73), and 'From this time forth / My thoughts by bloody, or be nothing worth' (IV. 4. 65–6).

393 *Acis* and *Polyphemus*: in Ovid, *Metamorphoses*, XIII, Galatea, a water-nymph, describes her passion for Acis. Polyphemus, seeing them together, throws part of a mountain at Acis and kills him; Galatea is permitted to transform Acis into a river-god, thus ensuring his immortality. Perhaps Conrad is referring specifically to the division of feeling that Galatea experiences

in Ovid: 'Him [Acis] did I love, but the Cyclops loved me with endless wooing. Nor, if you should ask me, could I tell which was stronger in me, my hate of Cyclops or my love of Acis; for both were in equal measure. O mother Venus, how mighty is thy sway!' (Ovid, *Metamorphoses*, tr. F. J. Miller, Heinemann, 1976, ll. 754–8).

407 *shades of death*: by turning to look at her as she was on the point of leaving Hades, Orpheus consigns Eurydice to the underworld.

408 *Achin war*: war fought (unsuccessfully) by the Achin people of Northern Sumatra to resist the Portuguese in the seventeenth century.

THE WORLD'S CLASSICS

A Select List

SERGEI AKSAKOV: A Russian Gentleman
Translated by J. D. Duff
Edited by Edward Crankshaw

A Russian Schoolboy
Translated by J. D. Duff
With an introduction by John Bayley

Years of Childhood
Translated by J. D. Duff
With an introduction by Lord David Cecil

JANE AUSTEN: Emma
Edited by James Kinsley and David Lodge

Mansfield Park
Edited by James Kinsley and John Lucas

Northanger Abbey, Lady Susan, The Watsons,
and Sanditon
Edited by John Davie

Persuasion
Edited by John Davie

Pride and Prejudice
Edited by James Kinsley and Frank Bradbrook

Sense and Sensibility
Edited by James Kinsley and Claire Lamont

CHARLOTTE BRONTË: Jane Eyre
Edited by Margaret Smith

Shirley
Edited by Margaret Smith and Herbert Rosengarten

FANNY BURNEY: Camilla
Edited by Edward A. Bloom and Lilian D. Bloom

Evelina
Edited by Edward A. Bloom

ANTON CHEKHOV: The Russian Master & Other Stories
Translated with an introduction by Ronald Hingley

Five Plays
Translated with an introduction by Ronald Hingley

WILKIE COLLINS: The Moonstone
Edited by Anthea Trodd

The Woman in White
Edited by Harvey Peter Sucksmith

JOSEPH CONRAD: Lord Jim
Edited by John Batchelor

The Nigger of the 'Narcissus'
Edited with an introduction by Jacques Berthoud

Nostromo
Edited with an introduction by Keith Carabine

The Secret Agent
Edited by Roger Tennant

The Shadow-Line
Edited with an introduction by Jeremy Hawthorn

Under Western Eyes
Edited by Jeremy Hawthorn

Youth, Heart of Darkness, The End of the Tether
Edited with an introduction by Robert Kimbrough

DANIEL DEFOE: Moll Flanders
Edited by G. A. Starr

Robinson Crusoe
Edited by J. Donald Crowley

Roxana
Edited by Jane Jack

BENJAMIN DISRAELI: Coningsby
Edited by Sheila M. Smith

Sybil
Edited by Sheila M. Smith

FËDOR DOSTOEVSKY: Crime and Punishment
Translated by Jessie Coulson
With an introduction by John Jones

Memoirs from the House of the Dead
Translated by Jessie Coulson
Edited by Ronald Hingley

JOHN GALT: The Entail
Edited with an introduction by Ian A. Gordon

The Provost
Edited by Ian A. Gordon

ELIZABETH GASKELL: Cousin Phillis and Other Tales
Edited by Angus Easson

Cranford
Edited by Elizabeth Porges Watson

North and South
Edited by Angus Easson

Ruth
Edited with an introduction by Alan Shelston

Sylvia's Lovers
Edited by Andrew Sanders

THOMAS HARDY: A Pair of Blue Eyes
Edited with an introduction by Alan Manford

Jude the Obscure
Edited by Patricia Ingham

Under the Greenwood Tree
Edited by Simon Gatrell

The Woodlanders
Edited with an introduction by Dale Kramer

HOMER: The Iliad
Translated by Robert Fitzgerald
With an introduction by G. S. Kirk

The Odyssey
Translated by Walter Shewring
With an introduction by G. S. Kirk

RICHARD JEFFERIES: After London *or* Wild England
With an introduction by John Fowles

GWYN JONES (Transl.): Eirik the Red and Other Icelandic
Sagas

GEORGE MEREDITH: The Ordeal of Richard Feverel
Edited with an introduction by John Halperin

ANN RADCLIFFE:
The Italian
Edited by Frederick Garber

The Mysteries of Udolpho
Edited by Bonamy Dobrée

MARY SHELLEY: Frankenstein
Edited by M. K. Joseph